NINE FEET FROM TIP TO TIP

Nine Feet from Tip to Tip

The California Condor Through History

by

Sanford R. Wilbur

Symbios Books: Gresham, Oregon

NINE FEET FROM TIP TO TIP
COPYRIGHT © SANFORD R. WILBUR

PUBLISHED BY:
SYMBIOS BOOKS
4367 S. E. 16TH ST.
GRESHAM, OR 97080

ISBN 978-0-9651263-4-2
LIBRARY OF CONGRESS CONTROL NUMBER
2012945916

PRINTED IN THE UNITED STATES OF AMERICA

TABLE OF CONTENTS

LIST OF ILLUSTRATIONS

PREFACE

In 1941, Harry Harris published "The Annals of *Gymnogyps* to 1900" [*Condor* 43(1):3-55, January 1941], a bibliographic survey of what was known of the early history of the California condor. Harris - born Joseph Henry Harris Jr. (1878-1954) - lover of both birds and books, had begun compiling condor records early in the 1930s, perhaps while serving at the California Institute of Technology as "honorary curator" of the Donald R. Dickey Library of Vertebrate Zoology. When Carl Koford - newly assigned to do the first in-depth field study of condors - visited Harris in March 1939, he found that Harris had accumulated "over 1000" references. Harris admitted to Koford that he had done no work on the bibliography "for about 2 years," but he expressed his intention to eventually publish it. "The Annals" were the result.

This is how Harris introduced his efforts: *"It has no doubt occurred to interested students as a remarkable and singular fact that not until the California Condor* (Gymnogyps californianus) *was on the very threshold of extinction has an adequately equipped and properly organized effort been made to secure a comprehensive body of data on its life history* [referring, no doubt, to the just-begun Koford study]. *It is true that sporadic and fragmentary contributions to this end have, throughout the years the bird has been known, resulted in an accumulation of much pertinent material, not all of which may be considered authentic..."*

Acknowledging as significant contributions the movies of condors taken by John Pemberton, and (without naming them) the condor nest site photography of William Finley and Herman Bohlman, Harris continued: *"The present writer has not escaped the general enthusiasm aroused by these and other current efforts on behalf of* Gymnogyps *and has been impelled thereby to review an unfinished bibliography of the species* [that seen by Koford in 1939] *for the purpose of compiling a more or less continuous record of civilized man's relations with this bird. Such an account, like the complete life history of the bird itself, has never been brought together in one place, and in the hope that it may in some small measure assist in sustaining the interest already centered around the species, as well as in emphasizing the imminence of its total extirpation, the story is given here as it has been found reflected in the bibliography."*

"The Annals" are remarkable. Prepared long before the Internet and the World Wide Web; before records had been amassed into convenient library and archive collections; and when information gathering was done very slowly by traveling, telephones, and stamped envelopes, Harris managed to capture the vast majority of early references to the California condor. He abstracted the information with care, and arranged it in a very readable format. He made a few errors of fact and interpretation, but also identified and showed to be erroneous part of the written record that was (as he called it) *"pertinent material, not all of which may be considered authentic."* Before publication of Carl Koford's monograph in 1953, Harris' review was by far the most complete and most authoritative document available concerning one of the world's rarest birds. It is still very useful.

* * *

In the 70 years since "The Annals," nothing comparable has been prepared. Carl Koford and I both covered parts of the story in some depth, but there is no comprehensive history that completes Harris' efforts, and carries on from 1900. That such a document is needed is evident from the incomplete, misinterpreted, and sometimes erroneous information included in most the publications about condors - both scientific and popular - published in the last quarter-century.

I began compiling a California condor bibliography in 1970, as part of my ten-year research project on the wild population of condors. Starting with Harris' information, and supplemented by the records accumulated by Carl Koford and Fred Sibley, my list of references that specifically mention the California condor has grown in the past 40 years to almost 2,000 citations. Included are books, journal and magazine articles, newspaper items, diaries, field notes, manuscripts, museum data, and historic correspondence. Supplementing these condor references are almost 1,000 additional items covering such topics as Pacific Coast history, biography, ethnology, paleontology, agriculture and livestock, chemical pesticides, and local faunas and floras. Following Harry Harris' lead, I've woven all this material into an expanded annals of *Gymnogyps*.

Harry Harris started his "Annals" from 1602, the apparent date of first contact with the California condor by Europeans. He did not explore the fossil record, as he was dealing only with *"man's relations with this bird."* He made the decision not to explore Indian lore, feeling that going back into *"the ethnozoologic phase of the story"* as he called it, was *"too involved and speculative a field for any but a trained and experienced specialist to deal with authoritatively."* Prehistory and the involvement with condors by the indigenous people of North America are difficult subjects to cover, but both are important for an understanding of what came after. I've taken my best shot at both of them.

I chose to end my narrative in the early 1980s. There was still a small population of wild California condors at that time, but it seemed destined for extinction if left to its own devices, and the U. S. Fish and Wildlife Service had shifted most effort to saving the species through captive propagation. That is developing into a fascinating story, and perhaps one day another historian will tell that tale in a second supplement to "the annals of *Gymnogyps."*

INTRODUCTION
WHAT IS THE CALIFORNIA CONDOR?

Ten thousand years ago, a large condor now identified as *Gymnogyps* was found in (at least) what are now those portions of the United States designated as Oregon, California, Nevada, Arizona, New Mexico, Texas, Florida, and New York, and also in northern Mexico [1]. One assumes that at some point the range of the birds included the area between Texas and Florida, but no evidence of that has yet been found [2]. So far, the one record from New York State is an anomaly, with nothing to suggest that *Gymnogyps* condors at any time occupied an uninterrupted range from south to north in eastern portions of North America.

Were the *Gymnogyps* condors of 10,000 years ago the same species today called the California condor? The fossil condors were first described by Loye Miller as a separate species, *G. amplus,* separated from a later appearing *G. californianus* on the basis of their larger bone size [3]. Miller's sample from a northern California cave was small, but after comparing skulls of a number of fossil and recent *Gymnogyps,* Harvey Fisher had no hesitation agreeing with Miller *"that the fossil California Condor is a species distinct from the Recent* Gymnogyps californianus" [4]. However, as more bone samples became available from both "species," and as additional measurements were taken, it seemed that there wasn't a significant size difference, after all. After an expanded study of vulture skeletons, Fisher concluded [5] that *"it has been found impossible to distinguish the two species,* californianus *and* amplus, *of the cathartid genus* Gymnogyps *on the basis of any qualitative characters in skeletal elements other than those of the skull."* However, 34 different measurements and ratios of bones *"demonstrate conclusively that we are dealing with two distinct forms...* (and) *"bear out the belief that two subspecies are involved..."*

More recently, Steven Emslie came to a similar conclusion [6]: *"It appears appropriate, however, that the fossil form be recognized as a large, temporal subspecies,* G. californianus amplus, *an opinion expressed by numerous other avian paleontologists and anatomists ... The designation of this fossil subspecies necessitates the establishment of an equivalent rank for the modern, post-Pleistocene species, hereby referred as* G. c. californianus.*"*

The classification of fossil and recent California condors as only subspecies has not gone unchallenged. After performing a broader set of measurements on many more bones than were analyzed by previous researchers, and subjecting the results to more rigorous statistical tests, Valerie Syverson and Donald Prothero concluded [7] that, while there is an overlap in most measurements taken of Pleistocene and modern condors, some dimensions are consistently different enough to warrant treatment as distinct species. They went on to suggest, based on one especially robust bone sample found in the youngest Rancho La Brea excavations [Holocene radiocarbon age of 9,000 years] that the two condors might have co-existed for some time beyond the Pleistocene. If so, it would seem improper to consider them subspecies. The debate will no doubt continue.

* * *

The *Gymnogyps* vultures, of which several fossil forms have now been identified [8], are grouped in the family Cathartidae with the other vultures now found in the Western Hemisphere. As a convenience, the Cathartidae are often called New World vultures, to separate them from the accipitrid vultures of Eurasia and Africa. However, fossil "New World" vultures have been found in Europe, and "Old World" vultures were once found in North America, so the terminology realistically applies only to modern representatives of the two groups. The more important point is that they are quite different types of birds, although each group fills the comparable niche for principal avian scavengers within their geographic ranges [9].

While there has never been any serious challenge to classifying the Old World vultures with the eagle-like raptors, there have long been doubts about the relationships of the Cathartidae to the "birds of prey." As early as 1873, it was suggested that - based on certain anatomical features – the cathartids might be more closely related to herons and storks. Later investigators found additional reasons to separate the New World vultures from their traditional classification with diurnal raptors, most favoring an alignment with storks or pelicans rather than eagles and hawks [10]. This eventually led the American Ornithologists' Union in 1998 to move the New World vultures from the Falconiformes to Ciconiiformes [11]. However, continuing genetic studies indicated the move was likely incorrect, and in 2007 the A. O. U. tentatively moved them back into the Falconiformes, but with a caveat: *"the New World vultures are not closely related to the storks, although their precise phylogenetic relationship to the Falconiformes is yet undetermined"* [12]. The debate goes on.

* * *

On the basis of the one specimen brought to England by Archibald Menzies in 1797 [Chapter 4], the California condor was first assigned to the genus *Vultur,* the same as the Andean condor of South America [13]. Most subsequent taxonomists felt that there were differences between the two types that were significant enough to warrant a separation. Through time, a number of different names were in vogue [14] – *Sarcoramphus, Vultur, Cathartes, Gypagus, Oenops, Pseudogryphus* – with Robert Ridgway's *Pseudogryphus* being favored through the last quarter of the 19th century [15]. In 1901, Charles Richmond published a note identifying *Gymnogyps* as the earliest generic designation assigned to the California condor [16]. That name had been applied by René Lesson in 1842, but had been published in a relatively obscure journal, and was therefore unknown to most of the early avian taxonomists [17].

A final note on taxonomy and nomenclature: Although Charles Bonaparte used the name condor for the North American species in 1833 [18], it was apparently not used again until Alexander Taylor's popular series of articles in the 1850s [Chapter 8]. The South American species was referred to as *the* Condor (assumed derived from the Quechuan word *cuntur*), while the North American bird was the Californian Vulture. It was not until after 1900 that California condor became the generally accepted name.

* * *

By far, the best source for information on the basic biology and behavior of California condors is Carl Koford's monograph, the result of detailed field work between 1939 and 1946 [19]. Some information especially pertinent to understanding the history of the condor population is highlighted here.

California condors, like all vultures, are predominantly scavengers of dead animals. While their beaks are sharp and good for tearing at carcasses, they differ from the Old World vultures in not having grasping feet. This limits their ability to capture and kill animals, and makes it impossible for them to fly with prey in their talons. Old newspaper stories of California condors carrying off fawns, calves, lambs, and occasional babies are products of very little knowledge and a whole lot of imagination.

California condors have been known to feed occasionally on fish and rarely on birds, but throughout recorded history they have fed predominantly on dead mammals. More specifically, large mammals (deer, cattle, and sheep in recent times) have been their principal source of food. While deer and calves have been said to be "preferred" [20], the choice of what they eat has probably always been largely dictated by availability and accessibility, and only secondarily by preference. California condors obtain their food by sight, not by smell, and large animals would generally be much easier than small ones to see from the heights at which condors forage. Also, the caloric needs of a 20 pound bird with a nine feet wingspan are such that it would take many small mammals to sustain it; selecting larger prey when available would be far more energy efficient. Practically speaking, much of the smaller food is not available to condors. Although condors are incredible fliers once they are aloft, their very high wing loading (the ratio of weight to wing area) prevents them from becoming airborne as early as other avian scavengers (turkey vultures, ravens, golden eagles). They must wait until the air has warmed sufficiently to generate thermal "lift." By the time condors are on the wing, the smaller birds have often had an hour or more to clean up any small carcasses that the coyotes didn't consume overnight.

California condors don't attain adult plumage (orange head, black body with white triangles under the wings) until about six years of age, first passing through various patterns of head and feather coloration that can be used in a general way to estimate the age of younger birds. No wild condor was known to breed before it was six years old, and it may be that the usual age of first reproduction in the wild was older than that. California condors in captivity have lived to be more than 30 years old (two have reached 45 years). Condors had no regular natural enemies, and died mainly from accidents and old age (except when helped along by us humans). It was probably not unusual for wild condors to live 20 years, and longevity of some likely rivaled their zoo relatives. However, there are no certain records of longevity in the wild.

One usually thinks of California condors as nesting in caves on precipitous cliffs. Many did, but the "cave" was sometimes a mere crevice between rocks or even a burned out cavity in a large tree. The "cliff" was sometimes a slope, accessible to almost anyone. (One condor egg was taken from its nest by a little girl on a family picnic [21].) A clutch consists of one egg, laid between February and May. Incubation lasts 54-58 days, after which the nestling condor is confined to the nest cave for about 20 weeks, being fed with regurgitated food brought by the adults. For another 10 weeks, the fledgling would still be nearly flightless, and would be fed by the parents in the vicinity of the nest. Even after fledging, the young condor was partially dependent on its parents for some months. This wasn't because the young bird couldn't forage on its own, but because of the social hierarchy that developed at a carcass; *i.e.,* adults kept the immatures from feeding with them. Because of the long reproductive cycle, it was unusual for condors to lay eggs in consecutive years. Sometimes they did, but most pairs nested every other year.

In later chapters, I discuss how some of these life history characteristics affected the survival of individual condors and, ultimately, the entire California condor population.

CHAPTER NOTES

1. Pages 12-13 *in:* Wilbur, S. R. 1978. The California condor, 1966-76: a look at its past and future. North American Fauna Number 72, U. S. Fish and Wildlife Service.

Emslie, S. D. 1987. Age and diet of fossil California condors in Grand Canyon, Arizona. *Science* 237:768-770.

Emslie, S. D. 1990. Additional Carbon 14 dates on fossil California condors. *National Geographic Research* 6(2):134-135.

Steadman, D. W., and N. G. Miller. 1987. California condor associated with spruce-jack pine in late Pleistocene of New York. *Quaternary Research* 28(3):415-426.

2. On the other hand, considering the great climatological and land form differences between Florida and the North American Southwest – even in prehistoric times – one might question whether California condor habitat was continuous across the southern United States. The presence of *Gymnogyps* condors in Cuba and South America might suggest another route for condors to have arrived in Florida (although Emslie believes *Gymnogyps* originated in North America, and later spread south).

Emslie, S. D. 1988. The fossil history and phylogenetic relationships of condors

(Ciconiiformes: Vulturidae) in the New World. *Journal of Vertebrate Paleontology* 8(12):212-228.

Suárez, W. 2000. Contribución al conocimiento del estatus genérico del cóndor extinto (Ciconiiformes: Vulturidae) del Cuaternario Cubano. *Ornithologia Neotropical* 11:109-122.

Suárez, W., and S. D. Emslie. 2003. New fossil material with a redescription of the extinct condor *Gymnogyps varonai* (Arredondo, 1971) from the Quaternary of Cuba (Aves: Vulturidae). *Proceedings of the Biological Society of Washington* 116(1):29-37.

3. Miller, L. H. 1911. Avifauna of the Pleistocene cave deposits of California. *University of California Bulletin of the Department of Geology* 6(16):385-400.

4. Fisher, H. L. 1944. The skulls of the cathartid vultures. *Condor* 46(6):272-296.

5. Fisher, H. L. 1947. The skeletons of recent and fossil *Gymnogyps*. *Pacific Science* 1(4):227-236.

6. Emslie 1988 *op. cit.*

7. Syverson, V. J., and D. R. Prothero. 2010. Evolutionary patterns in late Quaternary California condors. *Palarch's Journal of Vertebrate Palaeontology* 7(1):1-18.

8. Emslie 1988, *op. cit.*

9. Good discussions of the New World-Old World vulture relationships are found in:
Cracraft, J., and P. V. Rich. 1972. The systematics and evolution of the Cathartidae in the Old World Tertiary. *Condor* 74(3):272-283.
Amadon, D. 1977. Notes on the taxonomy of vultures. *Condor* 79(4):413-416.
Rich, P. V. 1983. The fossil history of vultures: a world perspective. Pages 3-25 *in:* Wilbur, S. R., and J. A. Jackson (editors), Vulture biology and management. Berkeley, California: University of California Press.

10. The early evolution of thought on the classification of the Cathartidae is summarized in:
Rea, A. M. 1983. Cathartid affinities: a brief overview. Pages 26-54 *in:* Wilbur, S. R., and J. A. Jackson (editors), Vulture biology and management. Berkeley, California: University of California Press.

11. Pages 51-53 *in:* American Ornithologists' Union. 1998. Check-list of North American birds, 7th edition. Washington, D. C.: American Ornithologists' Union.

12. Banks, R. C., R. T. Chesser, C. Cicero, J. L. Dunn, A. W. Kratter, I. J. Lovette, P. C. Rasmussen, J. V. Remsen Jr., J. D. Rising and D. F. Stotz. 2007. Forty-eighth supplement to the American Ornithologists' Union Check-list of North American birds. *Auk* 124(3):1109-1115.

13. Shaw, G., and F. P. Nodder. 1797. Vivarium naturae, or Naturalist's Miscellany. Ninth volume. London, England: Nodder and Company.

14. A good summary of California condor nomenclature over time appears on pages 17-18 *in*: Harris, H. 1941. The annals of *Gymnogyps* to 1900. *Condor* 43(1):3-55.

15. Pages 336-343 *in:* Baird, S. F., T. M. Brewer, and R. Ridgway. 1874. A history of North American birds. Volume 3, Land birds. Boston, Massachusetts: Little, Brown and Company.
   Ridgway, R. 1880. Notes on the American vultures (Sarcorphamphidae), with special reference to their generic nomenclature. *Bulletin of the Nuttall Ornithological Club* 5(2):77-84.

16. Richmond, C. W. 1901. On the generic name of the Californian condor. *Condor* 3(2):49.

17. Lesson, R. P. 1842. Index ornithologique. *L'echo du monde savant,* series 2, 6(44), col. 1037.

18. Pages 1-21 *in:* Bonaparte, C. L. 1833. American ornithology; or, The natural history of birds inhabiting the United States not given by Wilson. Philadelphia, Pennsylvania: Carey & Lea.

19. Twenty-five years of captive propagation have refined knowledge of some aspects of California condor biology, but Carl Koford had it essentially correct: Koford, C. B. 1953. The California condor. Research Report Number 4. New York, New York: National Audubon Society.

20. Koford *op. cit.,* page 53.

21. W. L. Chambers data slip accompanying the condor egg, Western Foundation of Vertebrate Zoology (Camarillo, California).

CHAPTER 1
THE CONDOR BEFORE HISTORY

Whether considered species or subspecies, all prehistoric "California" condors date from longer than 9,000 years ago. Most bones have been radiocarbon-dated at 11,000 to 13,000 years before present (B.P.), and a number of samples exceed 30,000 years in age [1]. At about 9,000 years B.P., the condor record fails and remains empty for 5,000 years. Almost certainly, the aboriginal people of the Pacific Coast knew condors during some of that time (see Chapter 2), but so far the earliest radiocarbon dates for archaeological sites where condor remains have been found are around 4,000 years B.P. [2]. The first specific date of the condors' return to the record is at about 2,900 years B.P., the radiocarbon date applied to a condor metatarsus found on Pender Island, British Columbia, Canada [3].

What was happening with the condors in those intervening 5,000 years? Perhaps that will never be known any more clearly than it is today, but some speculation may be worthwhile.

Popular accounts of the California condor often state or imply that condors were found prehistorically throughout much of North America. Except for one discovery of three bones in New York State [4], there is no reason to think that the species was ever regularly found east of Nevada and Oregon, or north of Arizona, New Mexico, Texas, and Florida. There is also no reason to think that California condor populations survived past the late Pleistocene or middle Holocene in any location more than about 200 miles from the Pacific Ocean. Every sight record beyond that area is suspect in some way [5]; no condor relics have been found in any archaeological sites east of California; and I have not located any information to suggest that condors were known to aboriginal populations beyond the West Coast [6].

As long ago as 1912, Loye Miller suggested that Pleistocene scavengers decreased in numbers, and in some cases vanished, because of food supply shortages following extinction of large mammals [7]. Sixty-seven years later, I made a similar observation, adding to megafauna extinctions the additional loss of food resulting from the effects on the remaining mammals of increasing aridity in the Southwest [8]. In 1990, Steven Emslie restated the case, now armed with radiocarbon dating of condor bones that showed condor presence in the West at the same time as the Pleistocene megafauna [9]. Such observations are intuitive – less food, lower carrying capacity for scavengers – but clearly it was not that simple. First, megafaunal extinctions in North America may have happened over a long time period, and at different times geographically, as they did in Europe [10]. Scavenger populations likely had considerable time to adjust to the changing food supply [11]. Second, although the "megafauna" (the very large mammals) died out in the late Pleistocene or early Holocene, a wide variety of large and small mammals survived to the present time [12]. Populations of condors and other scavengers would have had to adapt to a diminished food base, but it's unlikely they were left entirely without food anywhere in their known prehistoric range. Perhaps a more interesting question is why did California condors ultimately disappear from all former habitat except along the Pacific Coast? The answer may rest in the climate of the middle Holocene.

There is general agreement among climatologists, botanists, zoologists, and archaeologists that most of western North America was exceptionally warm and dry during the middle Holocene. There is not complete accord on the timing or duration of the drought – in fact, it appears that timing did vary geographically, and that there were intervals of greater or lesser drought – but the period of greatest aridity is usually identified as between approximately 8,000 to 3,000 years B.P. The magnitude and intensity has been described as *"the greatest aridity the Great Basin has seen in the last 10,000 years, and perhaps for the last 100,000 years or more"* [13]. *"A variety of analyses show that this period was in general far warmer and drier than what came before or what followed, at least in part a response to the fact that summer precipitation decreased at the same time as temperatures increased"* [14]. Middle Holocene aridity was not confined to the Great Basin, although it may not have been as severe in other areas. Evidence for such aridity has been identified in (among other locations) the Pacific Northwest [15], California [16], Wyoming [17], Arizona [18], New Mexico and Texas [19], Oklahoma [20], Missouri [21], and even Florida [22]. (Not all of these locations had condors; I note them to show that the drought event was so widespread that condors anywhere in the interior United States would likely have felt its impacts.) Manifestations of the drought included dried up lakes, springs and streams; retreat of temperate climate vegetation to higher elevations; decreased rates of sedimentation in marshlands; deposits of blowing sand following loss of vegetative ground cover; and reduced rates of stalagmite growth in southwestern caverns [23].

The length and intensity of the middle Holocene drought was such that human populations were disrupted. Apparently, large areas of the Great Basin were depopulated as people moved closer to the few remaining locations with dependable water [24]. On the plains of west Texas, Oklahoma, and eastern New Mexico, people dug water wells to help cope with the drought, and even then may have had to eventually vacate the most severely affected areas [25]. In Arizona *"the Santa Cruz Valley and the rest of the desert lowlands of the Southwest were largely abandoned by people"* [26].

Humans were not the only mammals affected. At Homestead Cave in north-central Utah, Donald Grayson found that *"the Middle Holocene small mammal faunas of this area underwent a decrease in species richness and evenness, driven largely by a series of local extinctions and near-extinctions coupled with a dramatic increase in the abundance of taxa well-adapted to xeric conditions"* [27]. Of greater significance to condors were the effects on the

10

artiodactyls ("big game" – deer, elk, pronghorn, bison, sheep – of the mammalian Order Artiodactyla). This group of mammals has been shown to be strongly sensitive to variations in temperature and moisture. *"The primary links between artiodactyl population growth and climate patterns stem from the effects of temperature and precipitation on forage quality and the availability of drinking water. In arid regions, environmental productivity and forage quality correlate positively with effective precipitation and soil moisture... The availability of high-quality forage, in turn, influences maternal condition, initial offspring survival, birth weight, growth rate, survival through the first winter, resistance to disease, overall recruitment rates and, ultimately, herd size... The availability of high-quality forage also affects the extent that animals require free drinking water. In times of drought, low-quality forage containing little water can tether herds to scarce free water sources and eventually restrict herd size... Several studies document the positive effects of cool and moist weather and the negative effects of hot and dry conditions on the reproductive success of artiodactyl species in a variety of contexts across the arid West"* [28].

In support of those findings on the effects of heat and dryness on artiodactyls, the archaeological record of the middle Holocene suggests major decreases in those species in such diverse locations as eastern Washington [29], southwest Wyoming [30], western Texas and eastern New Mexico [31], Utah [32], southern Arizona [33], and northern California [34]. With the return of more moderate climatic conditions in the late Holocene, some artiodactyl populations rebounded. Probably the return of more dependable food conditions came several centuries too late for Southwest condor populations.

* * *

If it is true that California condors disappeared from much of their former habitat because of lack of food, then why were they able to survive through the arid middle Holocene along the Pacific fringe of the continent? The answer seems to be that, even though areas west of the Sierra Nevada and Cascade Range felt the effects of the middle Holocene drought, the effects were moderated by proximity to the coast. *"Climatically influenced changes in terrestrial environments along the coast during the Middle Holocene appear to have been less drastic than in the interior, particularly in central and northern California"* [35]. The California coast, San Francisco Bay, and the Sacramento-San Joaquin delta have been considered "climatically complacent," implying they were likely to have been less affected by changing climatic conditions than more interior locations [36]. It is probably not coincidental that much of the evidence of human occupation of California between 8,500 and 5,500 B.P. has been found in coastal and near-coastal locations [37].

Artiodactyls appear to have become considerably less common in interior western California during the middle Holocene. However, their rapid increase

11

following the establishment of a more temperate climate regime suggests that a significant population survived through the drought [38]. Along the central California coast, there may have been little or no reduction in abundance of black-tailed deer [39]. Even in the Pacific Northwest, both coastal and inland archaeological sites show evidence of local populations of deer, elk, pronghorn, sheep and bison throughout the Holocene [40]. Condors living within regular foraging distance of the seacoast would have had access to marine mammal carcasses throughout the Holocene, as well [41]. Avian scavengers on the Pacific Coast might not have had the quantity or variety of foods they had during the late Pleistocene, but every indication is that they had much more than did the condors of the interior Southwest.

The earliest European explorers to reach the Pacific Coast in the late 1500s and early 1600s reported seeing large numbers of big game; many similar reports followed in the 1700s. Declines in artiodactyl populations may have occurred in the middle Holocene due to climate, and later from aboriginal hunting [42], but they were clearly back in abundance by the 17th century. It seems likely that condors increased along with the increase in large mammals, but that is intuitive. By the time Lewis and Clark reached the Pacific in 1806, condors were probably found from Canada to Mexico. Whether they were there all the time, or whether condors expanded their range following the Holocene hard times, are unanswerable questions at this time.

CHAPTER NOTES

1. Emslie, S. D. 1987. Age and diet of fossil California condors in Grand Canyon, Arizona. *Science, New series* 237(4816):768-770.

Emslie, S. D. 1990. Additional Carbon 14 dates on fossil California condors. *National Geographic Research* 6(2):134-135.

Syverson, V. J., and D. R. Prothero. 2010. Evolutionary patterns in late Quaternary California condors. *Palarch's Journal of Vertebrate Palaeontology* 7(1):1-18.

2. Simons, D. D. 1983. Interactions between California condors and humans in prehistoric far western North America. Pages 470-494 *in:* Wilbur, S. R., and J. A. Jackson. Vulture biology and management. Berkeley, California: University of California Press.

3. Specimen at the Royal British Columbia Museum, Victoria, British Columbia, Canada.

4. Steadman, D. W., and N. G. Miller. 1987. California condor associated with spruce-jack pine in late Pleistocene of New York. *Quaternary Research* 28(3):415-426. The bones were identified by competent paleontologists, and there is no reason to doubt that these were bones of a *Gymnogyps* condor. Still, bones have been initially attributed to condors that were later assigned to other species. This would be an extreme range extension for *Gymnogyps* – one that seems highly unlikely geographically, ecologically

and climatologically - and I will feel much more comfortable when some linkage is found to close the 1,000 mile gap between these bones and others from the species.

5. There are nine sight records of California condors east of California, Oregon, or Washington that are regularly cited in books and articles.

Idaho: In 1879, General T. E. Wilson saw two birds at a sheep carcass near Boise, which were *"much larger than turkey buzzards,"* and which *"hissed at me and ran along the ground for some distance before they were able to rise in flight."* [Lyon, M. W. Jr. 1918. Report of the Secretary, Biological Society of Washington, 20 October 1917. *Journal of the Washington Academy of Sciences* 8(1):25-28.] Although this was reported almost 40 years after the fact, it was a first-hand record and moderately detailed. Probably, there were still condors in western Oregon at that time, and non-breeding condors could possibly have foraged that distance on occasion. There is no support for the added hearsay report that condors were previously *"not uncommon"* in the area.

Alberta, Canada: John Fannin reported seeing two condors west of Calgary in 1896. [Fannin, J. 1897. The California vulture in Alberta. *Auk* 14(1):89.] In a letter to Harry Harris 6 March 1931, Major Allan Brooks claimed that Fannin had later recanted the sighting, on the basis that at the time he had not known that immature golden eagles had white under their wings. [I examined the letter at the Bancroft Library (Berkeley, California) in 1971, but have been unable to relocate it recently.]

Utah: Henry Henshaw reported a bird *"believed to be this species"* in Utah in 1872 [page 428 *in* Henshaw, H. W. 1875. Report upon the ornithological collections made in portions of Nevada, Utah, California, Colorado and New Mexico during the years 1871, 1872, 1873 and 1874. Volume 5, U. S. Geographical Survey west of the 100th Meridian. Washington, D. C.: U. S. Government Printing Office.] However, he later claimed not to have seen a living California condor until 1884 in California [Henshaw, H. W. 1920. Autobiographical notes (continued). *Condor* 22(1):7-10].

Arizona: (A) *"Resident in Southern Arizona. Individuals observed at Fort Yuma, in September 1865"* [Coues, E. 1866. List of the birds of Fort Whipple, Arizona. *Proceedings of the Academy of Natural Sciences of Philadelphia* 18:39-100]. Fort Yuma is actually on the California side of the Colorado River, not in Arizona. Although an unlikely desert location for condors, it is less than 100 air miles from condor habitat in the Cuyamaca Mountains of San Diego County, California, and the Sierra Juarez in Baja California Norte, Mexico. Samuel Rhoads claimed to have seen one condor in the Sierra Cocopah, in Baja California Norte not far south of Fort Yuma, in 1905 [Stone, W. 1905. On a collection of birds and mammals from the Colorado Delta, Lower California. *Proceedings of the Academy of Natural Sciences of Philadelphia* 57:676-690]. Interestingly, the Sierra Cocopah was the location of a much-repeated story of a "condor" observed by Edgar A. Mearns' International Boundary Commission surveyors in 1895 [For example: Anonymous. 1895. Some rare western birds. Interesting discoveries of Dr. Mearns of the United States Army. *New York Times* 26 May 1895]. The bird in question was fighting a rattlesnake: *"The big bird had seized the snake behind the head, and was struggling upward with its writhing, deadly burden. The snake's captor appeared aware that its victim was dangerous. The burden was heavy, as the reptile was nearly five feet long. The great pinions of the vulture waved rapidly as it slowly ascended from the mountain mesa. Although large in size, these vultures are not as strong as they appear to be. Up and up and up went the bird and the rattlesnake. The grip of the bird on the snake's body was not of the best. The snake seemed to be squirming from its captors talons at least sufficiently to enable it to strike at the great bird. The triangular head of the snake was seen to recoil and dart at the mass of feathers. It did this once or twice, and then, with a shriek, the vulture dropped its prey. The bird was then probably 500 feet or so above the observers. The astonished men below were then treated to a spectacle seldom seen anywhere. Few birds but the vulture could accomplish such a feat. The instant the snake escaped from the bird's clutches it dropped earthward like a shot. And like a shot the bird dropped after it, catching the astonished snake in midair ere it touched the ground, with a grip that caused death. At any rate the snake ceased to wriggle and the vulture soared away to a mountain peak to devour its hard-earned meal."*

The Mearns story proves that presumably "reliable sources" can be wrong. On the other hand, the Fort Yuma and Cocopah records considered together may lend some support to there being condors along the lower Colorado River.

(B) *"A large Vulture seen at Cave Creek* [Chiricahua Mountains, far southeastern Arizona] *March 7* [1881], *was thought by Mr.* [Frank] *Stephens to be* Pseudogryphus californianus" [Brewster, W. 1883. On a collection of birds lately made by F. Stephens in Arizona. *Bulletin of the Nuttall Ornithological Club* 8(1):21-36]. In his field notes and autobiography, the first certain mention I find of Stephens observing condors was in 1886 in California.

(C) *"In March 1881, three men, Bill Johnson, Joe Henderson and Miles Noyes* [at Pierce's Ferry, northwestern Arizona, observed] *a pair of Vultures... Noyes fired a shot from a model 76 Winchester and struck one breaking its wing near the body... It was described as being 'of a dark brown color with purplish warts on the neck.' The men had no rule, so measured it with a gun. It was over a gun length in height and more than three gun lengths in the spread of its wings."* [Brown, H. 1899. The California vulture in Arizona. *Auk* 16(3):272.] This second-hand report, recorded almost twenty years after the fact, is too vague to evaluate. The "purplish warts on the neck" suggest a bare head, but not a condor's head.

(D) Jack Alwinkle, *"an excellent hunter and reliable observer"* who reportedly had seen condors in California, shot one at "Mt. Lemon" [Lemmon] *"several years ago"* before 1891 [Rhoads, S. N. 1892. The birds of southeastern Texas and southern Arizona observed during May, June and July 1891. *Proceedings of the Academy of Natural Sciences of Philadelphia* 44:98-126]. No description was offered other than that it was *"twice as large as a buzzard."*

(E) One condor reported feeding on a dead horse, 26 March 1885, "between Ash Creek and Bumblebee, Arizona [near Payson?] [Edgar A. Mearns, manuscript cited in: Phillips, J. Marshall and G. Monson. 1964. The birds of Arizona. Tucson, Arizona: University of Arizona Press.] No other details available.

(F) One condor seen ca 1924 near Williams, Arizona [E. C. Jacot, manuscript cited in: Phillips, J. Marshall and G. Monson *op. cit.*] No other details.

6. Claude E. Schaeffer [Was the California condor known to the Blackfoot Indians? *Journal of the Washington Academy of Science* (1951), 41(6):181-191] compiled a number of stories from early Montana and Alberta about "big eagles" that occasionally visited the region. All but one of the stories described the birds as eagle-like, not vulturine. One mentioned a neck ruff and bald head, but others described features such as brown stripes or dark spots on the tail feathers, "elongated" tail, and brownish head

"feathers – none of which are condor characteristics. The big birds were considered by some to be aggressive and predatory, not vulture-like, and their arrival in the region was sometimes tied to portentous events (a subsequent earthquake, and warriors dying in battle shortly after the big bird appeared). Taken individually or as a group, there is nothing in this record that suggests the sightings and stories were about condors.

7. Miller, L. H. 1912. Contributions to avian paleontology from the Pacific coast of North America. *University of California Bulletin of the Department of Geology* 7(5):61-115.

8. Page 13 *in:* Wilbur, S. R. 1978. The California condor, 1966-76: a look at its past and future. North American Fauna Number 72. Washington, D. C.: U. S. Fish and Wildlife Service.

9. Emslie 1990 *op. cit.*

10. *"The loss of some 35 genera of North American mammals toward the end of the Pleistocene continues to be hotly debated... Although the timing of the losses is unclear, there is no reason to think that any lasted significantly after ≈10,500 ^{14}C years ago, whereas 16 of the mammals are known to have existed beyond 12,000 ^{14}C years ago. Some, however, cannot be shown to have survived the last glacial maximum, some 22,000 to 18,000 ^{14}C years ago."* [Grayson, D. K. 2008. Holocene underkill. *Proceedings of the National Academy of Sciences of the U.S.A.* 105(11):4077-4078.] Note: As an update to the above, Donald Grayson (personal communication, October 2011) informed me that the official figure for lost genera of North American mammals is now 36.
For a longer, more detailed review, see: Grayson, D. K. 2007. Deciphering North American Pleistocene extinctions. *Journal of Anthropological Research* 63(2):185-213. Grayson shows that in Europe, extinctions of various species sometimes had occurred over thousands of years, disappearing completely from some regions while remaining in others.

11. Samples of California condor bones from Arizona and New Mexico were carbon dated at around 9,600 yr B.P. [Emslie 1987, *op. cit.*]. If most of the megafaunal loss had occurred by 10,500 yr B.P., this suggests that condor populations in at least some areas had already survived 1,000 years on reduced food resources.

12. A few references to the presence of mammals following the megafaunal extinctions, both in and out of the known condor range:
Minor, R., and A. F. Pecor. 1977. Cultural resource overview of the Willamette National Forest, western Oregon. *Anthropological Papers No. 12, University of Oregon.* Eugene, Oregon. Pages 106-107, deer and elk bones in western Oregon radiocarbon dated to 7910 yrs B.P.
Wolverton, S. 2005. The effects of the hypsithermal on prehistoric foraging efficiency in Missouri. *American Antiquity* 70(1):91-106. White-tailed deer bones in Missouri with radiocarbon dates as early as 8678+/-74 yrs B.P.
Lyman, R. L., and S. Wolverton. 2002. The late Pleistocene-early historic game sink in the northwestern United States. *Conservation Biology* 16(1):73-85. *"Along the*

15

Lower Snake River between its mouth and the Washington-Idaho border, ungulate remains outnumbered those of small mammals during each 2,000-year period between 10,000 and 100 B.P."

Walker, D. N. 2000. Pleistocene and Holocene records of *Antilocapra Americana*: a review of the FAUNMAP data. *The Plains Anthropologist* 45(174):13-28. Review of all palaeontological and archaeological sites showed that pronghorn have been well distributed in North America since the Pleistocene.

Meltzer, D. J., and M. B. Collins. 1987. Prehistoric water wells on the Southern High Plains: clues to altithermal climate. *Journal of Field Archaeology* 14(1):9-28. *"Following megafaunal extinction (ca. 10,500 b.p.), bison emerged as the largest and most abundant mammal on the High Plains* [of the Texas-New Mexico border area] *not to mention the primary constituent of the human diet in the early Holocene."*

Jones, T. L., J. F. Porcasi, J. W. Gaeta, and B. F. Codding. 2008. The Diablo Canyon fauna: a coarse-grained record of trans-Holocene foraging from the central California mainland coast. *American Antiquity* 73(2):289-316. *"At Diablo Canyon, a reliable population of deer provided a primary target for hunting for nearly 10,000 years."*

Spencer, L. M., B. Van Valkenburgh, and J. M. Harris. 2003. Taphonic analysis of large mammals recovered from the Pleistocene Rancho La Brea tar seeps. *Paleobiology* 29(4):561-575. Ten specimens of modern pronghorn and 21 of black-tailed deer were found in Pit 91.[The bones themselves were not carbon-dated, but Pit 91 has two depositional layers, one at 45,000 to 35,000 yr B.P., and another at 26,500 to 23,000 B.P.]

Codding, B. F., J. F. Porcasi, and T. L. Jones. 2010. Explaining prehistoric variation in the abundance of large prey: a zooarchaeological analysis of deer and rabbit hunting along the Pecho Coast of central California. *Journal of Anthropological Archaeology* 29(1):47-61. Black-tailed deer remains were found in all 11 time periods investigated (9,000 to 500 yrs B.P.). *"The overall trend throughout the Holocene (was) a general increase in the abundance of deer in the Early-Middle Holocene with relative stability through the Middle-Late Holocene."*

13. Louderback, L. A., D. K. Grayson, and M. Llobera. 2010. Middle-Holocene climates and human population densities in the Great Basin, western USA. *The Holocene* 21(1):366-373.

14. Grayson, D. K. 2000. Mammalian responses to Middle Holocene climatic change in the Great Basin of the western United States. *Journal of Biogeography* 27(1):181-182.

15. Butler, V. L., and S. K. Campbell. 2004. Resource intensification and resource depression in the Pacific Northwest of North America: a zooarchaeological review. *Journal of World Prehistory* 18(4):327-405.

Lyman, R. L., and S. Wolverton. 2002. The late Pleistocene-early historic game sink in the northwestern United States. *Conservation Biology* 16(1):73-85.

16. Benson, L., M. Kashgarian, R. Rye, S. Lund, F. Paillet, J. Smoot, C. Kester, S. Mensing, D. Meko, and S. Lindstrom. 2002. Holocene multidecadal and multicentennial droughts affecting northern California and Nevada. *Quaternary Science Reviews* 21(4-6):659-682.

Kennett, D. J., J. P. Kennett, J. M. Erlander, and K.G. Cannariato. 2007. Human

16

responses to Middle Holocene climate change on California's Channel Islands. *Quaternary Science Reviews* 26 (3-4):351-367.

17. Byers, D. A., C. S. Smith, and J. M. Broughton. 2005. Holocene artiodactyl population histories and large game hunting in the Wyoming Basin, USA. *Journal of Archaeological Science* 32(1):125-142.

18. Hasbargen, J. 1994. A Holocene paleoclimatic and environmental record from Stoneman Lake, Arizona. *Quaternary Research* 42(2):188-196.
   Grimm, E. C., S. Lozano-Garcia, H. Behling, and V. Markgraf. 2001. Holocene vegetation and climate variability in the Americas. Pages 325-370 *in*: Markgraf, V. (editor), Interhemispheric climate linkages. Academic Press.

19. Holliday, V. T. 1989. Middle Holocene drought on the Southern High Plains. *Quaternary Research* 31(1):74-82.
   Meltzer, D. J., and M. B. Collins. 1987. Prehistoric water wells on the Southern High Plains: clues to altithermal climate. *Journal of Field Archaeology* 14(1):9-28.

20. Hall, S. A. 1988. Environment and archaeology of the central Osage Plains. *Plains Anthropologist* 33(120):203-218.

21. Wolverton, S. 2005. The effects of the hypsithermal on prehistoric foraging efficiency in Missouri. *American Antiquity* 70(1):91-106.

22. Watts, W. A., B. C. S. Hansen, and E. C. Grimm. 1992. Camel Lake: a 40,000-yr record of vegetational and forest history from northwest Florida. *Ecology* 73(3):1056-1066.

23. A summary of some of the principal evidences of middle Holocene drought is given in Louderback, Grayson and Llobera 2010 *op. cit.,* and in: K Kennett, D. J., B. J. Culleton, J. P. Kennett, J. M. Erlandson, and K. G. Cannariato. 2007. Middle Holocene climate change and human population dispersal in western North America. Pages 531-557 *in*: D. G. Anderson, K. A. Maasch, and D. H. Sandweiss (editors), Climate change and cultural dynamics: a global perspective on mid-Holocene transitions. Academic Press.
   Lack of stalagmite growth: Polyak, V. J., and Y. Asmerom. 2001. Late Holocene climate and cultural changes in the southwestern United States. *Science,* new series, 294(5540):148-151.

24. Benson, L., *et al.,* 2002, *op. cit*; also, Louderback, Grayson and Llobera 2010, *op. cit.*

25. Holliday 1989, *op. cit;* Meltzer and Collins 1987, *op. cit.*

26. Pages 97-100 *in:* Mabry, J. (editor). 2005. Feasibility study for the Santa Cruz Valley National Heritage Area. Tucson, Arizona: Center for Desert Archaeology.

27. Grayson 2000, *op. cit.*

28. Byers, Smith and Broughton 2005, *op. cit.*

29. Lyman and Wolverton 2002, *op. cit.*

30. Byers, Smith and Broughton 2005, *op. cit.*

31. Holliday 1989, *op. cit;* Meltzer and Collins 1987, *op. cit.*

32. Byers, Smith and Broughton 2005, *op. cit.*

33. Mabry 2005, *op. cit.*

34. Broughton, J. V. 1994. Declines in mammalian foraging efficiency during the late Holocene, San Francisco Bay, California. *Journal of Anthropological Archaeology* 13(4):371-401.
    Broughton, J. M., and F. E. Bayham. 2003. Showing off, foraging models, and the ascendance of large-game hunting in the California middle archaic. *American Antiquity* 68(4):783-789.
    Broughton, J. M., M. D. Cannon, and E. J. Bartelink. 2010. Evolutionary ecology, resource depression, and niche construction theory: applications to central California hunter-gatherers and Mimbres-Mogollon agriculturalists. *Journal of Archaeological Method Theory* 17:371-421.

35. Kennett *et al.,* 2007, *op. cit.*

36. Moratto, M. J., T. F. King, and W. B. Woolfenden. 1978. Archaeology and California's climate. *Journal of California Anthropology* 5(2):147-161.

37. Glassow, M. A. 1992. Archaic cultural development in California. *Revista de Arqueología Americana* 5:201-229.

38. Broughton, J. M., D. A. Byers, R. A. Bryson, W. Eckerle, and D. B. Madsen. 2008. Did climatic seasonality control late Quaternary artiodactyl densities in western North America? *Quaternary Science Reviews* 27(19-20):1916-1937.

39. Jones, T. L., J. F. Porcasi, J. W. Gaeta, and B. F. Codding. 2008. The Diablo Canyon fauna: a coarse-grained record of trans-Holocene foraging from the central California mainland coast. *American Antiquity* 73(2):289-316.
    Codding, B. F., J. F. Porcasi, and T. L. Jones. 2010. Explaining prehistoric variation in the abundance of large prey: a zooarchaeological analysis of deer and rabbit hunting along the Pecho Coast of central California. *Journal of Anthropological Archaeology* 29(1):47-61.

40. Butler, V. L., and S. K. Campbell. 2004. Resource intensification and resource depression in the Pacific Northwest of North America: a zooarchaeological review. *Journal of World Prehistory* 18(4):327-405.

18

41. It has been suggested "*that the restriction of the range of condors to the Pacific coast after the Pleistocene megafaunal extinction was largely controlled by the presence of a 'fall-back' food source, marine mammals*" [Chamberlain, C. P., J. R. Waldbauer, K. Fox-Dobbs, S. D. Newsome, P. L. Koch, D. R. Smith, M. E. Church, K. L. Sorenson, and R. Risebrough. 2005. Pleistocene to recent dietary shifts in California condors. *Proceedings of the National Academy of Sciences* 102(46):16707-16711]. Condors have undoubtedly always fed on dead seals, sea lions, whales, porpoises, dolphins, and sea otters whenever they were available. Just as clearly, marine mammals were not the only food available to post-Pleistocene condors in the Far West. In any event, such food would have only been available on a regular basis to condors that lived within effective foraging distance of the coast, say less than 50 miles. Sea mammals may have been important to some condors, but they were not vital to the survival of the condor population.

42. For compiled references to early wildlife observations, see Broughton 1994 *op. cit.,* and especially pages 95-98 *in:* Burcham, L. T. 1981. California range land. Center for Archaeological Research at Davis, Publication Number 7. Davis, California: University of California.

43. Broughton, J. V. 1994. Declines in mammalian foraging efficiency during the late Holocene, San Francisco Bay, California. *Journal of Anthropological Archaeology* 13(4):371-401.
   Broughton, J. V. 1994. Late Holocene resource intensification in the Sacramento Valley, California: the vertebrate evidence. *Journal of Archaeological Science* 21(4):501-514.

Figure 1. California condor skin dance outfit, and feather suit made from condor, bald eagle and golden eagle feathers. Collected by I. Voznesenskii in California 1840-1841. The dance outfit was acquired in the Sacramento Valley, origin of the feather suit unknown. Location: Zoological Institute, St. Petersburg, Russia. Photo courtesy L. A. Portenko.

CHAPTER 2
CONDORS AND INDIANS

Assessing the relationships between West Coast Indians and California condors – and identifying impacts early humans may have had on the condor population - is not easy to do. Probably three-quarters of the Oregon and California Indians were gone before 1850, victims of disease and murder. Some local groups were eradicated; most southern California Indians were brought under the control of the Spanish Catholic missionaries. Many of the individuals left in Oregon and northern California were herded to reservations, often intermixed with people from other geographical areas with no close kinship ties. Indian communication and documentation were oral, rather than written, and community continuity was required to preserve and pass on history. Loss of the people meant loss of information on past customs and culture. Reservation life, with its breaking down of traditional relationships, often made it impossible to continue to practice - and, eventually, even to remember - living as it had been done. By the beginning of the 20th century, when scholars began to seriously seek out and write down aboriginal history, there were few Pacific Coast Indians alive who had first- or even second-hand knowledge of what had gone on in the pre-European or early European days [1].

What is known about aboriginal contact with California condors is spotty geographically, with absolutely no information from some areas and "pretty good" information from others. For every local population, it is almost a certainty that knowledge is incomplete. It was gathered largely by non-Indians who, while struggling with Indian language, endeavored to translate Indian concepts to non-Indian documentation; whose primary interests and mode of questioning might or might not have elicited information on condors; and who often obtained all their local information from one or a few Indian informants. Chances are high that some of the "facts" were misinterpreted or are just plain wrong, and that other equally important knowledge was completely missed.

Added to the sketchiness of data and the chance of error, one also has to deal with a body of misinformation on condor-Indian interactions that has grown up in popular, and in some cases scientific, literature. Two of the most repeated stories of Indians and condors are clearly untrue. (I have to share the blame in my own earlier writings for helping - through incomplete research - to keep these "legends" alive.) With these shortcomings in mind, the following gives some idea of the tie between West Coast Indians and the California condor.

OREGON, WASHINGTON, AND BRITISH COLUMBIA.

The only prehistoric record of condors north of California links them to the aboriginal dwellers of the banks of the Columbia River in Wasco County, Oregon. During archeological excavations of Indian middens at Five Mile Rapids (also known as The Dalles Roadcut), more than 9,000 bird bones were unearthed. Included were remains from at least 22 different condors. Considering the extent of the site, it seems likely that additional excavation would yield bones from additional condors. Obviously, even twenty-two dead condors in one location is unlikely to have been a natural event; humans undoubtedly killed them for a purpose. Those particular condors died some 10,000 years ago; all were full-grown, not nestling or early fledgling, birds; and about twenty percent of the condor bones sampled showed signs of the feathers having been purposely removed. It is probably of significance that the sample included a large number of bald eagle bones, also, and that some of the eagle bones show signs of feather stripping [2]. So far, there are no clues as to what that significance might be.

Two other archaeological finds join condors and Northwest Indians in late Holocene or early recent history. Both consist of individual condor bones found with other aboriginal artifacts: one from Pender Island, British Columbia, Canada (carbon dated at ca 2,900 years B.P.) [3], and the other from a shell mound near Brookings, Curry County, Oregon. The latter, first described as being found with *"cultural material which is not very old, though entirely pre-caucasian"* [4], appears to be less than 1,100 years old [5].

Beyond these archaeological associations, the aboriginal story of condors in the Northwest is unclear. Only two words are known that were used to specifically identify condors in the region [6], both in the Sahaptin language of the middle Columbia River area. The terms, *canahúu* and *pachanahú*, have been described as *"nearly obsolete"* [7], relating to a bird that *"is very imperfectly known today and borders on the legendary"* [8]. Both descriptions suggest the words may have had their origin with the prehistoric denizens of the Columbia. Other possible references to condors are speculative; for example, designs on hand-woven baskets of *"large figures with out-spread wings"* could represent condors, but they *"usually are labeled eagles or butterflies"* [9]. "Grandfather Buzzard," possibly meant to identify the condor in a legend attributed to the Kalapuya of the Willamette Valley [10], is also the identity of one of the main characters in the well-known and much repeated Creation story of the Cherokee of the southeastern United States [11]. A story presumably from the far distant past of baby condors being kept in Columbia River camps *"to keep the thunder and lightning from striking"* [12] is almost certainly a more modern "remembrance" developed from outside information. The probable source of the story was the raising of golden eagles for eventual sacrifice, a widespread practice in the Southwest, which has been erroneously linked to the keeping of condors (see below).

California condors were present in the Pacific Northwest well into the 19th century, so they were certainly known to the Indians of the Columbia River and Willamette Valley areas. The weakness of the record suggests that there was much less contact there between people and condors than there was in California. However, it might be that the details have not survived. By 1840 – before great numbers of Caucasians had arrived in the region - many Indian bands were near extinction, the result of severe, widespread disease. By the 1870s the majority of survivors had been moved to reservations, sometimes well outside of their historic environment, and pooled with the remnant members of other near-extinct groups. By 1900 there were fewer than 2,000 Indians within the probable historic range of the condor in Oregon [13]. Little information on interactions with wildlife survived the drastic reduction in Indian numbers and the disruption of traditional activities.

FAR NORTHERN CALIFORNIA

Most of the aboriginal groups on the far northwest coast of California and in the mountains surrounding the upper Sacramento Valley seemed to know, or know of, the California condor. Most at least had a name by which they identified the species [14]. Only among the Indians of Humboldt. Del Norte, and western Trinity counties did the condor seem to have been important culturally.

Condors figured in myths, tales and religious beliefs handed down by the Yurok, Wiyot, Hupa, and Karok. "Condor" was not always a bird, but sometimes the human ancestor [15]. In Wiyot mythology, the forebear Condor has the role of the Judeo-Christian Noah, he and his sister being the only ones saved when Above Old-Man flooded the world, thereby making them the ancestors of all humans [16]. As a bird, condors in these stories were sometimes endowed with tremendous physical prowess *("so big and powerful he can lift a whale:"* Tolowa [17]; *"so big that when he flaps his wings he makes the wind:"* Wiyot [18]).

Principally, condors were noted for the potent spiritual strength inherent in them and their feathers. Shamans often gained some of this power by confronting a condor in dreams or mysterious circumstances [19], and condor feathers were used as part of the curing processes of the Indian doctors [20]. None of the Indians of the Northwest coast appear to have had ceremonies or dances directed specifically to condors. However, condor feathers were worn by Yurok, Wiyot, Hupa, Chimariko, and possibly Tolowa, in other rituals, such as the White Deerskin Dance and the Jump Dance [21]. Apparently, the usual practice was to splice condor wing (or tail?) feathers together to make especially long plumes to attach to other head ornaments [22]. In addition to shamans using individual condor wing feathers in their curing ceremonies, Wiyot shamans wore headbands that were decorated with condor body feathers, shells, and other ornaments [23]. For the Hupa Kick Dance (held at

23

the conclusion of a new doctor's training), the shaman had "a bunch" of condor feathers that she held [24].

I found only one reference to how these northwestern people obtained their condor feathers. One contemporary Yurok informant said that condors were never killed, and that all feathers were picked up where the birds had shed them [25]. Condors regularly used the same roosts and nest sites, so it might have been relatively easy for people with the knowledge of those locations to supply themselves with the few feathers needed each year. I found no indication that condor feathers were discarded after use. (Some central California Indians believed condor feathers could be "dangerous" if used improperly or for too long. See below.) Therefore, it might not have been necessary to regularly obtain replacements. Even without a strict taboo on killing condors throughout the region, the reverence in which the birds were held would have precluded all but the most necessary taking. The needs of a relatively few dancers and shamans (in a total area population of perhaps as few as 2,500 Indians by the late 1800s) would not have required the sacrifice of many birds.

SACRAMENTO VALLEY, NORTH CENTRAL COAST, AND NORTHERN SIERRA FOOTHILLS

As in far northwestern California, most Indian groups in this area knew the California condor by name [26], and many included condors in their mythology (Cahto, Yuki, Maidu, Konkow, Patwin, Nisenan, Pomo, Miwok) [27]. Surprisingly, because this is not generally thought of as "condor country," there are more documented cultural and ceremonial ties between Indians and condors in this region than anywhere else in California. A number of archaeological sites around the lower Sacramento Valley have yielded condor bone artifacts, including whistles and decorated tubes [28]. Also, this is the only area of the state in which Indian involvement led to regular killing of condors.

Indians that performed dances in which an entire condor skin was worn, or enough feathers that a condor would have to have been killed to acquire them, included the Pomo (all groups?), Northern Maidu, Konkow, Valley Nisenan, River Patwin, Miwok (all but Southern Sierra Miwok?), and perhaps Coast Yuki [29]. Among Indians embracing the Kuksu religion, condor dances were sometimes part of a dance cycle [30], but in general the condor dances seem to have been opportunistic, occurring whenever a condor was killed. The rituals were not deeply spiritual, but were imitations of the condor, or of the gods that the condor represented (*Sul* or *Sulak* of the Coast Range Indians, *Moluk* of the Miwok and Sacramento Valley groups). While performed in a widespread area, the actual dances may have occurred in a relatively few villages. There are reports of condor dancers performing exhibitions for groups that did not have their own dance [31], and of a village that "owned" the rights to the condor dance "selling" the dance to another village [32]. Condor dances were rarely performed after 1900, and even then they were considered ancient, with the details mostly forgotten. Their rarity was inevitable by then, because most Indians and most condors were gone from that area, both victims of the rapid expansion of California's non-Indian population that began with the Gold Rush (Chapter 7).

It is impossible to judge the number of California condors that were killed annually in the region. Factors that might have kept the number low were the relatively few Indians in the area (perhaps 50,000 pre-European, as few as 5,000 by 1900); the fact that condor dances were usually not part of a regular cycle and so condor killing was not a scheduled requirement; the difficulty of killing condors with snares or bow and arrows (because Indians were prohibited by White law from using firearms); and the fact that killing condors or handling their feathers was considered "dangerous," believed to sometimes lead to sickness or even death [33]. On the other hand, because condor feathers were "dangerous," they were not preserved from year to year, so new condors had to be killed for each new dance.

Did Indian exploitation of the condors hasten their disappearance from the Sacramento Valley and adjacent hills? There is no way to tell, but this is the only part of the California condor range in which it seems possible.

SAN JOAQUIN VALLEY AND SIERRA FOOTHILLS

Yokuts, Monache, and Tubatulabel all recognized condors by name [34], and Condor was a fairly prominent personality in several myths of the Yokuts and Monache (North Fork Mono) [35]. Shamans of all groups in this region were said to have worn ceremonial capes made of condor feathers [36]. Apparently no capes and no details of their use have survived. I found no suggestion that condor feathers were used by other than shamans, or that there were any dances or ceremonies in which the condor was a significant feature. Also, no condor bone artifacts have been recovered from archaeological sites in this region.

The San Joaquin-southern Sierra area never had a dense aboriginal population, and there were perhaps as few as 25,000 people in the area prior to the European invasion. The San Joaquin Valley Indians were not spared the effects of Spanish mission enslavement (see below), but real disaster arrived in the form of severe disease epidemics spreading through the area in the 1830s and 1840s [37].The Gold Rush followed in the late 1840s and early 1850s, highlighted for the Indians by more disease, murder, and displacement from their homelands, and the native inhabitants all but disappeared. By 1854, there may have been as few as 2,000 Indians in the entire San Joaquin area. If their activities had an adverse effect on the condor population before the European invasion, any impact after 1850 would have been minimal.

CENTRAL AND SOUTHERN COASTAL CALIFORNIA

The Indians of California from San Francisco Bay south to the Mexican border, and west of the San Joaquin Valley and the Mojave Desert, were the earliest to be affected by the arrival of Europeans. At the start of the Spanish Catholic mission era (1770), there were an estimated 72,000 Indians in that area. "Enrollment" (mostly forced) of Indians into mission society resulted in virtual slavery, major disruption of community and family ties, and drastic loss of individuals to disease and murder. *"By 1830* [a few years before the missions were secularized] *there were approximately 10,000 neophytes* [Indian "converts"] *enrolled at the missions and few, if any, unconverted heathen left in the territory."* In the following years many more Indians were lost to disease, murder, and destruction of their food supplies. By 1900, this vast area probably supported less than 2,500 Indians [38].

This is the region that one usually thinks of in relation to California condors, the area that certainly supported the greatest numbers of condors for at least the last 150 years of their wild existence. Therefore, it would seem logical that the species would figure prominently in local Indian mythology, ritual or religion. This seems not to have been the case. Most groups had names by which they recognized the condor [39], but condors or condor-like entities show up in myth only among the Chumash ("*Holhol,*" possibly a condor or condor-man) [40], and perhaps Cahuilla ("a bird which is larger than a buzzard") [41]. Use of condor feathers for dance regalia or ceremonial purposes is known only from the Chumash (dancing skirt, feather bands of uncertain use), Luiseño (dancing skirts), and Tipai-Ipai (dancing skirt) [42]. Whistles made from condor bones have been discovered in Costanoan territory at San Francisco Bay [43], and individual unmodified bones of condors have been found in archaeological sites at Avila Beach (San Luis Obispo County) and on San Nicholas Island [44]. There are two Chumash rock paintings that have been suggested as representations of condors; one certainly qualifies, but to see a condor in the other takes a powerful imagination [45].

During archeological excavations of Costanoan shellmounds around San Francisco Bay, a number of condor bones have been found. Also discovered were two skeletons of condors. One was complete and intact; the other was a disarticulated series of bones, but all the bones seemed to be from one bird. The condition of the skeletons suggested to the researchers *"special or ritual sepulture, perhaps mortuary treatment similar to that accorded humans"* [46]. If the condors were ritually buried, they are the only ones so far known to have received such treatment.

* * *

Two well known, often-repeated stories of condors ceremonially sacrificed appear to be entirely untrue, those of the "royal eagle" of Pajaro River, and the "Panes," or "Shoshonean condor cult," of coastal southern California.

The incident giving rise to the "Royal Eagle" story occurred in Costanoan territory. On 8 October 1769 at the Pajaro River crossing near the border of present-day Monterey and San Benito counties, Miguel Costanso, diarist of the Portola Expedition, wrote (English translation of the original Spanish):

"Here we saw a bird that the natives had killed and stuffed with grass; it appeared to be a royal eagle; it was eleven palms from tip to tip of its wings. On account of this find we called the river the Río del Pájaro" [47].

For centuries, the golden eagle had been known to the Mexican people as the royal eagle (*águila royal*). The soldiers with Costanso thought the stuffed bird looked like a royal eagle. Its wingspan of "eleven palms" was a little over seven feet, just right for a golden eagle. Neither Costanso's record, nor the similar diary entry of Fr. Juan Crespi [48], provided further details that suggest the bird was a condor. Why is this incident included in almost every story written about the California condor?

Credit for it becoming a condor story probably belongs to Harry Harris, and his "annals of *Gymnogyps*" [49]. Harris thought that the Pajaro River incident was an early record of the *panes* festival practiced by southern California Indians, an event believed at that time to involve the sacrificial killing of condors taken from their nests (see below). With the *panes* in mind, he surmised that a mere seven-foot wingspread only meant the specimen was a condor not yet full-grown. As further support, he noted that Pedro Fages' narrative of the Portola Expedition included comments about "eagles" with wings measuring "fifteen spans" (eleven feet), and of natives raising young eagles in their villages [50]. Harris failed to acknowledge that these observations were unrelated to the Pajaro River incident; it isn't clear where they occurred, as Fages did not elaborate, and no other diarist with the expedition commented similarly. Also, Fages wrote of seeing "vultures" and "buzzards" (hawks?), suggesting he was able to tell a large vulture (condor) from an eagle. There is no evidence that anyone on the Portola Expedition actually measured a bird with a "fifteen spans" wingspread (or any other wingspan). The literature is full of "eyeball" estimates of condors with wingspreads of 10, 12 and even 14 feet. By the same token, a normal seven feet of eagle wing could easily be estimated as 11 feet.

At the Pajaro River, the Spaniards may have witnessed part of an eagle-killing ceremony similar to that practiced by the southern California Gabrieliños, Luiseños, Serranos, Cahuillas, and Tipai-Ipais. The rite, often associated with the toloache (jimson weed) cult and the worship of the god Chingichnish ("Chinigchinich"), was early believed to involve condor sacrifice. This was shown to be erroneous in 1908, but the story continues to be regularly repeated in popular books and articles on the condor, and also in ornithological and ethnological papers.

* * *

In the early 1800s, at Mission San Juan Capistrano, the Catholic priest Geronimo Boscana observed an Indian ceremony in which a large bird was sacrificed. His description, first published in English by Alfred Robinson in 1846 [51], read as follows:

"The most celebrated of their [San Juan Capistrano Indians] *feasts, and which was observed yearly, was the one called the 'Panes,' signifying a bird feast. Particular adoration was observed by them, for a bird resembling much in appearance the common buzzard, or vulture, but of larger dimensions."*

In 1811, the Spanish government in Mexico asked the Catholic priests in California to answer various questions about life at the missions. Portions of the reply, translated in 1908 by A. L. Kroeber and J. T. Clark [52], contained similar descriptions of a bird sacrifice (perhaps some of the information prepared by Boscana, himself):

"They [Indians at Mission San Diego] *have a great desire to assemble at a ceremony regarding a bird called vulture (gavilan)... they kill it, and for its funeral they burn it... In the following year they search for another vulture, and do the same with it."*

"We know that they [Indians at Mission San Juan Capistrano] *adore a large bird similar to a kite, which they raise with the greatest care from the time it is young, and they hold to many errors regarding it".*

"We have not observed any other idolatry among these Indians [at Mission San Luis Rey] *than that connected with certain birds which they call azuts, which really are a kind of very large vulture... they very slowly kill the birds... They skin the birds and throw their flesh on the fire... They keep the feathers of the birds* [and] *make a sort of skirt of them... We made the most careful efforts to ascertain the purpose of this ritual, but we have never been able to extract anything else than that thus their ancestors made it".*

Even as he translated, Kroeber noted that a *"gavilan"* was not a vulture, but more likely an eagle *"which the word gavilan properly indicates."* He also noted that *"azuts are not really vultures, that is, condors, but eagles. Ashwut is Luiseño for eagle, yungavaiwot for condor."* Kroeber's Indian informants *"always mentioned the eagle as the bird connected with this ceremony."* Nevertheless, Boscana *"describes the bird as much resembling the common buzzard, but larger, which clearly makes it a condor."* Kroeber's conclusion was that probably both eagles and condors were used in the ceremony.

Shortly after Kroeber published his comments on the *Panes* story, another famous ethnologist, C. Hart Merriam, offered objections and corrections. *"As a matter of fact, the word gavilan means neither eagle nor vulture, but among Spanish and Spanish-Mexican people is the ordinary common every-day word for hawk... There is no doubt, however, that several of the early Mission Padres failed to distinguish the eagle from the large hawks, and used the name gavilan indiscriminately for both; hence Dr. Kroeber is entirely right in assuming that the ceremonial bird of the Mission Indians of Southern*

California is the eagle. It is the golden eagle (Aquila chrysaetos)".

"In another place in the same article... Dr. Kroeber states: 'Boscana, however, describes the bird as much resembling the common buzzard, but larger, which clearly makes it a condor.' This seemingly natural inference is entirely erroneous. Buzzards are large hawks - not vultures - and the bird we in America call 'turkey-buzzard' is not a buzzard at all, but a vulture. Boscana's 'common buzzard' is a large hawk closely related to our red-tail, and the bird he described as 'much resembling the common buzzard, but larger,' was of course the golden eagle. Had he meant the turkey-buzzard he would have used the Spanish-Mexican word aura (pronounced ow'-rah), which is the name by which the turkey-buzzard is known among the Spanish-speaking people of California" [53].

In 1934, John P. Harrington provided a new translation of Boscana, one that showed the entire discussion of buzzard, vulture, and condor to be irrelevant. The pertinent passage reads:

"Among all the feasts which they celebrated every year, among the principal and most solemn ones is one which they called the feast of the Pames, which means the feast of the bird, for they gave a kind of worship and veneration to a bird which has the same form and size as a kite, although somewhat larger. It is a kind of carnivorous hawk, but very sluggish and stupid" [54].

A look at the Spanish of Boscana's original manuscript shows that the Harrington translation is correct. Boscana spoke of the ritual only as a bird festival (*fiesta del Pajaro*) involving an adored and venerated species of bird of prey (*una especia de adoracion, y veneracion á un pajaro... una especie de gavilan carnisero*), similar to but larger than a kite (*que tiene la misma forma y grandeza, aunque algo mas, de un Milano*). "Kite" (signifying a hawk of the genus *Milvus*) is a better translation of "Milano" than "buzzard (a *Buteo* hawk). Either could be described as a small eagle, but neither looks anything like a vulture. Robinson's use of the term "vulture" was not actually part of the translation, but his own erroneous attempt to further define "buzzard" [55].

[An aside: The festival known as "Panes" was actually called "Pames." Robinson spelled the word correctly the first time he used it in his translation, but it was misspelled the rest of the time. This is clearly shown in the original Spanish.]

Even before Kroeber's translation of the Mission Indian report, one author had used Boscana's description to link the Pames to a "Shoshonean condor cult" [56]. Among ethnologists, Kroeber's and Merriam's explanations put an end to discussions of a southern California condor-based religion, but a number of researchers (myself included) continued to entertain the possibility that condors might occasionally have been used in lieu of eagles. A close look at the history of the ceremony shows that to be unlikely.

A Luiseño myth tells of Ouiot (pronounced *wee-ote*), the first person ever to die. The people held a ceremony at Ouiot's death, and were told that they

Figure 2. Luiseño dance skirt made of California condor feathers, San Diego (California) Museum of Man. Photo by Janet A. Hamber.

should continue to have "fiestas for the dead" every year, with a sacrificial offering. They selected Ash-wut the Eagle-Man, "a big man and a very great captain," to be the one killed. Ash-wut objected. *"To escape his fate, he went north, south, east, and west; but there was death for him everywhere, and he came back and gave himself up"* [57].

The Cahuilla believed that the eagle *"symbolized the constant life of [their] lineage. The eagle is said to live forever, and yet, from the 'beginning' allowed himself to be 'killed' so the people were assured of life after death. As lineage members died each year but the lineage continued in perpetuity, so it is with the eagle"* [58].

Descriptions of the bird-killing ceremony from the Cupeño, Serrano, Luiseno, Tipai-Ipai (Diegueno), Desert Cahuilla, Pass Cahuilla, and Mountain Cahuilla all include the same elements [59]: eaglets were obtained from eyries owned by the chiefs; they were reared in the villages, then at annual mourning ceremonies for the dead were sacrificed by suffocation. The eagle feathers were saved for ceremonial costumes, and to become part of the village's "sacred bundle" of religious items. From legend to conclusion of the ceremony, it is all about eagles. There could be no justification for substituting a condor or any other bird. It was not like having a ham instead of a turkey at Thanksgiving; the eagle was the revered bird.

Southern California Indians did kill condors on occasion. Examples of

Luiseño dance skirts made of condor feathers are preserved in several museums [60], and there are feather bands (of uncertain use) originating with the Chumash or Tatavium people [61]. Condors are seldom mentioned in southern California Indian lore, and there is no indication that condor killing was based on anything more than occasional need for feathers. Indian culture in this region was disrupted so early in the European invasion that it is impossible to know how accurate is that assessment.

* * *

So, what can be said about the effects of Indian activities on the California condor? Excepting only the inhabitants of the lower Sacramento Valley and nearby Coast Ranges, it appears that most California and Oregon Indians had little reason to kill condors, and they didn't. Some apparently had taboos against killing them. Even when permitted, killing was constrained by group rules concerning what individuals were allowed to do the taking, and by spiritual beliefs that it could be physically dangerous to handle condor feathers. Firearms of any kind were rare on the Pacific Coast prior to the Gold Rush, and early European settlers quickly passed laws barring Indians from owning or using guns. Indians had to shoot condors with bow and arrow, or snare them at baited sites [62]. Both were achievable, certainly, but - in contrast to what could be accomplished with firearms - constraints of talent and time clearly imposed limits on the amount of mayhem that could be caused.

There were limits on condor killing imposed by the habits and numbers of Indians in condor habitat, as well. Contrary to popular belief, Indians did not belong to big "tribes" occupying large areas of land. They lived in discrete communities, and seldom strayed far out of their local environment. Some trading was done for materials not found at home (including at least one case of importing condor feathers [63]), but in general Indians made use of what was available locally. A condor could only be killed if it was found nearby.

Indian population densities in most areas were low, even before European settlement. Condors had much of the countryside to themselves most of the time, with little likelihood of meeting up with Indians who wanted to kill them. By the mid-19th century, Indians had been nearly eradicated from much of California and Oregon. After that, it would have been rare for an Indian to kill a condor.

The reasoning outlined above may not apply to that region of California occupied by the Miwok, Pomo, and neighboring groups. Among these Indians, there was a steady demand for condor skins to wear in dances, with the need recurring because old "dangerous" skins and feathers needed to be replaced. The fragmentary record suggests that condor dances occurred only at scattered locations, and that villages hosting condor dances did not have them every year. Still, it looks to me like Indians killed enough condors in that region to have caused long-term reductions in condor numbers there.

31

The authors of one recent book on California condors opined that California Indians killed 700 condors each year [64]. They presented no basis for this opinion. It is clearly far from the truth. From the information available, a pre-European loss of condors to Indians might not have exceeded a dozen or so annually, with almost all that mortality occurring north of the San Francisco Bay area. Indians cannot be exonerated from contributing to the decline of California condors, but their impact was minor except in highly localized situations.

CHAPTER NOTES

1. I reviewed a large number of sources of Pacific Coast Indian populations over time, and the reasons for reductions in numbers. Some of the ones I found particularly pertinent were:

Coan, C. F. 1921. The first stage of the federal Indian policy in the Pacific Northwest. *Quarterly of the Oregon Historical Society* 22(1):46-86.

Cook, S. F. 1955. The epidemic of 1830-1833 in California and Oregon. *University of California Publications in American Archeology and Ethnology* 43(3):303-326.

Cook, S. F. 1971. The aboriginal population of upper California. Pages 66-72 *in*: R. F. Heizer and M. A. Whipple. The California Indians, a source book. Berkeley, California: University of California Press.

Cook, S. F. 1978. Historical demography. Pages 91-98 *in*: R. F. Heizer (editor), Handbook of North American Indians. Volume 8, California. Washington, D. C.: Smithsonian Institution.

Kroeber, A. L. 1925. Population. Pages 880-891 *in*: Handbook of the Indians of California. Washington, D. C.: Bureau of American Ethnology.

Thornton, R. 1980. Recent estimates of the prehistoric California Indian population. *Current Anthropology* 21(5):702-704.

2. Findings at The Dalles Road Cut are described in:

Cressman, L. S., D. L. Cole, W. A. Davis, T. M. Newman and D. J. Scheans. 1960. Cultural sequences at The Dalles, Oregon: a contribution to Pacific Northwest prehistory. *Transactions of the American Philosophical Society* 50(10):1-108.

Miller, L. H. 1957. Bird remains from an Oregon kitchen midden. *Condor* 59(1):59-63.

Hansel-Kuehn, V. J. 2003. The Dalles Roadcut (Fivemile Rapids) avifauna: evidence for a cultural origin. Master of Arts thesis. Pullman, Washington: Washington State University.

3. Specimen at the Royal British Columbia Museum, Victoria, British Columbia, Canada.

4. Miller, A. H. 1942. A California condor bone from the coast of southern Oregon. *Murrelet* 23(3):77.

5. Madonna L. Moss (University of Oregon, Eugene, Oregon) wrote 27 October 2011:

"Jon Erlandson and I [carbon]dated the Lone Ranch site in the 1990s as part of our Oregon Coast project, We obtained one historic date (280+/60 RYBP) and a pre-contact date of 1010 +/ 80 RYBP from Lone Ranch. No telling which is a better age estimate of the condor bone."

6. The term *ach'ig chiq* has been used in some recent reports, but is a Wasco word for the mythical Thunderbird, and has no known association with actual condors. [Page xviii *in:* Aguilar, G. W. Sr. 2005. When the river ran wild! Indian traditions on the mid-Columbia and Warm Springs Reservation. Portland, Oregon: Oregon Historical Society Press.] Similarly, *oma_xsapítau*, the name of a giant bird of Blackfoot legend, has occasionally been suggested as referring to the condor [Schaeffer, C. E. 1951. Was the California condor known to the Blackfoot Indians? *Journal of the Washington Academy of Sciences* 41(6):181-191].

7. Hunn, E. S. 2000. Review of linguistic information. Chapter 4, Kennewick Man, cultural affiliation report. National Park Service.

8. Hunn, E. S. 1991. Sahaptin bird classification. Pages 137-147 *in:* Pawley, A. (editor), Man and a half, essays in Pacific anthropology and ethnobiology in honour of Ralph Bulmer. Aukland, New Zealand: The Polynesian Society.

9. Pages 65-66 *in:* Schlick, M. D. 1994. Columbia River basketry: gifts of the ancestors, gifts of the earth. Seattle, Washington: University of Washington Press.

10. Moen, D.B. 2008. Condors in the Oregon Country: exploring the past to prepare for the future. Masters degree project, Portland State University (Portland, Oregon).

11. For example, see: Pijoan, T. 1992. White Wolf woman: Native American transformation myths. Little Rock, Arkansas: August House. 167 pages.

12. Schlick 1994 *op. cit.*

13. Estimates of the aboriginal population of the Pacific Northwest vary widely. Thirty-two thousand Indians along the Columbia River and in the Willamette Valley originally seems a well-researched figure. That number was reduced to 2,100 by the late 1830s: Boyd, R. L. 1975. Another look at the "fever and ague" of western Oregon. *Ethnohistory* 22(2):135-154.

Indians were not enumerated in early federal censuses unless they paid taxes, which reservation Indians did not do. However, an 1894 government report included less than 5,000 in the state of Oregon, less than 1,000 of those in the Willamette Valley. Less than 500 were estimated for the Washington side of the Columbia River: Pages 559-571 and 603-616 *in:* Anonymous. 1894. Report on Indians taxed and Indians not taxed in the United States, 1890. Washington, D.C.: Department of the Interior.

Interesting sources of information on the decline of the Pacific Northwest Indians are: Cook, S. F. 1955. The epidemic of 1830-1833 in California and Oregon. *University of California Publications in American Archeology and Ethnology* 43(3): 303-326.

Spores, R. 1993. Too small a place: the removal of the Willamette Valley Indians, 1850-1856. *American Indian Quarterly* 17(2):171-191.

14. Between 1900 and 1930, C. Hart Merriam gathered names of plants and animals from Indian groups throughout California. His notes are at the Bancroft Library (Berkeley, California): C. Hart Merriam Papers, Collection Number BANC MSS 80/18c.

Merriam listed about 20 names for condors from northwestern California, chiefly variations of one of the following (phonetically rendered): *Ke-yow'-min-nah'-ho-lan*; *Kin'-te-ah*; *Che-osh'-cho*; *Shah-tah'-ish*.

15. Among the California Indians, "Condor" – whether bird or human forebear – was always clearly identified. In contrast, in the Pacific Northwest some thought that the condor was the real species that gave rise to mythical creatures like the Thunderbird, but there was never a definite linkage. This suggests to me a more distant knowledge of the species among the more northern Indians than that had by the California people.

16. Page 83 *in*: E. W. Gifford and G. H. Block. 1930. California Indian nights entertainments. Glendale, California: Arthur H. Clark Company.
Also, pages 111-112 *in*: D. A. Leeming and J. Page. 1998. The mythology of native North America. Norman, Oklahoma: University of Oklahoma Press.

17. Page 187 *in*: C. H. Merriam and R. F. Heizer. 1967. Ethnographic notes on California Indian tribes. *Reports of the University of California Archeological Survey.* Berkeley, California: Department of Anthropology, University of California.

18. Merriam and Heizer *op. cit.,* page 180.

19. Pages 149-150 *in*: A. L. Kroeber. 1925. Handbook of the Indians of California. Washington, D. C.: Bureau of American Ethnology.
Driver, H. E. 1939. Culture element distributions: X. Northwest California. *University of California Anthropological Records* 1(6):297-433.
Pages 238-250 in: E. Sapir and V. Golla. 2001. Hupa texts, with notes and lexicon. The collected works of Edward Sapir, Volume 14. Berlin, Germany: Mouton de Gruyter.

20. Page 85 *in*: Curtis, E. S. 1924. The North American Indian. Volume 13. Cambridge, Massachusetts: Norwood Press.
Kroeber 1925 *op. cit.,* pages 117-118.
Simons, D. D. 1983. Interactions between California condors and humans in prehistoric far western North America. Pages 470-494 *in*: S. R. Wilbur and J. A. Jackson, Vulture biology and management. Berkeley, California: University of California Press.

21. Kroeber 1925 *op. cit.,* pages 55-56. Also: Waters, H. 2009. Fixing the world. *North Coast Journal* (Eureka, California) 16 July 2009.

22. Driver 1939 *op. cit.;* Kroeber 1925 *op. cit.,* pages 55-56.

23. Such a headband is preserved in the Phoebe Hearst Museum of Anthropology,

34

University of California-Berkeley (Catalogue number 1-11618); pictured in: C. D. Bates, J. A. Hamber and M. J. Lee. 1993. The California condor and the California Indians. *American Indian Art Magazine* 19(1):40-47.

24. Sapir and Golla *op. cit.*, pages 223-229, 260-267.

25. Barnard, J. 2009. Yurok Tribe works for return of condor to Northwest to help fix world gone wrong. The Los Angeles (California) *Times*, 18 August 2009: quoting Tiana Williams of the Yurok.

26. Some of the more common names for condors in this area, as gathered by Merriam (see Note 14, above): *sool', e-soon, mol'-luk, mol'-luk-ko.*

27. Some of the references reviewed were:
Barrett, S. A. 1906. A composite myth of the Pomo Indians. *Journal of American Folklore* 19(72):37-51.
Dixon, R. B. 1902. Maidu myths. *Bulletin of the American Museum of Natural History* 17(2):33-118 (condor, pages 98, 265, 302).
Goddard, P. E. 1909. Kato texts. *University of California Publications in American Archeology and Ethnology* 5(3):65-238 (condor on pages 71-77, 122-133).
Kroeber, A. L. 1929. The Valley Nisenan. *University of California Publications in American Archeology and Ethnology* 24(4):253-290 (condor, page 276).
Kroeber, A. L. 1932. The Patwin and their neighbors. *University of California Publications in American Archeology and Ethnology* 29(4):253-423 (condor, page 306).
Merriam, C. H. 1910. The dawn of the world, myths and tales of the Miwok Indians of California. Cleveland, Ohio: Arthur Clark Company.
Ortiz, B. 1989. Mount Diablo as myth and reality: an Indian history convoluted. *American Indian Quarterly* 13(4):457-470.

28. Simons 1983 *op. cit.*

29. Some of the references reviewed were:
Gifford, E. W. 1926. Miwok cults. *University of California Publications in American Archeology and Ethnology* 18(3):391-408.
Gifford, E. W. 1955. Central Miwok ceremonies. *University of California Anthropological Records* 14(4):261-318.
Gifford, E. W. 1965. The Coast Yuki. Publication No. 2, Sacramento (California) Anthropological Society.
Gifford, E. W., and A. L. Kroeber. 1937. Culture element distributions: IV, Pomo. *University of California Publications in American Archeology and Ethnology* 37(4):117-254.
Kroeber 1932, *op. cit.*, pages 339-342.
Loeb. E. M. 1926. Pomo folkways. *University of California Publications in American Archeology and Ethnology* 19(2):149-405 (condor dance, pages 384-385).

30. Loeb, E. M. The Eastern Kuksu Cult. *University of California Publications in American Archeology and Ethnology* 33(2):139-232.

35

31. Gifford 1965 *op. cit.,* pages 84-85; Loeb 1926 *op. cit.,* pages 384-385; Bates, Hamber and Lee *op. cit.,* page 43.

32. Kroeber 1929 *op. cit.,* page 269.

33. DuBois, C. 1935. Wintu ethnography. *University of California Publications in American Archeology and Ethnology* 36(1):1-147 (danger of condor feathers, page 91-93).
Kroeber 1932 *op. cit.,* pages 341-342; Merriam and Heizer *op. cit.,* page 280; Bates, Hamber and Lee *op. cit.,* page 44.

34. In the northern San Joaquin area, the usual name for the condor was *mol'-luk* or *mol'-luk-ko;* in the southern regions, most groups recognized the condor as *we'-its* or *weets* (Merriam, Note 14, above).

35. Gayton, A. H., and S. S. Newman. 1940. Yokuts and Western Mono myths. *University of California Anthropological Records* 5(1):1-110.
Gifford, E. W. 1923. Western Mono myths. *Journal of American Folklore* 36(142):301-367.
Gifford and Block *op. cit.,* pages 91-94.
Kroeber, A. L. 1906-1907. Indian myths of south central California. *University of California Publications in American Archeology and Ethnology* 4(4):167-250 (condor myths, pages 205-231).

36. Aginsky, B. W. 1943. Culture element distributions: XXIV Central Sierra. *University of California Anthropological Records* 8(4):393-468 (condor regalia, page 447).
Driver, P. 1937. Culture element distributions. VI Southern Sierra. *University of California Anthropological Records* 1(2):53-154 (condor regalia, pages 105 and 144).

37. Cook 1955 *op. cit.*

38. This section is summarized from information in the literature cited under Chapter Note 1. The quote is from Cook 1978 *op. cit.*

39. Names applied to the condor in west-central and southern California (after Merriam, Note 14, above): *Titch', wah'-sak* and *Wah-sak-kah* (central coast); *Yung-ah'-ve-wit* and *pah'-ke-ut* (southern California).

40. Page 84 *in*: Hudson, T., and E. Underhay. 1978. Crystals in the sky: an intellectual odyssey involving Chumash astronomy, cosmology and rock art. Santa Barbara, California: Ballena Press.

41. Page 376 *in*: Hooper, L. 1920. The Cahuilla Indians. *University of California Publications in American Archeology and Ethnology* 16(6):315-380.

42. Bates, Hamber and Lee *op. cit.;* photos of Luiseño dance skirts, pages 42-43.

Page 147 *in*: Blackburn, T. 1963. A manuscript account of the Ventureno Chumash. *Archeological Survey Annual Report* 5:139-158. University of California, Los Angeles.

43. Morejohn, G. V., and J. P. Galloway. 1983. Identification of avian and mammalian species used in the manufacture of bone whistles from a San Francisco Bay archeological site. *Journal of California and Great Basin Anthropology* 5(1-2):87-97.

44. Simons 1983 *op. cit.*

45. Lee, G. 1979. The San Emigdio rock art site. *Journal of California and Great Basin Anthropology* 1(2):295-305.
   Lee, G., and S. Horne. 1978. The Painted Rock site (SBa-502 and SBa-526): Sapaksi, the House of the Sun. *Journal of California Anthropology* 5(2):216-224.

46. Howard, H. 1929. The avifauna of the Emeryville shellmound. *University of California Publications in Zoology* 32(2):301-394.
   Wallace, W. J., and D. W. Lathrap. 1959. Ceremonial bird burials in San Francisco Bay shellmounds. *American Antiquity* 25(2):262-264.

47. Teggart, F. J. 1911. The Portola Expedition of 1769-1770. Diary of Miguel Costanso. *Publications of the Academy of Pacific Coast History* 2(4):1-167.

48. Page 210 *in*: H. E. Bolton. 1927. Fray Juan Crespi, missionary explorer of the Pacific Coast, 1769-1774. Berkeley, California: University of California Press.

49. Pages 6-7 *in*: Harris, H. 1941. The annals of *Gymnogyps* to 1900. *Condor* 43(1)

50. Pages 12 and 77 *in*: Priestly, H. I. (translator). 1972. A historical, political, and natural description of California by Pedro Fages, soldier of Spain, dutifully made for the Viceroy in the year 1775. Ramona, California: Ballena Press.

51. Page 291 *in*: "An American" [Alfred Robinson]. 1846. Life in California: during a residence of several years in that territory. New York, New York: Wiley & Putnam.

52. Pages 4, 7 and 11 in: Kroeber, A. L. 1908. A mission record of the California Indians. *University of California Publications in American Archeology and Ethnology* 8(1):1-27.

53. Merriam, C. H. 1908. Meaning of the Spanish word gavilan. *Science* 28(709), New Series, page 147.

54. Page 39 *in*: Harrington, J. P. 1934. A new original version of Boscana's historical account of the San Juan Capistrano Indians of southern California. *Smithsonian Miscellaneous Collections* 92(4):1-62.

55. Reichlen, H., and P. Reichlen. 1971. Le manuscrit Boscana de la Bibliotheque Nationale de Paris. *Journal de la Societe des Americanistes* 60(1):233-273.
   A "revised and annotated version" of Alfred Robinson's translation of Chinigchinich

37

was published in 1978 by the Malki Museum (Banning, California). Curiously, that version reverts to Robinson's original error of equating "buzzard" with "vulture." The extensive annotations by J. P. Harrington add to the confusion by giving lengthy comments supporting Robinson's original errors in bird identification.

56. Pages 397-399 *in*: Hodge, F. W. (editor). 1907. Handbook of American Indians north of Mexico. Washington, D. C.: Bureau of American Ethnology.

57. DuBois, C. 1906. Mythology of the Mission Indians. *Journal of American Folklore* 19(72):52-60.

58. Pages 138-140 *in*: Bean, L. J. 1974. Mukat's people: the Cahuilla Indians of southern California. Berkeley, California: University of California Press.

59. Principal references to the southern California eagle-killing ceremony:
Bean *op. cit.,* pages 138-140
Pages 182-183 *in*: DuBois, C. G. 1908. The religion of the Luiseño Indians of southern California. *University of California Publications in American Archeology and Ethnology* 8(3):69-186.
Strong, W. D. 1929. Aboriginal society in southern California. *University of California Publications in American Archeology and Ethnology* 26:1-358 (eagle-killing ceremony on pages 32-34, 83-84, 119-120, 177-179, 261-262, and 307-309).
Pages 314-320 *in*: Waterman, T. T. 1910. the religious practices of the Diegueno Indians. *University of California Publications in American Archeology and Ethnology* 8(6):271-358.

60 Bates, Hamber and Lee, *op. cit.*

61. Elsasser, A., and R. F. Heizer. 1963. The archeology of Bowers Cave, Los Angeles County, California. *University of California Archeological Survey Reports* 59:1-45.

62. Pages 101 and 133 *in*: Barrett, S. A. 1952. Material aspects of Pomo culture. *Bulletin of the Public Museum of the City of Milwaukee* 20(1).
Gifford 1926 *op. cit.,* page 395.
Kroeber 1932 *op. cit.,* page 279.

63. Gifford and Kroeber 1937 *op. cit.,* pages 169-170.

64. Pages 43-44 *in*: Snyder, N. F. R., and H. Snyder. 2000. The California condor: a saga of natural history and conservation. San Diego, California: Academic Press.

CHAPTER 3
EARLY BIRDS?

The first Europeans to reach California condor country probably didn't kill any condors, but some of the slightly later ones might have. Possibly the first casualty occurred in the winter of 1602-1603, when the Spaniard Sebastian Vizcaino sailed his ships into Monterey Bay. No one in his party left a day-to-day journal of the time spent there (16 December 1602 to 3 January 1603), but both Vizcaino and the Catholic padre Antonio de la Ascencion wrote down some of their impressions of the area and its wildlife.

Vizcaino was brief: *"There is much wild game, such as harts, like young bulls, deer, buffalo, very large bears, rabbits, hares, and many other animals and many game birds, such as geese, partridges, quail, crane, ducks, vultures, and many other kinds of birds which I will not mention lest it become wearisome"* [1]. Ascencion added a few more names to the list: *"There are many of these animals [tirando: reindeer; elk?] here, and besides them there are large deer, stags, jackrabbits, and rabbits, and wild-cats as large as kids. There is an abundance of birds of all kinds, geese, doves, thrushes, sparrows, linnets, cardinals, quail, partridges, magpies, cranes, and buzzards, all like those of Castile."* He went on to name a few birds of the seashore and also some of the local marine life. The lists are interesting (one wonders what Vizcaino saw that he thought were bison, and what birds Ascencion saw that were like the "cardinals" [*cardenales*] of Castile), but the condor connection lies in Ascencion's next two sentences:

"There are some other birds here of the shape of turkeys, the largest I saw on this voyage. From the point of one wing to that of the other it was found to measure seventeen spans (more than a yard)" [2].

The English translator of Ascencion's notes thought these birds had to be California condors, and with a wingspread of seventeen spans [a span being approximately 9 inches], what else could they be? But there were problems: Ascencion added after the measurement of seventeen spans that this was "more than a yard" (*de mas de a vara:* a vara being about 33 inches). Clearly, the translator said in a footnote, there was an error in Ascencion's journal, because *"seventeen spans is more than eight feet"* [3]. Yes, it is; seventeen spans is almost thirteen feet. But where exactly was the error?

Looking at the original Spanish of Ascencion's report, the word translated as "span" is *palmo* [4]. There are two palm measurements: *palmo mayor* is about 8 1/4 inches, and *palmo menor* about 3 inches. Using the large palm measurement instead of the span measure, the big bird's wingspread decreases from thirteen feet to a more likely (taking into account the imprecision of such field estimates) eleven and one-half feet. But, using the *palmo menor,* the wingspan becomes 4 feet, or "more than a yard." Was he seeing "turkeys" with eleven-foot wings or four-foot wings?

The Vizcaino expedition had departed Acapulco, Mexico, in March 1602, and had visited a number of locations in Mexico and present-day California. These "turkey-like" birds were "the largest" seen "on this voyage." Surely, they had seen some big birds on the trip, turkey vultures perhaps (with a 5 1/2 feet wingspan)? If so, then clearly the record would favor a bird with the condor-size wingspan. Neither Vizcaino nor Ascencion mentioned vultures until they reached Monterey, but there Vizcaino noted that they saw "vultures," and Ascencion reported "buzzards." There is often some confusion in the early American literature as to what is meant by the term "buzzard" (Chapter 2), but the word used by Ascencion, *buitres*, translates as vulture, not hawk or eagle. So, it would seem that Ascencion observed something larger than a turkey vulture.

There are other questions to be resolved. For instance, if Ascencion could identify turkey vultures, wouldn't he have thought that a condor was more like a large vulture than it was like a turkey? And here we run into another oddity: the word that Ascencion used that was translated as turkey, *gallina,* actually means "chicken." I can understand a turkey, in body shape and size and baldish head, reminding someone of a short-winged condor, but a chicken does not bring that comparison to mind. Ascencion's description actually sounds like the 17th century description of turkey vultures penned by the Russian explorer Langsdorff. The English translation:

"Among the feathered species, I observed the vultus aura. *The feet of this bird are very different from those of any other; the claws are thin and small, and the three foremost are united by a sort of half-web, so that to judge by the feet, it seems to belong to the class of marsh birds, but according to the bill, it should belong to birds of prey... These vultures are gregarious; they are slow in flight, and feed upon carrion, which, in company with the ravens, with whom they live upon friendly terms, they devour in great quantities"* [5].

No chicken-like bird has a wingspread of more than a yard, so Ascencion must have been describing a large hawk (4 feet), turkey vulture (5 1/2 feet), bald or golden eagle (7 feet), or condor (9 feet). He had already noted seeing vultures (*buitre*), so presumably the unidentified chicken-like birds were something else. They probably weren't hawks or eagles, because they were feeding on a dead whale... Oops, wait a minute.

Probably every story written about Ascencion's "condor" sighting has described the birds as feeding on a dead whale. The only problem is that Ascencion never saw such a sight - or, if he did, he didn't write about it. The misinformation arose from the first person to overlook the whimsy in Harry Harris's account of Ascencion's sighting, and was carried on by the hundreds of writers who quoted the misquoter. Concerning the mystery birds, Ascencion wrote only what I've quoted above. In another part of his description of the natural resources of Monterey, he wrote:

"There are oysters, lobsters, crabs and burgaos (snail, or whelk?) *among the rocks, and many large seals, or sea-calves, and whales. One very large one recently dead had gone ashore on the coast in this port and the bears came by night to dine on it"* [6].

Harris took the two quotes, and wove them into a memorable (but imaginative) quote of his own:

"The record begins with the published diary of a barefoot Carmelite friar, Fr. Antonio de la Ascension, who in 1602, from the tossing deck of a tiny Spanish ship, observed on a California beach the stranded carcass of a huge whale (conceivably and probably) surrounded by a cloud of ravenous condors. Here indeed is material with which to stir the most dormant imagination; civilized man for the first time beholding the greatest volant bird recorded in human history, and not merely an isolated individual or two, but an immense swarm rending at their food, shuffling about in crowds for a place at the gorge, fighting and slapping with their great wings at their fellows, pushing, tugging at red meat, silently making a great commotion, and in the end stalking drunkenly to a distance with crop too heavy to carry aloft, leaving space for others of the circling throng to descend to the feast!" [7].

Great writing, but "conceivably and probably" does not a condor feeding on a whale make.

Did the Vizcaino party observe California condors? I think they probably did; no matter the number of questions one raises about the record, there don't seem to any other logical alternatives. Did they kill a condor, or at least find one dead? Again, I think the answer has to be yes; "*from the point of one wing to that of the other it was found to measure seventeen spans*" sounds like an actual (albeit crude) measurement, not an "eyeball estimate."

* * *

After Ascencion, the California condor record is barren of European influence for almost 200 years. The first confirmed specimen was collected in 1792 or 1793 (Chapter 4), but there was a possible condor killed a year or so earlier. Harry Harris, in his "Annals of *Gymnogyps*," made a case for this specimen.

"Traversing the entire distance from the Cape region of Lower California to the San Francisco Bay district, [the botanist Jose Longinos Martinez] *collected much miscellaneous information and a number of specimens, including at least one California Condor. On his return by ship from Monterey to San Blas he mailed from a port on the coast of Lower California advices to a friend in Madrid that he was forwarding a shipment of specimens. The letter, dated San Borja, Old California, April 15, 1792, addressed to Professor Antonio Porlier, Madrid, Spain, was attached to a manifest containing an itemized list of fourteen species of birds. The first bird on the list (specimen No. 1) is given the strange name of* Vultur Harpyia *(variety:* Monstruosa*), which is without much question the first systematic name ever applied to*

41

Gymnogyps californianus; and that, above all things, a trinomial! ...The specimen of the condor is of course lost; at least no further mention of it has yet been uncovered, and it is presumed the name was never published. The evidence is explicit enough that this early specimen was taken in California sometime in 1791 or early 1792 and that it therefore antedates the type" [8].

Harris made some mistakes interpreting the timing and route of Longinos' travels, which raises doubts about his conclusion. Making mistakes with the Longinos manuscript is easy to do. It is neither a journal nor a diary, but is a narrative of various observations Longinos made while in "Old California" (present-day Baja California, Mexico) and "New California" (the modern-day state of California). There are no dates in the narrative, and an appended "itinerary" is merely a list of place names and the distances (in leagues) from one to the next. (The manuscript editor L. B. Simpson noted in his Preface that the itinerary is clearly inaccurate; to have followed the route identified, Longinos would have *"accomplished journeys that would be next to impossible, not to say altogether irrational, as a reference to a map of the territory will convince the investigator"* [9]) Only two sources indicate the timing of the trek, the 15 April 1792 letter noted by Harris, and a letter of 22 November 1792 cited by Simpson in his Preface.

From the April letter, we learn that, in 1791, Longinos had traveled from Mexico City to San Blas, on the Pacific coast of mainland Mexico, and was in San Blas in June 1791. There is no specific record of his whereabouts for the next six months, but part of that time was spent around Cabo San Lucas, in extreme southern Baja California. He left Cabo San Lucas *"three months ago"* (mid-January 1792), and traveled north up the peninsula. On 15 April 1792, apparently from a Gulf of California port near San Borja, he sent two boxes of biological specimens to Spain. In the transmittal letter, he advised that he planned to continue north through "Old" and "New" California, arriving in Monterey in September 1792 [10].

From his narrative, it appears that Longinos carried through with his plan to travel north to Monterey. (Once, he mentioned tar pits in the area between Monterey and San Francisco, but it isn't clear from the narrative that he actually saw them, or just heard about them.) By 22 November 1792, he was back in San Blas, having reached there aboard the frigate *"Concepcion,"* commanded by Don Francisco Eliza. (This information is in a letter from Eliza to the Mexican viceroy, correspondence Simpson discovered in the National Archives of Mexico.)

Longinos did not send his biological specimens to Spain on his return from Monterey, as Harris believed, but only three months into his journey through Baja California. It's possible that some of the specimens were collected in mainland Mexico during the three months for which there are no specific records. Any specimens taken between January and April 1792 would have come from Baja California Sur, between Cabo San Lucas and San Borja. If

Longinos did send a California condor skin to Spain, it didn't come from "Upper" California, but from Mexico at least 150 miles south of any other record of California condor, and in a desert terrain much different than any other known condor habitat.

Did Longinos collect a condor? Considering just the latitude and the habitat involved, I would be inclined to look elsewhere for the identity of *Vultur Harpyia* (variety: *Monstruosa*). My initial vote would have gone to the caracara. However, in a brief description of the birds of "Old California," Longinos identified as being among the *"most abundant"* he had observed *"the crows (those called gueleles or quebrantahuesos—bonebreakers), a species of vulture* (Vultur Harpia)...*hawks* (Falco)..." [11]. Quelele is another name for the caracara, whose appearance does bear similarities to the Old World lammergeyer (*quebrantahuesos*). That appears to rule out the caracara as the "mystery bird." The inclusion of *Vultur Harpyia* with the "most abundant" birds seen by Longinos tells us that, whatever species it was, it was not some rarity in the area.

Later, in "New California," Longinos mentioned seeing "vultures," but with no further description of them [12]. One might have expected him to identify them as *Vultur Harpyia,* if they were, but the list in which the vulture is included identifies only one bird species with a Latin name. The identity of the "New California" vultures remains undetermined.

Two additional points, although neither really helps. First, Harris thought that Longinos had coined a new name for the California condor, but *Vultur harpia* [actually, *harpja*] was already in use. Linnaeus considered the harpy eagle to be a vulture, and had given it that Latin name in 1758 [13]. Longinos appears to have merely claimed a subspecific identity for his bird. That being the case, he must have thought that he had seen and collected the harpy eagle, but a very big one (variety *Monstruosa*).

Second, Simpson translated Longinos as naming the bird *"a species of vulture* (*Vultur Harpia*)*,"* which to most people would suggest a (more or less) bald-headed bird. A very large, bare-headed vulture would have to be a California condor. But Longinos did not write what Simpson "translated." The original Spanish says only that he saw *"especie de Vultur Harpia;"* Simpson added "of vulture," presumably as a clarification [14]. Longinos was not reporting that he saw vultures; he saw birds he though were harpy eagles. It may be significant that he mentions vultures and hawks in his narrative, but not eagles (other than the harpy). Golden eagles are quite common in both Baja California and California; was his "gigantic harpy" a golden eagle?

The next identification gets a lot easier.

CHAPTER NOTES

1. Vizcaino, S. 1916. Diary of Sebastian Vizcaino. Pages 52-103 *in:* H. E. Bolton, Spanish exploration in the Southwest 1542-1706. New York, New York: Charles Scribner's Sons. The wildlife references are on pages 91-92.

2. Page 361 of: Wagner, H. R. (translator). 1928. Father Antonio de la Ascension's account of the voyage of Sebastian Vizcaino. *California Historical Society Quarterly* 7(4):295-394.

3. Wagner *op. cit.,* page 391.

4. Thanks to Alison Hinderliter (Manuscripts and Archives Librarian, The Newberry Library, Chicago, Illinois) for providing me with a copy of Ascension's original Spanish manuscript entry. It is on page 83 of: *Relación de la jornada que hizo el general Sevastian Vizcayno d[e]l descubrimiento de las Californias el año de 1602* [Newberry Library Call Number VAULT Ayer MS 1038 - Special Collections].

5. Pages 480-481 in: Von Langsdorff, G. H. 1817. Voyages and travels to various parts of the world during the years 1803, 1804, 1805, 1806 and 1807. Carlisle, Pennsylvania: George Philips.

6. Wagner *op. cit.,* page 361.

7. Page 4 in: Harris, H. 1941. "The annals of *Gymnogyps* to 1900." *Condor* 43(1): 3-55.

8. Harris *op. cit.,* page 8.

9. Pages xi-xii in: Simpson, L. B. 1938. California in 1792. The expedition of Jose Longinos Martinez. San Marino, California: Huntington Library. 111 pages.

10. Simpson *op. cit.,* pages 101-103.

11. Simpson *op. cit.,* page 9.

12. Simpson *op. cit.,* page 35.

13. Oberholser, H. C. 1919. *Thrasaetos* versus *Harpia. Auk* 36(2):282.

14. Thanks to Omer "Greg" Whitman for visiting the Huntington Library (San Marino, California), and examining for me the original Spanish of the Longinos manuscript (MSS HM 321).

Whether or not the Ascencion and Longinos birds were California condors, there is no question about the identity of the first of the species to be introduced to the scientific community. That specimen, the one from which the California condor received its first published recognition, still exists in the Natural History Museum at Tring, United Kingdom [1]. It is a fairly disreputable looking study skin of an adult California condor, but how could it not be somewhat the worse for wear? Consider that it was obtained (probably shot) in what is now California in 1792 or 1794; was aboard a sailing ship, probably stored in alcohol, for a minimum of one year and perhaps as long as three years; was prepared by a taxidermist and put on display with sunlight, dust and bugs to deteriorate it for 100 years or so; and then stored in a dark cabinet for the rest of its 220-year existence. Actually, comparing photos of it today with some taken in 1934, it looks like someone has done rehabilitation work on it sometime in the last 75 years.

If you search for information on when and where this condor was killed, you will probably find that it was obtained 5 December 1792 at Monterey, California. That was the conclusion of Joseph Grinnell, after studying the published California journal of Archibald Menzies, surgeon and botanist on Captain George Vancouver's ship *"Discovery,"* on their around-the-world cruise in 1791-1795 [2]. Grinnell's opinion was based on two items of information: first, Menzies had only a few opportunities to collect a condor in 1792-1793; and second, on 5 December he wrote in his journal that they had shot *"a new species of Hawk,"* the only instance in the journal where he mentioned a bird that might have been a condor [3]. Grinnell's surmise was probably incorrect. I can't provide the real date and place that the condor was procured, but I can tell you why I think Grinnell was wrong, and I can open the door to a few other possibilities.

Very little is known about this condor specimen. Presumably it was aboard *"Discovery"* when the ship returned to England in October 1795. It appears likely that Menzies had it in his possession until early 1796, as his mentor Sir Joseph Banks explained in a letter 3 February 1796 to the King's Home Secretary, the Duke of Portland: *"Mr. Menzies* [has been employed] *in arranging the various articles he collected during the Voyage, a Catalogue of these I have the honor to enclose... They are now at my house, and the greater part of them quite ready to be sent any place your Grace shall choose to direct"* [4].

The Duke of Portland presented Menzies' "Catalogue of Curiosities" to the King, and it was decided that the specimens listed should be placed in the British Museum. Unfortunately, the catalogue was not specific about what birds were included, but merely identified *"a Collection of Birds preserved in*

Spirits from California &c." [5]. We can probably safely assume that the condor was part of that collection, for within a short time the bird was being examined by George Shaw, Keeper of the Zoological Department at the British Museum. In September 1797, as part of his "Vivarium naturae" series, Shaw published the first description of the California condor. Shaw gave minimal information about the origins of the bird: *"This Vulture was brought over by Mr. Menzies during his expedition with Captain Vancouver, from the coast of California, and is now in the British Museum"* [6] So far, no one has found any additional data. Of Menzies' bird collection, only one other species has proven identifiable. A pair of California quail, the type specimens, were recently rediscovered after having been misplaced for well over 100 years [7].

Figure 3. First depiction of California condor: Shaw's Miscellany

46

In the 1970s, when I was first investigating California condor mortality, I corresponded with Richard C. Banks of the National Museum of Natural History, concerning Menzies' condor. Dick expressed doubts about Grinnell's conclusions. He wrote to me: *"I think it highly unlikely that a naturalist of Menzies' stature, who gave excellent descriptions of many birds in his journals and even applied manuscript scientific names to some, would have passed off the Condor as merely 'a new species of hawk' and not made some other comment... I have scoured through Vancouver's journal, and nowhere does he mention anything that might be a Condor, though he has a good bit of information including mention of two kinds of eagles, cranes, swans, ducks and teal, etc. Anyone who could separate ducks from teals would surely separate Condors from anything else."*

At the time, I knew little about Menzies and his qualifications as an ornithologist, but agreed with Dick that *"a new species of hawk"* was an odd way for anyone to describe a condor. Still, Grinnell was correct in his statements that Menzies had few chances to collect birds in California in 1792-1793, and that Monterey in December 1792 seemed a likely place and time to have obtained the condor. Whatever my and Dick's doubts, there seemed to be no way to further the discussion. Then, in September 2008, in the archives of the National Library of Australia (Canberra), I located Menzies' unpublished journal for 1794-1795 [8]. Apparently no one interested in Menzies' natural history observations in California knew of the existence of this manuscript. Finding it opened the door for a new look at Menzies' condor.

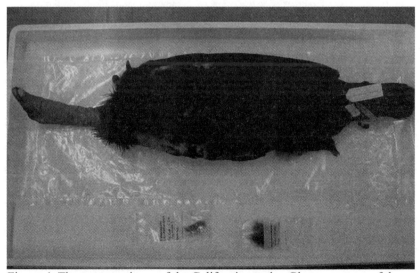

Figure 4. The type specimen of the California condor. Photo courtesy of the Natural History Museum (Tring, United Kingdom).

Would Menzies have called a California condor *"a new species of hawk?"* It seems unlikely. Although Menzies' principal training and interest was in botany, his journals show that he had a wide knowledge of natural history, and that he could identify many birds by type, if not by species. Typical of his written comments: *"We also saw a number of Birds such as Auks Divers & Shags"* [9]. *"We shot several Plovers and other small birds. We saw on the Lagoon large flocks of Pelicans & vast flights of common Curlews flying about..."* [10]. But other notations show that he was much more than just a "bird watcher:" *"On rowing a little distance from the ship I shot one of the large brown birds which were at different times seen in the course of this passage & found it to be a species of Albatross agreeing nearly in its characteristics with the* Diomedia fuliginosa *but as I was somewhat doubtful of its being the same bird, I have here subjoined the following brief description of it. This bird is about 7 feet between the tip of its wings moderately extended / & three feet in length including the Bill which is 4 inches & of a chocolate colour, the upper mandible is longer than the under & hookd at the end: The front--a small spot under each eye pointing backwards; the rump, crissum inner half of the tail & shafts of the quills are white; the rest of the head neck & tail together with the upper parts of the body & wings are of a dark brown, but the gullet & belly are of a dusky cinereous colour; the legs toes & claws are black; the trides dark hazley"* [11].

And on another occasion: *"...the Vessels had been visited by a few Natives who had nothing to dispose of but a few Water Fowls particularly a brackish colourd species of Auk with a hornlike excrescence rising from the ridge of its Bill, & as it appeard to be a new species I named it* Alca Rhinoceros *& describd it"* [12].

A person who could make these kinds of observations seems like someone who could tell that a condor was a type of vulture, not a hawk. In fact, Menzies' journal entry at Monterey 29 November 1794 shows that (at least by the end of the voyage) he did know.

"The country swarmed at this time with a vast variety of birds both land & aquatic; many of them had migrated to these regions from the northern parts of the coast, to [escape?] the severity of the weather. Among the larger were eagles hawks vultures <u>two</u> <u>species</u> [my underlining], *cranes white & blue, Canadian Geese, Ducks, Teal, Widgeons, Quails, Plovers, Curlews, Ravens Crows etc. & of small birds a numerous catalogue; so that sporting parties had sufficient amusement, in addition to the variety of excellent repast afforded to our tables by their industry"* [13].

The two species of vultures could only be the California condor and the turkey vulture, and the *"new species of hawk"* was probably a species of hawk. There would have been a number of possibilities at Monterey in late fall but, without Menzies' list, there is no justification to speculate.

* * *

As pointed out by Grinnell, there was limited opportunity to obtain specimens in California in 1792-1793, even taking into account that Menzies was not the only one in the party killing birds. Still, there was ample time at several locations to kill a condor if one had been available. Also, Grinnell did not know about the 1794 visit, which offered additional chances.

The *Discovery* was in San Francisco Bay 15 November to 25 November 1792. Menzies was recovering from a serious illness, and only took a few short walks near the bay shore during that time, but Captain Vancouver and some of the crew were three days on horseback visiting the Mission Santa Clara [14].

At Monterey 27 November 1792 to 14 January 1793, Menzies and others spent considerable time on shore. He noted in early December that *"those who were fond of shooting & sporting were suffered to indulge in their favorite pursuits without the least restraint, so that parties were out daily traversing the Country in almost every direction for ten or twelve miles round"* [15]. After his walk to Point Pinos on 5 December (the day they collected the *"new species of hawk"*), Menzies wrote: *"The two following days I remaind on board examining drawing & describing my little collection & such other objects of natural history as were brought me by the different parties who traversd the Country, & who were in general extremely liberal in presenting me with every thing rare or curious they met with. The sporting parties were particularly successful in killing a vast variety of Game with which the Country abounded & which were now in full perfection"* [16].

From Monterey, the *Discovery* sailed to the Hawaiian Islands and did not return to California until 2 May 1793, when they landed at Trinidad on the far northwest coast. They stayed two days, but apparently no one ventured far from the ships, and all were busy taking on water and refitting the vessels. The expedition went north from Trinidad, and did not touch land in California again until 20 October 1793, when a party including Menzies landed at Bodega Bay for a short visit. Menzies wrote: *"We strolled about on the low land between the Bay & the Lagoon which was composd of sandy banks & small hillocs on which we shot several Plovers & other small birds. We saw on the Lagoon large flocks of Pelicans & vast flights of common Curlews flying about, but both were so shy that we could not get near enough to have a shot at them"* [17].

At San Francisco Bay 21-24 October 1793, Menzies did not leave the ship. Some of the crew went ashore, but the Spaniards were much less hospitable to the English than on their previous visit, and no one went far. Similarly at Monterey 1-6 November, the Spaniards were uncooperative, and apparently no observing or collecting were done on shore. The *Discovery* was welcomed at Santa Barbara, and in the period 10-18 November 1793 Menzies made several trips into the countryside on foot and horseback. He noted on 12 November that *"the thickets swarmd with squirrels & quails & a variety of other birds which afforded some amusement in shooting them as I went along... I did not persevere to gain the summit of the ridge but returnd on board in the afternoon with what collection I was able to make of Plants & Birds"* [18].

The expedition put in at San Diego 27 November to 9 December 1793, but the Spanish would allow the English on shore only between the beach and the presidio. Menzies wrote that he botanized, but there is no indication that any bird collecting was done. From San Diego, the ships returned to the Hawaiian Islands.

Menzies' last visit to California occurred in November 1794. The *Discovery* reached the Pacific coast near Cape Mendocino on 3 November, and headed south. The expedition had intended to visit Drake's Bay, but bad weather prevented the side trip. They bypassed San Francisco Bay, and arrived at Monterey the afternoon of 6 November. This time, the Spaniards were friendly, and the exploring party was given unrestricted access to the area. A number of days were taken up with diplomacy and working on the ships' supplies, but between 9 November and 29 November, Menzies *"continued making almost daily excursions in various directions."* He mentioned riding to Mission San Carlos, and to a hill some 12-15 miles east of Monterey. We know from Capt. Vancouver's writings that some of the party made a longer trip into the interior, perhaps reaching the San Benito Pinnacles, later found to be a nesting area for condors. Menzies did not make mention of that trip in his journal, and apparently stayed at Monterey. The *Discovery* departed Monterey 2 December 1794, finally on its way back to England. No other stops were made in California or Baja California [19].

Menzies' condor could have been collected at Trinidad in May 1793; at Bodega Bay in October 1793; around San Francisco Bay November 1792 or October 1793; at Monterey November or December 1792, January 1793, November 1793 or November 1794; at Santa Barbara November 1793; or at San Diego November or December 1793. Because it would only take an opportunistic moment to kill a condor, none of those places or times can be completely ruled out. Practically speaking, the hostility of the Spanish government in 1793 severely limited the possibilities at San Francisco and Monterey. There was very little time at Trinidad in 1793, and the short time at Bodega Bay in 1793 was well-documented in Menzies' journal without reference to condors. San Francisco Bay in 1792 and San Diego in 1793 were better possibilities, although the restrictions imposed by the Spaniards at San Diego certainly reduced travel and (probably) collecting activity. By far, the best opportunities to procure a California condor would have been at Monterey during the winter of 1792-1793, at Santa Barbara November 1793, or at Monterey November 1794.

Of the three possibilities, perhaps the first visit to Monterey is the least likely. One would think that acquiring a California condor would be more noteworthy than *"a new species of hawk,"* and would have been granted some acknowledgment in Menzies' journal. The only reason to give Monterey in November 1794 a slight edge over Santa Barbara in November 1793 (both of which were logical locations at logical times) is that the last visit to Monterey was the only time in his journal that Menzies mentioned vultures. The evidence is too slim, however, to rule out Santa Barbara.

* * *

It was a rare writer in the 19th century who did not wax eloquent at merely the sight of a California condor. One has to wonder why Menzies - one of the first Europeans to see, let alone possess, a condor - did not mention the bird in his journal, and why we only know about the specimen because it still exists, and because an 18th century zoologist published a brief description of it. I think the answer is that there are - or were - more of Menzies' records to be found.

Menzies' journals include various comments on fauna and flora observed, but most of them are rather general. He seldom mentioned a specific collecting incident, and even his botanical notes are often superficial. Reading through the journals, I come away with the impression that he was recording specific details somewhere else. For example, at San Francisco Bay 15 November 1792, he wrote: *"I saw likewise* [in addition to plants] *several Birds which were new to me, but I shall be able to speak of them more particular hereafter"* [20]. Nowhere in his known journals is there any further elaboration. Of his examination of a rhinoceros auklet in Washington's San Juan Islands on 6 June 1792, he wrote: *"...as it appeared to be a new species I named it* Alca Rhinoceros *& describd it"* [21]. The description has not been found. We don't know how many specimens actually reached England, but his "Catalogue of curiosities" included *"a collection of birds,"* which to me implies more than one California condor and two California quails. We know from his journals that he regularly collected birds, and that other people brought him specimens. He wrote about *"examining drawing & describing my little collection,"* but those details are not included in any known documents. Much points to Menzies keeping two sets of notes, as later scientists (myself, included) often did. The "journals" have been found, the "species accounts" have not.

Controversy surrounds various logs and journals written by other members of the Vancouver expedition. Portions of these are missing, or are written in much less detail than one would expect, and there has been speculation that sections were purposely destroyed to suppress evidence of a certain controversial disciplinary action aboard ship. Menzies' 1794-1795 journal was thought to have fallen victim to that same suspected purging of evidence. Vancouver did, in fact, order Menzies to give him his journals, but this may have been more an issue of jealousy and chain of command than part of any other controversy. Although a member of Vancouver's staff, Menzies had received his orders from Sir Joseph Banks, and was directed to give all of his papers and specimens directly to Banks. Menzies refused to give his records to Vancouver, and may have sent some of his materials to Banks even before the expedition ended. He wrote to Banks from Valparaiso, Chile, in April 1795:

"When the Journal of the Voyage etc are demanded by Captain Vancouver I mean to seal up mine and address them to you, so that you will receive them I hope through the same channel as the most part of my correspondence during the Voyage" [22].

From Ireland, just before the end of the voyage, he again wrote to Banks: *"Though Captain Vancouver made a formal demand of my Journals etc before he left the ship; I did not think myself authorized to deliver them; in my present situation* [he was in the brig for insubordination] *particularly till I should hear from you or the Secretary of State from the Home Department; when I shall be ready to deliver up everything I have written, drawn or collected during the whole voyage, agreeable to the tenor of my instructions"* [23].

Menzies' "insubordination" may have saved his 1794-1795 journal from destruction, and it seems likely that it never became an official part of the expedition record. Although his specimens were presented to the British Museum in early 1796, Menzies was still working on finalizing his reports on the trip two years later. He wrote to Sir Banks in January 1798: *"My sincerest thanks for your friendly admonitions and solicitations respecting the finishing of my Journal before Captain Vancouver's is published. It is what I most ardently wish, for more reasons than one, and therefore have applied to it very close... The Volume I am now at work upon (and which is nearly finished) I once thought would include the whole of the remainder of the Narrative, but I find it will not, although it is much larger than either of those you have got"* [24].

In June 1798, he apologized to a friend for not answering his correspondence, attributing the delay *"to my being so much occupied on the business of our late voyage"* [25]. In 1799 he was appointed surgeon on HMS *Sanspariel,* and did not return from the West Indies until late 1802. Shortly after, he married and opened a surgeon's practice. It may be that, with the passage of time and the press of other business, Menzies never finalized some of his accounts from the Vancouver Expedition. The fact that I found the 1794-1795 journal among the Banks archives in Australia offers some hope that other Menzies papers may yet be rediscovered.

* * * *

One might ask why the British Museum did not keep better records of Menzies' collections. The answer seems to be that, from its beginnings in Dr. Hans Sloane's Museum in 1753 into the early 19th century, the institution was very poorly run, not an unusual situation for early museums. Many specimens were lost through lack of care, and records were superficially kept [26]. The first catalogues of ornithological specimens were not prepared until the 1830s. Prior to that, the only records for bird accessions were the Minute Books of the

Trustees' Standing Committee (where the note on Menzies' "catalogue of curiosities" was found) and donation records, the Catalogue of Benefactors to the British Museum. Unfortunately, the "Benefactions Book" is not *"the contemporary, up-to-the-minute, record which might be assumed but was compiled after the Trustees' Meetings, probably at times a good deal after the meeting. The Trustees resolved on 27 June 1760 that the Benefactions Book be written up when there was sufficient copying to employ the writer for one day"* [27]. Apparently, the Menzies data (if there ever was any further information given to the Museum) got lost along the way.

CHAPTER NOTES

1. Page 52 in: Knox, A. G. and M. P. Walters. 1994. Extinct and endangered birds in the collections of the Natural History Museum. London, England: The British Ornithologists' Club.

2. Eastwood, A. 1924. Archibald Menzies' journal of the Vancouver Expedition. *California Historical Society Quarterly* 2(4):265-340.

3. Grinnell, J. 1932. Archibald Menzies, first collector of California birds. *Condor* 34(6):243-252.

4. This letter is in the Botany Department, Natural History Museum (Tring, United Kingdom), Joseph Banks Correspondence, Dawson Turner transcripts 10:15-16; the portion quoted was reproduced on page 23 of: Galloway, J. D., and E. W. Groves. 1987. Archibald Menzies MD, FLS (1754-1842), aspects of his life, travels and collections. *Archives of Natural History* 14(1):3-43.

5. The "Catalogue of curiosities" is included as Item PN1 in the Sir Joseph Banks collection of the Sutro Library (San Francisco, California). My thanks to Martha Whittaker, Sutro Senior Librarian, for examining the files for me. The entire list of "curiosities" is included in: Dillon, R. H. 1951. Archibald Menzies' trophies. *British Columbia Historical Quarterly* 15(3-4):151-159.

6. Shaw, G., and F. P. Nodder. 1797. Vivarium naturae, or Naturalist's Miscellany. Ninth volume. London, England: Nodder and Company.

7. California quail information from Robert Prys-Jones (Head, Bird Group, Natural History Museum, Tring, United Kingdom), who will publish details.

8. Menzies, A. 1794-1795. Journal of Archibald Menzies, 1794-1795. Unpublished manuscript in the collections of the National Library of Australia [Canberra, Australia], 260 pages.

9. Page 4 in: Newcombe, C. F. (editor). 1923. Menzies' journal of Vancouver's voyage April to October 1792. Victoria, British Columbia, Canada: British Columbia Provincial Library.

10. Eastwood *op. cit.*, page 303.

11. Newcombe *op. cit.*, page 3.

12. Newcombe *op. cit.*, pages 46-47.

13. Menzies 1794-1795 *op. cit.*

14. Menzies' itinerary in 1792-1793 is from Eastwood *op. cit.*

15. Eastwood *op. cit.*, page 285.

16. Eastwood *op. cit.*, page 286.

17. Eastwood *op. cit.*, page 303.

18. Eastwood *op. cit.*, page 317.

19. Menzies 1794-1795 *op. cit.*

20. Eastwood *op. cit.*, page 268.

21. Newcombe *op. cit.*, pages 46-47.

22. Galloway and Groves *op. cit.*, pages 21 and 38.

23. Galloway and Groves *op. cit.*, pages 22 and 38.

24. Letter to Sir Joseph Banks 3 January 1798, from Archibald Menzies. Included in archive Letters of Sir Joseph Banks, Series 61, Number 35. State Library of New South Wales (Sydney, New South Wales, Australia).

25. Galloway and Groves *op. cit.*, pages 25 and 38.

26. Pages 83-84 of Sharpe, R. B. 1906. Birds. Pp. 79-515 *in* The history of the collections contained in the Natural History departments of the British Museum, Volume 2. London, England: Trustees of the British Museum.

27. Wheeler, A. 1996. Zoological collections in the early British Museum--documentation of the collection. *Archives of Natural History* 23(3):399-427.

CHAPTER 5
BUZZARD OF THE COLUMBIA

Perhaps surprisingly, the first good description of the California condor came from the Pacific Northwest, not from California. Also, the first significant losses of condors caused by Europeans occurred north of California. Between 1805 and 1835, 11 condors are known to have been killed. There is good reason to suspect the total number might have been significantly higher.

On 30 October 1805 on the Columbia River near present-day Cascade Locks, Oregon, William Clark wrote in his journal: *"this day we Saw Some fiew of the large Buzzard Capt. Lewis Shot at one, those Buzzards are much larger than any other of ther Spece or the largest Eagle white under part of their wings &c."* [1]. This was the introduction of the California condor to the members of the "Corps of Discovery," the Lewis and Clark Expedition, who had traveled across the United States on their way to the Pacific Ocean. Three weeks later, near Cape Disappointment, Washington, they killed their first one. In his journal for 18 November 1805, Patrick Gass wrote: *"They killed a remarkably large buzzard of a species different from any I had seen. It was 9 feet across the wings, and 3 feet 10 inches from the bill to the tail."* Captain Clark's entry was more descriptive: *"Rubin Fields Killed Buzzard of the large Kind near the meat of the whale we Saw: W. 25 lb. measured from the tips of the wings across 91/2 feet, from the point of the Bill to the end of the tail 3 feet 10 1/4 inches, middle toe 5 1/2 inches, toe nale 1 inch & 3 1/2 lines, wing feather 2 1/2 feet long & 1 inch 5 lines diameter tale feathers 14 1/2 inches, and the head is 6 1/2 inches including the beak."*

Later in November, the party saw *"the large Buzzard with white under their wings"* near present-day Astoria, Oregon. In early January 1806 along the beach south of Astoria, they noted the continuing presence of *"the beautiful buzzard of the Columbia."* On 16 February 1806, a second condor was killed. This one was brought wounded to the Corps of Discovery campsite, and Clark had the opportunity to examine a live bird at close range. His description of this bird, along with a line drawing of the condor's head, was preserved in his journal.

"Shannon and Labiesh brought in to us to day a Buzzard or Vulture of the Columbia which they had wounded and taken alive. I believe this to be the largest Bird of North America. It was not in good order and yet it weighed 25 lbs. Had it have been so it might very well have weighed 10 lbs. more or 35 lbs. Between the extremities of the wings it measured 9 feet 2 Inches; from the extremity of the beak to that of the toe 3 feet 9 inches and a half. From hip to toe 2 feet, girth of the head 9 inches 3/4. Girth of the neck 7 1/2 inches; Girth of the body exclusive of the wings 2 feet 3 inches; girth of the leg 3 inches. The diameter of the eye 4 1/2/10ths of an inch, the iris of a pale scarlet red, the

pupil of a deep Sea green or black and occupies about one third of the diameter of the eye. The head and part of the neck as low as the figures 1 2 [referring to drawing] is uncovered with feathers except that portion of it represented by dots forward and under the eye. (See likeness on the other Side of this leaf). The tail is composed of twelve feathers of equal length, each 14 inches. The legs are 4 3/4 inches in length and of a whitish colour uncovered with feathers, they are not entirely Smooth but not imbricated; the toes are four in number three of which are forward and that in the center much the longest; the fourth is short and is inserted near the inner of the three other toes and rather projecting forward. The thigh is covered with feathers as low as the Knee.   The top or upper part of the toes are imbricated with broad scales lying transversely; the nails are black and in proportion to the Size of the bird comparatively with those of the Hawk or Eagle, Short and bluntly pointed—.   The under Side of the wing is Covered with white down and feathers. A white Stripe of about 2 inches in width also marks the outer part of the wing, embracing the lower points of the feathers, which [c]over the joints of the wing through their whole length or width of that part of the wing. All the other feathers of whatever part are of a Glossy Shining black except the down, which is not glossy, but equally black. The Skin of the beak and head to the joining of the neck is of a pale orange Yellow, the other part uncovered with feathers is of a light flesh Colour. The Skin is thin and wrinkled except on the beak where it is Smooth. This bird flies very clumsily. Nor do I know whether it ever Seizes it's prey alive, but am induced to believe it does not. We have Seen it feeding on the remains of the whale and other fish which have been thrown up by the waves on the Sea Coast. These I believe constitute their principal food, but I have no doubt but that they also feed on flesh. We did not meet with this bird until we had descended the Columbia below the great falls; and have found them more abundant below tide water than above. This is the Same Species of Bird which R. Field killed on the 18th of Novr. last and which is noticed on that day tho' not fully described then I thought this of the Buzzard Species. I now believe that this bird is rather of the Vulture genus than any other, tho' it wants Some of their characteristics particularly the hair on the neck, and the feathers on the legs.   This is a handsome bird at a little distance. It's neck is proportionably longer than those of the Hawks or Eagle.

Shannon and Labiesh informed us that when he approached this Vulture after wounding it, that it made a loud noise very much like the barking of a Dog. The tongue is long firm and broad, filling the under Chap and partaking of its transverse curvature, or its Sides forming a longitudinal Groove; obtuse at the point, the margin armed with firm cartilagenous prickles pointed and bending inwards."

As the Expedition started back up the Columbia River, condors continued to be seen, and three more were killed. On 16 March 1806, Patrick Gass reported:

"Yesterday while I was absent getting our meat home, one of the hunters

killed two vultures, the largest fowls I have ever seen. I never saw such as these except on the Columbia River and the seacoast" [2].

On 6 April 1806, another condor succumbed: *"Jos. Field killed a vulture of that species already described."* This, the last condor reported by the group, was shot in the Columbia Gorge near Rooster Rock, not far from where the species was first encountered on the trip down the river the previous fall.

Although the Corps of Discovery was a military expedition and did not include "scientists" in the accepted sense of the word, the leaders of the expedition were not without interest and ability in natural history [3]. Meriwether Lewis (1774-1809) had learned the rudiments of botany from his mother, who collected medicinal plants, and had grown up hunting and exploring the outdoors. During two years as President Thomas Jefferson's personal secretary, Lewis prepared for the upcoming expedition by spending time with such specialists as Dr. Benjamin Rush (basic medical training), Dr. Benjamin Smith Barton (botany), and Dr. Caspar Wistar (paleontology). William Clark (1770-1838), co-leader of the expedition, was less educated than Lewis, but added many zoological, botanical and geological comments to his maps and journals. Several other members of the party kept journals, often copying the "official" records (apparently planned, to guard against important data being lost, should the formal expedition records be destroyed), but also adding their own perspectives. Lewis carried a number of natural history books with him, including botanical works by Linnaeus. There is nothing to show that Lewis had special training in zoology, but the party brought back excellent descriptions of the mammals and birds encountered, including a far better description of the California condor than had been written based on Archibald Menzies' bird (previous chapter).

The expedition apparently did not succeed in bringing a condor specimen back to the East Coast. That large a bird may have been too cumbersome to carry all the way across the country, or it may be that a condor was among the specimens lost on the way home. Some parts of a condor were deposited in Charles Wilson Peale's Philadelphia Museum, but it isn't clear what parts. In the literature, the remains are variously described as: a head; a skull and primary feather [4]; a bill and talons [5]; and a bill and a quill-feather [6]. The latter description, from Charles Lucian Bonaparte who actually examined the remains, is likely the accurate one. Peale's Philadelphia Museum was disbanded in the late 1840s and the collections sold in 1850 to a number of institutions and individuals [7]. There are no certain records of the Lewis and Clark condor artifacts after the 1830s, and they probably have not survived.

* * *

There were no scientific ventures into the Columbia River country for almost 20 years after the Corps of Discovery, but there was a steady stream of fur trappers and adventurers traveling the river valleys. Some of them saw condors, and a few journal records have been preserved. The fur trapping party

57

of Alexander Henry and David Thompson observed *"extraordinarily large vultures"* circling their camp near The Dalles, Oregon, on 20 January 1814, and they saw condors again in the Willamette Valley on 25 January 1814 [8]. No condors are known to have been killed during this period, but I think it would be surprising if there hadn't been regular mortality. The men of the Lewis and Clark party obviously were not loath to shoot condors for sport, but there may have been a more personal and practical reason for dispatching some. For example, on 28 March 1806, Meriwether Lewis wrote:

"This morning we set out very early and at 9 A. M. arrived at the old Indian Village on Lard side of Deer Island where we found our hunters had halted and left one man with the two canoes at their camp; they had arrived last evening at this place and six of them turned out to hunt very early this morning; by 10 A. M. they all returned to camp having killed seven deer... the men who had been sent after the deer returned and brought in the remnent which the Vultures and Eagles had left us; these birds had devoured 4 deer in the course of a few hours... Joseph Fields informed me that the Vultures had draged a large buck which he had killed about 30 yards, had skined it and broken the back bone."

William Clark's account: "[The men] *sent after the deer returned with four only, the other 4 haveing been eaten entirely by the Voulturs except the Skin. The men we had been permitted to hunt this evening killed 3 deer 4 Eagles & a Duck."*

John Ordway's notes: *"the grey Eagles are pleanty on this Island they eat up three deer in a short time which our hunters had killed... some of the hunters killed Several of them".*

Living off the land was seldom easy for these early Northwest travelers. Finding their hard-earned and much needed food devoured by condors and eagles would have been frustrating, for sure, but could also have been life-threatening if it was a regular occurrence. Reducing condor and eagle populations may have been both retaliatory (for past deeds) and preventative (to forestall future problems). Other writers reinforce this idea. Alexander Henry, writing from the Willamette Valley 25 January 1814:

"I sent for the eight deer killed yesterday. The men brought in seven of them, one having been devoured by the vulturs. These birds are uncommonly large and very troublesome to my hunters by destroying the meat, which, though well covered with pine branches, they contrive to uncover and devour" [9].

Writing more generally later in the century, Andrew Jackson Grayson expressed similar anti-condor sentiments:

"In the early days of California history it [the condor] was more frequently met with than now, being of a cautious and shy disposition the rapid settlement of the country has partially driven it off to more secluded localities. I remember the time when this vulture was much disliked by the hunter because of its ravages upon any large game he may have killed and left exposed for

only a short length of time. So powerful is its sight that it will discover a dead deer from an incredible distance while soaring in the air" [10].

* * *

In 1825, two more condor collectors arrived on the Columbia River. Dr. John Scouler and David Douglas had traveled together on the Hudson's Bay Company ship, *William and Ann,* Scouler as ship surgeon and naturalist, and Douglas as botanist under the auspices of the Hudson's Bay Company and the Royal Horticultural Society of London. Both were protégés of botanist William Jackson Hooker, who was apparently instrumental in getting them their appointments.

John Scouler (1804-1871) was born in Glasgow, Scotland, and studied medicine at the University of Glasgow. He came to the attention of Dr. Hooker because of his botanical skills, but he had a broad interest in natural history and ethnology [11]. His time on the Columbia River was relatively brief, from 8 April to 1 June 1825 and (after a voyage north to the Queen Charlotte Islands) from 3 September to 25 October 1825. His journal does not include any observations of live condors, only a 22 September 1825 record of acquiring one specimen:

"This morning we breakfasted at the Kowlitch [Cowlitz] *village & we were treated with much civility, although they were in a very unsettled state and were preparing for war in consequence of the circumstances formerly alluded to* [a dispute between two families of Indians]. *On arriving on board the ship much of my time was employed in procuring & preserving birds. The incessant rains we experienced at the advanced period of the year rendered the accumulation of plants hopeless. The river at this season was beginning to abound in birds. I obtained specimens of Pelecanus onocrotalus, Falco & a species of Vultur, which I think is nondescript. My birds are principly obtained from the Indians who would go through any fatigue for a bit of tobacco"* [12].

Scouler returned to Great Britain in early 1826 (I haven't found an arrival date for him), and within the year his condor was at Benjamin Leadbeater's taxidermy establishment in London. It was displayed at a 12 December 1826 meeting of the Zoological Club of the Linnean Society in London [13]. About the same time, Charles Lucien Bonaparte saw the specimen at Leadbeater's, describing it as *"a specimen from the Oregon, the second known in any collection"* [14]. Leaving England shortly thereafter, Bonaparte went directly to visit Dutch ornithologist Coenraad Jacob Temminck at the Rijksmuseum van Natuurlijke Historie at Leiden, The Netherlands [15]. He probably told Temminck about the condor, because the Rijksmuseum acquired the specimen in 1827 or 1828. It is still at Leiden [16].

One wonders why Scouler's condor went so quickly to Leadbeater, rather than being donated to some institution in Scotland or England. There seems to be no answer to that question. Scouler was back in Britain only a short time before he obtained a position as ship's surgeon on a voyage to Calcutta.

59

Perhaps he needed to quickly divest himself of his North American specimens, and Leadbeater was a ready receiver. After returning to Scotland, Scouler wrote many papers on natural history, geology and ethnology, but seems never again to have mentioned his "nondescript" vulture from the Columbia.

* * *

David Douglas (1799-1834), born in Perth, Scotland, was more of a botanical specialist than Scouler, but was also well versed in other aspects of natural history. When Scouler left the Columbia River for Canada in June 1825, Douglas remained. Through the winter of 1825-1826, he made various excursions up and down the Columbia, and also traveled south into the Willamette Valley. In spring and summer 1826, he extended his travels far up the Columbia into what is now northeastern Washington, returning in the fall to Fort Vancouver. In September 1826 he traveled up the Willamette River once again, this time crossing into the Umpqua River drainage before returning to Fort Vancouver for the winter. In March 1827, he started inland, eventually crossing the Rocky Mountains and visiting Hudson's Bay before sailing back to Great Britain in October 1827 [17].

Douglas' journal does not include any references to condors before the winter of 1825-1826, but then he apparently saw them regularly near the west end of the Columbia Gorge. In the Willamette Valley in October 1826, he found them "common," with nine condors seen in one group [18]. In spring 1827 Douglas' friend George Barston noted that condors were "ever hovering around" along the Columbia River [19]. Douglas killed his first in January or February 1826, probably near Fort Vancouver. In a general summary of his winter collecting activities, he wrote:

"When opportunity favored I collected woods, and gathered Musci &c., and from this time to March 20th I formed a tolerable collection of preserved animals and birds, but this desirable object was frequently interrupted by heavy rains. Among the birds and animals deserve to be mentioned Tetrao Sabine, T. Richardsonii, Sarcoramphus californica [the condor], Corvus Stelleri, an endless variety of Anas, several species of Canis, Cervus, Mus, and Myozus" [20].

Later, he elaborated on acquiring the condor specimen:

"On the Columbia there is a species of Buzzard, the largest of all birds here, the Swan excepted. I killed only one of this very interesting bird, with buckshot, one of which passed through the head, which rendered it unfit for preserving; I regret it exceedingly, for I am confident it is not yet described. I have fired at them with every size of small shot at respectable distances without effect; seldom more than one or two are together... I am shortly to try to take them in a baited steel-trap" [21].

His next close encounter came in mid-October 1826, on the divide between the Willamette and Umpqua rivers, probably in present-day Lane County,

60

Oregon. He wrote:

"This morning we passed a hill of similar elevation and appearance to that passed yesterday. Several species of Clethra were gathered – one in particular, C. grandis, was very fine – and many birds of Sarcoramphus californica and Ortyx californica, and two other species of great beauty were collected" [22].

Clearly, Douglas didn't mean that he collected "many" condors (*Sarcoramphus*) and quail (*Ortyx*). Likely, he meant to say that while gathering plants (*Clethra,* and possibly "two other species of great beauty"), he observed many condors and quail. If he did kill a condor on that trip, it was not preserved.

Douglas killed his last condors in the late winter and spring of 1827. Only one is mentioned in his journal, on an unspecified date in February:

"Killed a very large vulture, sex unknown. ... Of a blackish-brown with a little white under the wing; head of a deep orange colour; beak of a sulphur-yellow; neck, a yellowish-brown varying in tinge like the common turkey-cock" [23].

Apparently, this was one of the two condors he described in more detail in an 1829 journal article:

"Specimens, male and female, of this truly interesting bird, which I shot in lat. 45. 30. 15., long. 122. 3. 12. were lately presented by the Council of the Horticultural Society to the Zoological Society, in whose museum they are now carefully deposited."

"The length of the bird is 56 inches; the measure round the body 40 inches. Weight 25 to 35 pounds. Beak 3 ½ inches long, bright glossy yellow. Head 9 inches round, deep orange, with a few short scattered feathers on the fore part, at the root of the beak. Iris pale red. Pupil light green. Neck 11 inches long, 9 round, of a changeable color, brownish yellow with blue tints. Body 24 inches long, black or slightly brown. Collar and breast feathers lanceolate, decomposed, white on the outside near the points. Quills thirty-four, the third the longest. Extent between the tips of the wings 9 feet 8 inches. Under coverts white; upper coverts white at the points. Tarsi 4 ¾ of an inch long, bluish black. Claws black, blunt, having little curvature. Tail 14 feathers, square at the ends, 15 inches long. In plumage both sexes alike; in size the female is somewhat larger" [24].

If his latitude and longitude readings were accurate, these birds were killed somewhat southeast of Fort Vancouver, perhaps in the Sandy River drainage east of present-day Gresham, Oregon.

There is some confusion in the record at this point. Douglas claimed that he killed both of the condors he brought back to England, but another writer at Fort Vancouver in the spring of 1827 told of a condor that was given to Douglas:

"One morning a large specimen [condor] was brought into our square, and

we had all a hearty laugh at the eagerness with which the Botanist pounced upon it. In a very short time he had it almost in his embraces fathoming its stretch of wings, which not being able to compass, a measure was brought, and he found it full nine feet from tip to tip. This satisfied him, and the bird was carefully transferred to his studio for the purpose of being stuffed. In all that pertained to nature or science he was a perfect enthusiast" [25].

This may have been a third condor, or Douglas may have claimed credit for shooting two birds just to simplify the record (a not uncommon practice). If there was a third mortality, the specimen almost certainly was not preserved. As Douglas reported, the two condors he took back to England were given to his sponsors at the Royal Horticultural Society of London, who in turn presented them to the newly-formed Zoological Society of London [26].

Apparently no official records survive of Douglas' two condors at the Zoological Society Museum. An 1835 guide to the Zoological Society live animal exhibits made passing mention of the museum mounts as *"two noble specimens... the only pair in Europe"* [27]. I found no record of them after that date. In 1841 the Society gave up its lease on the building housing their greatly overcrowded Museum, and the entire collection was packed away in a warehouse until a new building was available in 1844. Lack of adequate funding for the museum, coupled with vast improvements at the British Museum (Natural History) that made the Zoological Society museum less important, led the Society to begin closing down their facility. In 1849, they began to dispose of duplicate specimens to other collections, and in 1850 voted to sell all the specimens to the Government. An upswing in member interest in the museum postponed that decision, but in 1855 the museum closed. Type specimens were given to the British Museum, and the rest of the collection was sold to various other museums and private collectors [28]. Unfortunately, there seem to be no surviving records of those sales. Probably Douglas' condors were sold in 1855, and probably they are either at the Museum d'Histoire Naturelle in Paris, or at the Institut Royal des Sciences Naturelles de Belgique in Brussels. The Paris birds came from the collection of Charles Lucien Bonaparte in 1858, and the Brussels condors were purchased from the Verreaux Brothers in November 1857. Either Bonaparte or the Verreaux brothers would have been logical bidders on the Natural History Society specimens - and it's unlikely there were other condors available in Europe at that time - but neither museum has any accession paperwork.

* * *

In May 1833, William Tolmie (a medical doctor in the employ of the Hudson's Bay Company), saw *"some large vultures"* on the Cowlitz River in Washington, not far from its junction with the Columbia. Except for a possible sighting in northern British Columbia, Canada, this was Tolmie's only written record of condors [29]. To this point in time, most of the people leaving records of condors had broad naturalist skills and interest, but for none of them was ornithology their chief concern. This changed in 1834 when John Kirk Townsend (1809-1851), at the invitation of ornithologist and botanist Thomas Nuttall, joined the Nathaniel Wyeth expedition across the country to the Columbia River. The party reached the Columbia near Walla Walla, Washington, in early September, stayed along the river until 11 December 1834, then traveled to the Hawaiian Islands for the winter. They returned to the Columbia in late April 1835. Nuttall left the area in September 1835 to return to the eastern United States, via Hawaii and California. Townsend stayed on, seldom traveling far from the main Columbia River valley between Walla Walla and the Pacific coast, until December 1836, when he sailed for Hawaii enroute to the East Coast [30].

According to Townsend, he did not see any California condors until he returned from Hawaii in the spring of 1835 [31]. His records are confusing. The only reference to condors in his published journal is as a name on an appended list of birds seen on the trip [32]. In answer to an inquiry from John James Audubon, he wrote that condors were *"seen on the Columbia only in summer, appearing about the first of June,"* but also that they were *"most abundant in spring"* [33]. Townsend's one published account of condors mentioned only the spring, when he *"constantly saw the Vultures at all points where the Salmon were cast upon the shore."* The one condor he shot was killed in April 1835, on the Willamette River near present-day Oregon City, Oregon. The tale of the killing seems a little larger than life, but the specimen still exists.

"In a journey of exploration which I made to the Willammet, in the month of April, when the river was crowded with Salmon, making their way up against the stream, urged by an abortive instinct to pass the barriers of the thirty feet fall, I observed dozens of Turkey Vultures constantly sailing over the boiling surges, with their bare heads curved downwards as if in search of prey. As I gazed upon them, interested in their graceful and easy motions, I heard a loud rustling sound over my head, which induced me to look upward; and there, to my inexpressible joy, soard the great Californian, seemingly intent upon watching the motions of his puny relatives below. Suddenly, while I watched, I saw him wheel, and down like an arrow he plunged, alighting upon an unfortunate Salmon which had just been cast, exhausted with his attempts to leap the falls, on the shore within a short distance. At that moment I fired, and the poor Vulture fell wounded, beside his still palpitating quarry. My prize being on the opposite side of the river, I lost no time in removing my clothing and plunging into the stream. A few vigorous strokes carried me across; I sprang upon the shore, and ran, with delighted haste, to secure the much coveted and valuable specimen. But I soon discovered that I had still something to do before the operation of skinning him was to commence. The huge creature had been only wing-broken, and as I approached him, seemed determined not to yield himself a willing captive. My gun had been left behind;

63

I was in a state of absolute nudity, and at that moment, the inhabitants of an Indian village near, consisting of men women, children and dogs, startled by the sound of my gun, were flocking out to see what was the matter. I looked about in vain for a stick; none was to be found, and my only weapons were stones, with which I continued, for a considerable time, to pelt the Vulture, who sometimes hobbled awkwardly away, when attacked, and at others dashed furiously at me, hissing like an angry serpent, and compelled me likewise to run. It must have been an amusing scene for the Indians looking on, and I heard more than once, the loud, obstreperous laugh of the women, when the Vulture was flapping after me and I throwing sand in his eyes with my naked feet. After perhaps half an hour spent in this way, I was fortunate enough to hit him fairly on the head with a large stone, which stunned him, and he fell. In an instant I alighted upon him, sitting upon his body; and firmly grasping his neck with my hands. One of the Indians, at my request, brought me a knife, and I soon dispatched him by severing the spine. I hired one of the boys to cross the river in a canoe to bring over my clothes and gun, and when dressed, skinned my prize with the Indians crowding around me, curious to see the operation" [34].

The history of Townsend's condor is not clear. Because it was killed in April 1835, before Thomas Nuttall left the Columbia, it probably was among those specimens that Nuttall delivered to The Academy of Natural Sciences in Philadelphia in the summer of 1836. Less likely is that Townsend kept the condor with him until he arrived in Philadelphia in November 1837. In either event, it appears that the condor skin was sold to John James Audubon along with most of Townsend's Western collections. The story of Audubon's acquisition is confusing, being told a little differently by everyone who related it [35].

Audubon was in the final stages of publishing *Birds of America* when the first part of Townsend's collection reached Philadelphia. Audubon wanted badly to examine, paint, and describe the new species so they could be included in his book. Those at the Academy refused to let him do more than see the specimens, thinking (rightly, it seems to me) that the absent Townsend should be allowed to do what he wanted with his collection when he returned from the West. Audubon was insistent and, enlisting the aid of Thomas Nuttall and other prominent men, he finally persuaded the Academy to sell him 93 Townsend specimens, presumably only those for which there were duplicates. (Probably the condor was not sold to Audubon at that point, as it was not a "duplicate.") As part of the agreement to sell, Audubon and Nuttall published a paper in the Academy's journal (in Townsend's name), describing the several new species. When Townsend returned to Philadelphia the next year, hard up for money and with much of his potential glory having already been usurped by Audubon, he agreed to sell Audubon the rest (or most of) his Western collection. The condor was probably included in that second sale.

Except for a brief description of the *"young individual obtained from Dr. Townsend"* [36], I've found no specific mention of Townsend's condor among Audubon memorabilia. (As it was an immature bird, it was not the one Audubon used as his model for the *Birds of America* painting It's likely that he had access to David Douglas' mounted specimens when in England.) Audubon's collection was housed for awhile with John G. Bell, a New York taxidermist and good friend of Audubon, then later was at Audubon's home on the Hudson River. Spencer Fullerton Baird was given about 40 of Audubon's "duplicates" in 1845, and another (apparently larger) gift in April 1846. Baird's daughter, Lucy Baird, wrote:

"I have often heard my father say that Mr. Audubon finding him to be modest in selecting from the collection only such birds as he thought Mr. Audubon could readily spare, told him that that was not what he meant, that he was to take any that he really wished, and, finally, he, Mr. Audubon went through the collection himself and took out with his own hand many additional specimens, and among them some of the most valuable in the entire collection" [37].

Presumably this latter gift included the Townsend condor. When Baird moved from Carlisle, Pennsylvania, to Washington, D. C. in 1850, as Assistant Secretary of the Smithsonian Institution, he took his bird collection with him. Included was the Townsend condor.

* * *

The United States Exploring Expedition, under the leadership of Charles Wilkes, reached the mouth of the Columbia River 18 July 1841. They traveled up the Columbia to Fort Vancouver; went south through the Willamette Valley to the Umpqua River and eventually the Rogue River; continued over the Siskiyou Mountains into California; then traveled south down the Sacramento Valley, reaching Mission San Jose 24 October 1841 [38]. Scientists on the trip were Charles Pickering and Titian Ramsay Peale. Unfortunately, none of Pickering's Oregon and California field notes have been found, and Peale lost his journals covering July through late September 1841. Only casual remarks are available concerning the wildlife of the Columbia River and Willamette Valley. In his summary of the trip, Peale noted that the condor *"cannot be considered a common bird in Oregon; we first saw it on the plains of the Willamette River, but subsequently observed that they were much more numerous in California"* [39]. The first record in his existing journals came on 24 September 1841, when the party was near the divide between the Umpqua and Rogue watersheds: *"Crossed rolling prairie land bordered by round hills... Saw numbers of Lewis's Partridge* [mountain quail]... *Besides them we saw today Goldenwing woodpeckers (red var.)* [flickers], *Ravens, Crows, Stellers & Florida* [scrub] *Jays, Californian Vultures, and a few larks."* He did not mention condors again until 5 October, in the mountains near the head of the Sacramento River: *"I saw two species of marmots, and several birds not*

65

seen before. Sevl Californian Vultures, etc"[40]. In John Cassin's compilation of the expedition ornithology, he noted *"several allusions to this bird by Dr. Pickering,"* but only mentions one specific record: an immature-plumaged condor flying with *"other specimens"* (adults) near the Sutter Buttes 16 October 1841 [41].

CHAPTER NOTES

1. Many versions of the Lewis and Clark Expedition journals have been published. An excellent recent edition is: Moulton, G. E. (editor). 2002. The journals of the Lewis and Clark Expedition. Lincoln, Nebraska: University of Nebraska Press. Thirteen volumes. Because of the many versions, I have noted observations by date, rather than specific page numbers.

2. Gass, P. 1904. Gass's journal of the Lewis and Clark Expedition. Reprint of the edition of 1811. Chicago, Illinois: A. C. McClurg and Company.

3. A number of authoritative biographies have been written of Lewis, Clark, and other members of the Corps of Discovery. My principal source has been: Cutright, P. R. 2003. Lewis and Clark: pioneering naturalists. Lincoln, Nebraska: University of Nebraska Press.

4. Page 17 in: Harris, H. 1941. The annals of *Gymnogyps. Condor* 43(1):3-55.

5. Pages 35-36 in: Nuttall, T. 1832. A manual of the ornithology of the United States and Canada. Cambridge, Massachusetts: Hilliard and Brown.

6. Page 16 in: Bonaparte, C. L. 1833. American ornithology; or, The natural history of birds inhabiting the United States not given by Wilson. Philadelphia, Pennsylvania: Carey & Lea.

7. Burns, F. L. 1932. Charles W. and Titian R. Peale and the ornithological section of the old Philadelphia Museum. *Wilson Bulletin* 44(1):23-35.

8. Pages 808 and 817 in: Coues, E. 1897. The manuscript journals of Alexander Henry and David Thompson, 1799-1814. Volume II. New York, New York: Francis P. Harper.

9. Coues *op. cit.,* page 817.

10. Page 52 in: Bryant, W. E. 1891. Andrew Jackson Grayson. *Zoe* 2(1): 34-68.

11. Keddie, W. 1874. Biographical notice of the late John Scouler, M. D., LL.D., F.L.S., some time President of the Society. *Transactions of the Geological Society of Glasgow* 4:194-205.

12. P. 280 in: Scouler, J. 1905. Dr. John Scouler's journal of a voyage to northwest

America. *Oregon. Historical Quarterly* 6(3):276-287.

13. Anonymous. 1827. Proceedings of the Zoological Club of the Linnean Society. *Zoological Journal* 3(10): 298-303.

14. Buonaparte, C. L. 1828. Supplement to the Genera of North American Birds, and the Synopsis of the Species found within the territory of the United States. *Zoological Journal* 3(9): 49-53.

15. Page 86 in: Stroud, P. T. 2000. The emperor of nature, Charles-Lucien Bonaparte and his world. Philadelphia, Pennsylvania: University of Pennsylvania Press.

16. G. F. Mees wrote to me from the Museum 10 March 1971: *"Underneath the socle* [the stand for the specimen] *appears a lot of pencil writing, much of it rubbed out, and difficult or impossible to read. I deciphered the words "1827 de Soudrey.' At least, I am sure of 1827, but the Soudrey might be a different name. Presumably this means that the specimen was acquired in 1827 from a person named Soudrey."* From other records, it is clear that "Soudrey" was Scouler.

17. Douglas, D. 1914. Journal kept by David Douglas during his travels in North America 1823-1827. London: William Wesley & Son.

18. Douglas 1914 *op. cit.,* page 216.

19. Fleming, J. H. 1924. The California condor in Washington: another version of an old record. *Condor* 26(3):111-112.

20. Douglas 1914 *op. cit.,* pages 62.

21. Douglas 1914 *op. cit.,* pages 154-155.

22. Douglas 1914 *op. cit.,* page 67.

23. Douglas 1914 *op. cit.,* page 241.

24. Douglas, D. 1829. Observations on the *Vultur Californianus* of Shaw. *Vigor's Zoological Journal* 4(1):328-330.

25. Fleming *op. cit.*

26. Douglas 1829 *op. cit.*

27. Pages 2-3 in: Bennett, E. T. 1835. The gardens and menagerie of the Zoological Society delineated. Cheapside, England: Thomas Tegg and Son.

28. Pages 98-123 in: Scherren, H. 1905. The Zoological Society of London, a sketch of its foundation and development and the story of its farm, museum, gardens, menagerie and library. London, England: Cassell and Company, Limited.

29. Pages 185-186 *in:* Tolmie, W. F. 1963. William Fraser Tolmie, physician and fur trader. Vancouver, British Columbia: Mitchell Press Ltd.

30. Townsend, J. K. 1999. Narrative of a journey across the Rocky Mountains, to the Columbia River, and a visit to the Sandwich Islands, Chili, &c. Corvallis, Oregon: Oregon State University Press.

31. Townsend, J. K. 1848. Popular monograph on the accipitrine birds of N. A. --No. II. *Literary Record and Journal of the Linnaean Association of Pennsylvania College* 4(12): 265-272.

32. Townsend 1999 *op. cit.,* page 249.

33. Pages 240-245 in: Audubon, J. J. 1839. Ornithological biography, Volume 5. Edinburgh, Scotland: Adam & Charles Black.

34. Townsend 1848 *op. cit.*

35. Stone, W. 1899. Some Philadelphia ornithological collections and collectors, 1784-1850. *Auk* 16(2):166-177.
 Rhoads, S. N. 1903. Auduboniana. *Auk* 20(4):377-383.
 Stone, W. 1916. Philadelphia to the Coast in early days, and the development of western ornithology prior to 1850. *Condor* 18(1):3-14.
 Branch, M. P. 2008. John Kirk Townsend. Pages 373-380 *in* D. Patterson, R. Thompson and J. S. Bryson (editors), Early American nature writers: a biographical encyclopedia. Westport, Connecticut: Greenwood Press.

36. Pages 244-245 in: Audubon, J. J. 1839. Ornithological biography, Volume 5. Edinburgh, Scotland: Adam and Charles Black.

37. Pages 134-135 in: Dall, W. H. 1915. Spencer Fullerton Baird, a biography. Philadelphia, Pennsylvania: J. B. Lippincott Company.

38. Wilkes, C. 1844. United States exploring expedition during the years 1838, 1839, 1840, 1841, 1842 under the command of Charles Wilkes, U. S. N. Volume V. Philadelphia, Pennsylvania: C. Sherman.

39. Page 58 *in:* Peale, T. R. 1848. Mammalia and ornithology. United States exploring expedition during the years 1838, 1839, 1840, 1841, 1842 under the command of Charles Wilkes, U. S. N. Volume VIII. Philadelphia, Pennsylvania: C. Sherman.

40. Poesch, J. 1961. Titian Ramsay Peale 1799-1885 and his journals of the Wilkes Expedition. Philadelphia, Pennsylvania: American Philosophical Society.

41. Page 72 *in:* Cassin, J. 1858. Mammalogy and ornithology. United States exploring expedition during the years 1838-1842 under the command of Charles Wilkes, U. S. N., Volume VIII. Philadelphia, Pennsylvania: J. B. Lippincott and Company.

CHAPTER 6
DISCOVERING CALIFORNIA

Scientists, explorers, trappers, traders, and eventually homesteaders continued to visit the Pacific Northwest. Some reported seeing condors, but none are known to have been killed in the area for the next quarter-century. Interest in California condors shifted south.

* * *

By the 16th century, the presumed Holocene shortage of large mammals (Chapter 1) was a condition of the distant past, and wildlife abounded throughout western California. Sir Francis Drake's party put ashore near San Francisco Bay in 1579, and found *"herds of deer by a thousand in a company, being most large, and fat of body"* [1]. (The large, fat deer were almost certainly tule elk.) Already noted (Chapter 3) were the Vizcaino and Ascension comments from the winter of 1602-1603 of *"much wild game"* at Monterey [2]. In the southern San Joaquin Valley in 1772, there was *"plentiful game, such as deer, antelope, mule deer, bear, geese, cranes, ducks, and many other species of animals both terrestrial and winged"* [3]. There was a *"large drove"* of pronghorns near Ventura in 1776, and *"many"* in the Salinas Valley that same year [4]. A one-day hunt in the mountains north of Monterey in November 1833 resulted in the killing of 93 black-tailed deer, verified by the hunters displaying all 93 tongues [5]. In October 1841 in the Sacramento Valley, members of the Wilkes Expedition found that *"game abounded, elk, antelopes, deer and bears;"* they observed *"numerous bands of animals now covering the plains;"* and saw *"many small herds of antelopes and elk"* [6]. In April 1844, John C. Fremont found the San Joaquin Valley near the Merced River *"crowded with bands of elk and wild horses."* The party *"frequently started elk, and large bands were seen during the day, with antelope and wild horses"* [7]. In the northern San Joaquin Valley in September 1846, Edwin Bryant saw *"large droves"* of antelope, elk, deer, and wild horses, and commented that *"game of all kinds appears to be very abundant in this rich valley"* [8].

This abundance of potential food was obviously good for scavengers, and with apparently little impact on condors from the California natives (Chapter 2), the first 200 years of European presence in the West meant little to the birds. The few explorers who stopped at various coastal locations did not stay long or venture far into condor habitat. When change eventually came, it was initially quite favorable for condors.

In 1768, becoming worried about possible English or Russian colonization along the Pacific Coast, the King of Spain authorized settlement of "Upper California," the area that would later become the State of California. The first of the Spanish parties arrived in 1769 – two groups by ship to Monterey, and two overland from the Jesuit communities of southern Baja California. The overland groups brought with them some 200 head of cattle, the nucleus of herds meant to support the new Californians at the string of Franciscan missions planned to extend from San Diego to the San Francisco Bay area.

Livestock numbers were slow to increase, and in 1773 there were still only about 200 head at the five southernmost missions. More cattle, along with other livestock, were brought overland from Sonora, Mexico in 1776. As husbandry improved, the herds grew rapidly, and by 1830 there were several hundred thousand cattle associated with the missions [9]. Added to this number that could be roughly documented, wild cattle and horses had spread throughout the hills and valleys of central and southern California. Near the Merced River in 1833, the prairies were *"in many places swarming with wild Horses,"* [10]. The numbers so impressed Lieutenant George Derby that his 1849 map of the Sutter Buttes – Butte Creek area north of Sacramento includes the notation *"large herds of wild cattle and horses"* [11]. Edwin Bryant in the northern San Joaquin Valley in 1846 noted *"the herds of cattle... scattered over the plain,"* and commented that *"beef in California is so abundant, and of so fine a quality, that game is but little hunted, and not much prized"* [12].

The sheer numbers of native and domestic animals must have been a major attraction for condors, but another aspect of the early California livestock picture made it even more of a scavenger bonanza. Beef obviously provided food for the Spanish settlers, but by 1830 the non-Indian population of all California had grown to only 4,200 people; by 1840, it was still less than 6,000 [13]. Consequently, most livestock were killed for their hides and tallow, alone, with the meat left where the animals were slaughtered. There is no reliable record of how many livestock were killed for these purposes, but there is no question the numbers were immense. Estimates for the hide harvest between 1800 and 1848 range from 1.5 million to 5 million, with perhaps 100,000 hides shipped in 1834, alone [14]. Despite this harvest and the adverse effects on livestock of several severe droughts, livestock remained abundant on the California ranges into the 1840s.

* * *

The California environment remained benign for condors. With vast areas essentially unpopulated, and with firearms scarce [15], there was probably very little shooting of condors and other large birds for sport. There was some limited scientific collecting.

In addition to Menzies' type specimen (Chapter 4) and the condors collected in the Pacific Northwest (Chapter 5), another nine California condor specimens are known to have been in Europe before 1845. Five are of more or less certain origin. The other four are puzzling, in that there appear to have been few opportunities for collecting in California in the first 45 years of the 19th century. Looking first at the "known" condors, they include one collected by Ferdinand Deppe about 1835, and several taken by Ilya Voznesenskii in 1840-1841.

Ferdinand Deppe was employed as a horticulturist in the royal gardens near Berlin, Germany, when he was selected to join Count Albert von Sack on a trip to Mexico to acquire natural history specimens for the local zoological museum. Deppe collected in Mexico from December 1824 to February 1827, mostly on his own as the Count turned out to be a difficult traveling companion. He spent 1827 and early 1828 in Berlin, then returned to Mexico in late summer 1828. Apparently he made his first trip to California in October 1829, then visited several more times before he sailed for the Hawaiian Islands in late October 1836. At various times, he visited (at least) San Diego, San Gabriel, Santa Barbara, Monterey, San Juan Bautista, San Jose, Santa Clara, and San Francisco [16].

There is no question that Deppe secured a condor specimen - it still exists in the Museum für Naturkunde in Berlin. Unfortunately, the date and place of the acquisition are unknown. I suspect 1832 and 1835 are the most likely years, because these appear to be the years when Deppe spent the most time traveling in California. (The majority of his trips were probably as supercargo on the hide ships of his employer, Henry Virmond, with little time spent onshore.) Deppe sent a shipment of natural history specimens to Hamburg, Germany, from San Diego in May 1836, which might have included the condor [17]. However, no manifest has been found. None of Deppe's trips are well documented. Concerning California condors, he reported only that they were found in the mountains that paralleled the Pacific coastline [18]. So far, nothing has been found in writing that specifically addresses the collection of his one known condor specimen.

* * *

Ferdinand Deppe was a prolific collector, sending back to Germany from Mexico over 20,000 specimens (mostly insects and plants, but almost 1,000 birds) in just one year [19]. A similar type of naturalist was the Russian Ilya Gavrilovich Voznesenskii who visited California in 1840-1841. He is perhaps best known for the ethnographic materials (garments, utensils, weapons) he sent back to Russia from California and Alaska, but he also collected nearly 4,000 vertebrates (including almost 3,000 birds), 10,000 insects, and about 2,000 plants [20]. Among his birds were at least four California condors, plus a full condor skin used in Indian dances, and a robe constructed of condor, bald eagle and golden eagle feathers [21].

The travels of Voznesenskii in northern California are well documented in his journals. He sailed from Sitka, Alaska, 7 July 1840 on the Russian ship *"Elena,"* landing at Bodega Bay (on the coast just north of San Francisco Bay) 20 July 1840. He was at Bodega Bay until 30 July 1840, then moved to the nearby Russian settlement at Fort Ross. He collected intensively over the next couple months, making a long trip north to Cape Mendocino in September or

71

early October, and in October 1840 sent 10 crates of California biological and ethnological specimens to Russia on the *Nicolai I* headed from San Francisco to Sitka. On 23 October 1840 he rode horseback to San Rafael, then canoed to San Francisco. Between October 1840 and mid February 1841, he visited all parts of the San Francisco Bay area. On 20 February 1841 he went by boat to Sutter's Fort (at present-day Sacramento), and explored and collected in the vicinity until 2 April 1841. He returned to San Francisco, and on 11 April 1841 rode horseback from San Rafael back to Fort Ross. He collected many birds around Fort Ross in the next few months. In May and June 1841, he traveled the entire length of the Russian River, and on 16 June 1841 made what was apparently the first ascent by Europeans of Mt. Saint Helena, a rugged 4,400 foot peak on the border of present-day Napa and Sonoma counties. In July 1841, the Russians sold Fort Ross to John Sutter, and moved to Bodega Bay to begin their evacuation of California. Voznesenskii continued exploring and collecting in the area until he sailed for Sitka 5 September 1841 [22].

As detailed as is this itinerary, it only provides a general idea of where and when Voznesenskii obtained his condors. Only one of his condors has a currently known collection date: 17 May 1841 [23], when Voznesenskii was in the Russian River area of Sonoma or Mendocino counties. He obtained his dance skin (*mollok,* named for the Indian deity represented by the condor) while in the Sacramento Valley in March 1841 [24]. The best we can say of the others is that they came from northern California between July 1840 and September 1841.

I'm tantalized by the thought of what additional information on condors [and other California birds!] might be in the Voznesenskii journals. Only fragments have been published, mainly by ethnologists, and I am told that his notes were written in pencil and are now mostly indecipherable. Still, those who have tried to read them have been able to transcribe some wonderful passages about the lands he visited, and the people and wildlife he saw. If the published passages are an indication of the general richness of his narrative, then there is likely valuable zoological and botanical information that would be worth trying to extract. Perhaps someday someone will do more work on the journals.

* * *

The four European condors of unknown origin were, respectively, in the London collection of John Flint South; exhibited in Scotland in 1837; in the Austrian collection of Christoph Fellner von Feldegg; and in the Duc de Rivoli collection in France.

(1) John Flint South (1797-1882) was a London anatomist, medical lecturer, and physician, associated with St. Thomas's Hospital and the Royal College of Surgeons. He accumulated a considerable collection of skeletal material of animals, including the full skeleton of a California condor. I have found

nothing in his memoirs or in writings about him that addresses this collection. He developed an interest in comparative anatomy early in his surgeon apprenticeship (at age 16), and by late 1814 *"became a very diligent visitor of the College museum"* [25]. In 1820 he was appointed conservator of the museum, and in 1823 was a demonstrator of anatomy at the college. It is probably safe to say that his collection was well underway by this point. When he sold it to the Royal College of Surgeons in 1835, it included 70 skeletons and seven skulls [26]. The condor skeleton was identifiable at the Royal College Hunterian Museum as late as 1891 ("Californian Turkey-Vulture, *Rhinogryphus californianus"*) [27]. Probably it was destroyed during World War II, when the College was bombed and two-thirds of their collection was lost [28]. I haven't found any clues as to how South acquired his bird.

(2) The story of the Scottish condor is a short one, so far. At the 18 February 1837 meeting in Edinburgh of the Wernerian Natural History Society, *"there were exhibited to the meeting a very fine red orang-outang of Borneo, the great sloth from South America, a new species of eagle from Northern India, and the great Californian vulture"* [29]. No condor specimens were known in Scotland at that time. The only name I have found of someone linked to both the Wernerian Society and condors is John James Audubon, but he was not in Scotland at the time of the California condor exhibit.

(3) The third early European mystery condor was in the collection of Christoph Fellner von Feldegg by 1842. Feldegg (1779-1845) apparently began collecting birds while serving in the Austrian army. Combining his own collecting with various purchases, he amassed some 4,500 specimens. After his death, the collection was auctioned off, and in 1852 the condor was among a number of Feldegg specimens acquired by the National Museum in Prague, Czech Republic, where it remains to this day. The condor specimen was included in an 1842 catalogue of Feldegg's collection, but no information was given except that it was obtained in "Neu-Californien" (the area of the current state of California) [30].

(4) The fourth California condor of unknown origin was in the Paris, France, collection of Victor Massena, Prince d'Essling, Duc de Rivoli. In 1846 Dr. Thomas B. Wilson, working through his brother Edward Wilson (who lived in England), bought the entire Rivoli collection of some 12,500 bird specimens. Although Wilson kept legal possession until 1860, the Rivoli birds were immediately placed in the Academy of Natural Science of Philadelphia (Pennsylvania), and Wilson even provided funds to build additional space at the Academy to house the acquisitions [31].

The California condor specimen had the number 948 in the Rivoli collection; unfortunately, the only other information that came with the bird was that it was collected in California [32]. The Academy initially gave it number 14 in their collection [33]; later renumbering changed its designation to Academy specimen number 42 [34]. This condor was identifiable in the Academy collection as late as 1905 [35], but had disappeared before 1941.

* * *

Where and when could these four California condor specimens have originated? Perhaps we can eliminate (or, at least, ignore) the John Flint South skeleton by assuming (perhaps erroneously) that it belonged with one of the several condor skins in the London area at that time. Flint certainly knew the museum people around London, and his collection was a logical repository for a skeleton. That still leaves three condors with no obvious ties to anyone or anywhere else.

Between 1786 and 1842, a dozen or so European ships with some level of scientific staff on board landed in California. Most remained only a week or so, and most visited only San Francisco Bay or Monterey. (Two parties traveled inland to the vicinity of Sacramento.) Most visitors left enough of a written record for present-day researchers to feel confident that - except in the cases of Menzies, Deppe and Voznesenskii - California condors were not collected and taken back to Europe [36]. There is one possible exception: Paolo-Émilio Botta.

Botta (1802-1870) is best known as an archeologist, famous for his discovery of the ancient site of Ninevah (at present-day Mosul, Iraq), and later as French Consul in Mosul. But as a member of the crew of Captain Auguste Duhaut-Cilly's ship *Le Heros,* he visited a number of ports in California in 1827 and 1828, and collected a number of animal specimens. From the information given in Duhaut-Cilly's journal, I estimate the crew spent some 32 weeks ashore, divided roughly as follows: San Francisco Bay area, 45 days; Santa Cruz, 7 days; Monterey, 57 days; Santa Barbara, 23 days; San Pedro Bay - Los Angeles area, 27 days; and San Diego Bay, 68 days [37].

No list of Botta's California specimens has been found, and it has been assumed that his collecting effort was minor [38]. The amount of time spent on-shore, coupled with some of Duhaut-Cilly's journal entries, suggest otherwise. For example, while at San Francisco Bay in January 1827, he wrote of the "large number" and "astonishing variety" of ducks, sea birds, quail, rabbits and hares that they shot for the dinner table. He continued:

"As for the collection I was engaged in with Dr. Botta, our quests were not less fruitful: on the seashore a swarm of beautiful shore-birds; in the woods and on the hills, several fine species of hawk and other birds of prey; in the thickets, magpies, blackbirds, sparrows and several frugivorous birds all different from ours; finally, in the heath, a pretty species of humming-bird, perhaps the smallest existing, with a head and throat of glowing fire" [39].

At Santa Cruz in early February 1827, Duhaut-Cilly described his pleasure in seeing kingfishers, "red-ducks" [cinnamon teal?], and white herons [egrets]. He then jestingly suggested they were all in danger from Botta:

"There would be, truly, some offset if Dr. Botta were to renew frequently his collection of skins of California birds; for during the two days he passed at Santa Cruz, he threw a little confusion into the habits of these poor creatures; and I even believe I should, in justice, blame myself for a part of this cruel invasion" [40].

At San Pedro Bay in early March 1827, they *"shot some rabbits and a small species of owl which makes its nest upon the ground and lives in families"* [41]. Later, in March at San Diego, they described the roadrunner; it and Anna's hummingbird are Botta's best known specimens [42].

Unless further information is found on Botta's activities, we'll never know if he took a condor back to Europe. It is suggestive that he collected *"several fine species of hawk and other birds of prey;"* that at least two of Botta's birds went directly into the collection of the Duc du Rivoli [43]; and that the Rivoli collection contained a California condor. To me, Botta seems the best source for the Rivoli condor.

* * *

Who else could have taken condors to Europe before 1845? Options seem to be limited to Ferdinand Deppe and Ilya Voznesenskii.

Common belief is that Deppe collected only one California condor, the one still located in Berlin. It is true that Deppe was collecting primarily for the Berlin museum, and that many of his specimens went to that institution. What isn't generally known is that Deppe, through his brother Wilhelm Deppe, was trading and selling specimens elsewhere. Concerning his collections in Mexico in 1828-1829: *"While a part of these natural history treasures were acquired by Berlin institutions, Wilhelm Deppe did his best trying to sell the rest of the objects for his brother's and [Wilhelm] Schiede's benefit to London, Paris, Vienna, St. Petersburg, Copenhagen, Leiden and various German collections"* [44]. An 1830 price list of 169 specimens of natural history and ethnographic items has also been found, signed by Wilhelm Deppe [45]. These two lists predate Deppe's time in California, and it isn't known if later specimens were offered for sale, but it does suggest that Deppe could have been the source of more than one condor in Europe.

Voznesenskii collected at least four California condors, only two of which are still at St. Petersburg. One of the missing birds is almost certainly in Paris, at the Museum National d'Histoire Naturelle, received in trade from St. Petersburg in 1856. It has been suggested that the Feldegg-Czech Republic bird is the other. In the 1840s, the St. Petersburg museum exchanged specimens with the Frankfurt/Main Museum in Germany. Feldegg exchanged specimens with the Frankfurt Museum about that time [46]. Could one of Voznesenskii's specimens have reached Feldegg in time to be included on his 1842 collection list? It seems barely possible. We don't know when Voznesenskii killed his first condor, but his first shipment of specimens from California was placed on a Russian-bound ship at San Francisco 16 October

1840 [47]. His voyage from Russia to the west coast of North America had taken eight months. Assuming a similar time for the return trip (and with weather delays, ship repairs, and business en route it seems unlikely the trip could have taken less time), the shipment would not have reached Russia before May or June 1841. Allowing for unpacking time, some minimal curating, and communication between the exchanging museums, the condor would have been a very last minute addition to Feldegg's 1842 collections list. Unfortunately, Feldegg's list did not place his acquisitions in chronological order, so "barely possible" is the best that can be said.

CHAPTER NOTES

1. Page 213 *in:* Payne, E. J. (editor). Voyages of the Elizabethan seamen. Select narratives from the "Principal Navigations" of Hakluyt. Oxford, England: Clarendon Press.
2. Vizcaino, S. 1916. Diary of Sebastian Vizcaino. Pages 52-103 *in:* H. E. Bolton, Spanish exploration in the Southwest 1542-1706. New York, New York: Charles Scribner's Sons. The wildlife references are on pages 91-92.
   Page 361 of: Wagner, H. R. (translator). 1928. Father Antonio de la Ascension's account of the voyage of Sebastian Vizcaino. *California Historical Society Quarterly* 7(4):295-394.

3. Bolton, H. E. 1931. In the south San Joaquin ahead of Garcés. *California Historical Society Quarterly* 10(3):211-219.

4. Pages 247 and 320 *in:* Bolton, H. E. 1930. Font's complete diary of the second Anza expedition. Volume IV, Anza's California expeditions. Berkeley, California: University of California Press.

5. Page 195 *in* Wagner, W. F. (editor). 1904. Adventures of Zenas Leonard , fur trader and trapper, 1831-1836. Cleveland, Ohio: The Burrows Brothers Company.

6. Pages 195-196 *in:* Poesch, J. 1961. Titian Ramsay Peale 1799-1885 and his journals of the Wilkes Expedition. Philadelphia, Pennsylvania: American Philosophical Society.

7. Pages 360-361 *in:* Fremont, J. C. 1850. The exploring expedition to the Rocky Mountains, Oregon and California. Buffalo, New York: Geo. H. Derby.

8. Page 301 *in:* Bryant, E. 1859. What I saw in California: being the journal of a tour in the years 1846, 1847. New York, New York: D. Appleton & Company.

9. Details of the early days of California livestock are given on pages 38-42 and 118-127 *in*: Burcham, L. T. 1981. California range land: an historico-ecological study of the range resources of California. Publication Number 7, Center for Archaeological Research at Davis (California).

10. Wagner 1904 *op. cit.,* page 183.

11. Farquhar, F. P., and G. H. Derby. 1932. The topographical reports of Lieutenant George H. Derby. *California Historical Society Quarterly* 11(2):99-123.

12. Bryant 1859 *op. cit.,* pages 302 and 305.

13. Pages 698-699 *in:* Bancroft, H. H. 1886. History of California. Volume III, 1825-1840. San Francisco, California: The History Company.

14. Burcham 1981 *op. cit.,* pages 126-127.
A dramatic first-hand account of the operation of the California hide and tallow business is given in: Dana, R. H. 1840. Two years before the mast. (Many editions and reprints.)

15. Lack of ammunition was regularly cited as the reason for not fighting battles, or for withdrawing from battles that had started. For example, in 1829 Mexican soldiers from the San Francisco presidio reportedly abandoned their battles with San Joaquin Indians because they ran short of ammunition (Gray, T. 1993. The Stanislaus Indian wars: the last of the California Northern Yokuts. Modesto, California: McHenry Museum Press). In September 1846, at the "Battle of Chino," a small group of Americans were taken prisoner by Californians. The American loss was blamed on failure of reinforcements to show up because of lack of ammunition (page 52 *in:* White, M. C., and T. Savage. 1956. California all the way back to 1828. Los Angeles, California: Glen Dawson).

16. Ferdinand Deppe is mentioned regularly in the literature of early California, but usually just in passing with little substantive information. More detailed references are:
Bankmann, U. 2002. A Prussian in Mexican California: Ferdinand Deppe, horticulturist, collector for European museums, trader and artist. *Southern California Quarterly* 84(1):1-32.
Stresemann, E. 1954. Ferdinand Deppe's travels in Mexico 1824-1829. *Condor* 56(2):86-92.
Pages 111-127 *in:* Robinson, A. 1891. Life in California during a residence of several years in that territory. San Francisco, California: William Doxey, Publisher. Alfred Robinson described a number of trips he took with Ferdinand Deppe, apparently all in 1832. (Robinson did not date any of his narratives!)

17. Pages 318-319 in: Ogden, A., and A. Robinson. 1944. Business letters of Alfred Robinson. *California Historical Society Quarterly* 23(4):301-334.
"I have embarked in the Alert *[the name of the ship] Boxes containing specimens of Natural History addressed to your care [Bryant and Sturges, Boston] & to be embarked in Boston the first opportunity for Hamburg. The Owner is a particular friend of Mr [William A.] Gale & undoubtedly ere this you may have had the pleasure of his acquaintance - he having left this Coast in January last to return to his Country via Los Estados Unidos del Norte in company with Baron Merryhoff & Ladd.*
"Respecting the freight the House in Hamburg will satisfy all expenses & it is the request of Mr Deppe that the Cases may not be opened in the Custom House if possible

to avoid it - enclosed you will find a small scrap of paper on which is written the address of the House to which the Boxes are consigned."

18. Anonymous (H. Lichtenstein?). 1847. Ferdinand Deppe's reisen in Kalifornien. *Zeitschrift fur Erdkunde, als vergleichende Wissenschaft* 7:383-390. An English translation, erroneously titled "Ferdinand Deppe's travels in California in 1837" (the information is from 1836) was published in 1953 by Glen Dawson (Los Angeles, California).

19. Bankmann *op. cit.,* page 9.

20. Pages 104-105 *in*: Alekseev, A. I. 1987. The odyssey of a Russian scientist: I. G. Voznesenskii in Alaska, California and Siberia 1839-1849. Translation by W. C. Follette. Kingston, Ontario: The Limestone Press.

21. The feather cape and dance skin are shown in Figure 1.

22. Aleskeev *op. cit.,* pages 15-26.

23. Two of Ilya Voznesenskii's California condors are still at the Zoological Institute, St. Petersburgh, Russia (confirmed by Wladimir Loskot, Curator of the Department of Birds, 28 April 2008). Two others have been gone from the Institute for many years, probably traded to other museums within a few years of Voznesenskii's return to Russia.

24. Aleskeev *op. cit,* page 21.

25. Page 75 *in*: Feltoe, C. L. 1884. Memorials of John Flint South. London, England: John Murray.

26. Page 434, of the 30 June 1835 report of the Board of Curators, Hunterian Museum, Royal College of Surgeons.

27. Page 204 in: Sharpe, R. B. 1891. Catalogue of the specimens illustrating the osteology of vertebrated animals, recent and extinct, contained in the Museum of the Royal College of Surgeons of England. London, England: Taylor and Francis.

28. Information provided in 2010 by Sarah Pearson, Curator of The Hunterian Museum, Royal College of Surgeons of England.

29. Anonymous. 1838. Proceedings of the Wernerian Natural History Society. *The Edinburgh New Philosophical Journal* 24:203-209.

30. The information on Christoph Fellner von Felldeg and his California condor was given to me by Jirí Mlíkovsky, Research Curator of Ornithology, National Museum, Prague, Czech Republic.

31. Stone, W. 1899. Some Philadelphia ornithological collections and collectors, 1784-1850. *Auk* 16(2):166-177.
Pages 9-11 *in*: Ennis, J., J. H. B. Bland, and J. F. Knight. 1865. A memoir of Thomas Bellerby Wilson, M. D. Philadelphia, Pennsylvania: The Entomological Society of Philadelphia.

32. Verreaux, J. 1846-1847. Catalogue of birds in the collection of the Duc de Rivoli purchased by Thomas B. Wilson in 1846. Academy of Natural Sciences of Philadelphia (Pennsylvania), Archives Collection 53, Folder 4.

33. Coues, E. 1876. Catalogues, Raptores - Cathartidae - Falconidae. Manuscript, Academy of Natural Sciences of Philadelphia (Pennsylvania), Archives Collection 54, Box 1, Folder 3.

34. Stone, W. ca 1893. Systematic catalogue of mounted collection. Raptors. Manuscript, Academy of Natural Sciences of Philadelphia (Pennsylvania), Archives Collection 54, Box 5, Volume 1.

35. Letter 4 April 1905 from Witmer Stone (Academy of Natural Sciences of Philadelphia, Pennsylvania) to W. Lee Chambers (Santa Monica, California). Chambers Collection, Bancroft Library, University of California, Berkeley.

36. Excellent summaries of these early explorations, accompanied by an extensive bibliography, are included in: Beidleman, R. G. 2006. California's frontier naturalists. Berkeley, California: University of California Press. I have read most of the major references to assure myself that condor observations were not missed in the summaries.

37. Duhaut-Cilly's journal covering the time spent in California was published as: Carter, C. F. (translator). 1929. Duhaut-Cilly's account of California in the years 1827-28. *California Historical Society Quarterly* 8(2):130-166, 8(3):214-215, 8(4):306-336. Days spent in port are relatively easy to estimate from the journal, but time taken with ship duties, diplomacy, bad weather or sickness are seldom identified. Days when specimen collecting was possible were probably a fairly small percentage of the total shore days.

38. Palmer, T. S. 1917. Botta's visit to California. *Condor* 19(5):159-161.

39. Carter *op. cit.*, page 146.

40. Carter *op. cit.*, page 150.

41. Carter *op. cit.*, page 166.

42. Carter *op. cit.*, page 221.

43. Palmer *op. cit.* We know that Botta's specimens of roadrunner and Anna's hummingbird went into the Rivoli collection because René Lesson examined them when he wrote the first descriptions of these species in 1829. Lesson undoubtedly

examined other Botta specimens, but presumably these two were the only ones from California that were new to science, and had not been previously described in a scientific publication.

44. Bankmann *op. cit.,* page 9.

45. Bankmann *op. cit.,* pages 11-12.

46. Information provided by Jirí Mlíkovsky, Research Curator of Ornithology, National Museum, Prague, Czech Republic.

47. Aleskeev *op. cit.,* page 16.

CHAPTER 7
RANDOM SHOTS

For the time period 1794 through 1844, I've accumulated 22 records of condor mortality. Certainly those weren't all of the human-related condor deaths in those 50 years - I continue to locate records not on my earlier lists, and surely not everyone who killed a condor in those years left a written report of it. Nevertheless, considering how few people were on the Pacific Coast, where they lived, and what opportunities were available to them for killing condors, I think it's safe to conclude that the overall take was small. That was not true of the next 50 years, as previewed in just the next fifteen.

It took only ten years after 1844 to exceed (by four) the previous 50-year total of 22 mortality records, and in the next five years (1855-1859) 18 more were added. Some of this loss was attributable to the same random, opportunistic natural history collecting of earlier years, but two new reasons for killing condors were added in the late 1840s and the 1850s. The first, collecting to specifically meet a growing demand for condor specimens, will be discussed in later chapters. The second, accounting for nearly half of the documented losses between 1845 and 1860, was the killing of condors merely for sport or out of curiosity.

In 1840, there were less than 10,000 non-Indian people in what would become the states of Washington, Oregon and California. By 1850, as a result of the California "Gold Rush" and the continuing westward movement of settlers, the Pacific Coast "European" population was over 100,000; by 1860, 400,000; and by 1870 it was over 600,000 [1]. The mere increase in human numbers in the condors' range would likely have resulted in increased condor losses, but the arrivals of the "Gold Rush" period had two attributes that proved deadly to the condors: they came with an amazing number of firearms, and with lots of time on their hands to use the artillery.

As one contemporary author described the westward movement: *"The emigrants were walking arsenals, armed to the teeth with rifles, shotguns, and revolvers, supposedly to hunt buffalo and defend themselves from Indians"* [2]. The guidebooks read by the emigrants urged every man to take *"a good rifle, and , if convenient, a pair of pistols, five pounds of powder, and ten pounds of lead"* [3]. *"Ignorant of guns and camping life except for what they had heard or read in legend and literature, thousands of city and rural men studied John C. Fremont's famous* Report of the Exploring Expedition to the Rocky Mountains in the Year 1842 and to Oregon and North California in the Years 1843-'44 *and accounts of other western travelers. In part motivated by such reading and by the traditional fear of Indians, these emigrants purchased a remarkable number of guns, an impulse encouraged by the U. S. War Department's February 1849 offer to sell pistols, rifles and ammunition at cost to California (and Oregon) emigrants"* [4].

So many firearms in the hands of inexperienced owners resulted in a high incidence of gunshot injuries and deaths; in fact, one researcher rated guns as causing the greatest number of wagon train accidents (ahead of drowning, being crushed by wagon wheels, and being injured handling domestic animals) [5]. The novelty of the new firearms, and lack of the supposed legitimate reasons for having them (killing food and shooting Indians), encouraged the travelers to amuse themselves. One "Forty-niner" beginning his trip west by riverboat described some extracurricular activities:

"We have amused ourselves all the way down the river shooting at wild ducks, and when no men were around, we would shoot at hogs, dogs, etc. on the shore. Thirty or forty rifles fired all at the same time would hurry a dog some! By the time we get among the Pawnees, we will be able to take their eyes out without much trouble" [6].

Not all these firearms made it to California. By the time the travelers reached western Nebraska and eastern Wyoming, the need to lighten their loads resulted in discarding everything that wasn't essential. This included many weapons. At Fort Laramie, *"rifles are thrown by the dozen into the river and worthless white beans almost cover the ground and old stoves almost without number are thrown away"* [7]. By the time they reached the Humboldt River in Nevada *"few men carried guns--in fact, most rifles had been thrown away"* [8].

Despite all this load lightening, many firearms made it over the mountains to California. In testimony before the United States Senate, Navy Lieutenant W. May wrote: *"When I left California* [in November 1849], *the country was completely glutted with every description of weapon.."* [9].

This excess of weaponry in the turmoil of newly-established mining camps led to many armed confrontations and deaths. In the decade of the 1850s, Tuolumne County (in the heart of the Mother Lode) alone had 156 homicides, many of them gun-related. The communities were settling down somewhat by the 1860s, but Tuolumne County still registered 96 homicides [10]. From 1865 through 1869, Tuolumne County with a population of 8,150 had 38 homicides; the entire state of Vermont (population 330,551) had two [11].

Of course, men shooting one another in mining camps had no direct relationship to condors being killed. But the factors leading to the lawlessness of California at the turn of the 19th century also increased the potential for condor losses: large increases in human populations, many guns, men away from their families with few diversions, hard work with very little profit for most of them in the gold fields, and long periods when they could not mine because of dry streams in the summer and inclement weather in winter. The means (lots of guns) and the motives (boredom, coupled with a curiosity to see these giant birds up close) came together in California in the middle of the 19th century.

There didn't seem to be any animosity or maliciousness in the condor shooting; it was just something to do. The reports were matter-of-fact. J. D. B. Stillman wrote about an incident near the confluence of the Sacramento and Feather rivers in September 1849: *"Just before night, Mark* [Hopkins] *shot a large bird in the top of a tree, which we thought was a wild turkey. It was directly over our heads, and fell into the water alongside the boat. It measured nine feet from tip to tip of wings, and its head and neck were bare of feathers and of a yellow color. It was of the vulture family, though we pronounced it a 'golden eagle' for want of a better name"* [12].

A month later, in the hills northeast of Hopkins' locale, J. Goldsborough Bruff made passing reference to a condor shooting in his trip notes of an average day on the trail: *"6 dead and 1 abandoned ox on road... Saw on the road side a small black & yellow fox, dead, also a dead deer, and numerous remains of them. Shot a large very brown Vulture, measuring 9 feet from tip to tip"* [13].

The editor of the Sacramento *Daily Union* embellished his personal story a bit, but the basic tale was the same - condor shot and measured: *"A vulture of enormous proportions was shot on the American river, near the store of Woods & Kenyon, in El Dorado county, a few days since, which measured nine feet from tip to tip of its wings. A friend presented us with a quill, which is a quill from one of its wings, with the remark that it was handed to us as a weapon with which to defend the rights of the people. We shall endeavor to apply it to that purpose"* [14].

Later the same summer, another condor yielded a primary feather to a newspaper editor: *"The Editor of the Marysville* Herald *may well 'plume himself' on the receipt of a vulture's quill measuring twenty-four inches in length. The bird measured nine feet four inches from tip to tip of the wings. It was shot near Chico"* [15].

Alfred Doten, later to become owner and editor of the Gold Hill (Nevada) *Daily News,* had his own close encounter with a condor near the south end of San Francisco Bay in 1858: *"Seth* [Morton] *shot a big black Eagle measuring 9 feet and an inch from tip to tip of his wings – the largest bird I ever saw – he is, I think, properly called the 'California Condor' instead of 'baldheaded eagle' as Emerson calls it – it weighed nineteen pounds "* [16].

* * *

These random records from journals and newspapers certainly document an increase in condor mortality, but they don't tell us the magnitude of the increase. Did most of the losses get documented, or is the record I've developed so far just a small view of a much bigger scene? Obviously, many (most?) people shooting condors would not have been keeping journals with details of their shooting activities, and most would not have had a local newspaper editor to whom they could present a condor feather. On the other hand, killing and measuring *"from tip to tip"* made a popular news item through the 1850s, 1860s and 1870s. Because there was no stigma attached to shooting a condor, probably more of the deaths made the news than was the case toward the start of the 20th century, when the activity was becoming less "politically correct."

Figure 5. Frank Holmes with California condor, probably shot by Henry Hopken in Monterey County circa 1898. Photo courtesy of Betty Ryon (Holmes' granddaughter).

I think it's possible - I'm almost willing to say likely - that the loss of condors during the Gold Rush and early post-Gold Rush period was substantially greater than the existing records indicate. The social and economic situation in one small area of central California, the East Bay redwoods, was repeated in many other communities. The impact on condors at Redwoods may be illustrative of what occurred in other areas, as well.

* * *

When I was growing up in Oakland in the 1940s and 1950s, I often hiked in Redwood Regional Park and adjacent Joaquin Miller Park, and enjoyed the cool wildness of steep canyons filled with redwood trees. At the time, I had no idea that these groves were the remnants of what had been a substantial

84

redwood forest. Even though I was avid in my interest in birds, I was unaware that my favorite hiking area had once been habitat for what was apparently a significant population of California condors. In the 1840s, both were facts.

Commercial logging began in the East Bay redwoods in the early 1840s, undertaken (not always entirely legally) by seamen who had deserted their ships in San Francisco Bay [17]. However, Santa Cruz redwoods were much nearer the coast, making shipping more economical; also, John Sutter was beginning to develop lumber mills in the Sierra Nevada. Cutting in the East Bay waned, but picked up again about 1845 as American immigrants arriving in California sought work. Gold fever caused desertion of the woods for awhile, but before long the demand for lumber was evident, and operations began anew. The likelihood of making a fortune in the gold field fell rapidly [18]. *"Soon many a disillusioned miner was hurrying back to the redwoods of the East Bay hills"* [19]. In late 1849, the human population of "Redwoods" was 100 or more. The 1853 election rolls show that there had been 300 to 400 people in the woods, enough to have established a Redwoods voting precinct, but the community was already in decline. In December 1853, James Lamson reported drastic changes in his part of the woods.

"An important change has been in progress for some time past in the Redwoods. Three or four months ago I was surrounded by a deep, dense forest, in which was a busy population at work. But this industry fast swept away the forest, and as the timber grew scarce, they began to remove to other places. They continued to go until our society was reduced to ten men, living in a little cluster of four cabins. But even this colony has taken a sudden resolution to migrate, and this morning the last man went, and I am left alone. So now, nothing remains for me but to go too, which I shall do as soon as I can determine where" [20]. By 1857 almost all the redwoods and almost all the people were gone, not just from Lamson's community but throughout the area [21].

Luckily, for historical information on the condors of the East Bay, Lamson did not immediately leave Redwoods. He stayed through 1854, visiting with the few people remaining in the area, and observing the condors that obviously were using the area as a major roosting site. On 9 February 1854, he wrote in his journal:

"I saw six or eight vultures perched on the trees, sitting in perfect idleness, and scarcely moving. A man was cutting up a fallen tree near one of them, but his labors did not seem in the least degree to disturb the bird. Another one sat on a low tree which I approached. When I arrived within less than gunshot distance he half spread his wings and stood up, as if preparing to fly. But after a moment's hesitation he folded his pinions again, and seemed to have come to the conclusion that there was no danger from a man with only a stick in his hand. As I continued to approach the tree on which he stood, he thrust his head down below his body, and turned it about most whimsically, while he

kept his keen eye fastened upon me, as though he were quizzing me; but still he showed no disposition to fly. I now began to shout at him, and to swing my cap; and in faith, it seemed as if my noise and gesticulations served rather to amuse than to frighten him. Then I threw my cane up in the air towards him, but he only gave his head an extra cant, and continued peering at me with such an impudent, derisive no-ye-don't sort of a look, that I almost expected to see him raise his thumb to his nose and shake his fingers at me. Finding him thus firmly resolved not to be driven from his position, I left him, firmly believing that if a man wants to hunt California vultures, their shyness will be no obstacle to his success" [22].

Two days previously he had written that he had observed *"a scattering flock of more than fifty California Vultures [that] flew over the forest in the morning. Seeing them sailing past in greater numbers than I had before observed them, and all in one direction, I began to count them. In a few moments I counted twenty-five, while those that preceded them and those that followed, all within an hour, must have exceeded that number."* Given the condors' habit of circling back and forth, and dropping below the ridge line and reappearing, he may not have seen fifty different birds. He obviously saw quite a few.

Lamson's 9 February comment about the ease with which condors could be killed was not idle speculation. Already in 1854, he knew of five California condors that had been shot at Redwoods. On 2 February, he wrote: *"I was standing at the door of my cabin, when I heard the report of a rifle, and turning my eyes in the direction of the sound, I saw a California Vulture fall to the ground. I hastened up the cañon, and speedily purchased the bird of the owner, who did not place a very high value on it."*

On 4 February: *"I went up the cañon to see the man, Mr. Currie, Kentuckian, of whom I had bought the California Vulture. I saw there a young man, Currie's son, who told me he had shot another Vulture three weeks before, and had thrown it away. He directed me where to find the body, and I went in search of it, intending to preserve the skeleton, but when I found it a very important portion of the bird, the head, was wanting, which rendered it worthless for a skeleton. So I cut off the wings and tail, which I took home."*

His 9 February journal entry had begun with three other condor shootings: *"In a long walk a few days since I encountered an old man by the side of the road engaged in making shingles. He was a very coarse looking fellow, with a dark complexion, and a black bushy beard that more than half covered his face,... He was an old Kentucky rifleman, and, as I afterwards learned, a first rate marksman. He had shot a vulture some days before, and it was lying near his cabin half decayed. Some quills were scattered over the ground, and I picked up two or three of them, when he ordered me in the rudest manner to leave them. I then proposed to buy some of them, but he would neither sell nor give them away.. Today I passed his cabin again, and he accosted me with considerable civility. A sort of grim smiled played on his harsh features, his manners were wonderfully softened, and the gruff old savage seemed to have been suddenly transformed into a half civilized being. He had shot two vultures yesterday, though one of them, which he had only wing tipped, and tied to a stake, had made his escape. He had been thinking of me since he killed the bird, and wished I had it, for he perceived that I was very desirous to obtain a specimen. He now offered to sell it to me, and the payment of five bits made me its owner."*

Lamson tried to preserve this purchased condor skin, but the excessively fat and greasy carcass thwarted his amateur efforts, and he threw it away. On 22 March: *"Anxious to procure another skin to replace that of the California Vulture I had lost, I borrowed a rifle yesterday, and took it up the mountain to young Currie, the Kentuckian. His father had gone up the bay and carried his rifle with him. Currie had found an opportunity to use the rifle and this morning he came down the mountain bringing a Vulture he had just shot. It was not quite so large as the last, its alar extent being but nine feet and its weight 20 pounds."*

I haven't found any information on what happened to that condor carcass, nor to the last one Lamson mentioned as having been in his keeping. On 30 October 1854 a teamster brought him a live condor that had been lassoed while feeding on a cow carcass. Lamson kept the condor four days, but it died *"having probably been wounded in his capture."*

* * *

The condor situation at Redwoods was almost certainly unusual; probably not many communities sprang up in the middle of a major condor roosting area. Because there were so many condors in such vulnerable circumstances, the kill was probably unusually high. But if the condor situation was unique, the human situation at Redwoods was typical of many areas in California during and just after the Gold Rush. Even when mining was relatively good, there was of necessity a lot of idle time. As the easy gold played out, or as disillusion and discouragement built, miners moved on to other situations. Some returned to their homes in the East, but many couldn't afford the trip and many were ashamed to be returning as "failures." They moved to somewhere like the East Bay redwoods; stayed until the job ran out; waited around with nothing to do until a new opportunity arose or they decided it was time to go; then moved on again [23]. There may have been no more situations quite like Redwoods, but opportunities for idle shooting were everywhere.

After California settled down following the initial excitements of the Gold Rush, shooting out of idleness and boredom gave way to shooting as organized sport, with the condor sometimes a recognized target. For example, a sporting club in San Bernardino announced a competitive hunt to take place on Thanksgiving Day in 1887, with points to be awarded for each species killed. Points ranged from one for each robin, dove, lark, or killdeer through (among

87

others) *"mountain quail five; hawk three...curlew four...teal duck five...mallard seven...cranes, swan or pelicans twenty each...weasel or mink twenty each...coyote forty; deer, antelope or mountain sheep seventy-five each; California vulture or eagle seventy-five each; panther, mountain lion or bear one hundred each"* [24]. I haven't found any report on how successful was the hunt, but a few years later two mounted condors graced the roof of the San Bernardino old log cabin at festival time [25].

CHAPTER NOTES

1. Population estimates are taken from the histories of Hubert Howe Bancroft, and from the U. S. census figures of residents used to apportion seats in Congress each ten years.

2. Page 90 *in*: Mattes, M. J. 1969. The Great Platte River Road: the covered wagon mainline via Fort Kearny to Fort Laramie. Lincoln, Nebraska: Nebraska State Historical Society.

3. Pages 6 and 10 *in*: Disturnell, J. 1849. The emigrant's guide to New Mexico, California, and Oregon; giving the different overland and sea routes, compiled by reliable authorities. New York, New York: J. Disturnell.

4. Page 52 *in*: Holliday, J. S. 2002. The world rushed in: the California gold rush experience. Norman, Oklahoma: University of Oklahoma Press.

5. Mattes *op. cit.*, pages 90-91.

6. Holliday *op. cit.*, quoted on page 70.

7. Holliday *op. cit.*, page 170, quoting William Swain.

8. Holliday *op. cit.*, page 230, quoting William Swain.

9. U. S. Senate report republished in an unnumbered appendix, Colburn's United Service Magazine and Naval Military Journal, 1852, Part II.

10. Page 7 *in*: McKanna, C. V. Jr. 2002. Race and homicide in nineteenth-century California. Reno, Nevada: University of Nevada Press.

11. McKanna *op. cit.*, page 104.

12. Johnson, K. 1967. The Gold Rush letters of J. D. B. Stillman. Palo Alto, California: Lewis Osborne (entry of 19 September 1849).

13. Page 204 (20 October 1849) *in*: Reed, G. W., and R. Gaines, editors. 1949. The journals, drawings and other papers of J. Goldsborough Bruff, April 2, 1849-July 20, 1851. New York: Columbia University Press.

14. Anonymous. 1854. California vulture. Sacramento (California) *Daily Union,* 11 March 1854.

15.Anonymous. 1854. A California vulture. Sacramento (California) *Daily Union,* 21 June 1854.

16. Page 402 (17 January 1858) *in*: Clark, W. V. T. (editor). 1973. The journals of Alfred Doten 1849-1903. Reno, Nevada: University of Nevada Press.

17. Details of the East Bay redwood harvest are from: Burgess, S. D. 1951. The forgotten redwoods of the East Bay. *California Historical Society Quarterly* 30(1):1-14.

18. Page 5 *in*: Vaught, D. 2007. After the Gold Rush: Tarnished dreams in the Sacramento Valley. Baltimore, Maryland: Johns Hopkins University Press.
   By the end of 1848, some 6,000 miners had found $10 million worth of gold. [So, the "average miner," if there was such a person, might have made $1,500 to $2000.] *"The amount tripled in 1849, but the number of miners to share it grew by a factor of seven. By 1852, the peak year, the output was $80 million and the number of miners exceeded 100,000."* [In four years, the expectation had dropped to around $750 per person.] As the return per miner decreased, *"the more the glory of El Dorado faded. Letters from home, stories in newspapers, and entries in diaries increasingly focused on the dark side of life in the mines--exhausting work, wildly inflated prices, overwhelming loneliness, illness and disease, and prevalence of death."*

19. Burgess *op. cit.,* page 5.

20. Page 129 *in*: Lamson, J. 1878. Round Cape Horn, voyage of the passenger-ship *James W. Paige,* from Maine to California in the year 1852. Bangor, Maine: O. F. & W. H. Knowles.

21. Burgess op. cit., page 11.

22. Lamson devoted two sketches in "Round Cape Horn," *op. cit.,* to the California condor (pages 152-155). Additional information is included in Lamson's 1852-1861 manuscript diary, the original of which is at the North Baker Library, California Historical Society, San Francisco, California.

23. The population turnover in California communities during the 1850s was often nearly complete, even in towns that stayed prosperous after the main "rush" was over. In Nevada City and Grass Valley, *"almost none of the men who had enjoyed the two camps' flush times were still there* [a few years later]... *Of the populations of both camps in 1850, only about five out of every hundred can be located in these towns by 1856."* Pages 492-494 *in*: Mann, R. 1972. The decade after the Gold Rush: social structure in Grass Valley and Nevada City, California, 1850-1860. *Pacific Historical Review* 41(4):484-504.

24. Anonymous. 1887. Thanksgiving sport. Riverside (California) *Daily Press,* 25 October 1887.

25. Anonymous. 1901. The old log cabin at the street fair - most interesting exhibit that was filled with suggestions of the old pioneer days. Riverside (California) *Morning Enterprise*, 19 May 1901.

CHAPTER 8

DOCTOR TAYLOR OF MONTEREY

Through the first third of the 1850s, with the exception of whatever condors may have been acquired by Indians for their social and religious needs, no one was specifically seeking condors. Explorers and naturalists killed condors randomly and opportunistically, in the same way they collected other specimens of fauna or flora they encountered. Early miners, ranchers and homesteaders shot condors not because they were condors, but because they were big and made good targets, or because they were big and curiosity demanded a closer look. In the 1850s in Monterey, California, the first two true "condor people" emerged, Alexander Smith Taylor and Colbert Austin Canfield. Chapter 10 is devoted to Canfield.

Taylor, born in Charleston, South Carolina 16 April 1817, son of Alexander Taylor and Mary Chapman, was first on the scene. His grandfather, Capt. James Taylor, emigrated from Aberdeen, Scotland, and had settled in Charleston, South Carolina, by 1785 [1]. His father was apparently born in Charleston about 1786, but married in England in 1812. He gained some fame in the War of 1812 when the privateer *Saucy Jack* captured a major British cargo ship, *Pelham,* and Taylor was named prize master [2]. The father died in either 1821 or 1823 [3]. Almost the total of what is known about Alexander's first thirty years of life was given by him in one long sentence in a letter he wrote to the American Antiquarian Society 22 July 1866:

"I left my native city of Charleston, So. Carolina, in 1837 (only returning for a few days in 1839), when in my 21st year, and since that time have wandered over the West Indies, England, India, the Red Sea, China, Singapore and Ceylon" [4].

What he did in those places, and how he made a living, remains unknown. Considering that his grandfather, father, and three uncles were all mariners, it seems reasonable to assume he was shipboard much of that time. Finally, on the brig *Pacific,* coming from Hong Kong, he landed at Monterey 8 September 1848 [5]. He lived at Monterey until 1860, then relocated to Santa Barbara, California. There he married Josepha Hill (daughter of Daniel Hill and Rafaela Olivera de Ortega), sired at least six children, and died 27 July 1876 [6].

If it's possible for a person to be both well-known and unknown, Alexander S. Taylor fills the bill. Other than in the works of Hubert Howe Bancroft, his name is nearly absent from early histories and biographies of coastal California. His occupation in the 1850 census was given as "physician" (hence, "Dr. Taylor"), but no record has been found that he actually practiced medicine. The 1860 census labeled him a "druggist," and he did indeed have an apothecary on Alvarado Street in Monterey from 1849 to 1860. He also served as local agent for the Pacific Express Company [7], and was a clerk in the U. S. District Court at Monterey [8]. He was nominated by the Democratic Party in Monterey County for State treasurer [9], but did not make the ticket.

Sharply contrasting with his little-known private life, for many he was the voice of the west coast of North America in the 1850s. He wrote for newspapers; he corresponded with scientists, historians and politicians. He gathered information on Indians, on the Spanish and Mexican periods of California history, on agricultural history, and on geography. He sent natural history specimens to England and to the museums of the eastern United States. He was one of the organizers of the first California historical society [10], was elected a member of the American Antiquarian Society, and was made an Honorary Member of the California Academy of Sciences [11]. There were no limits to his interests [12]. One result of this shotgun approach to life and learning was that he became the first widely-quoted "authority" on the California condor.

Apparently, Taylor's first communication about California condors came in 1852, when he wrote a brief newspaper note, describing a condor killed near Monterey [13]. (In 1851, a letter he wrote to England about the animals of California mentioned "the red-headed buzzard" - likely the turkey vulture - but not the condor [14].) He followed with a newspaper series in *"The California Farmer and Journal of Useful Science,"* covering the California condor, Andean condor, and king vulture [15]. The California condor information, supplemented by other articles and new observations, was published nearly simultaneously as a new series in *"The Overland Monthly"* [16]. Parts of his writings were republished widely in other newspapers, in books on birds and natural history, and even in scientific journals.

Hubert Howe Bancroft, the renowned California historian, called Alexander Taylor *"a literary and historical dabster,"* who *"knew much; but credit was given him for knowing much more than he did know"* [17].

"[It was] *as an investigator and writer on the ethnography, bibliography, and history of Cal. that he deserves particular notice; and in these respects he was a remarkable man. Without having any special aptitude by nature or education for such work, he developed a fondness for it almost amounting to a mania. His zeal in face of the most discouraging obstacles is worthy of all praise, though it must be confessed that the result was wellnigh valueless. He was not content with being a collector or even translator and narrator, but had a most unfortunate passion for working the results of his observations and study into what he regarded as a scientific form, the result being too often an absurd jumble of bad Spanish, worse Latin, and unintelligible affectations"* [18].

Few matched Bancroft's style of criticism that sliced to the bone but, unfortunately, agreement was general that Taylor's work was prodigious but mostly of little usefulness [19]. Interestingly, one modern-day reviewer believed that *"'The Great Condor of California' was a careful study in natural history, and is yet of considerable value"* [20]. Oh, if that was only true! Actually, Taylor's writings on condors are the same hodgepodge of fact and fancy that characterized most of his work. He shares with the botanist David Douglas honors for introducing a most amazing amount of nonsense into the early record of condors [21].

Taylor was quoted liberally on both sides of the Atlantic for 30 years in the second half of the 19th century, when no other "authorities" were writing about condors. Few zoologists or historians recognize his name today - and almost everything he wrote has been shown to be either incorrect or unlikely - yet his writings still color the way that the history of the condor is perceived. Because his is the principal influence behind modern-day pronouncements on subjects as varied as condor poisoning, and storing gold in condor quills, we need to look closely at his sources of information and his presentation.

Taylor seems not to have traveled far from Monterey during his years there (1848-1860), and his personal realm of condor reference included little beyond Monterey and Santa Cruz counties. Other than his descriptions of condor specimens he had in his possession, and an occasional comment on a bird or two seen by him in the wild, everything came from other sources. His principal written reference was John James Audubon's 1839 "Ornithological Biography" [22], with its extensive quotes from David Douglas and John Kirk Townsend. He cited Thomas Jefferson Farnham [23], but Farnham had merely quoted David Douglas. Although not identified by name, some version of Goldsmith's "A history of the earth and animated nature" - with its potpourri of writings on the Andean condor [24] - appears to have been one of Taylor's sources. Word of mouth information came from "a hunter," "a fifteen year resident of California," "a friend," and various unidentified vaqueros and rancheros. The "fifteen year resident" told him that the condor's egg was pale blue with brown spots (they are white and unmarked), and that it was placed on the ground *"in the ravines in the mountains, and generally near the roots of the red-wood and pine trees."* The "hunter" reported that the clutch consisted of two eggs, which condors *"sometimes lay on the ledges of high rocks, but quite as often on tall trees, in the old nests of hawks and eagles."* The same informant told Taylor that the female condor was smaller than the male, *"and this is without doubt, as he has often observed them"* [25].

When a large number of sea lions died, Taylor reported that *"a friend of ours informed us that he saw a few days ago, as many as three hundred of these creatures* (condors) *near such feeding ground"* [26]. This is perhaps not impossible, but no one but Taylor ever reported hundreds of condors at one location. Taylor used the number 300 on another occasion, in even more improbable circumstances: *"A friend of ours engaged in the cattle trade, informs us, that in going from the Mission of Santa Clara towards San Francisco, in 1850, he accidentally dropped a quarter of fat beef from his cart, while a number of the Condor were in sight. On discovering his loss, after a*

93

THE CONDOR, OR GREAT VULTURE OF CALIFORNIA.—A friend writes us that a fine specimen of this gigantic bird, the *Sarcoramphos Californiensis* of ornithologists, was killed on the hills of the San Lucas range, near Monterey, the other day. His measure was as follows:—From the end of the tail feathers to top of beak, 4 feet 3½ inches; from tip to tip of the wings, 8 feet 3 inches in breadth; from the outer joint to end of feather, 1 foot 9 inches: i. e. breadth of a wing. A feather measured 2 feet 4 inches; from point of beak to commencement of feathers on shoulder, 1 foot; the length of head, 7 inches; 2½ inches thick from crown of head to bottom of lower beak; breadth 2 6-8 inches; the tail, 1 foot 4 inches; legs and feet from fore joint, 10 inches. The bird is found, according to travellers and naturalists, along the whole coast of Northwest America, and throughout the Rocky Mountains, and inhabits the heights of the sierras and most unfrequented parts. He is easily attracted in parts which he frequents by a dead bullock or deer, and sometimes steals the salmon and trout from the Indians when fishing. It is said to be among birds second only to the condor of the Andes of South America, and nearly resembles it in size and appearance. Farnham, in his work on California, says:—

"It builds its nests among the woody districts, on the tops of the highest trees, in the most inaccessable parts of the mountain vallies." The color of feathers of this specimen answers to Farnham's description, being of a uniform brownish-black. The bill is a mottled black, the skin of the head and neck yellow, without feathers to the approach of the shoulders. Its egg is nearly as large as that of the ostrich.—*San Francisco Herald.*

Figure 6. A typical Alexander Taylor newspaper piece, 1853.

few minutes, he turned back and observed the Condor in numbers, which he estimated at over three hundred, hovering over and near his lost beef. On coming up with it, he was surprised to find that the fat and kidneys of the quarter, with all the inner meat, had completely cleaned off the bones, and the piece of meat had lost more than half its weight" [27].

Miscellaneous vaqueros and rancheros allegedly told Taylor that condors were captured by hiding in animal skins, and grabbing the condors' feet when they landed; that condors were often pitted in cock fight-like circumstances against bears, dogs and eagles (he had *"never had the opportunity to witness any of these fights;"* neither did anyone else, at least as documented in print); that a group of condors separated a calf from its mother, then killed it; and *"they are often known to kill lambs, hares and rabbits"* [28].

Some of Taylor's more bizarre statements seem to have no basis anywhere in the historical record. Take for example his comments on condor feeding habits: *"It* [the condor] *is particularly fond of fish, and is often found on the sea-shore watching for fish thrown on the beach, or even steals from the Indians when catching salmon and mountain trout in the lakes and rivers of the Great Plains and of the Coast. A dead whale thrown ashore is sure to bring some of them in sight, and a hunter killing a deer in the mountains is confident of their appearance as soon as the beast is wounded. They are also said to attack wounded deer and other animals, and kill them, and sometimes carry off alive smaller creatures. They are also stated to carry off fish caught in river, sea and lake shallows; and though they will eat dead meat, they will not, like a buzzard, eat carrion - but the last is a mistake"* [29].

To add to Taylor's problems of general credibility, he often contradicted himself, and made no effort to reconcile or explain differences. For example, when he was presented with an authentic condor egg (the first certain one known), his description made a point of refuting Douglas' famous black egg information [30]. Yet, in an accompanying article in the same magazine, he presented the egg as pale blue with spots, as told to him by the "fifteen year resident of California" [31]. Perhaps this was just an example of the "kitchen sink" approach [32] that was common in natural history writing in information-starved 19th century America; *i.e.,* everything ever said or written about a topic, with no attempt to evaluate, correct, or criticize. However, it may also be another of several instances in which it is clear that he melded several articles without bothering to edit. This shows up in his comments on condors feeding on sea lion carcasses. The language he used in his 1859 article - *"A friend of ours informed us that he saw <u>a few days ago</u>..."* (my underlining) - is exactly the same as he wrote in that same story in a newspaper article in August 1855 [33]. Even considering the shortage of good information on condors in the second half of the 19th century, one wonders how his writing could have been taken seriously in natural science circles. Yet, he was quoted extensively in the work of the leading ornithologists in both the United States and Europe [34].

* * *

Bird study didn't seem to be one of Alexander Taylor's strongest interests. I've only been able to find one article he wrote on a bird - the roadrunner - that wasn't a vulture [35]. Although it appears that he personally collected invertebrates, reptiles, and small mammals on occasion, there is no evidence that he shot any birds. I have wondered how his interest in condors developed, and how he came to send seven California condors and three turkey vulture specimens to England (the only bird specimens I have found that are attributed to him). The answer seems to rest in his long-time friendship with John Henry Gurney.

Gurney (1819-1890), renowned for his collection of raptorial bird specimens at England's Norwich Museum, in 1851 published some notes on California wildlife that he had received *"from a friend of mine, who is resident at Monterey"* [36]. The friend was not named, but the writing style is clearly Alexander Taylor's. "Friend" could have been merely a form of address for a correspondent, but I think the evidence is good that Gurney and Taylor actually were friends. Taylor, who was only two years older than Gurney, wrote that he left South Carolina in 1837, sailed to the West Indies, returned home briefly in 1839, and then traveled to England [37]. Gurney's father, Joseph John Gurney, toured through the eastern United States and Canada 1837-1840, visiting various establishments of the Society of Friends. Before returning to England, he sailed to the West Indies and visited a number of islands, then returned to the United States before sailing home. *"Accompanied by his young friend Alexander S. Taylor, Joseph John Gurney embarked on board the 'Roscius,' on the twenty-sixth of the seventh month [July 1840]"* [38]. I have found no details of what brought Alexander Taylor and Joseph Gurney together, but a subsequent meeting between Alexander Taylor and Joseph's son John seems inevitable. When Taylor "discovered" the condor, and Gurney began to build his collection of raptorial birds into the largest in the world, they would have developed a clear mutual interest.

Taylor probably sent Gurney his first California condor in early 1853; that was also the year that Gurney reportedly began to actively build his "bird of prey" collection [39]. One story is that Gurney had no special interest in raptors when he began to stock the Norwich Museum, but fate stepped in with the auctioning off of the Zoological Society of London's museum collection. Gurney sent an agent to the sales *"with some money to buy a selection of the birds for the Norwich Museum. The sale commenced in scientific sequence with the* Accipitres, *and the agent bid with diligent persistence until all his money was gone, with the result that he bought only Birds of Prey. With this foundation Gurney determined to devote himself to a special study of these birds, and made the collection of* Accipitres *at Norwich the most famous in the world"* [40]. Whether or not the story is true, it is a fact that Gurney put the major share of his efforts into the raptor collection, and by his death it had grown to include almost 5,000 specimens, representing almost 600 species and subspecies [41].

Only one of the Taylor-Gurney condors remains at Norwich today, the skeleton of one of the first two birds obtained by Taylor [42]. The others, including the first California condor egg and the first nestling ever collected [43], are now in the Natural History Museum (Tring, United Kingdom). Two condors were transferred in an exchange before 1874 [44]; the rest came in the 1950s [45]. From Taylor's newspaper stories it is possible to identify approximately when condors were killed. Unfortunately, no specific collection data accompany the specimens, so one can only guess which bird goes with which news story, based mainly on age or sex. Given that Gurney reportedly *"did not care much for duplicates at any time unless they were from different countries"* [46], one could speculate that the first two condors exchanged out of the collection were the last two that Taylor sent to him. Alas, we will probably never know.

CHAPTER NOTES

1. Anonymous (Alexander Taylor?). 1868. Something about the "Saucy Jack." Charleston (South Carolina) *Courier,* 19 August 1868.
   It isn't yet clear when James Taylor actually arrived in North America. He married Margaret (Davies) Laidler in St. Augustine, Florida, in 1779.

2. *Niles' Weekly Register* (Baltimore, Maryland), 6(144):225.

3. Pages 743-744 *in*: Bancroft, H. H. 1890. History of California. Volume V - 1846-1848. San Francisco, California: The History Company.
   Anonymous. 1855. The late Admiral Price and the Saucy Jack. Charleston (South Carolina) *Courier,* 13 March 1855.

4. Death notice pages 263-265 in: *Proceedings of the American Antiquarian Society,* New Series, Volume 3 - October 1883 to April 1885. Worcester, Massachusetts.

5. Cowan, R. E. 1933. Alexander S. Taylor, 1817-1876: first biographer of California. *California Historical Society Quarterly* 12(1):18-24.

6. Bancroft 1890 *op. cit.;* Cowan 1933 *op. cit.* Also, U. S. Federal censuses: 18 September 1850, Monterey; 2 June 1860, Monterey; 25 September 1870 Santa Barbara; and 21 June 1880 Santa Barbara.

7. Information provided October 2011 by Dennis Copeland, Museum and Archives Manager, City of Monterey, California.

8. Page 74 *in*: Barrows, H. D., and L. A. Ingersoll. 1893. Memorial and biographical history of the coast counties of central California. Chicago, Illinois: The Lewis Publishing Company.

9. Anonymous. 1857. Monterey County Democratic nominations. *Daily Alta California*. San Francisco, California. 11 August 1857.

10. Howell, W. R. 1942. News of the Society: meetings. *California Historical Society Quarterly* 21(2):183-184.

11. Cowan *op. cit.*

12. Taylor's larger efforts on Spanish history, Indians, the literature of Alaska and California, etc., are discussed in Cowan *op. cit.,* and Bancroft 1891 *op. cit.* Just a sampling of some of the other fields in which he gained recognition:
   Ahearn, C. G. 1995. Catalog of the type specimens of Seastars (Echinodermata: Asteroidea) in the National Museum of Natural History, Smithsonian Institution. Washington, D. C.: *Smithsonian Contributions to Zoology*, Number 572 - Page 9, Taylor credited with providing two specimens of echinoderms to the National Museum.
   Cope, E. D. 1900. The crocodilians, lizards, and snakes of North America. Report of the U. S. National Museum for the year ending June 30, 1898 - Page 676, two specimens of legless lizard from Taylor.
   Gill, T. 1862. Description of a new species of Alepidosauroidae. *Proceedings of the Academy of Natural Sciences of Philadelphia* 14:127-132 - Page 131, Taylor credited with discovering a new fish in Baja California, Mexico.
   Gray, J. E. 1866. Notes on the skulls of sea-bears and sea-lions (Otariadae) in the British Museum. *Annals and Magazine of Natural History* 18:228-237 - Page 232, Taylor provided a sea lion skull to an English museum.
   Hanna, G. D. 1956. Distribution of West American deposits of fossil diatoms. *Bios* 27(4):227-231 - Page 228, "beautifully preserved diatomite collected near Monterey" sent to England.
   Lyon, M. W. Jr., and W. H. Osgood. 1909. Catalogue of the type-specimens of mammals in the United States National Museum, including the Biological Survey collection. United States National Museum Bulletin 62 - Page 290, Taylor provided the type specimen of a bat species.

13. San Francisco (California) *Herald,* 12 December 1852, widely reprinted in newspapers around the United States in the following several months.

14. Gurney, J. H. 1851. Notes on the zoology of California. *The Zoologist* 9:3297-3299.

15. Taylor, A. S. 1859. Condors of Chile and California. *California Farmer and Journal of Useful Science* (San Francisco, California): 20 May (page 122), 27 May (page 132), 3 June (page 138), 10 June (page 146), 17 June (page 156), 24 June (page 162), and 1 July (page 170).

16. Taylor, A. S. 1859a. The great condor of California. *Hutching's California Magazine* 3(12):540-543, 4(1):17-22, 4(2):61-64.

Taylor, A. S. 1859b. The egg and young of the California condor. *Hutching's California Magazine* 3(12):537-540.

17. Pages 497-498 *in*: Bancroft, H. H. 1891. Literary industries, a memoir. San Francisco, California: The History Company.

18. Bancroft 1890 *op. cit.*, page 743.

19. Davis, H. 1886. Alexander S. Taylor. *The Overland Monthly* 7(41):553-554. Also: American Antiquarian Society *op. cit.*; Cowan *op. cit.*

20. Cowan *op. cit.*, page 21.

21. Douglas, D. 1829. Observations on the *Vultur californianus* of Shaw. *Zoological Journal* 4(1):328-330. Despite his excellent work overall as a naturalist, Douglas will always live in condor annals as the man who passed along the hearsay that California condors build large stick nests like eagles; lay two spherical, jet-black eggs; and are most numerous and soar the highest just prior to (Oregon's non-existent!) hurricanes.

22. Pages 240-245 *in:* Audubon, J. J. 1839. Ornithological biography, or an account of the habits of the birds of the United States. Volume 5. Edinburgh, Scotland: Adam & Charles Black.

23. Pages 388-389 *in:* Farnham, T. J. 1844. Travels in the Californias, and scenes in the Pacific Ocean. New York, New York: Saxton & Miles.

24. For example, pages 62-70 *in:* Goldsmith, O. 1840. A history of the earth and animated nature. Volume III, Part I. Edinburgh, Scotland: A. Fullarton and Co.

25. Taylor, A. S. 1855. Notes on the great vulture of California. *Zoologist* 13:4632-4635.

26. Taylor 1859a, *op. cit.*, page 19.

27. Taylor 1859a, *op. cit.*, page 19.

28. Taylor 1859a, *op. cit.*, pages 17-22.

29. Taylor 1859a, *op. cit.*, page 541.

30. Taylor 1859, *op. cit.*

31. Taylor 1859a, *op. cit.*, page 541.

32. This is an saying dating back at least to World War I, used in any situation in which more was done than was needed or justified; *e.g.*, when they went on vacation, they took everything but the kitchen sink; the enemy attacked with everything but the kitchen sink.

33. Anonymous [A. S. Taylor]. 1855. The California condor. *Daily Placer Times and Transcript* (San Francisco, California), 9 August 1855.

34. For example: Baird, S. F. 1870. Ornithology of California. Sacramento: Geological Survey of California.
    Cassin, J. 1856. Ornithology of the United States: the American Vultures. *United States Magazine* 3(1):18-29.
    Gurney, J. H. 1855. Note on the great vulture of California (*Cathartes* vel *Sarcoramphus Californianus*), by Alexander S. Taylor. *Zoologist* 13:4632-4635.

35. Anonymous. 1854. The California snake-bird. *Friends' Intelligencer* 11(36):575-576.

36. Gurney 1851 *op. cit.*

37. American Antiquarian Society *op. cit.*

38. Page 378 *in*: Braithwaite, J. B. 1902. Memoirs of Joseph John Gurney: with selections from his journal and correspondence. London, England: Headley Brothers.

39. Page 58 *in*: Reeve, J. 1905. Norwich Castle Museum: the arrangement of the collections. *The Museums Journal* 4(2):57-62.

40. The story is on page 378 *of*: Sharpe, R. B. 1906. Birds. Pages 79-515 *in*: The history of the collections contained in the Natural History departments of the British Museum. Volume II. London: Trustees of the British Museum.

41. Southwell, T. 1891. Memoir of the late John Henry Gurney. *Transactions of the Norfolk and Norwich Naturalists' Society* 5(2):156-165.

42. Taylor 1859a, *op. cit.,* page 63; Dr. A. G. Irwin, Senior Curator of Natural History, Norfolk Museums personal communication 2 November 2009.

43. Sclater, P. L. 1860. Note on the egg and nestling of the Californian vulture. *Ibis* 2(7):278, Plates VIII and IX. Also, Taylor 1859b, *op. cit.*

44. Page 29 *in*: Sharpe, R. B. 1874. Catalogue of the Accipitres, or diurnal birds of prey, in the collection of the British Museum. London, England: Trustees of the British Museum.

45. Pages 51-53 *in*: Knox, A. G., and M. P. Walters. 1994. Extinct and endangered birds in the collections of the Natural History Museum. London, England: British Ornithologists' Club, Occasional Publications No. 1.

46. Page 7 *in*: Gurney, J. H. 1894. Catalogue of the birds of prey with the number of specimens in Norwich Museum. London, England: R. H. Porter.

CHAPTER 9
QUILLS OF GOLD

In 1855, Alexander S. Taylor wrote of the California condor that *"the plain diggers of Northern Mexico use the quills for putting their gold-dust in"* [1]. One hundred and forty-five years later, a book proclaimed that *"many condors may have been shot for their quills in the 19th and early 20th centuries;"* in fact, said the authors, shooting for quills *"may have been much more important than museum collecting in the past woes of the species"* [2]. In the years between, the story of quills of gold has appeared in many news articles, magazine stories, popular books on condors and endangered species, and some of the earliest American ornithology books. Usually, killing for quills is merely cited as one item in the long litany of bad things that happened to condors. The 2000 reference cited above is the first since 1923 [3] to suggest that the practice had a significant impact on the condor population.

Tales of gold carried in the quills of birds date far back in time. Describing early explorations of Africa, it was written [4]: *"The country of Kordofan, to the south-east of the Great Desert, affords a considerable quantity of gold. The precious metal found in that country is brought to market by the negroes, in quills of ostrich and vulture."* When Hernán Cortés arrived in Mexico in the early 16th century, he reportedly found the Aztecs carrying gold dust *"in tubes, or quills of aquatic birds, made transparent, so that the size of the golden grains could be seen"* [5]. Such containers served not only for storage and transport, but were believed to be part of a regulated currency system. *"Some natural unit (and by natural I mean some product of nature of which all specimens are of uniform dimension) is taken, such as the quill used by the Aztecs. The average-sized quill of any particular kind of bird presents a natural receptacle of very uniform capacity. These quills of gold dust were estimated at so many bags containing a certain number of grains. The step is not a long one to the day when some one will balance in a simple fashion a quill of gold dust against seed of cacao, and find how many seeds are equal in weight to the metal"* [6].

By what path did the story of condor quills full of gold enter California, and where did Alexander Taylor hear it? As noted in a previous chapter, Taylor was a grand gatherer of facts, stories, and miscellaneous bits of information. He wove these morsels into presentations, the substance of which was often far different than stated in the original items. But if he lost or exaggerated the real story, he must have heard something that caused him to mention it, in the first place.

Apparently, California Indians had no interest in gold as money prior to the arrival of European populations; a tradition of using quills for storage would not have originated with them. Rumors of gold in California circulated widely in the years before it was "officially" discovered in 1842, and it is from the 1820s or 1830s that I found the first mention of quill use:

"General M. G. Vallejo, who came to California about the year 1810, and whose remarkable and unimpaired memory is still a ready reference on all questions of local or general interest connected with the earlier annals of California, says that in the year 1824, while on a military expedition to the region of the Tejon, Tehachipe [sic], Kings, and Kern rivers, now Kern and San Bernardino counties, he found a Russian living there at a point between the two last-named rivers, who was then and had been for some time mining for gold. He was supplied with all then known appliances for separating the precious metal. About the same time and for some years later General Vallejo used to remit gold dust to the authorities at the city of Mexico in sealed quills of the vulture" [7].

Walter A. Skidmore, a government mining official, reported this as if he had heard it direct from General Vallejo, probably close to the time of Skidmore's publication of the information in 1885. I have found no similar references, and most historians deny the possibility that gold was being shipped from the area before the 1840s. Still, it is interesting in light of later reports, because "vulture" quills are specifically mentioned. Although the term "condor" was used in California in the late 1850s, it did not gain wide acceptance until near the end of the 19th century. "Vultures" were usually California condors; "buzzard" and the Spanish *buitre* or *aura* were names commonly used for the turkey vulture. If the gold shipments occurred, and if Vallejo's memory was correct about the time period and the species involved, then condor quills were probably the gold containers used.

Because Hubert Howe Bancroft and other early California historians did not write about Vallejo's gold, it was probably not the source of Alexander Taylor's 1855 mention of gold in condor quills. Also, Taylor described his condor quill users as "plain diggers of Northern Mexico" - and perhaps more descriptively in later publications as "placer diggers of Northern Mexico" [8]. Gold found in California before the 1840s would have been mined by locals, not immigrants.

John Bidwell saw, or heard of, condor or turkey vulture quills being used to carry gold dust in southern California in the 1840s, and his comments are among those most frequently cited in stories about California condors. Bidwell did not publish his information until 1900, but he was well known in early California, and traveled extensively through the state. There is a good chance he met Taylor; even if he didn't, tales undoubtedly passed freely among the sparse pre-Gold Rush population of California. Bidwell might have been the source of Taylor's assertion, if a word-of-mouth story in the 1850s was similar to what Bidwell published 50 years later [9]:

"It is not generally known that in 1841 - the year I reached California - gold was discovered in what is now a part of Los Angeles County. The yield was not

102

rich; indeed, it was so small that it made no stir. The discoverer was an old Canadian Frenchman by the name of Baptiste Ruelle, who had been a trapper with the Hudson's Bay Company, and, as was not an infrequent case with trappers, had drifted down to New Mexico, where he had worked in placer mines. The mines discovered by Ruelle in California attracted a few New Mexicans, by whom they were worked for several years. But as they proved too poor, Ruelle himself came up into the Sacramento Valley, and engaged to work for [John] *Sutter when I was in Sutter's service.*

"New Mexican miners invariably carried their gold (which was generally small, and small in quantity as well) in a large quill - that of a vulture or turkey buzzard. Sometimes these quills would hold three or four ounces, and, being translucent, they were graduated so as to see at any time the quantity in them. The gold was kept in by a stopper. Ruelle had such a quill, which appeared to have been carried for years."

* * *

When in the 1970s I evaluated the various causes of condor mortality, Bidwell's account was the only apparently first-hand California reference I could find to quills being used to store gold [10]. In the years since 1978, even with the advent of internet search engines and many on-line historical newspapers and books, I've been able to find only a few more instances.

From the American River near Sacramento, 1847 [11]: *"The Indians of whom there were many, came to our store wishing to buy serapes... They had much fine gold which they carried in vulture or goose quills."*

In a New York City magazine article, January 1849, summarizing everything then known about the "Gold Rush" [12]: *"The writer calculates the amount of grain gold received per month at over two millions of dollars. People carried the gold dust around in goose quills, for change."*

From Calaveras County, 1856 [13]: Ben Thorn arrested a Yaqui miner who refused to pay the "foreign miners' tax" on his gold. *"Thorn then turned over a confiscated goose quill full of gold dust, which Johnston weighed and found to be worth $5.75."*

From Monterey, ca 1850 (but maybe not an actual record) [14]: *"David Jacks's first job in Monterey was as clerk in the store kept by Joseph Boston.... By day David Jacks dealt with miners who brought their gold dust in condor quills. By night he pulled his bedding out from under the counter and slept in the shop."*

From southwestern Kern County, late 1800s [15]: *"J. D. Reyes, resident of Cuyama Valley since 1887, told me* [Carl Koford] *that the quills of condors and other large birds were formerly used for carrying gold dust and that they were sold for a dollar each."*

* * *

The best known and most widely quoted reference to California condor quills being used to carry gold dust was that of A. W. Anthony, who reported on his travels in northern Baja California, Mexico, in May 1893 [16]: *"Every Indian and Mexican gold miner is provided with from one to six of the primary quills of this species for carrying gold dust, the open end being corked with a plug of soft wood and the primitive purse hung from the neck by a buckskin string. All the dead birds that I saw in Lower California had been killed for their quills alone."*

For 42 years after Anthony's observations, I find no mention of quills and gold. Then, in 1935, C. D. Scott visited Baja California's Sierra San Pedro Martír looking for condors. He talked to various local residents, including *"one Antonio, a cattleman of the mountain who shot a Condor in 1933 and another in 1932. He said the birds spread disease among the cattle, but he sold all the quills to prospectors"* [17]. With that reference, and the later reported interview with J. D. Reyes [18], the gold dust saga ends.

Summarizing, in nearly 100 years of records (1841-1935), I found a maximum of eight (and probably only seven) specific instances of quills *of any species of bird* being used to carry gold dust within the range of the California condor. Two records did not mention condors at all, and three named condors as only one of the species whose feathers were used for gold storage. Only one of the records was from the main California "Gold Rush", when miners were most numerous and when the mining activity lasted for the longest time. Only two of the records might have involved "Yankee" miners, either non-Mexican residents of California or Europeans from "The States" (eastern North America) who came west as "Forty-niners." If not for the Bidwell and Anthony references, it would be easy to conclude that condor killing for quills was a very rare occurrence. We need to look at those instances in more detail.

* * *

The gold mining in Los Angeles County's Placerita Canyon usually gets the kind of fairy tale treatment that a "gold rush" should have. *"Either late in 1841 or early in 1842, Francisco Lopez, majordomo of the San Fernando Rancho, and a companion were in search of some stray cattle in the mountains near the ranch. Becoming tired they dismounted to rest in San Feliciano Canyon [sic: Placerita Canyon, then called Cañon de los Encinos]. Here Lopez whipped out his knife to dig some wild onions to eat and in the earth clinging to them he found particles of what appeared to him to be gold. Using his knife he continued to mine in the vicinity and found additional alluvial gold deposits. Following this gold find came the first rush in California history"* [19]. Actually, the discovery was probably less serendipitous than portrayed, because Lopez reportedly had some direction from Mexican mineralogist Don Andres Castillero in knowing what to look for in gold-bearing soil [20]. In any event, the find did attract immediate attention, first from local residents but *"within the year men of greater mining experience were imported from Sonora"* [21]. These Sonorans (almost certainly Taylor's "Northern Mexico placer miners") and people like Baptiste Ruelle (Bidwell's "New Mexican miners") were skilled in placer mining (separating gold dust and nuggets from loose soil, in contrast to hard rock mining of veins of ore) [22]. Initially, they were the only people in California who knew much about mining, *"and the value of their example and instruction made them welcome additions in and around the mines"* [23]. Presumably, these miners fresh from Mexico and the Southwest brought with them the tradition of storing gold dust in the quills of birds [24].

According to Bidwell, the Placerita mines *"attracted a few New Mexicans, by whom they were worked for several years"* [25], but *"were so poor as to create no excitement whatever"* [26]. This is an overly negative view of the situation, when in fact the mines operated profitably for several years [27]. However, the number of miners declined steadily after the first two rainy seasons, when *"some hundreds of people were profitably engaged in mining"* [28], to only 30 men when Bidwell visited the area in 1845 [29].

All accounts of the Placerita mines (Placerita itself, and a few smaller finds in nearby Los Angeles and Ventura counties) agree that miner numbers were few, the duration of activity was short, and the harvest of gold for the average miner was small; as Bidwell said, their gold was *"generally small, and small in quantity as well."* Although the New Mexican miners may have *"invariably"* carried their gold dust in quills (in lieu of some other type of container), they probably didn't need many quills. Bidwell's quintessential miner, Baptiste Ruelle, apparently had only one quill, that *"appeared to have been carried for years"* [30]. Considering this information, plus his comment that the quills were not always from condors - *"a large quill - that of a vulture or turkey buzzard"* - the probable impact on the California condor populations seems minor.

But there is more to question: Bidwell's account leaves the impression that he was at Placerita while Baptiste Ruelle was there, and that he saw some of the condor or vulture quills, himself. This appears not to be true. In fact, his first meeting with Ruelle likely occurred in 1843 at Sutter's Fort, after Ruelle's time in southern California. Bidwell did not visit Placerita until 1845 when, by his account, only 30 miners were still at work. It seems possible that the one quill Ruelle had, *"which appeared to have been carried for years,"* may have been the only one seen by Bidwell.

The quill itself is an enigma: was it a condor quill? Bidwell's 1900 publication did not say, nor did an earlier account of the first meeting with Ruelle, who was carrying *"an old quill, which looked as if it had been brought from New Mexico."* In the quill *"were a few particles of gold, which he said he found on the American river"* [31]. Was the quill in fact old, or did it just *look old*? Ruelle is believed to have arrived in California from New Mexico shortly before the Los Angeles County gold find; if the feather was old, he probably did not obtain it in California. If he brought it from New Mexico, it was not a condor feather.

105

Ruelle himself may not have been the most reliable of information sources. Bidwell credited him with discovering the Placerita mines. Clearly, he didn't, and I've found no one but Bidwell who even mentioned Ruelle's name in connection with Placerita or the other nearby finds. Were his stories of condor quills of gold mere inventions? His appearance at Sutter's Fort with gold that he said he obtained locally (on the American River, several years before its "discovery" in the region) made Bidwell doubt his veracity in some matters, at least:

"This excited the suspicions of Bidwell, who was present, and these suspicions were increased when the man asked for two pack-horses laden with provisions, and an Indian boy to attend him. He wished to go in search of gold, he said, and he would be absent for several days. There was a company of Canadian trappers in the vicinity about to start for Oregon. It was not known that Ruelle belonged to them, but it was feared that with so valuable an outfit he might forget to return. Hence his request was denied" [32].

I'm not prepared to entirely discard the Bidwell story of condor quills of gold, but I am ready to relegate it to the "probably not significant" files as a cause of condor mortality in California. There is one further justification for this decision: if Sonoran miners were the principal employers of quills (of all species) for their gold dust, whatever impact they had on the condor population would have been short-lived. The welcome given the Mexicans in 1848, because of their knowledge of mining techniques, soon turned to prejudice as the Mexicans were generally more successful miners than the Americans, and their claims were in areas that the Yankee miners coveted. By mid-1849, inter-racial violence was growing. Fear that too much of the gold was going to non-Yankees led to the passage in early April 1850 of taxes ($20 per month) on foreign miners. The growing antagonism and the heavy tax prompted an immediate exodus. *"By September 1850, from one-half to three-fourths of the Mexicans had left the area... The number of Mexicans in the southern mines had been estimated at about 15,000, of whom about 10,000 were in the Sonora [California] region alone..."* [33]. Presumably, most of the need for quills went with them.

That leaves Anthony's Baja California records to evaluate.

* * *

Anthony's information seems straightforward: he did find dead condors which he believed had been stripped of their larger quills [*"the dead birds... had been killed for their quills alone"*], and apparently he personally saw miners sporting strings of condor quills [each *"provided with from one to six of the primary quills of this species*]. But, looking a little closer at his records of trips into Baja California in 1887-1888 (*"two or three short trips")*, 1893 (two months) and 1894 (three months), he reported seeing only three dead condors [34]. Further, ignoring the typical 19th century hyperbole of declaring that *"every"* miner had quills (something he couldn't know, and almost certainly an

106

exaggeration), how many miners did that include? The record suggests the total was pretty small.

Near the end of the 18th century, the human population of the entire Baja California peninsula - approximately 150,000 square kilometers - was estimated at 8000 persons. By 1847, numbers had shrunk even further to 7,500 inhabitants. The native Indians of Baja California were near extinction, most of the inhabitants were immigrants from mainland Mexico, and most of the people lived in the towns at the extreme southern end of the peninsula. The major part of Baja California could be termed uninhabited [35].

Some gold mining occurred on the Baja peninsula in the early part of the 18th century, but *"mining activities had not in general developed to the same degree as they had in Sonora and other regions of Mexico. By the early decades of the nineteenth century, many gold and silver mines had been abandoned... Although the mining of precious metals in Baja California increased somewhat during the 1840s, the Mexican War interrupted such activities"* [36]. Placer gold was discovered at a number of locations in northern Baja California in the 1850s, prompting a number of short duration "rushes." These small excitements occurred in the central desert area south of El Rosario and San Fernando, near the Mexican border just south of San Ysidro, and in the Guadalupe Valley just northeast of Ensenada. Apparently, mining in all of those areas had ceased by 1860 [37].

I found no references to any significant gold mining in Baja California during the 1860s, but in the early 1870s a number of discoveries were made in extreme northern areas, between the Pacific coast and the western slopes of the Sierra Juarez. Gold mining activity also increased in the central desert areas near the boundary of Baja California Norte and Baja California Sur. By 1874, the placers on the west slopes of the Sierra San Pedro Martír at Socorro and Valladares were being worked [38]. During this period, the Sierra Juarez foothills saw the establishment of *"several boom towns of 500 to 1,650 people each"* [39], but in most areas the "rushes" were false alarms, or the readily available gold gave out in a few months. Only the mines of Real del Castillo southeast of Ensenada, the El Socorro-Valladares area, and the mid-peninsular desert placers lasted into the next decade.

In succeeding years, there were occasional excitements, but all were short-lived. For example, gold was discovered in the Santa Clara mountains some 60 miles southeast of Ensenada in December 1888. When word finally reached San Diego in February 1889, a major rush of Californians occurred. Between 4,000 and 5,000 miners were estimated to have been involved in the "boom," which lasted less than a month and yielded a grand total of perhaps $20,000 in gold! [40].

Lack of new discoveries, political upheaval, and the difficulty and expense of developing commercial enterprises in the remote areas of the peninsula brought active mining to a temporary end in most of Baja California. It would not revive for several decades.

* * *

Comparing this brief review of Baja California gold mining with Anthony's comments provokes some interesting observations. First, only one of Anthony's three dead condors was found within 50 airline miles of a gold mining area, active or inactive at the time. Also, the two condors not found near a mine site were in the desert at the extreme southern end of known or suspected condor range, and not in the direction of travel most miners would have used coming to or going from the placers. Apparently, none of the carcasses were recent fatalities, and no live condors were seen near any of them. One wonders why Anthony was so certain they were victims of gold miners.

We also need to question Anthony's statement that *"every"* miner had condor quills. Only in 1893 did he visit an active gold mining site, the Socorro-Valladeres area on the west slope of the Sierra San Pedro Martír. I haven't found any record of how many miners were there in 1893, but gold had been discovered there in 1874 so any "gold rush" was long over. Five or six years later, about 1898, owner-operator Harry Johnson was employing only ten men at the site [41]. If *"every miner"* that Anthony saw had *"one to six"* quills, they might have all come from one to two condors.

The Johnson Ranch at Sorocco was burned by rebels in 1911, ending for some time both gold mining and any threat to condors from that element. Some placers were being reworked on a small scale between 1920 and 1940 [42], providing at least a small market for the quills that C. D. Scott's informant said he sold in 1932 or 1933 [43]. Although the condors were reportedly killed because they were believed to spread disease to cattle, not specifically for their feathers, these losses might be considered in the "killing for quills" category. Even so, there probably was not much demand at that time.

* * *

It's curious that no other travelers on the Baja California peninsula in the 19th or early 20th centuries reported seeing quills (of condors or any other birds) used to store gold dust. A number of ornithologists visited the area before 1910 [44], and there was a steady procession of naturalists, explorers, and adventurers who left reports and memoirs of their travels. Some of these people visited more active mining camps than did Anthony. The sight of a string of condor quills would seem like something that would have been remembered and remarked upon. While I'm still inclined to give more credence to Anthony's Baja California records of condor quills full of gold dust than I am the California stories, the truth seems to be that mining activities had very little impact on California condors in any region.

CHAPTER NOTES

1. Taylor, A. S. 1855. Notes on the great vulture of California. *Zoologist* 13:4632-4635.

2. Pages 45-47 *in:* Snyder, N., and H. Snyder. 2000. The California condor: a saga of natural history and conservation. London and San Diego: Academic Press.

3. Page 1734 *in:* Dawson, W. L. 1923. The birds of California. San Diego, California: South Moulton Company.

4. Page 361 *in:* Jameson, R., J. Wilson, and H. Murray. 1830. A narrative of discovery and adventure in Africa from the earliest ages to the present time. Edinburgh, Scotland: Oliver & Boyd.

5. Page 700 *in:* Ober, F. A. 1883. Travels in Mexico and life among the Mexicans. Houston, Texas: Estes and Lauriat.

6. Page 93 *in:* Ridgway, W. 1889. How were the primitive weight standards fixed? *Journal of Hellenic Studies* 10:92-97.

7. Page 547 *in:* Skidmore, W. A. 1885. Gold and silver mining in California, past, present, and prospective. Pages 525-557 *in:* Report of the Director of the Mint upon the production of the precious metals in the United States during the calendar year 1884. Washington, D. C.: Government Printing Office.

8. Taylor, A. S. 1859. The great condor of California - Part I. *Hutching's California Magazine* 3(12):540-543.

9. Pages 95-96 *in:* Bidwell, J. 1900. Echoes of the past. Chico, California: Chico Advertiser.

10. Page 19 *in:* Wilbur, S. R. 1978. The California condor, 1966-76: a look at its past and future. North American Fauna Number 72. Washington, D. C.: U. S. Fish and Wildlife Service

11. Pages 131-132 *in:* Harlan, J. W. 1888. California '46 to '88. San Francisco, California: The Bancroft Company.

12. Page 62 *in:* Anonymous (Freeman Hunt?). 1849. The gold region of California. *The Merchants' Magazine* 20(1):55-64.

13. Page 117 *in:* Limbaugh, R. H., and W. P. Fuller. 2004. Calaveras gold: the impact of mining on a Mother Lode county. Reno, Nevada: University of Nevada Press.

14. Pages 6-7 *in:* Bestor, A. E. 1945. David Jacks of Monterey and Lee L. Jacks, his daughter. Stanford, California: Stanford University Press. In a footnote, the author explained that *"the fact of Jacks' employment at Boston's store rests upon family*

tradition... No document definitely records Jacks' employment in Boston's store, however." That raises the question of whether there is any document from the store that mentions condor quills, or if this was a mere poetic gloss to make the story more interesting. Joseph Boston did have a safe in his store in which he reportedly allowed customers to keep their gold.

15. Page 134 *in:* Koford, C. B. 1953. The California condor. Research Report Number 4. New York, New York: National Audubon Society.

16. Page 233 *in:* Anthony, A. W. 1893. Birds of San Pedro Martír, Lower California. *Zoe* 4(3):228-247.

17. Scott, C. D. 1936. Are condors extinct in Lower California? *Condor* 38(1):41-42.

18. Koford 1953 *op. cit.*

19. Cutter, D. C. 1948. The discovery of gold in California. Pages 13-17 *in:* Jenkins, O. P. Geologic guidebook along Highway 49--Sierra Gold Belt, the Mother Lode Country. California Division of Mines Bulletin 141. Sacramento, California.

20. Pages 47-50 *in:* Bancroft, H. H. 1888. California inter pocula. San Francisco, California: The History Company.

21. Cutter *op. cit.*

22. Placer gold was reportedly discovered in Sonora, Mexico, in 1799, and a number of placer areas were worked there until the late 1840s. Gold extraction continued after that date, but almost no placer mining, which perhaps gave incentive for the Sonorans to move north into California. [Pages 50-95 *in:* Hamilton, L. 1881. Border states of Mexico: Sonora, Sinaloa, Chihuahua and Durango. San Francisco, California: Leonidas Hamilton.]

Placer gold was discovered in what is now New Mexico in 1828, and was profitably mined until about 1835. At that time, the Mexican government prohibited mining by non-natives, which would have encouraged people like French-Canadian Baptiste Ruelle to move on to more hospitable areas. [Pages 21-22 *in:* Jones, F. A. 1904. New Mexico mines and minerals. Santa Fe, New Mexico: The New Mexico Printing Company.]

23. Morefield, R. H. 1956. Mexicans in the California mines, 1848-53. *California Historical Society Quarterly* 35(1):37-46.

24. I haven't been able to find any records of miners using quills for gold dust storage while actually in Sonora or New Mexico. California Indians apparently had no interest in gold mining prior to the arrival of Europeans, and Yankee miners are seldom mentioned as having used quills. With both Bidwell and Taylor descriptively tying quill possession to Sonorans and New Mexicans, it seems logical to assume that these miners brought the practice to California with them.

There are two Colorado records of "Yankees" using goose quills for gold storage, but they occurred well after the California "Gold Rush." The first: *"(L)ooking over a daily journal for 1859, I find recorded on the 5th day of January of that year then advent to Omaha from the Rocky mountains, of Al. Steinberger and Colonel Wynkoop, bringing the first gold from Cherry creek placers, where Denver now stands. The precious metal was in goose quills. The feather end had been cut off below the pith, right where the hollow trunk begins, and into this delicate, translucent receptacle the scale gold had been poured. There were not to exceed six quills full altogether, but there were enough to energize, organize, and enthuse a cavalcade of fortune hunters the succeeding spring which reached from the Missouri river to Pike's Peak."* [Morton, J. S. 1887. The discovery of gold in Colorado. Pages 315-316 *in: Transactions and reports of the Nebraska State Historical Society*, Volume II. Lincoln, Nebraska: State Journal Company.]

There is a footnote rebuttal to the above note, a claim from A. G. Barnes (Lincoln, Nebraska) that he was the first to bring gold to Nebraska from Colorado: *"On the 25th day of December, 1858, I landed at Plattsmouth, and in a quill from a mountain eagle I carried about fifty cents worth of gold dust which I had found and panned myself at what was called the Mexican diggings, three miles above the mouth of Cherry creek on the banks of the Platte river."*

25. Bidwell 1900 *op. cit.*

26. Page 55 *in:* Bidwell, J. 1904. Autobiography and reminiscences of John Bidwell. Autobiographies and reminiscences of California pioneers, Volume 7. San Francisco, California: Society of California Pioneers.

27. Cutter *op. cit.*

28. Pages 414-415 *in:* Del Mar, A. 1902. A history of the precious metals from the earliest times to the present. New York, New York: Cambridge Encyclopedia Company.

29. Bancroft 1888 *op. cit.*

30. Bidwell 1900 *op. cit.*

31. Bancroft 1888 *op. cit.*, page 52.

32. Bancroft 1888 *op. cit.*, page 52.

33. Morefield 1956 *op. cit.*

34. Anthony 1893 *op. cit.*, page 233: *"The first evidence I found of the occurrence of the condor in Lower California was the finding of a dead bird in Guadaloupe Valley, forty miles south of Ensenada and near the coast; later another carcass was found in the dry barren hills east of El Rosario..."*

Also, page 137 *in:* Anthony, A. W. 1895. Birds of San Fernando, Lower California. *Auk* 12(2):134-143. *"In 1887 I found the bones of a recently killed California*

111

Vulture...at a water hole about twenty miles north of San Fernando... after questioning a number of the natives, I concluded that its occurrence must have been very unusual..."

35. Leon-Portillo, M. 1973. Paradoxes in the history of Baja California. *Journal of San Diego History* 19(3):9-17.

36. Pages 463-464 *in:* Taylor, L. D. 2001. The mining boom in Baja California from 1850 to 1890 and the emergence of Tijuana as a border community. *Journal of the Southwest* 43(4):463-492.

37. Taylor 2001 *op. cit.,* pages 467-469.

38. Taylor 2001 *op. cit.,* page 475.

39. Page 109 *in:* Minnich, R. A., and E. F. Vizcaino. 1998. Land of chamise and pines: historical accounts and current status of northern Baja California's vegetation. Berkeley, California: University of California Press.

40. Flanigan, S. K. 1980. The Baja California gold rush of 1889. *Journal of San Diego History* 26(1).
   A 48-page "guide" to the Santa Clara gold rush was published, with details of travel routes, Mexican mining laws, Baja California climate, etc. It sold for 25 cents. The "rush" was probably over before it had very wide distribution: Stephens, B. A. 1889. The gold fields of Lower California, being a complete guide book with official maps, revenue and mining laws, etc., etc. Los Angeles, California: Southern California Publishing Company.

41. Page 74 *in:* Southworth, J. R.1899. El Territorio de la Baja California, su agricultura, comercio, minería é industrias (en Inglés y Español). San Francisco, California.

42. Pages 641-642 *in:* Minnich, R. A. *et al.* 1997. A land above: protecting Baja California's Sierra San Pedro Martír within a biosphere reserve. *Journal of the Southwest* 39(3-4):613-695.

43. Scott 1936 *op. cit.*

44. Wilbur, S. R., and L. F. Kiff. 1980. The California condor in Baja California, Mexico. *American Birds* 34(6):856-859.

CHAPTER 10
DR. CANFIELD

At first glance, Alexander Taylor (Chapter 8) and Colbert Canfield seem much alike. Both identified themselves as "doctor" and "druggist." Both were early arrivals at Monterey, California. Both lived relatively short lives, even in comparison with the standards of the times. Both were regular contributors to newspapers and magazines. Both had wide ranging interests in history and natural history. Both sent natural history specimens to museums and other collectors, both in the United States and abroad. Both had a strong interest in California condors. As similar as all that seems to make them, they were clearly very different types of individuals.

Colbert Austin Canfield, son of Austin Canfield and Lodemia Benton, was born at Chardon, Geauga County, Ohio, in 1829 [1, 2]. His was a farming family, but he received a medical education at Western Reserve Academy (Hudson, Ohio) [3]. He worked for a year or so with Dr. Sherman Goodwin in Chardon [4], but in March 1853 he joined a friend, Wallace John Ford, on a trip to California via New York and Panama. In California in early 1854, he went with Ford from San Francisco to Los Angeles, to bring a herd of cattle north. He may also have worked with Ford hauling merchandise to northern California towns [5]. By 1855 he was living in Monterey County, and before long had established a medical practice there [6]. Reportedly, he was "*the first resident physician at The Presidio*" (although it's unlikely he was actually a part of the military staff) and also "*an official at the old customs house in Monterey*" (although this statement may relate to his later political positions) [7].

Dr. Canfield's first few years in Monterey appear to have been involved mostly with establishing his medical practice and starting a family. In 1858, he married Anita Watson, daughter of James Watson and Maria Anna Escamilla, and their first of five children was born 5 February 1859 [8]. The first written account I have found for him was in January 1858, when Alexander Taylor (of all people!) described a possible stage route from San Francisco to Fort Tejon, based on information he had received from Dr. Canfield [9]. Later that same year, Canfield made his first personal appearance in print, with a letter to the editor correcting the story of how many children a certain California lady (a patient of his) had borne (twenty-four, not thirty-six!) [10]. But it was a letter he wrote to Spencer F. Baird, Assistant Secretary of the Smithsonian Institution, on 10 September 1858, that gives us our first look at Dr. Canfield, the naturalist.

Canfield had just read Dr. Baird's account of the pronghorn antelope in Volume VII of the "Pacific Railroad Surveys" [11]. Knowing from his own observations that some of what Baird had written was incorrect, and that he obviously knew some things about pronghorns that Baird didn't, Canfield wrote Baird a long description of the pronghorns he had observed in central California [12]. He explained that he had *"some new facts that will sufficiently interest you to repay your for the trouble of learning them."* He went on:

"I take the liberty of saying this because I have observed the Antelope for several years, have hunted them and killed a number of them (perhaps 150 of all ages and sexes), have caught and raised young ones, and am as familiar with them as most people are with goats and sheep."

What followed was a well written, scholarly but easily understandable account of the morphology, reproduction, habits and habitat of the pronghorn. He concluded:

"Much more could be added to the above, relative to the habits, &c., of the Prong-horned Antelope; but this must suffice; and if what I have written you will be of any value to science, you are at liberty to make such use of it as you think proper."

Interestingly, Baird did not "think proper" to use any of it, and Canfield's information did not come to the attention of the zoological community for another eight years. Apparently, the problem was that Baird could not accept Canfield's information that pronghorns shed their horns annually. J. D. Caton explained the issue:

"The first allusion which I find to the deciduous character of the horns of this antelope is in the letter-press of Audubon and Bachman ['Quadrupeds of America'], *where they say, 'It was supposed by the hunters of Fort Union that the Prong-horned Antelope dropped its horns; but as no person had ever shot or killed one without these ornamental and useful appendages, we managed to prove the contrary to the men at the fort by knocking off the bony part of the horn and showing the hard spongy membrane beneath, well attached to the skull, and perfectly immovable.'*

"The hunters were right, and the scientists were wrong... Some years later, on the 19th of April, 1858, Dr. C. A. Canfield, of Monterey, California, in a paper which he sent to Professor Baird of the Smithsonian Institute, communicated many new and interesting facts concerning the physiology and habits of this animal; and, among others, the surprising announcement that although it has a hollow horn, like the ox, yet this horn is cast off and renewed annually. This statement by Dr. Canfield was considered by Professor Baird so contradictory to all zoological laws, which had been considered well established by observed facts, that he did not venture to publish it, till the same fact was further attested by Mr. Bartlett, superintendent of the gardens of the Zoological Society of London, who, in 1855 [sic - 1865], repeated the fact in a paper published in the Proceedings of that society. In the February following, the paper which Dr. Canfield, eight years before, had furnished the Smithsonian Institute, containing the first well attested account of the interesting fact, was published in the Proceedings of that society.

"At the time I gave an account of Mr. Bartlett's observation, in a paper I read before the Ottawa Academy of Natural Sciences in 1868, and which was published by that society, I was not aware that the same fact had been previously communicated by Dr. Canfield to Professor Baird, else I should have taken pleasure in mentioning it" [13].

Although Baird chose not to publish Canfield's pronghorn observations, the letter may have been the catalyst to stir Canfield to a more active role in natural history pursuits, and also the impetus for the next fourteen years of interaction with the Smithsonian Institution. Within a year, Dr. Canfield had been recruited as one of ten Smithsonian weather observers in California (only four California stations had been established earlier) [14], a responsibility he maintained for ten of the next twelve years [15]. Local histories later identified him as *"the Pacific coast agent and representative of the Smithsonian Institution"* [16]. I find no record that such a formal position or relationship existed; I suspect he was merely *a* (volunteer) representative, not *the* representative. Nevertheless, his contributions were substantial, and duly recognized. He supplied over 100 specimens of birds and birds' eggs to the national collection, also a few mammals and invertebrates [17]. Through Dr. Baird, he was able to send specimens to other museums in Europe and the United States. Also, he acted as local guide and assistant to Smithsonian scientists working in the Monterey area. One such instance was cited by William. H. Dall:

"While acting as Chief of the Scientific Corps of the Western Union Telegraph Expedition, in 1865-6, I obtained leave of absence for three weeks, and proceeded to the town of Monterey, some ninety miles south of San Francisco, on the coast of California. This was in the month of January. During my stay, I devoted my entire time to the examination of the Mollusk fauna of that locality, which is very rich and varied. The results of much arduous labor (I was unable to dredge), in which I was most kindly seconded by Dr. C. A. Canfield, of Monterey, may be found summed up in the Proceedings of the California Academy of Sciences [Volume III, p. 271, 1866] " [18].

Dall honored Canfield by naming *Gibbula Canfieldi*, one of the newly-discovered mollusks, after him: *"One specimen of this modest little shell was found dead on the beach at Monterey. I take pleasure in dedicating it to Dr. C. A. Canfield of Monterey, who has done much for science with very slender means"* [19]. A cursory search of the invertebrate literature yielded citations for seven other species named for Canfield, by Smithsonian scientists Dall and Richard Rathbun. (After Canfield's death, his personal collection of nearly 3,000 shells, was purchased by the State Normal School in San Jose [now San Jose State University] for $500 [20]; unfortunately, the "Canfield Collection" was destroyed in a fire at the school in 1880 [21].)

June 26, 1866.

Dr. J. Hamilton, F.L.S., in the Chair.

The Secretary called the attention of the Meeting to a fine specimen of the Californian Vulture (*Cathartes californianus*, Shaw), recently added to the Society's living collection. This scarce bird had been presented to the Society by Dr. Colbert A. Canfield, of Monterey, California, through the intervention of Prof. Baird of the Smithsonian Institution, Washington, and kindly assisted in its passage across the Isthmus of Panama by Capt. J. M. Dow.

Cathartes californianus

Figure 7. The first live California Condor outside the United States.

Through the 1860s, Colbert Canfield's name appeared regularly in the newspapers of central California. He provided detailed observations on the New Idria quicksilver mines, showing a good knowledge of mining practices [22]; wrote about the effects of current weather on crops and livestock [23]; and described the deleterious effects of wind-driven sand in the Salinas Valley [24]. He was quoted as knowledgeable on the ocean currents and temperatures of the Monterey Bay area, and on the iron springs existing on the coast [25]. His journal article on using the juice of the plant *Grindelia robusta* to relieve the symptoms of poison oak [26] was widely quoted, as was his information on the pronghorn antelope after it was presented to the Zoological Society of London [27] and the California Academy of Sciences [28] in 1866. His increasing scientific stature earned him the elected status of "corresponding member" of both the Zoological Society and California Academy [29, 30].

Dr. Canfield's involvement with California condors came fairly late in his career. Alexander Taylor cited him as having seen large numbers of condors in what is now San Benito County in the early 1850s [31], but the next record is from December 1864, when the local newspaper reported on the death of a condor:

"Some person, through accident or design, some few days since poisoned a pet vulture belonging to Dr. Canfield. The poison used was strychnine, and was probably administered in a piece of meat. The vulture was about eight months old, and measured across its wings, from tip to tip, 8 feet 9 1/2 inches" [32].

This condor may have been destined for the aviaries of the Zoological Society of London, and it wasn't long after the bird's death that Canfield procured a second live condor, a young bird taken from its nest in 1865. The bird was kept at Monterey through the winter of 1865-1866, then shipped to London by way of the Isthmus of Panama [33]. The Zoological Society of London received the condor in June 1866, the first live California condor ever in a public institution [34]. It lived in the Zoological Society aviaries two years, but died in late 1868 (cause unknown). The skeleton of that bird is preserved in the Natural History Museum (Tring, U. K.).

Spencer Baird and the Smithsonian had negotiated the Zoological Society condor acquisition [35]. In 1866, they arranged a specimen exchange with the Naturhistorisches Museum (Vienna, Austria) that sent a Canfield-procured study skin to Europe [36]. They may have acted as intermediary in the transfer of another condor skin in 1866, from Canfield to the Field Museum of Natural History (Chicago, Illinois) [37], and possibly a live condor from Canfield to the Royal Zoological Society aviaries in Dublin, Ireland in 1867 [38].

Dr. Canfield secured one condor egg for the Smithsonian in 1866 [39], and another condor skin in 1868. His final condor was another live bird, taken from its nest and raised at Canfield's home in Monterey. The local news

117

carried a story about the bird in August 1871. *"The Monterey Republican of the 10th inst., says: Chained to a post in Dr. Canfield's front yard may be seen one of those rare birds known as the 'California Vulture.' He was captured in the hills south of Carmel Valley. This specimen is some six months old, and is two-thirds grown, and is quite a formidable looking youngster. The doctor intends shipping him to the Zoological Society of London"* [40].

A month later, there was a follow-up story: *"Dr. Canfield's California vulture still stands guard in his front garden. The day after his arrival he nearly fell victim to the mischievous malevolence of the Monterey embryo 'Hoodlums,' who pelted him with a pitiless storm of small projectiles. Now he is respected as an old resident, and as he is likely to remain at his post for the next four months, it is consoling to be able to relate that juvenile curiosity respecting his vultureship has quite subsided, and hopes are entertained that he may reach the hands of Dr. Sclater, of the Zoological Society of London, who will so dispose of him that he may feast his eyes on princes, if he cannot feast himself on princes' eyes"* [41].

That condor, apparently destined to replace the bird that died in London in 1868, was never shipped to England. Perhaps it died before it could be delivered, or perhaps Dr. Canfield himself became too ill to complete the transaction. The remains of what are probably that bird are in the U. S. National Museum.

In each of the eight cases in which Dr. Canfield had California condors in his possession - and with the 100 or so other specimens he contributed to the National Museum - he has been listed in the official records as the "collector." As it was common practice for agents, salesmen, and even museum preparators to list themselves as the actual procurer of specimens, it raises the question of how many of these birds Dr. Canfield actually killed or captured himself. He had a full-time career, not only as a physician, but also as the elected Monterey County coroner [42]. He served as his political party's secretary, was the city clerk of the Board of Registration and Election, and even found himself taking on such jobs as *"directing and supervising the location of a road from this town to the Point Pinos Lighthouse Reservation."* [43].

It seems likely that some of his songbird specimens were brought to him by others. (He noted in the above-cited letter to Spencer Baird that *"while writing this last line, a boy comes bringing me a nest & eggs of some unknown bird, for which I give him a bit."*) It also seems likely that - because of the time required to find condors, particularly nesting ones - Canfield hired hunters to procure some of his condors, or at least let it be known that he was looking for condor specimens. On the other hand, he was clearly an outdoor person who enjoyed close contact with wildlife. His statement that he had killed over 100 pronghorns and that he had raised young pronghorns [44], and the fact that he had kept condors in captivity for months at a time, suggest that he was fully

118

capable of being the actual "collector." The truth is probably somewhere in the middle: that he obtained some of the condors himself, and procured some from other parties.

In 1870, at the age of 41, Colbert Austin Canfield's life must have seemed about as stressful as a life could get. He wrote a letter to Spencer Baird, apologizing for not sending some specimens that were expected from him. As noted above, he was supervising the locating of a road to the Point Pinos lighthouse (an unpaid favor to Colonel Williamson), he was making up the voting rolls for two upcoming elections, and was generally swamped with various political and governmental responsibilities. To this litany, he added (almost as an afterthought!) that his wife had just died in childbirth, leaving him with five children ranging in age from newborn to eleven years old, and he didn't know how he was going to afford domestic help to care for them. Still, he said, *"I am constantly adding to my collections of Monterey species, but principally of shells, quite a number of new ones not yet named;--411 species in all. I am getting more birds' nests and eggs again."* And: *"As soon as I can 'get things in order again' I will try to forward to you all that I have collected"* [45].

I haven't been able to determine if Dr. Canfield was able to *"get things in order again."* In late 1872 or early 1873, he died [46].

CHAPTER NOTES

1. U. S. Federal census 6 July 1850: Chardon, Geauga County, Ohio.

2. The death notice for Colbert Canfield's mother, Lodemia (Benton) Canfield appeared in the *Geauga Republic* (Chardon, Ohio), 14 May 1850.

3. Colbert A. Canfield is shown as a student of "Dr. Hamilton" in the 1848, 1849 and 1850 catalogues for Western Reserve College (Hudson, Ohio).

4. Page 478 *in*: Anonymous. 1880. Pioneer and general history of Geauga County with sketches of some of the pioneers and prominent men. The Historical Society of Geauga County.

5. Pioneer and general history of Geauga County *op. cit.*, pages 542-547.

6. I can find no definite date that Dr. Canfield settled at Monterey, but two records indicate 1855 as the most likely year.
   Taylor, A. S. 1858. The southern California stage route. Sacramento (California) *Daily Union*, 23 January 1858: Taylor noted that Dr. Canfield had resided in Monterey County "for the last three years."
   Canfield, C. A. 1866. Notes on *Antilocapra Americana* Ord. Paper read at the 5 February 1866 regular meeting of the California Academy of Sciences (San Francisco, California). "The following notes were taken from 1855 to 1858 in Monterey County..."

7. Pages 291-292 *in:* Anonymous. 1925. History of Monterey and Santa Cruz counties, California, cradle of California's history and romance. Volume II. Chicago, Illinois: S. J. Clarke Publishing Company.

8. Birth announcement, child of Dr. C. A. Canfield and Anita M. Watson, 5 February 1859. Sacramento (California) *Bee*, 3 March 1859.

9. Taylor 1858 *op. cit.*

10. Anonymous. 1858. Still a numerous family. San Francisco (California) *Bulletin*, 13 August 1858.

11. Page 666-670 *in*: Baird, S. F. 1857. Mammals. General report upon the zoology of the several Pacific railroad routes. Volume VII. Explorations and surveys for a railroad route from the Mississippi River to the Pacific Ocean. Washington, D.C: War Department.

12. Canfield, C. A. 1866. On the habits of the Prongbuck *(Antilocapra americana),* and the periodical shedding of its horns. *Proceedings of the Scientific Meetings of the Zoological Society of London* [27 February 1866], pages 105-110.

13. Pages 25-26 *in*: Caton, J. D. 1877. The antelope and deer of America. Antilocapra and Cervidae of North America. New York, New York: Hurd and Houghton.

14. Commissioner of Patents. 1861. Results of meteorological observations made under the direction of the United States Patent Office and Smithsonian Institution, from the year 1854 to 1859, inclusive. Volume I. Washington, D. C.

15. Page 87 *in*: Anonymous. 1874. Annual report of the Board of Regents of the Smithsonian Institution, showing the operations, expenditures and conditions of the institution for the year 1873. Washington, D. C.

16. History of Monterey and Santa Cruz counties, *op. cit.*

17. U. S. National Museum of Natural History specimen databases.

18. Page 93 *in*: Dall, W. H. 1871. Descriptions of sixty new species of mollusks from the West Coast of North America and the North Pacific Ocean, with notes on others already described. *American Journal of Conchology* 7(2):93-160.

19. Dall *op. cit.*, page 129.

20. Pages 53-54 *in*: Anonymous. 1889. Historical sketch of the State Normal School at San Jose, California. Sacramento: State Printing Office.

21. Historical sketch of the State Normal School, *op. cit.,* pages 74-75.

22. Anonymous. 1860. The New Idria quicksilver mines. San Francisco (California) *Bulletin*, 25 April 1860.

23. Canfield, C. A. 1864. The weather, crops, stock, etc., in Monterey County. San Francisco (California) *Bulletin*, 26 May 1864.

24. Canfield, C. A. 1864. Drifting sands. San Francisco (California) *Bulletin*, 29 June 1864.

25. Pages 85-89 *in*: Anonymous. 1875. The hand book of Monterey and vicinity. A complete guide book for tourists, campers and visitors. Monterey, California: Walton and Curtis.

26. Canfield, C. A. 1860. The poison-oak and its antidote. *American Journal of Pharmacy*, Third Series, Volume 8(5: 412-415.

27. Canfield 1866 [Note 12], *op. cit.*

28. Canfield, C. A. 1866. Notes on *Antilocapra Americana* Ord. A paper presented at the 5 February 1866 regular meeting of the California Academy of Sciences. Proceedings of the California Academy of Sciences 1866.

29. Page 5 *in*: Report of the Council of the Zoological Society of London, 29 April 1867. London: Taylor and Francis.

30. Proceedings of the California Academy of Natural Sciences (San Francisco, California), Regular meeting 19 February 1866.

31. Taylor, A. S. 1859. The great condor of California. *Hutching's California Magazine* 4(1):17-22.

32. Anonymous. 1864. A pretty pet! San Francisco (California) *Bulletin*, 21 December 1864 (quoting from the Monterey *Gazette* of 16 December 1864).

33. Renshaw, G. 1907. The Californian condor. *The Zoologist* (London), Fourth Series, 11(794):295-298.
   Page 340 *in*: Baird, S. F., T. M. Brewer and R. Ridgway. 1874. A history of North American birds. Volume III, land birds. Boston, Massachusetts: Little, Brown and Company.

34. Sclater, P. L. 1866. Living California vulture received in London. *Proceedings of the Zoological Society of London* 13:366.
   Anonymous. 1867. Report of the Council of the Zoological Society of London, read at the annual general meeting, April 29, 1867. London: Taylor and Francis.

35. Renshaw 1907 *op. cit.;* also, the 29 April 1867 report of the Council of the Zoological Society.

36. Letter 27 April 1971 from G. Rokitansky (Naturhistorisches Museum, Vienna, Austria) to S. R. Wilbur: "Specimen no. 40862... received in 1867 from Dr. C. A. Canfield, Smithsonian Institution, in exchange."

37. Specimen FMNH 95160 at the Field Museum of Natural History (Chicago, Illinois) does not have an identified source, but it was shot near Monterey in 1866, when only Colbert Canfield is known to have been collecting condors.

38. Sigwart, J. E., et al. 2004. Catalogue of raptors in the National Museum of Ireland. National Museum of Ireland database.

39. Some have given Colbert Canfield credit for collecting two California condor eggs, one in the collection of the U. S. National Museum, and one that was reportedly at the Academy of Natural Sciences of Philadelphia (Pennsylvania), but disappeared early. No official paperwork has ever been found concerning that egg, and Witmer Stone (Academy curator in the late 1800s and early 1900s) opined that there probably never had been a condor egg, but only a misidentified "foreign egg" (Letter from Stone to W. Lee Chambers, 4 April 1905; in the Chambers Collection, Bancroft Library, Berkeley, California).

40. Anonymous. 1871. A California vulture. *Daily Evening Bulletin* (San Francisco, California), 19 August 1871.

41. Anonymous. 1871. Matters in Carmel Valley. San Francisco (California) *Bulletin*, 9 September 1871.

42. Anonymous. 1867. Monterey County officers. *Daily Alta California* (San Francisco, California), 16 September 1867.

43. Letter of 20 May 1870 from Colbert A. Canfield to Spencer F. Baird: Smithsonian Institution Archives, Record Unit 7002, Box 17, Folder 2.

44. Canfield 1866 [Chapter Note 12], *op. cit.*

45. Canfield-Baird letter of 20 May 1870, *op. cit.*

46. I haven't found the date of Dr. Canfield's death, or his burial location. Only one reference so far found gives a relatively precise time.
    Anonymous. 1873. Death of Dr. Canfield. *Pacific Medical and Surgical Journal and Western Lancet* 6(9):488.
    "Colbert A. Canfield, M. D., died at his residence in Monterey, California, a few weeks ago. He was a man of considerable ability in his profession and a contributor, some years ago, to the columns of this Journal."

CHAPTER 11

POISONED CONDORS

The topic of poisons used to kill "predators" and "vermin" is an emotional one, which has added to the difficulty of trying to assess the role of poisons in the decline of the California condor population. A number of writers in the late 19th century alleged major condor mortality caused by feeding on strychnine-poisoned meat put out to kill predators. Later investigators concluded there was little basis for these earlier claims. In recent years, in the continuing controversy over the use of chemicals, most popular writers have chosen to ignore the 20th century analyses in favor of the earlier reports. It's odd, because nothing really new has come to light on the subject since the 1950s [1]. I guess once we begin to rewrite history, it's impossible to ever completely un-rewrite it.

OREGON AND WASHINGTON

Strychnine, or nux vomica (the only regularly used predator and rodent poison until well into the 20th century), made its first appearance in California condor range about 1839. That year, Dr. John McLoughlin, chief factor for the Hudson's Bay Company in the Pacific Northwest, requested poison to be used for wolf control on the Company's recently established farms located between Puget Sound and the Columbia River. The Company's governing committee complied, sending *"a small quantity of Strychnine made up in dozes [sic] for the destruction of Wolves; it should be inserted in pieces of raw meat placed in such situations that the shepherd's dogs may not have access to them, and the native people should be encouraged by high prices for the skins to destroy wolves at all seasons"* [2]. Although the chief purpose in providing strychnine was to protect livestock, it's clear from the directive that poisoning wolves for their pelts was also intended. Later, the Company did not allow its trappers to use strychnine because it damaged the animals' fur [3]. Perhaps in 1839 they didn't yet know about the degrading effects of the poison.

The "small quantity" was apparently all the strychnine available in the area until perhaps 1844. McLoughlin requisitioned 6 more ounces in 1842 or 1843, but Sir George Simpson intended to reduce the order to 1 ounce. Presumably he did this because McLoughlin had declared the earlier batch *"perfectly useless"* (Simpson's words: I haven't found McLoughlin's actual requisition), and *"if the article be useless as represented, much better expose the concern to the loss of one ounce than six, until it be ascertained whether the drug be efficacious or not."* This raises some question about how efficient wolf poisoning was at Fort Vancouver and elsewhere in western Washington, but the reply from McLoughlin was that *"the remark on the inferior quality, was that, a superior quality to the last might be sent"* [4]. This could be construed as McLoughlin saying that the poison worked, but that he thought it should work better. In any event, no more poison had been sent by the end of 1843.

The need for predator control on Hudson's Bay Company lands could not have been great. In 1828, the total numbers of livestock (cattle, goats, horses, swine) at Fort Vancouver were only about 500 head [5]. Between 1833 and 1839, other "farms" were established farther north at Fort Nisqually and the Cowlitz River, but when the first strychnine was ordered in 1839 there were still only 3,000 head of livestock in all western Washington. By 1846 the numbers had grown to about 14,000 head, 80 percent of those sheep, most of which were at Fort Nisqually. (The Cowlitz farm was devoted to raising crops, and never had more than a few hundred head of livestock.) [6]. Some predation by wolves, mountain lions, dogs, and eagles was documented, but sheep (and often cattle) were penned at night to keep them safe [7]. Even if poisoning was "heavy" on the Company farmlands, most of western Washington would have been strychnine-free, with the greatest use being in more northerly areas that appear to have been visited only irregularly by condors. The Company did not use strychnine for their minor livestock operations on the Oregon side of the Columbia River.

Strychnine used by Hudson's Bay Company was probably purchased in England. The Company was the likely source of strychnine being used at the Whitman Mission (at present-day Walla Walla, Washington) in 1841 [8], and they may have supplied the first known strychnine used in Oregon, available at Salem beginning in 1847. Thomas Cox, an immigrant to Oregon in 1846, established a mercantile store in Salem the following year, and the first sale of strychnine has been attributed to him [9]. It may be he purchased the strychnine from the Hudson's Bay Company, as he is known to have acquired some of his stock from John McLoughlin [10]. However, his supply may have come with him from Illinois; when he couldn't sell all the merchandise from his Illinois mercantile, he reportedly had 14 wagons specially constructed to haul the remainder across the plains to Oregon [11]. This amounted to a "respectable store" [12]. I don't know if strychnine was included in his load, but it was in use for killing predators in the Midwest as early as 1839. That winter in Wisconsin, J. MacNish reported [13]: *"I gave to a neighbor who had lost a cow, a few grains of strychnine (made from the strychnos calabrinum,) instructing him to cut out small baits, and insert into each, under a flap cut very thin, 1.8 of a grain of the poison. The body of the cow was drawn to a convenient spot on the banks of our Lake, and the prepared baits dropped at different distances around the carcass. The strategem resulted in the death of six wolves besides a number of foxes, raccoons and birds of prey. When these facts became known, I had many applications for the article; and so uniformly successful were these trials, that I can enumerate twenty-six wolves and one panther which have been destroyed by the strychnine, (only 60 grains) which I furnished that winter. One farmer in this town has $40 bounty for the wolves he killed with but one dollar's worth of the poison."* In the same time period in Cox's home state of Illinois, the gray wolf was *"being driven back by the approach of man, trapped and hunted, and more than all, poisoned by strychnine"* [14]. Some immigrants to Oregon were apparently bringing supplies of strychnine with them; as an example, at the crossing of the Snake River at Fort Boise in 1852 [15]: *"There was an Indian village near the crossing of the Snake River at this place. These Indians have been feasting on the dead carcasses of emigrant cattle. Some thoughtless emigrants whose cattle died near here cut the carcasses open and put in a bait of strychnine, as they said, 'to kill off some of those pesky coyotes,' but the Indians happened to get hold of these poisoned carcasses and died by the hundreds."*

Prior to 1840, there were less than 200 Caucasians in Oregon, almost all of them in the northern Willamette Valley [16]. Although localized farming got an early start there, the only livestock were a few leased from the Hudson's Bay Company. The Company would not sell livestock to settlers, which prompted the formation in 1837 of the Willamette Cattle Company. This local group organized a trip to California to bring cattle to Oregon. On the first overland drive in 1837, 600 of the 800 head of cattle purchased survived to the Willamette Valley. A second drive in 1843 included 1,250 head of cattle, 600 horses and mules, and 3,000 sheep [17]. By early that same year the first concerns were being expressed in the Willamette Valley over the destruction of cattle by wolves, bears, and mountain lions. At meetings held 2 February 1843 and 6 March 1843, a bounty system was established, requiring every participant to subscribe $5.00 to the bounty fund. Bounties were paid for scalps: *"for a small wolf, fifty cents; for a large wolf, $3.00; for a lynx, $1.50; for a bear, $2.00, and for a panther $5.00"* [18]. From the record, it's difficult to discern just how deep was the concern about predators; while there is no question that livestock loss was an acknowledged problem, the meetings had really been called to discuss the formation of a territorial government. *"The object of this war upon the wild animals was simply a ruse to get the French Canadians in the valley to join with the Americans in forming a government"* [19]. As further explained by J. Q. Thornton [20]: *"The wild beasts had become a very serious evil, because of their great destruction of domestic animals. A number of persons who had held a consultation at the house of Wm. H. Gray, to consider the expediency of organizing a Provisional Government, and who had, or at least supposed they had carefully reflected upon the various retarding influences, thought they saw in the fact mentioned in the beginning of this paragraph, an object of sufficient interest to all, to collect a large number of settlers who would probably adopt some line of harmonious action."* At the February meeting, a committee was appointed to make a predator proposal. Then, at the follow-up meeting in March: *"James A. O'Neil, who had come to Oregon with Capt. Wyeth in 1834, was privately informed of what was the* real *object sought to be accomplished by the meeting, and it was intimated to him that he would be called to the chair, in*

125

which he was desired to hasten as rapidly as possible over the wild beast and domestic herds, to the real object which in due time would be brought forward in a resolution."

* * *

Whatever the actual level of concern about predators, until 1847 the problem had to be handled with guns, dogs, and traps. Once strychnine became available, it appears to have been regularly used, but the actual amount distributed may have been far less that later popular histories implied. The few journals and reminiscences that mention strychnine are short on details. A typical entry (from pioneer John Arthur, but not necessarily a personal remembrance) [21]: *"In the early pioneer days, the wild beast of prey became a very serious evil, because of their great destruction of domestic animals. The extermination of them was an object to which the principal stock owners gave an encouraging word, and ample contributions of money... The big timber wolf did not only kill cows, but occasionally a poor horse, but they were soon extirpated mostly by the use of strychnine; but the bear, panther and coyote remained numerous a number of years."*

Daniel Waldo remembered that in the 1840s, *"the wolves ate up a lot of horses. They ate up 14 for our company one spring. Cattle would fight them, but horses would run; the wolves would run them. I got some nux vomica that killed them off in about two months. We just rubbed it on a file and put it on a piece of meat"* [22].

John Minto reminisced that [23] *"...the well-aimed bullet was the only way of killing these most destructive enemies of domestic stock [wolves], until in 1847, when Mr. Thomas Cox brought a lot of strychnine to Salem. It was but a year after the Cox family settled in the edge of the Santiam valley, until the hair-raising howls of the bands of big wolves ceased."*

The most specific account, recording use of strychnine in one area of what is now Douglas County, was in a letter written by Roselle Putnam in January 1852 (original spelling and punctuation retained): *"The wolves in this country are very large and numerous there has been a great many of them killed this winter, in this neighborhood with strycknine, Charles put out upwards to thirty doses of it, and I suppose every one killed a wolf at least the physician from whom we got it said it woud – we have seen two that died near the house – notwithstanding the quantity of poison they have taken – they are still to be heard every night or two howling round us & one impudent fellow has been in the habit of coming every night to pick up the scraps about the house & even in the porch a couple of nights ago – we gave him a dose of poison and he has not been back since – they have never killed any of our cattle though they do frequently kil cattle & horses"* [24].

Except for the account from Douglas County - which, compared to the Willamette Valley, was still "wilderness" in 1852 - the quotes above make it appear that the need for heavy use of strychnine was short-lived, because the nuisance animals were quickly eliminated. Such a conclusion seems to be supported by the lack of information on the subject in local newspapers [25]. In the Oregon press between 1846 and 1871, I found no mention of strychnine and only one item on predatory animals (a proposal to organize a *"Marion County Society for the destruction of wolves, cougars and panthers"* [26]). I found 18 news reports of livestock predators between 1872 and 1880, two of which were from far eastern Oregon where condors had never been known to occur. Seven of the reports mentioned strychnine, and four kills were made using dogs and guns; control methods were not listed in the other items. After 1880, news reports of strychnine use increased; most stories were about suicide and murder, but use for animal control was clearly increasing, particularly in eastern Oregon and Washington, and especially for ground squirrel control. For example, an 1893 item noted that county commissioners had awarded an eastern Washington pharmacist a contract to furnish 4,000 ounces of strychnine for squirrel control [27].

Obviously, newspapers and a few reminiscences can't tell the whole story of predator control in early Oregon. Still, a consideration of the numbers and distribution of the human population during the years that California condors might still have occurred in the region strongly suggests that strychnine was not a significant issue in the disappearance of the species.

In 1840 there were only 200 Caucasians - Americans and French-Canadians - in Oregon; in 1842, that number was unchanged until a wagon train with another 112 people arrived in the fall [28]. Each succeeding year brought additional immigrants, but by 1845 the white population of Oregon was still only 2,500, and by 1849 had not reached 9,000. Immigration continued, but was accompanied by a significant exodus to California during the "Gold Rush," so that the tally for the 1850 federal census was 12,000 Caucasians in the entire territory. In 1841, there had been no settlements south of the Salem area, and in 1850 there were still less than 2,000 people there, scattered in perhaps half a dozen small, widely separated settlements. Twenty-five percent of the total 1850 Oregon Territory population lived in urban areas [29].

Not only were there very few people in Oregon in the mid-1800s, and most of those town dwellers living in a very small portion of the territory, there were not that many livestock to protect. Cattle still numbered less than 20,000 in 1850, and there were only 5,000 sheep. The majority were located in the same small area in the northern Willamette Valley where most of the people resided, roughly present-day Portland south to Albany. Probably less than 3,000 cattle and 1,000 sheep were found south or east of there, and there were almost no livestock in the vast mountain area south of the Columbia River between Portland and the Pacific Ocean [30]. The last area in which condors were recorded in Oregon, the Umpqua River-Rogue River watersheds, in 1860 still had less than 4,000 residents; by 1900 there were fewer than 25,000 people scattered through some 8,000 square miles of rugged, mostly

127

uninhabited wilderness. While the total human population of Oregon increased from 52,000 to 415,000 between 1860 and 1900, over half of the people lived in the Willamette Valley, the majority of them within the cities, themselves.

No condor is known to have been killed by strychnine in Oregon or Washington, but that doesn't entirely rule out the possibility that some succumbed after eating poisoned meat. From the limited record that has been pieced together, it appears that condors had become rare in the region long before strychnine came into use. There were still some condors in southwestern Oregon into the early 1900s. With more people, more livestock, and apparently more strychnine in that area in the last two decades of the 19th century, poisoning may have been more of a threat than at any time previous. Nevertheless, the odds of a condor being poisoned in that vast areas seems small.

CALIFORNIA

Not having the early source of strychnine that was available to Oregonians, farmers and ranchers in California had to wait a little longer to have ready access to the poison. Reportedly the first shipment to California came as a mistake, resulting indirectly from the discovery of gold. Rosengarten and Denis, a Philadelphia company that had begun manufacturing strychnine in 1834, sent a cargo of it to a South American port. When word of the 1848 California gold discovery reached the ship, it was diverted to San Francisco and the strychnine was sold there [31]. Presumably other shipments soon followed, and by 1850 there were daily advertisements in California newspapers by druggists selling strychnine. How much was used for animal control in the early 1850s is unknown. There's no question that a lot of strychnine was in circulation; looking through the files of 15 California newspapers from 1850-1855, I found 26 records of strychnine use, including six murders, two attempted murders, 10 suicides, three malicious poisoning of dogs, one purposeful poisoning of horses, one pig poisoning, and one attempt to kill Indians suspected of stealing livestock. Also included was a record of Indians buying strychnine to poison arrow tips for squirrel hunting, and one of a Czech scientist who purposely poisoned himself, believing he had an antidote. He didn't.

The earliest accounts I have found of strychnine use for animal control in California were in 1854, one for ground squirrels alone, and one for both livestock predators and squirrels. Both observations were in the Los Angeles basin area. Carvalho wrote [32]: *"The whole country of Southern California, especially in Los Angeles county, is infested with millions of ground squirrels, which destroy vegetation, and are great nuisances to farmers, as well as to the community; they domesticate themselves in houses, and I have seen them jump on the dinner-table, overturning tumblers, etc. The country is overrun with them; various methods have been suggested to destroy them, but without effect; the most successful, however, is strychnine--large quantities of which are imported into California, for this express purpose. This virulent and active poison, for this reason, becomes an important article of trade."*

Nearby, Julius Froebel described activities in August on a ranch near Chino, California [33]: *"One day I rode to the hills, on which our mules were grazing... In this ride I also passed through a part of the cattle belonging to the estate, which covered the hills for miles. In these herds, many are killed by the wild beasts - wolves, bears, and cuguars [sic]. The proprietors use great quantities of strychnine to destroy these, the effect of which I witnessed. As I was riding out one day, I met one of the people of the estate throwing about poisoned meat; and, on my return a few hours later, there already lay a dead wolf in the road. In the same manner the Colonel has tried to destroy the earth-squirrels, which, together with the owls and rattlesnakes, live in holes in the ground, and are here the greatest enemies to the farmer. The Colonel strews corn, poisoned with strychnine, before the holes of these little animals."*

There were newspaper mentions of strychnine used for animal killing in 1856. That year, along with one murder, four suicides, and one purposeful poisoning of dogs, the newspapers carried reports of a grizzly bear killed with strychnine in Monterey County [34], a mountain lion killed near San Mateo [35], and ground squirrel poisoning in Santa Clara County [36]. In Mariposa County, grizzlies were thought to have killed 20 hogs, to which the news writer opined that *"a little strychnine could not be applied to a better use than in destroying these dangerous visitors"* [37]. A similar opinion was expressed by a Sacramento newspaper, this time concerning canids: *"We have heard of several instances of mad dogs and coyotes recently, and our farmers and rancheros should have a good supply of strychnine on hand to administer to these worthless brutes, that have been allowed to increase until the nuisance has become insufferable"* [38].

Newspaper reporting 1857-1859 showed use of strychnine similar to 1856. In the papers I reviewed were stories of four murders, three attempted murders, 38 suicides, seven failed suicide attempts, eight accidental poisonings of people, and five malicious poisonings of dogs and livestock. There were also two stories of Indians being poisoned, one apparently accidentally but the other purposely. Use of strychnine against animals involved mountain lions, ground squirrels, gophers, crows, and songbirds in orchards. Strychnine was believed to be ineffective against mountain lions in Trinity County [39], but near Santa Rosa four lions were killed after a rancher *"secreted a lot of strychnine"* into the carcasses of two sheep [40].

From the start, concern about ground squirrels and gophers damaging farm crops and rangeland seemed more important to Californians than predator control. By 1863, squirrel control legislation was being proposed because of growing problems in the Bay Area: *"Many acres have been left uncultivated for years because of the multitude of ground squirrels in the vicinity, and the* *negligence of the neighbors in taking no measures to destroy them. Large fields of grain have been destroyed, and great numbers of valuable fruit trees killed by these little pests... Poison is the favorite method [of killing ground squirrels], and thousands of dollars are annually spent for phosphorus and strychnine, which are almost as necessary to the farmer in Santa Clara as his plow or his seed wheat. Phosphorus is cheaper, and therefore the preferred material; costs $3.50 per pound in San Francisco... Strychnine costs $4 per ounce, and one drachm of it is enough for a half peck of wheat"* [41].

In addition to rodent concerns and a continuing litany of social mayhem (murders, suicides, domestic animal poisonings, accidental exposure to strychnine, poisoning of Indians), there were a number of news reports in the 1860s concerning predatory carnivores. A rancher in Siskiyou County lost 15 sheep and 20 lambs to wolves and mountain lions. *"He set a bait with strychnine, and succeeded in killing a huge panther and three wolves"* [42]. Strychnine wouldn't kill grizzlies that were destroying hogs and calves in Siskiyou County, so the rancher changed to *"a mixture of broken glass in meat"* [43]. Grizzly poisoning was successful in Walker Basin, Kern County, using strychnine in tallow balls inserted into pieces of fresh beef or mutton [44]. Mountain lions were dispatched with strychnine in Yuba County (two) [45] and Butte County [46]. A lion allegedly responsible for the deaths of six sheep and 39 lambs in Colusa County would not succumb to strychnine, but was finally caught in a leg-hold trap [47]. John Muir, writing from the Yosemite Sierra 13 August 1869, noted the apparently widespread practice of carrying strychnine, even in areas where it wasn't needed [48]: *"I visited our old Yosemite camp ground on the head of Indian Creek, and found it fairly patted and smoothed down with bear tracks. The bears had eaten all the sheep that were smothered in the corral, and some of the grand animals must have died, for Mr. Delaney, before leaving camp, put a large quantity of poison in the carcasses. All sheep men carry strychnine to kill coyotes, bears, and panther, though neither coyotes nor panthers are at all numerous in the upper mountains. The little dog-like wolves are far more numerous in the foothill region and on the plains, where they find a better supply of food - saw only one panther track above eight thousand feet."*

* * *

In the 1870s, suicides, murders, and accidental poisoning by strychnine remained big news. There were a few specific accounts of large carnivores killed with strychnine - a mountain lion killing lambs in Yuba County [49], three bears (presumably grizzlies, as that was not black bear habitat) disturbing beehives near San Bernardino [50], and a wolf (coyote?) killing lambs in Sonoma County [51] - and a general article regarding predators and sheep on the Tejon Ranch in Kern County [52]: *"The grizzly does not usually attack sheep. The California lion, a strong but very cowardly beast, the wild cat, the fox, and the coyote, are the sheep's enemies. The last named is easily poisoned,*

130

with meal which has strychnine powdered over it. The others are hunted when the become troublesome." But the main poison stories involved ground squirrels and gophers.

In 1870: *"Gophers and squirrels are very numerous, this year* [in the San Francisco Bay area]*... The boys are out in force, earning ten and five cents a head from the county treasury. Strychnine is most efficacious, but a large proportion is lost to the boys by dying underground"* [53].

In 1871: *"It is not generally known that killing gophers has become an important business in several counties in California, including San Joaquin. Says the Stockton* Republican, *'There is a bounty of five cents on each scalp, and besides this the largest and best skins are readily sold for fifteen cents each. Several persons in the county have gone into the business systematically. Those most successful use wheat or other grain soaked in strychnine. On one ranch near this city, twenty-five hundred gophers were recently captured by using poisoned wheat. This number netted the captor at least $350. Large numbers of gophers are caught daily by boys, who generally use dogs and guns for that purpose'"* [54].

In 1873, a farmer (apparently in southern California) killed ground squirrels in his grainfield by mixing strychnine, vinegar and sugar, and distributing it around the field in little cups. *"During the warm parts of the day the rodents went to drink from these vessels by hundreds, and never had time to get to their holes any more; and so deadly is the poison, four bits worth of strychnine will lay out from three to four hundred rodents"* [55].

By late summer 1873, farm groups were meeting around the State to discuss the problem, and in October 1873 a "squirrel law convention" was convened, to draft legislation compelling landowners to control squirrels on their property [56]. Various ordinances were eventually passed, but penalties for noncompliance were eventually declared unconstitutional by the California Supreme Court [57].

Gopher control seemed to lose impetus after the 1870s, but poisoning ground squirrels with strychnine continued unabated into the 20th century, as did poisoning coyotes. I found several late 19th century reports of mountain lions and bears being killed by strychnine, but none after 1900.

* * *

As noted previously, newspaper accounts and occasional journal entries can't tell the complete story of strychnine use on the Pacific Coast during the 19th century. On the other hand, newspapers were the principal means of communicating local events in pioneer times, and - although the coverage was uneven - every aspect of human events was covered to some extent. Also, these 19th century newspapers were refreshingly open in their reporting - there was no shame in reporting a bear, mountain lion, or condor killing; in fact, the larger the mammal or the wider the wingspan, the more likely it was to make the news. Lacking the concrete, readily evaluated data we expect today, I think

131

it's worthwhile to compare these scattered but on-the-spot records against the stories about poisons and predators that developed later.

The zoologists of the 1850s who visited California, Oregon and Washington were mostly associated with the War Department surveys, assessing potential cross-country railroad routes. In none of their reports was there mention of birds killed by poisons [58], but there were brief comments on the use of strychnine to kill mammals:

"Formerly [the wolf] *was quite abundant in the vicinity* [Nisqually Plains, Washington], *much to the detriment of the sheep of the Puget Sound Agricultural Company, but, of late years, owing to the persuasive influence of strychnine, they together with the wolf-like Indian dogs, have become quite scarce"* [59].

"On the Columbia well dried, good [fox] *skins can be readily purchased for 25 cents apiece, and in the way of trade are even bought by the storekeepers for much less. They are principally taken in traps or killed with strychnine"* [60].

"They [California ground squirrels] *are very fine eating, and formerly sold well in San Francisco markets, but since strychnine has been used to kill them, no one will buy them for fear of being poisoned"* [61].

These comments by the Railroad Survey zoologists correlate well with the history of strychnine use in the 1850s, as outlined above: *i.e.,* strychnine was established in limited areas of western Washington and western Oregon, and was only beginning to be used in California. Yet, in 1859, Alexander Taylor wrote: *"The Condor is often killed by feeding on animals, such as bears and cattle, when poisoned with strychnine by the Rancheros--the poisoned meat kills them readily. The rancheros have very little fear in California of their depredations on young cattle and stock, though it has been known within my knowledge for five or six Condors to attack a young calf, separate it from its mother, and kill it; the Californians also say they are often known to kill lambs, hares and rabbits. But the cattle owners here have no such dread of them as the Haciendados of Chile have of the Southern Condor"* [62].

I've already described (in Chapter 8) Alexander Taylor's predilection for mixing fact and fancy in unpredictable and confusing ways, making almost everything he wrote slightly suspect. The paragraph quoted above is a good example: are we to accept the statement about strychnine, while ignoring his description of a gang of condors killing a calf, and also killing lambs, hares, and rabbits?

Between 1853 and 1860, Taylor published a dozen or more notes and articles on condors; other than that cited above, only one mentioned poison [63]: *"A short time ago quite a number of condors were found dead by the vaqueros of the Sur ranch in this county* (Monterey), *from the effects of eating the meat of a bear poisoned with strychnine."* This seems like a straightforward observation, and perhaps one made by Taylor, himself. However, it is the last sentence in a long paragraph about *"a friend of ours"* reporting what Taylor proclaimed in 1859 to be something that *"has been known within my knowledge;"* i.e., the attack on a calf by a group of condors. *"Six or seven or the birds had joined together to separate a calf from its mother, and having got it some distance off, succeeded in pecking to death with their powerful beaks, nothwithstanding the constant attempts of the dam to drive them away. The habits of our condor are precisely those of Chili and Peru, and though often stated to the contrary by bookmen, are distinctly different from the Cathartes, which never attack a living animal."* Because the "friend's" information is clearly erroneous, and because a significant loss of condors seems not to have been reported anywhere else, one wonders if this was an actual event, or more of Taylor's blending of miscellaneous bits of information.

Accurate or not, this was the only specific mention of condor poisoning Taylor made in print. Yet - in context with the calf killing incident - it appears to have been the source of his later, more inclusive statement that condors are *"often killed by feeding on animals...poisoned with strychnine."* His were the first statements linking condors and strychnine, and until 1890 (see below) he was the only person to cite a specific instance of condor poisoning. In fact, every reference to condors and strychnine between 1860 and 1890 can be traced back to Taylor. J. G. Cooper, in his 1870 "Ornithology of California," quoted Taylor directly, including the alleged calf killing [64]. "A history of North American birds," published in 1874 [65], not only quoted Taylor's statement on poison word for word, but erroneously attributed Taylor's remarks to Colbert A. Canfield, a reliable condor observer! H. W. Henshaw, in California in 1875, noted that *"opportunities for an acquaintance with this Vulture were most brief and unsatisfactory, and were limited to seeing two or three individuals warring on the wing in the mountains."* Yet, and after acknowledging receiving some of his information from Taylor, he wrote: *"As is well known, this bird is easily killed by strychnine, and as this poison has been in almost constant use for a term of years in the destruction of wild animals, it seems highly probable that great numbers of these birds have suffered a like fate from eating the carrion"* [66]. He never saw a condor feeding on a carcass, poisoned or otherwise - in fact, may not have personally seen a condor until 1884 [67] and only specifically mentioned seeing one carnivore, a grizzly, that had died of poison. In his report on the mammals seen in 1875, he made only general comments about the reported deaths from strychnine of coyotes, gray foxes, grizzly bears, and California ground squirrels [68].

Charles Bendire, in his 1892 "Life histories of North American birds," used Taylor as one of his sources of condor information, although he did not quote Taylor directly on the subject of poisons [69]. Of the apparent significant decrease in condor numbers, Bendire said that *"poison so far has been the*

133

principal agent." He gave no details, but outlined the reasons why he thought poisoning of condors had become so significant: *"Stockraising has increased enormously in southern California during the past twenty years, and these fastnesses* [*i.e., "the minor mountain ranges running parallel to the Sierra Nevada,"* the backcountry presumed to be the home of the condors] *have been completely overrun by stockmen to find pasturage for their flocks during the hot summers when everything is dried up in the valleys. Necessity compelled this invasion of the retreats of numerous predatory carnivora, like the grizzly bear, the panther, lynx, and the prairie wolf. These, as a matter of course, preyed on the calves and flocks of sheep that were to be found everywhere in the mountains at that time, to be had for the taking, and they naturally enough committed a great deal of damage. The simplest and certainly the safest way for the stockmen to get rid of such undesirable neighbors was to bait them with poisoned carcasses. This means was resorted to almost everywhere, and generally with considerable success. The Vultures, too, with their keen sight and scent, found many of these, to them, tempting baits, and being sociable in disposition many of these birds were destroyed by this means, so that at this time comparatively few are said to be left."*

The gist of the above statement appears to be that Bendire - who, it is worth noting, may never have spent any time in condor habitat - believed: (1) there had been substantial increases in California livestock in the previous 20 years (presumably, 1870 to 1890); (2) these increases had depleted the lowland food supply to the extent that in summer livestock had to be moved from the valleys to the higher hills to find forage; (3) this move brought the livestock into closer contact with predatory mammals, and increased the predation; (4) more strychnine was used in these *"minor mountain ranges"*; and (5) these ranges being the home of the condors, more condors succumbed to poisoned livestock carcasses. This explanation takes considerable liberties with both the history of California and the life history of the condor. First, while there were substantial increases in sheep numbers near the middle of the 1870-1890 period, and increases of beef cattle near the end, the total number of livestock in California in 1890 was less than in 1870 [70]. Second, the significant movement of livestock to higher elevations was not into the *"minor mountain ranges"* paralleling the Sierra Nevada; to escape the effects of the long, rainless California summer, livestock had to be moved into the high mountain areas, mostly well above 6,000 feet elevation. To repeat John Muir's comment [71], *"neither coyotes nor panthers are at all numerous in the upper mountains. The little dog-like wolves are far more numerous in the foothill region and on the plains, where they find a better supply of food - saw only one panther track above eight thousand feet."* Grizzlies were found in the highest mountains at times, but were generally much more numerous at lower elevations [72]. The perceived need for strychnine would certainly not have been any greater in the mountain meadows than in the lower elevations at other times of year. Finally,

134

the high country occupied by livestock in summer was not *"the fastnesses"* that were the principal habitat of the California condor. While condors occasionally ventured into the higher mountains (but apparently very seldom above 8,000 feet), almost all their nesting habitat and a large percentage of their feeding range was below 5,000 feet elevation. In other words, as a scenario for large losses of condors to strychnine, Bendire's description fails on all counts.

Curiously, Bendire's next two paragraphs noted that *"within the past few years these birds have again commenced to hold their own,"* and that in some areas *"they do not seem to be decreasing"* and are even *"still abundant,"* and *"may in time regain their former numbers."* This reversal of fortune, he said, was *"undoubtedly due to the breaking up of the large cattle ranches and their conversion to small farms. Poison, which has been resorted to on most of the large stock ranches to kill the carnivora, has certainly almost exterminated the California Vulture as well, and in more than one locality, where they were formerly abundant, their very perceptible decrease is, in my opinion, due to this cause"* [73]. Again, his understanding of California history and habitat was at fault; certain lowland valleys were developing more formal agriculture, but in 1890 California still had vast areas of rangeland that supported vast herds of livestock. From the written record, there is no indication that the use of strychnine was decreasing in 1890; the use for ground squirrels and coyotes probably was increasing. If, in fact, strychnine poisoning had been a significant cause of the condors' decrease in numbers, then there is no reason to believe it was suddenly less significant.

* * *

After 1890, Alexander Taylor was seldom quoted by name; Bendire became the chief authority, and statements very similar to those included in his 1892 publication have been repeated over and over, even up to the present time. However, there were dissenting voices. William Leon Dawson was the first [74]: *"We note that there is a widespread opinion that the disappearance of the Condor was occasioned by the use of poison. The cattle-men, frenzied by the depredations of the coyotes, poisoned their beef carcasses. The coyotes ate and were killed. Ergo, the Vultures, who feasted on them, must have perished by scores. It sounds very plausible, but I am not persuaded. Evidence is lacking to show that the Vultures did die of poison. The question should have been very easy to determine. Vultures lingered about their fallen prey and gorged to repletion. If they fell, they must have fallen in their tracks, or at least in the open. But there is no record of such destruction. There are two other alternatives. A Condor's stomach can stand a great deal of abuse. Ptomaines, for example, have no terror for it. Again, a bird has unusual facilities, up to a certain point, for 'unswallowing' food which disagrees with it. In such fashion I think our friend has succeeded in escaping the wholesale punishment so generously meted out for it - on paper. Perhaps I am wrong, but here at least*

135

is something to think about."

Carroll DeWilton Scott was the next to raise questions [75]: *"Practically every writer about the condor lays its dramatic exit to poisoning. Owners of cattle and sheep poisoned carcasses to kill coyotes, bears and cougars and the great birds died.*

"This tale may have originated with Bendire because he makes much of it. But he cites no evidence for his statements. Early naturalists often filled the gaps in their knowledge with stories from pioneers and some of the stories were fantastic. But the printed word has more lives than a tomcat. As far as I know, nobody who has repeated the poison story has ever offered a shred of evidence. Since the poison explanation is a theory, the burden of proof is certainly with the theorist.

"Biological evidence is against the theory. The condor is a vulture and, presumably, like the turkey vulture, is immune to poisons or can get rid of them by disgorging. It is the habit of condors, as well as buzzards, to linger at the banquet table for hours, even days, either on the ground or it neighboring trees. A cattleman in the Sespe, in the 'good old days,' once walked among a crowd of gorged condors and almost could have kicked several if he had wished. Mrs. Eugene Percy of Fillmore came upon a group of condors at a carcass, one afternoon a few years ago, that were so full they scurried under the trees, before they could take wing, like a flock of turkeys. Is it not reasonable to suppose that if somebody had ever laid eyes on poisoned condors he would have been sufficiently impressed with the spectacle to leave a record of it?

Both Dawson and Scott were naturalists and bird enthusiasts, and in no way apologists for livestock interests or the poison manufacturers. Neither was Harry Harris, who up to 1940 had made the most comprehensive review of California condor literature ever undertaken [76]: *"Dr. Cooper's casual reference to the decimation of vultures by poison (strychnine) during the cattle era of California history recalls that this was formerly so universally accepted as a fact that no writer, scientific or popular, ever deemed it necessary to cite supporting evidence. The rancheros poisoned meat to check the numerous mammalian predators, and thus the countless herds of horses and horned cattle inhabiting the range of* Gymnogyps *acted as a check rather than a benefit to the bird, as it also fed on the poison. This was a logical enough conclusion prior to a general knowledge of the toxic resistance possessed by vultures, and it is not strange that the long accepted dictum has only recently been challenged. Nor is it strange that the literature is so entirely barren of any eye witness corroboration of the lethal effect the poison was claimed to have had on the birds. Only a single reference is citable in this connection, and it rests on evidence too questionable to warrant discussing. The inference to be drawn from this, as well as certain other testimony, is that decimation of the species by poison was merely assumed to account for a seemingly sudden decrease in its numbers."*

Finally, Carl Koford's major field and library study of California condors in the 1930s and 1940s summed up his understanding of strychnine poisoning in a few short sentences [77]: *"The only reported 'observation' which indicates that a condor may have died from eating poisoned bait is given in a mimeographed pamphlet by Fry (1926:2). He claims that in 1890 he saw two dead condors which a sheepherder had found near a poisoned carcass."*

"In southern California, ranchers poison coyotes and other carnivores by putting out chunks of pork containing capsules of strychnine. It is conceivable that occasionally a condor eats one of these baits."

"To a limited degree, strychnine poisoned bait is used to poison squirrels. This poison acts very fast so that a high proportion of the squirrels die outside their burrows where they are accessible to carnivorous birds."

* * *

The questioners of the strychnine scenario were too sanguine concerning the dangers of poisons to vultures. It was generally assumed that, due to their food habits, vultures would be less vulnerable to contaminants than some other species. Now, we know that both New World and Old World vultures can get lethal doses of strychnine. But how often, and how many? In all the journals, manuscripts, government correspondence, books, magazines, and newspapers I have reviewed over the past 40 years, I have only found eight references that cite or allege a specific instance of condor poisoning with strychnine. One is almost certainly not an actual incident, and another is a death by strychnine not related to killing livestock predators.

1. Alexander Taylor's 1856 note *that "quite a number of the condors were found dead ... from the effects of eating the meat of a bear poisoned with strychnine"* [78].

2. *"Some person, through accident or design, some few days since poisoned a pet vulture belonging to Dr. Canfield. The poison used was strychnine, and was probably administered in a piece of meat. The vulture was about eight months old, and measured across its wings, from tip to tip, 8 feet 9 1/2 inches"* [79]. This 1864 incident was not a condor death related to killing predators, but I include it because it does show that condors can be killed with strychnine. This may have been a very concentrated dose of the poison, and not necessarily what condors would be exposed to in the wild.

3. *"On South Eel river, Humboldt county, Mr. Adams recently poisoned a bird of the vulture species which measured nine feet across the wings, four feet from beak to tail and eight inches from crown to tip of beak"* [80]. I haven't been able to find anything more about this 1880 incident, but the details certainly make it sound authentic.

4. Walter Fry, a Sequoia National Park naturalist, gave the first non-hearsay report of condor deaths from poison directly linked to predator poisoning. He doesn't name the poison, but it would almost certainly have been strychnine at

that time [81]: *"While I was stopping at Huron, Fresno Co., California, during January 1890, Mr. Manuel Cardoza, a sheep herder, brought in two beautiful dead Condors. These birds had died from eating poison. Coyotes had killed two of his sheep and he had poisoned the carcasses with the hope of killing the coyotes; but instead of getting the animals he got the two big birds that had been feeding on the dead sheep. Cardoza said that he had noticed several of the Condors around the poisoned sheep the day before and upon going out in the evening found the dead ones a few yards from the bait."*

5. C. Hart Merriam wrote in 1917: "Frank Hubbard, who has a large stock ranch in Isabel Valley on the east side of Mt. Hamilton, told me that during his boyhood Grizzlies and Condors were both common in the Mt. Hamilton region. For a long time the stockmen believed that Grizzlies and Condors like Turkey Buzzards were immune to poison, but later found that both were easily killed by poisoning sheep carcasses" [82]. This may be hearsay, but has an authentic feel.

5. From Mayne Reid: *"There are times when certain beasts of prey, more especially wolves and coyotes become pests to the ganaderias or grazing farms; and means have to be adopted for thinning their numbers. An old ganadero, whose testimony I can trust, tells me of his having employed strychnine to poison them. He did so by chopping up the flesh of several bullocks, and inspissating it with the poison. It was scattered here and there over his pastures, at places known to be frequented by the 'vermin.' On going one day to inspect the envenomed lure, he found not only a number of coyotes lying lifeless on the ground, but half a dozen large vultures, that had gorged themselves on the 'spiced beef.' The birds were not quite dead, but only stupefied, and looking, as he said, like pigeons that had been made drunk on wheat steeped on whiskey.*

"He had no ill-will toward the vultures, and would have allowed them to live; but it was too late. The strychnine had already done most of its work; and after fluttering a while over the ground, now getting up, now tumbling down again, and staggering about like so many drunken men, one after another at length lay prostrate upon the sward, turning stiff, almost as soon as they had ceased kicking!" [83].

This report sounds authentic, and yet I think it isn't. Mayne Reid (1818-1883) was an Irish author of children's adventure books. He apparently was fascinated by vultures, and they figure in many of his books, including two entire chapters (43 pages) discussing the natural history of New World vultures in "The Boy Hunters" [84]. He was well-read on the subject of California condors, and quoted most of the information (both fact and fancy) available at that time. In the 1869 article quoted from above, he even refuted some of the earlier erroneous information from Alexander Taylor, David Douglas, and others (although he never amended the false information that continued to be printed in the many later editions of "The Boy Hunters").

Reid lived in the eastern United States 1838-1849, and again 1867-1870, but as far as I can tell never got closer to the Pacific Coast than Veracruz, Mexico. Most of his books were written while living in London in the 1850s and 1860s. The chances are slim that he actually knew any *"old ganadero"* (rancher, or sheep herder) that could tell him anything about condors. I suspect he crafted this article the same way he said he wrote his children's books: *"While undertaking no responsibility for the truth of his story, the author of the 'Boy Hunters' claims consideration for the* truthfulness of the materials *out of which it is constructed... He makes bold to indorse the genuineness of the scenery and its* natural facts. *He is not conscious of having taken any liberty, for the sake of effect, with the laws of nature... Neither plant nor tree, bird nor mammal, has been pressed into service,* beyond the limits of its geographical range..." [85]. In short, he is saying that he didn't write anything that couldn't be true! And as further support for the probability that the *"old ganadero"* was just a literary prop used to tell a story, Reid identified other intelligence that was imparted to him by this person *"whose facts I can trust."* For example, in refuting Douglas' report that condor eggs were black, Reid's informant allegedly told him *"the eggs are not black, but of a yellowish white color, with a band of brown blotches around the large end, with other smaller specks distributed over the whole surface. This account corresponds exactly with the description given of an egg voided by a 'hen' vulture of the California species, in the* Jardin des Plantes *of Paris."* Yes, it does; it is the description of the egg of an unknown species of vulture provided by James Trudeau to Thomas M. Brewer, and erroneously published in Brewer's 1857 "North American Oology" as that of the California condor [86]. Reid's trusted informant also was said to have told him that condors had more than one young per nesting; that young condors were taken from their nests by Indians, fattened up, then eaten at certain festivals; and that *"many"* condors were *"annually disposed of"* by Indians who sold them to *"museums and Zoological gardens in different parts of the world."* I think Mayne Reid's trusted informant shouldn't be trusted about his strychnine story.

6. On 1 March 1950, three condors (two adults, one immature) were found near a Fish and Wildlife Service strychnine drop bait site east of Bakersfield, California. Strychnine-laced fat baits had been placed around a sheep carcass, to kill coyotes. One adult condor was dead near a coyote carcass, the other two birds were weak and unable to fly. The living birds were provided with horsemeat and water at the site from 2 March to 6 March, when the adult was able to fly away. The immature continued to run around the area, and came for food and water, but didn't fly for some time. It finally disappeared on 18 March. The predator control people searched for it, but couldn't find it. They assumed it flew away.

Analysis of the dead bird was done by the Bureau of Chemistry, California Department of Agriculture. There was only a trace of strychnine in its digestive tract. Fish and Wildlife Service concluded that it probably wasn't strychnine poisoning because of the small amount of strychnine found, and because the trappers didn't think the birds exhibited signs of strychnine poisoning [87]. Despite the official findings, it still looks to me as if the condors were poisoned, probably by feeding on a coyote that had eaten a strychnine-laced bait.

7. Quail hunters found a "sick" adult condor 2 January 1966 in Alisos Canyon near Los Alamos, Santa Barbara County, California. They reported their observation to the Department of Fish and Game, and on 3 January 1966 a game warden found the bird *"huddled under an oak tree, unable to fly and (it) seemed to be a very sick bird. (The warden) placed the bird in a burlap sack...and the bird was taken to Griffith Park Zoo... Upon arrival at the zoo the Condor was examined by a veterinarian and was found to be suffering from strychnine poisoning. The Condor was placed in a padded, darkened cage and treated (treatment unspecified) for several days. On Jan. 12 the Condor was taken to the locality where it was found and released. It seemed to have recovered from the effect of the strychnine."*

"Mr. Louis Dourdet, owner of the ranch, has stated that he poisoned these (calf) carcasses in an effort to relieve himself of a serious predator damage to his livestock and poultry. He bought 4 ounce of strychnine at a drug store in Solvang, cleaned the carcasses...and sprinkled 1/8 ounce in each carcass" [88].

A news release from the Department of Fish and Game said *"the diagnosis of strychnine poisoning as the most probable cause of the condor's illness was made by Dr. Nathan Gale and Dr. Charles Sedgwick of the Los Angeles Zoo, who treated the bird, and Eldridge G. Hunt, leader of the Department's Pesticides Investigations project"* [89]. Fecal samples from the condor did not show any strychnine, but that wouldn't be a very good test. No one did any other tests, so strychnine was only "probable." Apparently a number of the ranchers in the area were using strychnine-laced carcasses at the time. A popular summary of this incident was published in "Audubon Magazine" [90].

* * *

No one wrote about strychnine poisoning condors until Alexander Taylor penned one sentence on the subject in 1856, and one more sentence in 1859. In the first instance, he reported that he had heard of *"quite a number"* of condors dying in one poisoning incident; three years later, without any further specifics, he reported that condors were *"often killed"* by strychnine. It was 20 years later that another condor was thought to have died from strychnine (in northwest California), and another ten years after that when Walter Fry saw two condors in the San Joaquin Valley that he presumed were killed by strychnine. Assuming that Taylor's incident actually occurred, and that *"quite a number"* meant more than two or three condors, the more or less *confirmed* loss from strychnine in the 19th century was less than a dozen birds. Yet, even before the second report was published, Henshaw had declared - with no other sources than Taylor - it *"highly probable that great numbers"* of condors had died from strychnine. Two years after the third report, Bendire had dropped Henshaw's *"highly probable"* qualifier, and declared *"poison so far has been the principal agent,"* elaborating that *"many of these birds were destroyed by this means, so that at this time comparatively few are said to be left."* Bendire quoted a number of condor observers not interviewed by the earlier writers, but none volunteered any information on poisons. Alexander Taylor's penchant and talent for hyperbole notwithstanding, I doubt he could have imagined his two sentences on strychnine would be parlayed into a major indictment of the poison that has survived 150 years of public perception.

Even if Taylor's writing style had not made many of his pronouncements suspicious, his sources of information were limited. His principal written reference was John James Audubon's 1839 "Ornithological Biography" [91]. (Taylor quoted extensively from David Douglas and John Kirk Townsend, but only as Audubon had previously included them in his book.) Other than Audubon's compilation of condor fact (and fancy), Taylor had only local informants and the stories they provided him. He seems not to have traveled far from Monterey during his years there (1848-1860), and his personal realm of condor reference included little beyond Monterey and Santa Cruz counties. Audubon did not write about poisons, so any knowledge Taylor had of the use and effects of strychnine beyond those two counties would have been meager. He would have had little or no knowledge of what was happening in most of California. There is no way his knowledge could be construed as giving a true picture of any aspect of condor distribution, numbers, or threats to survival.

* * *

This lengthy review of the 19th century record of strychnine use in the Pacific states reconfirms, I think, that the early 20th century writers were correct: it is highly unlikely that strychnine poisoning was a major cause of California condor mortality. The timing and magnitude of strychnine use, the history of livestock in California, and the life history of condors do not correlate well with the statements of alleged losses. The fact that nothing really new or more substantive was ever added to the original 1856 and 1859 remarks of Alexander Taylor further weakens the case. Most troublesome to me, however, is the lack of actual records. I and others have said it before: birds the size of a turkey with a nine feet wingspan, lying sick or dead in a field, would have attracted attention. In the second half of the 19th century, they would have been reported in the newspapers.

Strychnine as a cause of California condor mortality was a reality, and almost certainly there were more deaths than the few that "made the news." The threat of strychnine to condors probably increased after 1915, when the federal government (through the Bureau of Biological Survey) implemented major predator and rodent control activities throughout the West. If it was not the major reason for decreases in the condor population, it was an additional problem at a time when the condors were facing a number of other threats. Any losses to poison would have further destabilized a species already in trouble.

CHAPTER NOTES

1. I think I showed clearly in evaluations in 1978 and 2004 that the 20th century writers were a lot closer to the truth about condor poisoning than were those from the late 19th century. See pages 21-22 *in:* Wilbur, S. R. 1978. The California condor, 1966-76: a look at its past and future. U. S. Fish and Wildlife Service, North American Fauna Number 72. Also, pages 209-224 *in:* Wilbur, S. R. 2004. Condor Tales: What I learned in twelve years with the big birds. Gresham, Oregon: Symbios.

2. Letter to John McLoughlin 31 December 1839 from Pelly, Colvile and Simpson. Explanatory footnote to 18 November 1843 letter from McLoughlin to Hudson's Bay Company, London. Page 164 *in:* Rich, E. E., and W. K. Lamb (editors). 1943. The letters of John McLoughlin from Fort Vancouver to the Governor and Committee. Second Series, 1839-44. Toronto, Ontario: The Champlain Society.

3. Anonymous. 1871. The fur trade. San Francisco (California) *Bulletin,* 10 November 1871. The Hudson's Bay Company destroyed furs that had been ruined by trappers baiting their traps with strychnine. *"By this means they are very successful in taking game, and the skins when brought for sale are to all appearances as good as if the animal had been captured in the usual manner; but after awhile the fur falls off from the effects of the poison."*

4. Letter of 18 November 1843 letter from John McLoughlin to Hudson's Bay Company, London. Page 164 *in:* Rich, E. E., and W. K. Lamb (editors). 1943. The letters of John McLoughlin from Fort Vancouver to the Governor and Committee. Second Series, 1839-44. Toronto, Ontario: The Champlain Society.

5. Pages 13-14 *in:* Maris, P. V. 1923. An agricultural program for Oregon. Oregon Agricultural Extension Service Bulletin 367. Corvallis, Oregon.
Pages 39-40 *in:* Gibson, J. R. 1985. Farming the frontier. The agricultural opening of the Oregon country 1786-1846. Seattle, Washington: University of Washington Press.

6. Gibson 1985 *op. cit.,* page 103.

7. Gibson 1985 *op. cit.,* pages 119-122. Also: Page 344 *in:* Wilkes, C. 1856. Narrative of the United States Exploring Expedition during the years 1838, 1839, 1840, 1841, 1842. Volume IV. New York, New York: C. P. Putnam & Co.

8. Pages 258-259 *in:* Marshall, W. I. 1911. Acquisition of Oregon and the long-suppressed evidence about Marcus Whitman. Seattle, Washington: Lowman & Hanford Company.

9. Minto, J. 1905. Wild animals in Oregon. *Oregon Teachers Monthly* 10(4):193- 195.

10. Pittock, S. J. Undated. Thomas Cox. 5 page manuscript. Salem, Oregon: Willamette Heritage.

11. Pittock, *op. cit.*

12. Geer, R. C. 1880. Occasional address for the year 1847. *Transactions of the Annual Re-union of the Oregon Pioneer Association* 7:32-42.

13. McNish, J. 1841. Poisoning wolves. *The Farmers' Register* 9(10):597-598.

14. Anonymous. 1855. The beasts of the prairie. *Putnam's Monthly* 5(29):526-532.

15. Page 485 *in:* Conyers, E. W. 1905. Diary of E. W. Conyers, a pioneer of 1852 now of Clatskanie, Oregon. *Transactions of the Annual Re-union of the Oregon Pioneer Association* 33:423-515.

16. As late as 1843, there were still only 215 white males in all of Oregon: Page 6 *in* Heider, D., and D. Dietz. 1995. Legislative perspectives, a 150-year history of the Oregon Legislatures from 1843 to 1993. Portland, Oregon: Oregon Historical Society Press.

17. Maris 1923, *op. cit.;* also, pages 976-977 *in:* Carman, E. A., H. A. Heath, and J. Minto. 1892. Special report on the history and present condition of the sheep industry of the United States. Washington, D. C.: Government Printing Office..
    The original Willamette Cattle Company agreement, signed 13 January 1837, is in the Oregon State Archives at Salem. Although the cattle drives were meant to break the livestock monopoly held by the Hudson's Bay Company in the Northwest, Company manager John McLoughlin advanced one-third of the money used by the Willamette Company for the livestock purchase.

18. Pages 107-109 *in:* Gaston, J. 1911. Portland, Oregon, its history and builders. Volume I. Chicago, Illinois: S. J. Clarke Publishing Company.

19. Gaston 1911 *op. cit.*

20. Thornton, J. Q. 1875. History of the provisional government of Oregon. Pages 43-96 *in:* Constitution and quotations from the register of the Oregon Pioneer Association. Salem, Oregon: E. M. Waite, Book and Job Printer.

21. Arthur, J. 1887. A brief account of the experiences of a pioneer of 1843. *Transactions of the Fifteenth Annual Reunion of the Oregon Pioneer Association,* pages 96-104.

22. Quoted on page 75 *in:* Bowen, W. A. 1978. The Willamette Valley, migration and settlement of the Oregon frontier. Seattle, Washington: University of Washington Press.

23. Minto 1905 *op. cit.*

24. Pages 255-256 *in:* Hargreaves, S. 1928. The letters of Roselle Putnam. *Oregon Historical Quarterly* 29(3):242-264.

25. By the time strychnine would have been in regular use in western Oregon, there were several local papers (*"Oregon Spectator"* 1846, *"Oregonian"* 1850, *"Oregon Statesman"* 1851). Also, Northwest news was being regularly reported in the main California newspapers (e.g., *"California Star"* 1847, *"Daily Alta California"* 1849, *"Placer Times"* 1849).

26. Letter from "W. P.," *Oregon Spectator* (Oregon City, Oregon Territory), 20 February 1851.

27. Anonymous. 1893. Spokane has a sensation. *The Dalles* (Oregon) *Daily Chronicle,* 28 April 1893.

28. Thornton 1875 *op. cit.,* page 45.

29. Bowen 1978 *op. cit.,* pages 13-16.

30. Bowen 1978 *op. cit.,* pages 79-88.

31. Page 325 *in:* Young, S. P., and E. A. Goldman. 1944. The wolves of North America, Volume 1. Washington, D. C.: American Wildlife Institute. The source of the story was a 30 June 1939 letter from Dr. James C. Munch (Temple University School of Pharmacology), in the archives of the U. S. Fish and Wildlife Service.

32. Page 250 *in:* Carvalho, S. N. 1857. Incidents of travel and adventure in the far West with Col. Fremont's last expedition. New York, New York: Derby and Jackson.

33. Page 548 *in:* Froebel, J. 1859. Seven years' travel in Central America, northern Mexico, and the far West of the United States. London, England, Richard Bentley.

34. Anonymous. 1856. The California condor. San Francisco (California) *Bulletin,* 16 May 1856.

35. Anonymous. 1856. A California lion killed by strychnine. San Francisco (California) *Bulletin,* 6 August 1856.

36. Anonymous. 1856. Farmers' pest. *Daily Union* (Sacramento, California), 11 April 1856.

37. Anonymous. 1856. Grizzlies. *San Joaquin Republican* (Stockton, California), 20 September 1856.

144

38. Anonymous. 1856. Mad dogs and wolves. *Daily Union* (Sacramento, California), 13 March 1856.

39. Anonymous. 1857. California lions. *Daily Union* (Sacramento, California), 9 April 1857.

40. Anonymous. 1859. Four panthers killed in Sonoma County. San Francisco (California) *Bulletin,* 21 March 1859.

41. Anonymous. 1863. Legislation relative to the destruction of ground squirrels. *Daily Alta California* (San Francisco, California), 21 January 1863.

42. Anonymous. 1861. Panthers and wolves. San Francisco (California) *Bulletin,* 1 March 1861.

43. Anonymous 1868. Yreka items. San Francisco (California) *Bulletin,* 9 September 1868.

44. Anonymous. 1867. How to poison grizzlies. *Daily Alta California* (San Francisco, California), 17 May 1867.

45. Anonymous. 1863. Lions. *Daily Union* (Sacramento, California), 13 May 1863.

46. Anonymous. 1864. Panthers in Butte. San Francisco (California) *Bulletin,* 27 July 1864.

47. Anonymous. 1867. Caught at last. *Daily Union* (Sacramento, California), 20 March 1867.

48. Muir, J. 1911. My first summer in the Sierra. Boston, Massachusetts: Houghton Mifflin Company.

49. Anonymous. 1872. Catamount killed. *Daily Union* (Sacramento, California), 8 March 1872.

50. Anonymous. 1878. [No headline: bears and beehives]. *Daily Union* (Sacramento, California), 1 June 1878.

51. Anonymous. 1879. [No headline: wolf at Santa Rosa]. *Daily Union* (Sacramento, California), 22 January 1879.

52. Anonymous. 1872. Herding in California. Friends' Review 26(7):99-100.

53. Anonymous. 1870. [No headline: squirrel and gopher control]. *Daily Alta California* (San Francisco, California), 2 September 1870.

54. Anonymous. 1871. Gopher slaughter. *Daily Alta California* (San Francisco, California), 15 June 1871.

145

55. Anonymous. 1873. The way to get them. San Francisco (California) *Bulletin,* 28 July 1873.

56. Anonymous. 1873. A discussion about squirrels. San Francisco (California) *Bulletin,* 20 August 1873.
   Anonymous. 1873. The squirrel law convention. *Pacific Rural Press* (San Francisco, California), 18 October 1873.

57. Pages 2157-2158 *in:* Deering, J. H. 1895. Digest of the reports of the Supreme Court of California, Volumes One to One Hundred Inclusive. Volume II. San Francisco, California: Bancroft-Whitney Company.

58. Newberry, J. S. 1857. Report upon the zoology of the route. Report of explorations and surveys to ascertain the most practicable and economical route for a railroad from the Mississippi River to the Pacific Ocean. Volume VI, Part 2:35-110. Washington, D. C.: Beverly Tucker.
   Heermann, A. L. 1859. Report upon the birds collected on the survey. Report of explorations and surveys for a railroad route from the Mississippi River to the Pacific Ocean, 1853-56. Volume X, Part 4:29-80. Washington, D. C.: Beverly Tucker.
   Cooper, J. G. 1860. Report upon the birds collected on the Survey. Chapter I, Land birds. Reports of explorations and surveys, to ascertain the most practicable and economical route for a railroad from the Mississippi River to the Pacific Ocean, made under the direction of the Secretary of War, in 1853-55. Volume XII, Book 2:140-291.Washington, D. C.: Thomas H. Ford, Printer.

59. Page 111 *in:* Suckley, G. and G. Gibbs 1860. Report of Dr. Geo. Suckley, U. S. A., and Geo. Gibbs, Esq. Reports of explorations and surveys, to ascertain the most practicable and economical route for a railroad from the Mississippi River to the Pacific Ocean, made under the direction of the Secretary of War, in 1853-55. Volume XII, Book 2:108-139.Washington, D. C.: Thomas H. Ford, Printer.

60. Suckley and Gibbs *op. cit.,* page 113.

61. Page 81 *in:* Cooper, J. G. 1860. Report upon the mammals collected on the Survey. Reports of explorations and surveys, to ascertain the most practicable and economical route for a railroad from the Mississippi River to the Pacific Ocean, made under the direction of the Secretary of War, in 1853-55. Volume XII, Book 2:73-107.Washington, D. C.: Thomas H. Ford, Printer.

62. Page 20 *in:* Taylor, A. S. 1859. The great condor of California--Part II. *Hutching's California Magazine* 4(1):17-22.

63. Anonymous. 1856. The California condor. San Francisco (California) *Bulletin,* 16 May 1856.

64. Page 500 *in:* Cooper, J. G. 1870. Ornithology. Sacramento, California: Geological Survey of California. In fairness to Cooper, he did question Taylor's report of condors

flying with prey in their talons, and disputed Taylor's claim that dark-headed birds were female condors, rather than immatures.

65. Page 342 *in:* Baird, S. F., T. M. Brewer, and R. Ridgway. 1874. A history of North American birds. Volume III, Land birds. Boston, Massachusetts: Little, Brown and Co.

66. Page 265 *in:* Henshaw, H. W. 1876. Report on the ornithology of the portions of California visited during the field season of 1875. Annual report upon the geographical survey west of the 100th meridian in California, Nevada, Utah, Colorado, Wyoming, New Mexico, Arizona and Montana. Appendix JJ:224-278. Washington, D. C.: Government Printing Office.

67. As early as 1872, Henry Henshaw reported a bird in Utah *"believed to be this species"* [*Explorations and Surveys West of the One Hundreth Meridian* 5(3):428], and the 1875 records from California could be construed as his own. However, he later claimed not to have personally seen a living California condor until 1884: Henshaw, H. W. 1920. Autobiographical notes. *Condor* 22(1):8.

68. Henshaw, H. W. 1876. Notes on the mammals taken and observed in California in 1875. Pages 525-532 *in:* Report of the Secretary of War to the Second Session of the Forty-fourth Congress: appendixes to the report of the Chief of Engineers, Volume II, Part III. Washington, D. C.: Government Printing Office.

69. Pages 158-159 *in:* Bendire, C. 1892. Life histories of North American birds. Washington, D. C.: Government Printing Office.

70. An excellent, fully documented history of livestock in California is presented in: Burcham, L. T. 1982. California range land. Center for Archeological Research at Davis, Publication Number 7. University of California, Davis.

71. Muir 1911 *op. cit.*

72. Pages 18-26 *in:* Storer, T. I., and Tevis, L. P. Jr. 1955. California grizzly. Berkeley, California: University of California Press.

73. Bendire *op. cit.*

74. Pages 1733-1734 *in:* Dawson, W. L. 1923. The birds of California. San Diego, California: South Moulton Company.

75. Scott, C. D. 1936. Who killed the condors? *Nature Magazine* 28(6):368-370.

76. Pages 41-42 *in:* Harris, H. 1941. The annals of *Gymnogyps. Condor* 43(1):3-55.

77. Pages 130-131 *in:* Koford, C. B. 1953. The California condor. National Audubon Society, Research Report Number 4. New York, New York.

147

78. Anonymous. 1856. The California condor. San Francisco (California) *Bulletin,* 16 May 1856.

79. Anonymous. 1864. A pretty pet! San Francisco (California) *Bulletin,* 21 December 1864.

80. Anonymous. 1880. State news in brief. San Francisco (California) *Bulletin,* 5 April 1880.

81. Fry, W. 1926. The California condor - a modern roc. *The Gull* (Golden Gate Audubon Society) 8(5):1-3.

82. C. H. Merriam California journals 1917 (pp. 31-32, 16 September 1917). Merriam Collection, Bancroft Library (Berkeley, California), BANC MSS 83/129c.

83. Reid, M. 1869. The vultures of America, a monographic sketch of these foul-beaked birds. *Onward, Mayne Reid's Magazine.* May 1869, pages 371-378.

84. Pages 377-420 *in:* Reid, M. 1853. The boy hunters, or adventures in search of a white buffalo. London, England: David Bogue.

85. Reid 1853 *op. cit.,* Preface.

86. Brewer, T. H. 1857. North American oology. Washington, D. C.: Smithsonian Institution.

87. U. S. Fish and Wildlife Service memorandum 24 March 1950, from H. Nelson Elliott (Sacramento, California) to Clarence Cottam (Washington, D. C.), subject: California Condor incident, Kern County, California.

88. U. S. Fish and Wildlife Service memorandum 21 January 1966, Riley D. Patterson (Bakersfield, California) to State Supervisor (Sacramento, California), subject: Condor poisoning in Santa Barbara County.

89. California Department of Fish and Game (Sacramento, California) press release, 22 January 1966, subject: Poison suspected in condor illness.

90. Borneman, J. C. 1966. Return of a condor. *Audubon Magazine* 68(3):154-157.

91. Pages 240-245 *in:* Audubon, J. J. 1839. Ornithological Biography, or An account of the habits of the birds of the United States of America. Edinburgh, Scotland: Adam & Charles Black.

CHAPTER 12
CAPTIVE CONDORS

Through the 1860s and 1870s, shooting for sport or curiosity continued to be the main source of California condor mortality. Two-thirds of the known losses during that twenty year period were random shooting deaths. Demand for condor specimens for museums and private collections was growing, but was not yet a major factor. A new interest was for live condors to display in public zoos. Collecting for zoos would reach its peak after 1900, but began during this period.

The earliest instances of confined condors were not for public display, however, but more for the fun of it. One wouldn't think that a giant carrion-eating vulture would be a logical choice for a pet, but apparently the attraction of having one was strong.

The first record I found was from 1854. Near the American River in El Dorado County, California, Alonzo Winship and Jesse Millikan surprised a roosting condor, threw a shovel at it, and broke its wing. A spirited pursuit followed, as related by Mrs. Millikan 46 years later [1]:

"The condor, thus rudely disturbed, jumped from its perch, and running under the flume, started down the mountain toward the American River with Mr. Winship following closely after. The condor's broken wing impeded its progress, and finding its pursuer was gaining upon it, it turned savagely upon him and he was compelled to take refuge on a granite boulder just out of its reach, realizing he had a dangerous enemy."

Millikan came to Winship's rescue, and between them they managed to subdue the injured condor. They set and bandaged its broken wing, then *"fastened a trace chain to one leg, securing the other end to a post..."* The owners of a nearby slaughterhouse wanted the bird, so *"with much difficulty the bird was once again secured, taken down the mountain and turned loose in the stockade of the corral..."* The condor lived there for some unstated time, then disappeared. *"A week later, a miner prospecting on the river bank found it more dead than alive from starvation, as its wing was not yet thoroughly healed. All the bird's fight was gone, and the miner, without the slightest difficult, conveyed it back to the stockade, where it was well fed and soon regained its former ferocity. Finally during the second autumn, it disappeared for good and they supposed it had gone south."*

That same autumn of 1854, at Redwoods (Contra Costa County, California; see Chapter 7), a teamster brought a live condor to James Lamson. It had been lassoed near a cow carcass, apparently unable to fly (*"though it ran with considerable fleetness"*) after gorging itself on beef. Lamson had a small menagerie at his camp, and he might have intended to study the behavior of the condor. It was not to be, as he reported three days later:

"While cleaning out the cages, one of my foxes -- I had six at this time -- slipped out and escaped to the woods, and having carelessly left the door of the cage unfastened, another one soon followed. As further illustration of the fact that 'When sorrows come, they come not as single spies, but in batallions,' my vulture died today, having probably been wounded in his capture. Still further, a third fox managed to draw a nail that had fastened his door and took French leave in the night" [2].

Between 1855 and 1940, I found records of 17 other captures of condors, apparently just for the novelty of catching and keeping a big bird. To this number can be added several more instances of sick or injured birds being taken into captivity, presumably to try and rehabilitate them. Like James Lamson's bird, most condors that weren't sick or injured were lassoed or otherwise captured by hand at animal carcasses, after the condors had fed heavily and could not immediately get airborne. A few condors were removed from their nests while still too young to fly.

* * *

Just as dead condors were popular news fodder, live condors were a novelty that couldn't be passed up. Take for example this story from Sacramento in 1857.

"Mr. Sutton, of the Western Hotel, corner of K and 10th streets, was presented a few days since with a young vulture, which he placed in the yard of his establishment. In order that our readers may estimate the size and powers of the bird, we give his dimensions as follows: Length of wings from tip to tip, about 10 feet 6 inches; length of head and beak, 7 inches; length of claws, from 7 to 9 inches. He is fed regularly and literally on raw heads and bloody bones, and can clean a skull or bone in the most approved style. Efforts have been made to induce several dogs to take hold of him, but his competitors have always respectfully declined. Sutton's dog (which has never been whipped) declined having anything to do with him, except to gaze and admire his stalwart proportions. The dog in question is the same that nursed a brood of chickens, and would permit no one to molest them. The vulture was caught on Mrs. Harrold's ranch, near this city" [3].

With a few notable exceptions, most condors taken by individuals lived only a few days or a few weeks after capture. Some were casualties of their injuries or illness; cause of death for most went unrecorded. Some causes were obvious:

"[A California vulture was] *brought alive to Mr. [Thomas] Shooter. It seemed at times to be troubled with a kind of asthma, which trouble seemed to increase, for it appeared to be a local complaint. A month later Mr. Shooter's assistant trying, alone, to move this powerful bird from one cage to another, was severely bitten, and in trying to save a finger being bitten off, broke the* bird's neck. The bird's skin was mounted and is now at the Chicago exhibition" [4].

Other deaths were documented, but still leave interesting questions; for example:

"A San Diego (Cal.) man caught a fine specimen of the California vulture and gave it to the proprietor of a small menagerie to keep for him. In the menagerie was a pet coon, and the vulture was placed in a tree above the box in which the coon was kept. In the morning, fur and feathers marked the spot, the vulture lay on its back, claws up, stiff in death, and the coon lay on his side still alive, but in a very dilapidated condition. The expression on his face suggested the remark attributed to the parrot after a somewhat similar experience with a monkey" [5].

Certainly the most famous condor to live only a short time in captivity was that lassoed by one of the employees of Richard Gird, famous Arizona miner, southern California agriculturalist, and founder of the town of Chino, California [6]. The story of Gird's condor ran in dozens (perhaps hundreds?) of newspapers in the United States and abroad, in spectacular detail.

"These birds are among the largest, if not the largest species that navigate the air. They have become nearly extinct in California, and to see one, much more to capture one, is a great rarity. This one is young, yet it stands about six feet high and has a wing expansion of ten feet. It is very broad in the breast and back, and has powerful beak and talons... It is said that these birds will fly twenty miles, straight as an arrow's course to a carcass, and will kill and devour a deer in very short order" [7].

"Richard Gird's ranch Superintendent has captured a rare prize in the hills south of here in the shape of a California vulture. It had just devoured a cow, and was unable to fly, and was lassoed and brought to Mr. Gird's stables. For tip to tip the wings expand twelve feet, and the bird stands about six feet high and weighs over 100 pounds. Mr. Gird says a vulture will fly twenty miles as straight as an arrow to a carcass, and easily kills cattle and deer, having a broad breast and back and powerful beak and talons"[8].

"A bird of prey as tall as a man! Such is the prize just captured by the superintendent of Richard Gird's ranch in the hills south of Chino, San Bernardino county, Cal. The prisoner is a magnificent specimen of the California vulture, without doubt the largest ever taken captive. From the crown of its ferocious-looking, red-wattled head to its strong, scaly talons it measures six feet. Its plucky captor is an inch or two shorter in his cowhide boots. The man has the advantage in weight, for the bird weighs 100 pounds. Still, that is a fair fighting weight to carry through the rarified upper air. In order to accomplish this feat the vulture is provided with wings that have a spread of twelve feet. Withal the ornithologists who have seen it say that it is merely a youngster" [9].

Mr. Gird intended to convert this alleged 100 pound, six feet tall condor with twelve foot wings (!!) *"into an affectionate and interesting household pet."* Unfortunately, although the news story lived to appear and reappear in papers across the country for at least three months after the capture, the condor did not. As reported in the local newspaper (but apparently nowhere else):

"The account of the vulture captured on the ranch a couple of weeks ago has created quite a sensation, having appeared in the Eastern newspapers and being commented on quite generally. Many people have driven to Chino to see the huge bird, which unfortunately died a few days after it was captured" [10].

* * *

The first captive California condor to excite the scientists as well as the general public was "Ben Butler." Taken from the mountains of Monterey County, California, when still a nestling, Ben lived in the San Jose area aviary of Frank H. Holmes from July 1896 to "his" (I don't think sex was ever determined) death in early 1901 [11]. Various ornithologists came to observe the big bird, including well-known Bay Area bird enthusiasts Otto Emerson and Donald Cohen [12]. In a unique tribute, Mrs. Holmes and her "pet" earned a story that ran to portions of five columns (with a picture) in the "women's section" of the San Francisco *Chronicle*. Here is a portion of the report [13].

"Ladies with a penchant for sweetly warbling canary birds would look with a sort of awe on the big, powerful playfellow which Mrs. Frank H. Holmes of Berryessa, Cal., thinks is a lovely, intelligent creature, and which she is not afraid to handle.

"Of all the strange pets which man has chosen from the animal creation as a subject for amusement and study, surely none, among the birds, at least, could be more outre than a California condor...."

"'I am not at all afraid of this big fellow,' said Mrs. Holmes; 'In fact, we are old friends, and he will come shuffling up to me in his queer way to be fed when he sees me. I was a little shy about approaching such a big creature at first, but he soon came to know me. Now we have frolics together sometimes. Although some persons say he is an ugly, fierce-looking pet to have, I am very fond of him, and he is real good-natured, and, though you would scarcely believe it, he is almost as playful in his big, lumbering way as a kitten.'

"'If he is annoyed about anything he will hiss like a goose, raising the ruff about his neck at the same time. He seems to like me better than anybody else, and when I enter his cage he always flies down from his perch and comes rubbing up against me like a kitten.'

"When the condor was a young bird and unable to fly he was allowed to roam about the yard. One of his favorite amusements was to go wading in the creek near the house, where he would bathe, afterward standing in the sun with widespread wings until dry. His attention is attracted at once to any small and bright object, and when Mr. Holmes was about to photograph him the rubber bulb of the camera shutter proved such an irresistible attraction that it was necessary to maintain a sharp watch to prevent its being 'punctured'

152

during the operation."

Frank Holmes reportedly took many photos of "Ben Butler," but only two are known to have been printed for the public to see. I searched for Holmes photos and notes in the 1970s, but could only determine that copies might have gone to the California Academy of Sciences in San Francisco. If they did, they were probably destroyed in the 1906 earthquake and fire. Recently, I learned of a letter written by Holmes to the Smithsonian Institution in 1898, in which he said [14]: *"I will also mail you a series of photos of a live condor in my possession, which may furnish some characteristic attitudes to assist in mounting* [the condor skins]." If the photos were sent, they cannot be located in Smithsonian files. Rollo Beck, a neighbor of Holmes, sent some of the Ben Butler photos to William Brewster in Cambridge, Massachusetts, accompanying condor skins Brewster had purchased from him. The Beck-Brewster correspondence survives in the Museum of Comparative Zoology, but the photos are not locatable.

It is a reasonable assumption that "Ben Butler" was saved as a mount or study skin after "his" death, but I haven't located the specimen. Frank Holmes condors are in the U. S. National Museum and the American Museum of Natural History (New York City), but "Ben" is not identifiable among them.

* * *

Not long after the short-term captives of 1854, and 40 years before "Ben Butler," live California condors made their first public appearances, as members of James Capen "Grizzly" Adams' "Pacific Museum." Adams, famous worldwide for his exploits with grizzly bears, brought his menagerie of live West Coast animals to San Francisco in the winter of 1855-1856 [15]. In addition to a dozen or so live grizzlies, the "Museum" reportedly included live wolves, mountain lions, bison, elk, a sea lion, and a variety of birds [16]. Among the birds were at least two California condors [17].

I haven't been able to determine where, when and how Grizzly Adams procured his condors. By his own account, he killed one condor near the Nevada-California border north of Mono Lake in May or June 1854 [18], but I haven't found any records of him capturing condors alive. His "Pacific Museum" had one living condor in March 1857 *("a large vulture worth seeing"* [19]), and possibly the same one in June 1859 *("a fine living specimen of this bird, and the only captive of its kind we know of"* [20]. In June 1860, Adams had two condors in his show.

Other than acknowledgments that the Pacific Museum did include live California condors, I've found only one specific reference to one of them [21]: *"Adams, the Museum man, while removing the last cage of his animals to the Old Mechanic' Institute Pavilion yesterday, experienced the kind of a bite which a vulture, or what is usually called the California condor, can inflict. This bird in some manner got loose, and as Adams caught him, it took a large piece of flesh, about the size of a thumb, out of the left hand. The old man*

153

seems destined to be eaten up alive by degrees. "

The Pacific Museum remained in San Francisco until the winter of 1859-1860, when Adams made his decision to move his menagerie to New York [22]: *"In the course of a few months, the people of New York, and the Atlantic States generally, will have an exhibition destined to excite great attention amongst them. This is the collection of wild animals of California, Oregon, Washington and Utah, gathered by Mr. Adams, and known as the Pacific Museum. It is proposed to ship the entire museum, in a short time, and Adams himself, the curiosity of all, will go with it... "*

In New York, Adams formed a partnership with the showman, P. T. Barnum, and the California Menagerie (as the Pacific Museum had been renamed) was exhibited in a large canvas tent at Broadway and Thirteenth Street. The show ran through the summer of 1860. Adams died 25 October 1860, the cumulative result of repeated injuries inflicted by his bears, and soon after Barnum reported that he sold most of the animals [23]. However, there are conflicting accounts [24]: *"The California Menagerie, recently under the management of 'Grizzly Adams,' whose sudden death was recently recorded, has been re-organized by Barnum, and shipped to Havana, where it is to be exhibited under the management of Colonel Wood. As the collection is perfectly unique, Barnum contemplates shipping them to England when their Cuban term is ended. An old California trapper will be the successor of 'Grizzly Adams' in the management of the bears. "* The Menagerie had, in fact, been shipped to Havana in mid-October 1860 [25], and returned to New York 25 January 1861 [26]. I have found no specific mention of condors after May 1860, so I don't know if they made the trip to Havana, and don't know what eventually happened to them. Barnum did eventually sell many of Adams' animals, and he lost many of his artifacts in structure fires. Adams' bears continued to be exhibited as part of a traveling menagerie for a number of years after 1861.

* * *

The first condor to reach a public zoo was the one supplied by Dr. Colbert Canfield to the Zoological Society of London in 1866 [Chapter 10]. The first live condors in a public institution in the United States were not acquired until August 1896, when two five-month old condors were delivered to the Philadelphia (Pennsylvania) Zoological Garden. These young birds were taken from nests in Monterey County, California, by Wallace Mathers (collector of a number of condor eggs: Chapter 16), and delivery to the Zoo was facilitated by Capt. Charles Bendire of the U. S. National Museum [27]. According to Philadelphia Zoo records, the Zoo paid $50 apiece for them. One condor lived two years, the other four and a half years [28]. Cause of death was not determined in either case.

Both Philadelphia condors were still alive when a third nestling condor was obtained, destined for a semi-public facility. After killing an adult condor near Santa Monica, California, in August 1898, Harry G. Rising discovered that there was a five-month old, nearly fledged condor near its nest. He captured the young bird, and kept it for several months [29]. He sold it to the National Home for Disabled Volunteer Soldiers at Sawtelle, California, where "Dewey," as the soldiers named it, lived for a number of years with a menagerie that included *"28 head of horses, 100 sheep, 800 head of hogs and 700 chickens. The menagerie consists of 7 monkeys, 12 ground squirrels, 1 gray squirrel, 1 California vulture, 1 gray eagle, 1 parrot and 100 canaries"* [30]. According to W. Lee Chambers: *"The bird thrived and in about two years assumed its full growth. It was confined in a cage large enough for it to fly from a high perch to the ground below and became quite a pet of the old soldiers. A short time ago* [February 1903] *it suddenly sickened without any apparent cause, and died; although all the medical skill at the Home attempted to cure it... The bird gradually became so weak that it could scarcely stand. He is now mounted and adorns a prominent place in the Home library"* [31].

* * *

Beginning in 1900, the demand for live condors increased, and in the next ten years eleven California condors were procured for zoos. The National Zoo (Washington, D. C.) received six, the Bronx Zoo (New York) four, and the Golden Gate Park Aviary (San Francisco) one. Only one of the zoo condors lived less than a year; four lived one to five years; and three lived seven to 10 years. The other three, all at the National Zoo, survived 36, 39 and 45 years in captivity. William B. Whitaker, a rancher and bee keeper from Piru, Ventura County, California, was the party responsible for procuring at least six (and almost certainly seven) of the 11 captives. The other four were acquired from individuals in Monterey, San Luis Obispo, Santa Barbara, and Los Angeles counties.

Acquiring a live California condor was not an easy task. Even when the species was still relatively common, nests were difficult to locate. Finding a nest site, assuring it was active, watching the area until sure there was a young condor in the nest, extracting the youngster safely from its precarious location, getting it back to "civilization," then shipping it to the other side of the continent: the process involved considerable time on the part of the collectors, and a great deal of luck [32]. William T. Hornaday, Bronx Zoo curator of birds, described the complications in a newspaper interview [33]:

"Five years ago, when I was consumed with the desire to obtain a California condor, I broke my usual practice [of waiting until a bird was offered to me] *and sent an order for one to a man who lives in the mountains of the southern part of the State, where is the habitat of this, the rarest and largest of North American birds of prey. How long do you think I had to wait before I received word that a young condor, taken from the nest, was on its way to me? Just a shade over four years. And I considered myself exceedingly lucky."*

Figure 8. One of the Bronx Zoo condors, circa 1906. New York Zoological Society photo, courtesy William G. Conway.

Hornaday's first California condor was reportedly taken from its nest by "several small boys," held at a San Luis Obispo County ranch for some time, then shipped by rail from San Francisco to New York, arriving there in mid-March 1905. Named "Search Me" by one news reporter (and "Sierra" by the same or another reporter two years later, although neither name appears anywhere else), he was given a memorable welcome by the press [34].

"With an aggressive sweep of his five-inch beak and a stretch of his fine wings that measured something like ten feet, Search Me, the first California condor ever brought alive to New York, and a baby type of the rarest bird of prey in North America, climbed on his perch at the New York Zoological Gardens yesterday afternoon and clamored for food.

"Search Me, like all healthy infants, was hungry. All he had had to eat since he left his mountain home, in Southern California, ten days ago, were 120 luscious pork chops. And because his transcontinental trip had been rushed by an over-zealous ornithologist, who wanted to bring a live American bird instead of a dead one for New Yorkers to admire, the bird arrived in this city

twelve hours ahead of time, before his hotel accommodations were ready for him.

"The astonished condor was met at the Grand Central Station by Director W. T. Hornaday and two assistants, who were profuse in their apologies for being 'taken unawares,' so to speak. The bird of prey listened to them in reserved, not to say sulky, silence. He never opened his lips -- or rather his beak -- while he was hoisted on a wagon and taken for a long drive through the Bronx to his future home. It was only when he was pushed into the Aquatic House that the California condor gave vent to his pent-up indignation. The language the fierce bird used was intelligible only to Director Hornaday, who is an expert on condors and such things. A liberal translation by Mr. Hornaday reads something like this:

"'To put me -- me -- a bird that soars to the skies; a bird born and bred in the crags of cliffs that the hardiest mountaineers dare not scale, into a cage with common ducks and pelicans! Think of it! Ducks are my abomination. We do not have them at home. They can't soar worth a cent. Ugh!'

"Director Hornaday explained to his distinguished guest that his quarters in the duck house were only temporary. An exclusive perch in the big wire aviary was reserved for him, where he can plume himself to his heart's content when the weather gets warmer. But at present, considering the chilly weather and the warm climate from which the bird came, the steam-heated duck house is perhaps more comfortable."

But there was apparent intrigue involved with the condor; the Pacific Coast Forest, Fish and Game Association accused Hornaday of stealing their bird. As reported in a California news story [35]:

"Who will get the condor? This is the question which is at present worrying the members of the Pacific Coast Forest, Fish and Game Association. R. E. Follett, who was at one time associated with the organization has the condor, and the association says that it has a prior claim on the bird.

"It all happened this way. A magnificent California condor was captured by a small boy, or, rather, several small boys, in the mountains some forty miles from Santa Maria, in San Luis Obispo county. The birds measures eleven feet from tip to tip and would have made a valuable acquisition to the exhibit. C. J. Russell, a prominent ranchero in San Luis Obispo county was commissioned to secure the bird, and he did. He drove out to the place and paid a deposit on the bird. He was not, however, satisfied, and so made a second trip, intending to pay for the bird and ship it to the city. When he got to his destination he found to his great amazement that the bird was gone. It had been sold to a man from San Francisco for $67.50 who, they say, gave the name of Fowler, and it was intended either for the Golden Gate Park or the Chutes [an amusement park in San Francisco].

"Mr. Russell immediately wrote to Dr. d'Evelyn, the chairman of the birds and game committee, who started to find out where the bird had gone. He

learned from the Wells Fargo people that the condor had arrived this morning and that it had been consigned to R. R. Follett. When Folett left here he had said he was going on a trip to Santa Barbara to pay a call on President Ripley of the Santa Fe, and now it is said that Follett went straight to Santa Maria, secured the bird and shipped it off to New York. As the bird's fare is only paid as far as Ogden, it is thought likely that the association will be able to get the great bird and exhibit it in due time at the Pavilion."

The condor was not stopped in Utah, but the Association continued to pursue the alleged "theft" of the bird. Frederick W. D'Evelyn, the Association's chairman of the Committee on Birds and Game, wrote to the New York papers [36].

"To the Editor of The Sun--Sir: I am indebted to a recent issue of your paper for certain valuable information, namely, the final destination of a specimen of the California condor, taken east by a gentleman recently in the employment of the above association but discharged therefrom for cause. I have tried to locate the condor, as it was the property of our association and removed from our custody without our knowledge. I have informed a Mr. Hornaday in New York to that effect as from telegram I saw in San Francisco it was presumed to be the consignee, but this he denied.

"Several months ago I had communicated with our agent at Santa Maria, Cal., who ultimately purchased the bird for our association. It was after this had been done that Mr. Follett obtained the possession of it, as the seller's friend states, by representing himself as an agent of your local park or zoo. Any information Mr. Follett gained of this specimen was while he was in the employment of the association. It took a long persuasion and by forcing a correspondence to convince the simple herder, the original owner of the bird, that he (Follett) was the rightful purchaser.

"Had our agent in Santa Maria telegraphed the abduction of our property instead of writing to us the condor would never have left California.

"These are simple facts, and now, when the final location of the bird is known, we shall take other measures to expose the undue ambition of a 'Naturalist from the East,' an ambition which could easily and truthfully be called by a more correct and less complimentary title. We have all the necessary data to institute proceedings."

A reporter from *The Sun* took the story to Hornaday, and included Hornaday's response in the news story with D'Evelyn's allegation:

"When this letter was shown to William T. Hornaday, the director of the Bronx zoo, he remarked, as soon as he saw the letterhead, that he could guess the contents.

"'Those Frisco people are trying to get a rise out of us,' he added. 'I can best reply to the charges contained in the letter by telling how we came to get the condor which recently arrived and which is now in one of the ostrich cages, doing very well.

158

"'C. K. Worthen, an animal dealer of Warsaw, Ill., wrote to me in the winter that one of his collectors had located a condor which could be had for $100. I wrote him that we would take the bird, but that it must not be delivered until the weather became milder. This acceptance Mr. Worthen transmitted to his collector in southern California, a man named [Arthur] Wilcox, instructing him to hold the bird until spring.

"'Meanwhile the Mr. Follett referred to in the letter wrote to me reporting on efforts he had been making to get certain kinds of animals for our zoo and asked if there was anything we wanted him to do. He added that he was coming East in a few weeks, and I told him to get the condor and bring it. At the same time I wrote to Mr. Worthen to telegraph to Follett the name of the man who had the condor. Follett had left the service of the Pacific Coast Forest, Fish and Game Association, but his mail and telegrams were still received at its office.

"'I am informed that the telegram was opened at the office of the association and held there for two days before it reached Follett. Moreover, this was the first intimation the association had of the condor's existence, but it set out to get the bird.

"'The condor was not then in the possession of Wilcox, Worthen's collector, but was still held by a boy, the son of a ranchman. Along came an agent of the association and offered the boy $45 for it and the boy agreed to sell. He did not deliver it, however, and when Mr. Follett arrived and offered $65 he got the bird and a bill of sale.

"'So we have the condor and feel entitled to it, because if Mr. Follett's telegram or letter had not been opened the San Francisco association would never have heard of the bird.'"

The reporter gave the condor what turned out to be the last word on the subject:

"Mr. Condor, who was found preening himself in the bird house, said that he had heard of the row over him and was quite chesty.

"'I feel like the Equitable surplus [37],' he added, for condors have a rare turn of humor as well as of speed."

* * *

The Zoo's "victory" was short-lived because their first California condor died a year and a half later, the result of swallowing a rubber band [38]. Curator Hornaday didn't have to wait four years for a replacement, however; he already had one on hand. In September 1906, William L. Finley had sold to the Zoo "General," who thanks to the writings and lectures of Finley, was destined to become the best-known California condor in the world.

Finley and his photographer partner, Herman T. Bohlman, on 10 March 1906 near Pasadena, California, had discovered a condor nest with one egg in it. They kept the nesting pair of condors under observation until the egg hatched 22 March, then regularly photographed the young condor into early

159

July. By then, the young condor they had named "General" was two-thirds grown, and on 6 July it was taken from its nest and transported to Finley's home in Portland, Oregon. "General" stayed in Oregon until late September 1906, then was sold to the New York Zoological Park [39].

"General" survived until 1916, then died of undocumented causes. Once in the zoo, the condor's life was unremarkable, but Finley kept interest alive with many popular articles in magazines and newspapers, and the excellent condor photographs taken by Herman Bohlman remain some of the best ever produced [40]. Finley apparently saw "General" only twice after "he" [41] was taken to New York, the last time in December 1908 [42].

* * *

Between 1903 and 1939, the National Zoological Park (Washington, D. C.) had three California condors housed together. Beginning in 1919 and continuing through 1932, these condors produced at least one egg each year, totaling about 17 eggs. Three more eggs were laid between 1935 and 1939. All were either broken or proved to be infertile. Because only one egg was laid most years, and because the zoo keepers could not always tell the birds apart, they never were sure if one of the birds was responsible for all the eggs, or if more than one was producing. Because none of the eggs hatched, there was speculation that all three condors were females. However, when the first of the three birds died in 1939, it proved to be a male [43]. Also, egg laying ceased after the death of the male condor.

Because the National Zoo, like most zoos in the early 1900s, was a mere menagerie, not a scientific operation, the egg-laying of rare California condors received little attention. It was never determined why none of the eggs hatched successfully. Newspapers picked up the story once when the Zoo reported that, because the condors were breaking their eggs, one was given to a domestic chicken to incubate [44]. (It proved infertile.) Unbroken eggs were salvaged and given to the U. S. National Museum; some were added to the Museum's permanent collection, and some were sold or traded to other institutions and private collectors. It was not until the late 1960s, when captive breeding of California condors began to be considered, that some of the details of the National Zoo experience became relevant. Condors had produced eggs in captivity, a condor continued to produce eggs for 20 years after reaching maturity, and a condor did on occasion lay more than one egg per season. This was useful information to have when developing a captive breeding proposal [45].

* * *

Nowhere near as famous as "General," but more of a star in other ways, was "Bozo," a California condor that lived in the Selig Park Zoo in Los Angeles from 1923 to 1928. Bozo, when barely a fledgling, had been found in her nest cave in the Sespe Creek area of Ventura County, where Joseph Herring and Frank Arundell had been shooting condors for museum displays (Chapter 15).

She was captured, and taken to the zoo [46].

In 1915, "Colonel" William Selig developed a combination movie studio and zoo in Lincoln Park, Los Angeles, California. Selig's studio, Selig Polyscape Company, produced films featuring Tom Mix and Tarzan. He reportedly had several hundred animals in the zoo, some of which he used in his films and rented out to other film makers. In at least one case, Bozo achieved a brief stardom. The 1926 movie, "The Night Cry," pitted Bozo (as the evil condor) against an animal hero, the famous dog star, Rin Tin Tin. As described in the movie ads, the story *"revolves around the intimate tale of a hopeful young rancher, his brave little wife, their cunning baby and the faithful shepherd dog, Rinty, their brave battle against circumstantial evidence, and the wild forces of nature... Among others in the cast are...Bozo, the only California condor in captivity in America, who portrays the role of the villain"* [47]. Not a very proud role for one of the world's rarest bird species, but fame is fame. Unfortunately, Bozo didn't get a chance to redeem herself on film; she died of unknown causes in 1928. Her skin and skeleton are in the collections of the Los Angeles County Museum of Natural History.

* * *

Since the mid-1980s, when the current captive breeding program was begun, California condors in zoos have become commonplace. For twenty years prior to that, however, only one condor was in captivity. When "Topatopa," the Matilija Canyon condor still alive in Los Angeles today (2011), was taken into captivity in February 1967 it truly was an unusual event. In the 20 years between 1946, when the last National Zoo condor died and "Topatopa's" capture, only two California condors are known to have been in captivity. Their combined incarcerations totaled less than two weeks. Both were victims of sickness or injury. One died while confined; the other, an apparent victim of strychnine poisoning, was rehabilitated at the Los Angeles Zoo and returned to the wild [48].

CHAPTER NOTES

1. Millikan, C. 1900. Capture of a condor in El Dorado Co., Cal. in 1854. *Condor* 2(1):12-13.

2. Lamson, J. 1852-1861. Manuscript diary of James Lamson, 30 October to 2 November 1854. Original at North Baker Library, California Historical Society, San Francisco.

3. Anonymous. 1857. Decidedly voracious. *Daily Union* (Sacramento, California), 24 September 1857.

4. Lawrence, R. E. 1893. *Pseudogryphus californianus. Auk* 10(3):300-301.

5. Anonymous. 1880. General notes. *Sentinel* (Indianapolis, Indiana), 27 March 1880.

6. Pages 77-124, Chapter 4, Life of Richard Gird, *in*: Bancroft, H. H. 1892. The builders of the Commonwealth, Volume III. San Francisco, California: The History Company.

7. Anonymous. 1896. (An untitled note.) *Chino Valley Champion* (Chino, California), 13 March 1896.

8. Anonymous. 1896. A California vulture story. *The Times* (New York, New York), 20 March 1896.

9. Anonymous. 1896. A bird that ate a cow. *Daily Inter Ocean* (Chicago, Illinois), 5 April 1896.

10. Anonymous. 1896. (Untitled note.) *Chino Valley Champion* (Chino, California), 27 March 1896.

11. Holmes, F. H. 1897. A pet condor. *Nidiologist* 4(6):58-59.
   Anonymous. 1901. (Untitled note on death of "Ben Butler.") *Condor* 3(3):79.

12. Cohen, D. A. 1899. Pet California condor. *Osprey* 3(5):78.

13. Anonymous. 1898. California condor as a lady's pet. Big specimen in the possession of Mrs. Frank H. Holmes of Berryessa. *Chronicle* (San Francisco, California), 20 May 1898.

14. Letter of 9 November 1898, Frank H. Holmes to C. W. Richmond. Smithsonian Institution Archives (Washington, D. C.), Record Unit 305, Folder 34469.

15. Anonymous. 1859. Adams and his museum for the East. *Daily Evening Bulletin* (San Francisco, California), 30 September 1859.

16. Pages 437-458 *in*: Benton, J. 1891. A unique story of a marvellous [*sic*] career. Life of Hon. Phineas T. Barnum. Philadelphia, Pennsylvania: Edgewood Publishing Company.

17. Anonymous. 1860. (Untitled report on Grizzly Adams' California Menagerie.) *The Star* (Los Angeles, California), 12 May 1860.

18. Pages 243-244 *in*: Hittell, T. H. 1861. The adventures of James Capen Adams, mountaineer and grizzly bear hunter of California. Boston, Massachusetts: Crosby, Nichols, Lee and Company.

19. Anonymous. 1857. Pacific Museum. *The Bulletin* (San Francisco, California), 19 March 1857.

20. Anonymous. 1859. Birds of California: No. 1, The vulture family. *Daily Alta Californian* (San Francisco, California), 2 June 1859.

21. Anonymous. 1859. Bitten by the vulture. *Daily Evening Bulletin* (San Francisco, California), 9 August 1859.

22. Anonymous. 1859. Adams and his museum for the East. *Daily Evening Bulletin* (San Francisco, California), 30 September 1859.

23. Benton 1891, *op. cit.*

24. Anonymous. 1860. Adams' California Menagerie. *Daily Evening Bulletin* (San Francisco, California), 4 December 1860.

25. Anonymous. 1860. (Untitled note, Adams' California Menagerie sailing for Cuba.) *Herald Tribune* (New York, New York), 15 October 1860.

26. Anonymous. 1861. Barnum's Museum. *Commercial Advertiser* (New York, New York), 25 January 1861.

27. Page 12 *in*: Zoological Society of Philadelphia. 1897. The twenty-fifth annual report of the Board of Director of the Zoological Society of Philadelphia. Philadelphia, Pennsylvania: Allen, Lane & Scott's Printing House.

28. Letter of 1 April 1971 from John A. Griswold (Curator of Birds, Philadelphia Zoological Garden) to Sanford R. Wilbur.

29. Rising, H. G. 1899. Capture of a California condor. *Condor* 1(2):25-26.

30. Anonymous. 1902. Soldiers Home, Los Angeles, Cal. *Ledger* (Longmont, Colorado), 16 May 1902.

31. Chambers, W. L. Handwritten manuscript on California condors, undated but probably about 1906. Willie Chambers Papers, BANC MSS 67/131c. The Bancroft Library (Berkeley, California).
    Also: Anonymous. 1903. The big condor is dead. Santa Monica (California) *Outlook,* 18 February 1903.

32. An entertaining (and probably only slightly exaggerated) account of capturing young condors is given in: Whitaker, G. B. 1918. Capturing the great American condor. *Overland Monthly* 71(5):390-392.

33. Brown, H. S. 1905. The traffic in rare birds, how they are procured for the zoological gardens. *Daily Picayune* (New Orleans, Louisiana), 23 July 1905.

34. Anonymous. 1905. A big young condor arrives at the Zoo. *The Times* (New York, New York), 17 March 1905.

35. Anonymous. 1905. After the big condor. *Morning Tribune* (San Luis Obispo, California), 12 March 1905.

36. Anonymous. 1905. That condor is our condor. Like to know how Frisco ever heard of it. *The Sun* (New York, New York), 9 April 1905.

37. "Equitable surplus" was an allusion to a headline news story of the day: the Equitable Life Insurance Society was the subject of a class action lawsuit, seeking to force the company to distribute to its shareholders surplus profits of some $80,000,000: a pretty big deal!

38. Anonymous. 1906. Condor killed by rubber diet. *Daily Times* (Seattle, Washington), 26 October 1906.

39. Finley, W. L. 1910. Life history of the California condor. Part IV, The young condor in captivity. *Condor* 12(1):5-11.

40. All the information available concerning "General" in captivity is included in Finley 1910 *op. cit.* However, Finley told the story of his condor many times in journals, magazines, and newspapers, and several of the periodical articles are noteworthy for their photographs of condors:
  Finley, W. L. 1908. Home life of the California condor. *Century* 75(3):370-380.
  Finley, W. L. 1909. General, a pet California condor. *Country Life* 16(1):35-38.
  Finley, W. L., and I. Finley. 1915. Condor as a pet. *Bird-lore* 17(5):413-419.
Information on "General's" nest life before capture is included in:
  Finley, W. L. 1906. Life history of the California condor. Part I. *Condor* 8(6):135-142.
  Finley, W. L. 1908. Life history of the California condor. Part III. *Condor* 10(2):59-65.

41. "General" is often referred to as "he," but I can find no evidence that the sex of the bird was ever known for certain.

42. Finley 1910 *op cit.*

43. There is no formal source of information on the condors' breeding activities. The records of egg-laying were pieced together from the annual reports of the U. S. National Museum, a few notes kept at the National Zoo, and one publication:
  Dixon, E. 1924. California condors breed in captivity. *Condor* 26(5):192.

44. Anonymous. 1926. Condor lays $750 egg in Washington Zoo; but ordinary hen gets job of hatching chick. *The Times* (New York, New York), 3 May 1926.

45. Pages 69-72, 115-120, and 281-287 *in:* Wilbur, S. R. 2004. Condor tales: what I learned in twelve years with the big birds. Gresham, Oregon: Symbios.

46. Wyman, L. E. 1924. A California condor in captivity. *Condor* 26(4):153.

164

47. Anonymous. 1926. Only one other in captivity. Seattle (Washington) *Daily Times,* 13 June 1926.

Anonymous. 1926. Rin Tin Tin, wonder dog, heads Rialto double feature program. *Jewish Chronicle* (Newark, New Jersey), 2 April 1926.

48. Borneman, J. C. 1966. Return of a condor. *Audubon Magazine* 68(3): 154-157.

Figure 9. Frank Blas McCormack, first to be paid for collecting California condors. Photo courtesy of Suzanne Pierce Taylor.

In the last two decades of the 19th century, the human assault on the California condors increased dramatically. For the 100 years prior to 1880, I found approximately 100 records of condor mortality. For 1880 to 1899, I have 167 records. Random shooting (for sport or curiosity) still ranked high as a mortality factor, accounting for about 30 per cent of the records. The major increase was in killing or capturing condors for what might be termed the collector trade: providing condors either in response to a specific request (e.g., for a zoo, public museum, or individual), or killing condors with the expectation that someone would want to buy them. Contracts from public institutions were still relatively uncommon (accounting for less than 10 per cent of the records during this period); killing on speculation had become the greatest source of mortality (40 per cent of the total) [1].

Before 1880, most mortalities involving condors were individual events. (A person shot a condor for sport, but he did not often shoot a second one. Someone collected a condor for a museum, but seldom collected more than one. A museum requested a condor specimen, but usually not more than one or two.) Exceptions to this were Alexander Taylor, who acted as agent for John Gurney to acquire a number of condors in the 1850s (Chapter 8), and Colbert Canfield, who located condors (both alive and dead) for several institutions in the 1860s (Chapter 10). No one had a similar role in the 1870s. In the 1880s and 1890s, three types developed: hunters who specialized in killing or capturing condors; people who acted as agents between the hunters and the collectors who wanted condors; and collectors who wanted to acquire more than one or two condor specimens for themselves.

* * *

Henry Wetherbee Henshaw (1850-1930) traveled throughout California in 1875 as a member of the Wheeler Survey, collecting natural history information. He returned to California and Oregon a number of times with the Bureau of American Ethnology, pursuing his interests in zoology, archeology, and Indian linguistics. He had been trying to acquire a condor specimen since at least early 1883, as noted in a letter to John Bidwell (Chico, California) in April of that year [2]: *"Please accept my thanks for your efforts on my behalf. Whether successful or unsuccessful I fully appreciate your kindness. The fact that the Vulture once so common has become rare, and that it is doomed at no very distant day to complete extinction has added much to my desire to procure specimens before it is too late."* Bidwell could not obtain a specimen for him and, in his memoirs, Henshaw wrote [3]: *"One of the notable California birds I particularly desired to see was the California Condor... Though I kept a sharp look-out for the bird [in 1875], it was not until several years later (1884) that I enjoyed the sight of a live vulture. While at the San*

Antonio Mission, in what is now Monterey County, September 27, engaged on Indian work, I saw four individuals circling about high in air and a notable sight they were. Finding that they were still not uncommon in the region I hired a hunter to obtain specimens, and in a few days was gratified by the possession of three. Two of them I measured and weighed. One weighed twenty pounds, and had a spread of wing of eight feet, nine inches; the other weighed twenty-three pounds with a spread of nine feet one inch. Females are no doubt still larger. It is a pleasure to record that at this time of writing [1920] *the condor is still extant in several of its native haunts, though apparently not so numerous as when I obtained my specimens."*

Henshaw did not name his condor hunter in his memoir, but museum records show that it was Frank Blas McCormack. McCormack was born about 1861 in Santa Clara County, California, second son of Lewis McCormack and Catherine Forbes [4]. In 1871 the family had moved to the San Antonio area of southeastern Monterey County. Frank McCormack spent most of the rest of his life in that part of the county, around San Antonio and later in King City. He died in Salinas 21 May 1953, and was buried in the Pleyto Cemetery near Lake San Antonio. He had three children with his first wife, Mary Govers (who died about 1902), and two with his second wife Mary (Carbajal) Bracisco, who brought an additional two children to the family from her first marriage. Some of the McCormack descendants still live in the area.

Figure 10. Frank Blas McCormack in Monterey County "condor country," 1930. Photo courtesy of Suzanne Pierce Taylor.

The inscription on Frank McCormack's gravestone at Pleyto labels him as miner and hunter, and from censuses and voting records it is clear he spent his life in the outdoors working for local ranchers, mining, farming, and supporting his family however he could. According to Suzanne Pierce Taylor, a great-granddaughter, he became a proficient hunter in his teens, and later had a number of contracts with Bay Area markets to supply wild game. *"The season he hunted with Barney Butte until October they took a great deal of dried meat to San Jose and sold it for 15 cents a pound. They also sold about 185 hides to a San Jose tannery... Some of Frank's customers were San Francisco's finest restaurants. They paid him top prices for wild game.."* [5]. Gold excitement in the nearby Los Burros area in 1887 attracted him to mining, an activity he pursued through his lifetime in Monterey County and also in central Nevada and northern California [6].

About the time Frank McCormack was hired by Henshaw to hunt condors, he was still unmarried and employed as a laborer on a ranch at San Antonio [7]. There appears to be no record of how Henshaw came to hire him, but chances are good that it was through the agency of James Alonzo Forbes. Forbes, foster brother of Frank McCormack's mother Catherine [8], was an attorney and justice of the peace for San Antonio Township. He acted as local interpreter and translator for Henshaw in 1884 [9]. It would have been logical for Henshaw to ask Forbes for the name of a condor hunter, and for Forbes to identify his nephew Frank McCormack.

Henry Henshaw loaned two of his condor specimens to the U. S. National Museum in December 1884, *"for exhibition in the mounted collection* [10]." The third apparently was not salvageable as a skin, and Henshaw donated a part of its skeleton to the National Museum [11]. Robert Ridgway requested more specimens for the museum, and in March 1885, Frank McCormack shipped five condor skins to Washington, D. C., in care of Henshaw [12]. The five skins and the skeletal parts are still in the National Museum; the two loaned mounts were returned to Henshaw. One went into the collection of his friend, William Brewster, and is now in the Museum of Comparative Zoology (Cambridge, Massachusetts). Henshaw sold his entire bird collection to the British Museum in 1885, and the final condor went to England, and is now in the Natural History Museum at Tring.

Frank Blas McCormack was the first person known to have been hired to collect a number of condors. There appears to be no record of how much money he received for his endeavors. In the 1890s, agents selling to museums and private collectors were being paid $20 to $30 for each condor skin. The hunters probably were given only a few dollars per bird, although McCormack likely did better than that with the skins that he sent direct to the National Museum. He is not known to have killed condors after March 1885, but it is possible that some later Monterey County specimens were taken by him [13].

* * *

169

The first person known to have acted as an agent between condor hunters and those who wanted to acquire condor specimens was Frank Stephens (1849-1937). Stephens' early years were spent in New York, Illinois, and Kansas, his move to California in 1875-1876 being partially financed by collecting birds along the way for Charles E. Aiken of Colorado [14]. He lived at various locations in southern California and Arizona before settling in San Bernardino County, California, in 1881. As had been the case on his first arrival in California, the return from Arizona to California in 1881 was partially financed by bird collecting, this time for William Brewster [15].

Other than a doubtful sighting of a California condor in far southeastern Arizona in March 1881 [16], Stephens appears not to have observed condors until 1886, when he recorded them near San Bernardino in April and June [17]. His interest in condors, and his opportunity to acquire them, developed as a result of his move in 1887 to Witch Creek in the Cuyamaca Mountains of San Diego County [18]. There, between 1888 and 1890, at least five condors passed through Stephens' hands. Two more were procured by him in 1899, and it's likely he was involved with two other specimens in 1900-1901. He also had a hand in collecting and selling two condor eggs [19].

I have found no indication that Stephens personally hired condor hunters, or that he had advance orders for condor specimens that he sought to fill. It appears that his collecting and selling were opportunistic. In the 1880s, there were only about 500 residents in the Witch Creek-Santa Ysabel-Ballena area of the San Diego mountains, and it wouldn't have taken long for everyone to hear that there was a taxidermist-bird collector living there. Killing of the condors he received also seemed random and opportunistic, with no overt motive to acquire the birds for sale. Frank Boring, a carpenter living in Julian, California, shot two; a third was killed at Julian by a William Decker [20]. Jeff Swycaffer, stagecoach driver, reportedly shot one with a pistol from the moving stage [21]. Massimo Morelli, a vaquero at Santa Ysabel, captured a condor with a lasso [22], and an unidentified Indian shot another [23]. As far as I can tell, Stephens only shot one condor, one found sick or injured that he later dispatched [24]. His 1886 field notes reveal that he shot twice at condors near San Bernardino, but failed to hit either [25].

Among those to whom Frank Stephens sold condors were William Brewster (Cambridge, Massachusetts), George Frean Morcom (Los Angeles, California), and the natural history specimen dealer Charles K. Worthen (Warsaw, Illinois). The relatively short time span covered by his condor collecting activities was not unusual among agents. Condors became scarce locally, condor hunters became unavailable, or the agents moved on to other pursuits. In Stephens' case, it is probably explained by his change in emphasis from birds to mammals. He spent almost all of 1894 away from San Diego, collecting mammals throughout California [26]. Much of his time through the late 1890s was spent in pursuit of mammals, and in drafting the manuscript for the book, "California Mammals," finally published in 1906 [27]. By then, condors were scarce in San Diego County; demand for condor specimens was high, but the supply had to come from other regions.

* * *

Twelve years after Frank McCormack collected condors in Monterey County, the area figured again in organized condor hunting. The principals this time were two men from Berryessa, Santa Clara County, California: Frank Holmes and Rollo Beck.

Frank Henry Holmes (1865-1924), son of Ahira Holmes and Emily C. Foye, was born in San Francisco, where his father had served as principal of several schools and was just completing a three-year term as the first Principal of the State Normal School [28]. Ahira Holmes retired from the education profession after 25 years at schools in California and Massachusetts, then spent 10 or 15 years as a stock broker in the San Francisco Bay area [29]. The family record between 1880 and 1890 is imprecise. About 1883, the family moved to Sebastopol, Sonoma County, California, and engaged in fruit growing there for three or four years [30]. This is borne out by records of Frank Holmes' bird collecting, showing considerable activity at Sepastopol in 1884, 1885 and 1886. However, Frank Holmes was also farming at Rio Vista, Solano County, during that time period, as shown by his bird records, and by letters from him cited in agricultural publications [31]. A further examination of realty and agricultural records would likely show that the family had farming businesses in both locations concurrently. About 1886, they moved south to San Jose, where they continued to grow fruit trees. Over the next 30 years, Frank Holmes developed and operated a major orchard and fruit packing business. He married Hattie Alma Lake in September 1890, and they produced two sons, both of whom eventually pursued farming interests in Santa Clara County and also in the San Joaquin Valley [32].

Farming and fruit packing did not command all of Frank Holmes' attentions. Automobiles attracted his early interest, and he reportedly owned the second car sold in the Santa Clara Valley, a Stanley Steamer, in 1899. He gained local fame in 1900 by making the first automobile trip over the mountains between San Jose and Santa Cruz, and a few weeks later drove across Pacheco Pass to Los Banos in the San Joaquin Valley [33]. Also in 1900, he and his brother Arthur E. Holmes became the first to drive a car into Yosemite Valley, *"a trip of almost 2,000 miles without a breakdown, going in and coming back on his own wheels and with his power* [34]." His automotive interest became more practical when he became involved in the building of the Sunset car in San Francisco about 1905. The 1906 San Francisco earthquake and fire completely destroyed the Sunset plant, and in 1907 the operation was moved to San Jose, incorporating under the name Victory Motor Car Company, with Frank Holmes as president and general manager [35]. After the company was dissolved, Holmes continued selling automobiles and automotive supplies, and in 1913 became distributor of Federal trucks, just then growing popular with California farmers [36].

Frank Holmes' business successes and general renown in the Santa Clara Valley undoubtedly figured into his later involvement with California condors, but his early interest in birds dated back to his youth in Oakland. As early as May 1883, he was collecting occasional bird specimens in Berkeley, some of them in company with Theodore S. Palmer, two years younger than Holmes and then a student at the University of California [37]. Perhaps Palmer introduced him to bird collecting [38]; in any event, by 1884 Holmes was collecting regularly at Rio Vista and Sebastopol. His observations of Sebastopol birds were cited 64 times in Belding's "Land birds of the Pacific District" [39]. He also was quoted by Walter Bryant and C. A. Keeler regarding his bird and mammal observations in northern California [40]. Although not a major figure in California ornithology in the 1880s, he was obviously becoming well-known.

After moving to San Jose about 1886, Frank Holmes' interest in personally collecting birds appears to have waned, and he is only known to have collected a few birds each year after that [41]. However, his own trophies were supplemented with other stuffed birds and natural history items. A grand-daughter recalled [42] that in the Holmes house there were *"six big cases of birds... My favorites are a snowy owl and a big flamingo... There was also a polar bear rug, a grizzly bear rug, and many mounted heads of animals. My seat at the table was under a moose head..."* Holmes also maintained a menagerie of live birds which included at various times the condor "Ben Butler" [Chapter 12], a golden eagle, a bald eagle, two red-tailed hawks, a peregrine falcon, a turkey vulture, and a raven [43]. He apparently traveled in conjunction with his bird collection, as he is credited with taking a series of photographs of the stuffed birds of Harry E. Austen in Halifax, Nova Scotia [44]. He became a member of the Cooper Ornithological Club in 1894 [45], but resigned in 1902 [46]. Although he is mentioned in a number of publications, I have only found two articles written by him, a report on "Ben Butler" [47] and a record of unusual waterfowl [48].

* * *

Hired by Frank Holmes in the late 1880s to pick fruit in his Berryessa orchards was a young man named Rollo Howard Beck (1870-1950). The son of blacksmith Thomas Beck and Laura Vance, Rollo Beck was born in the Los Gatos area of Santa Clara County, and had moved with his family to Berryessa about 1876 [49]. A high school dropout, Beck reportedly became interested in birds by observing Holmes' living and stuffed collections, and was taught bird identification and taxidermy by Holmes [50]. This story is almost certainly a simplification of history, as Holmes could not have hired him before 1886, and Beck had collected at least one bird as early as June 1885 (Specimen 125326, common nighthawk, U. S. National Museum). Nevertheless, Beck and Holmes became good friends, and Beck went on to a long career studying and collecting birds. He became famous in ornithological circles for his collecting trips to the Galapagos Islands and to the South Pacific, New Guinea, and Peru [51], and infamous for shooting nine of the 11 last remaining Guadalupe Island caracaras [52].

The involvement of Holmes and Beck in the California condor specimen trade apparently started with Holmes' acquisition of "Ben Butler" in 1896. There is no specific record of how "Ben Butler" was acquired, but likely the bird was taken from its nest by a young man living in Monterey County's Big Sur area. Henry Hopken, son of Henry and Johanna Hopken, was born about 1880, probably in Germany, before his family immigrated to the United States in 1882. In July 1898, Rollo Beck had written to William Brewster in regard to Henry Hopken, that Beck *"had camped at his place in Monterey Co. two or three seasons"* [53]. One might speculate that on one of these visits Beck had mentioned that Holmes might like a live condor for his aviary. In any event, Hopken and Holmes did meet, and eventually Hopken supplied him with six condor specimens. Their condor collecting relationship might have continued beyond those half dozen birds, but in June 1898 Hopken was shot to death in San Jose. The shooter, a Milpitas, California, constable (who was later shown to have been inebriated, and so was convicted of manslaughter) suspected Hopken of stealing his coat and coach whip, and pursued and killed him. Hopken was shown to be innocent of any crime; in fact, Frank Holmes had played an indirect role in the incident. According to coroner Lincoln Cothran, Hopken *"came to San Jose a few days ago. He had a unique occupation. He captured condors and eagles which he sold to societies and people who are interested in these rare birds. He brought two condors and an eagle to this city when he arrived a few days ago and sold them to Frank Holmes, an orchardist near Berryessa. He traded the birds for a horse, and it was intention to ride home today by way of Santa Cruz."* Hopken had been with Cothran less than half an hour before the shooting, when Hopken *"started to walk to Mr. Holmes' place, which is about six miles from town."* That was when he was killed [54].

Holmes' acquisition, and subsequent selling, of California condors was probably purely opportunistic: he found a source of condors, and found a buyer. He had placed an ad in the June 1898 *Osprey*, offering two condor skins for sale [55], and eventually sold five skins to the U. S. National Museum [56]. Other than the trade of condor skins for a horse, I don't know what Hopken was paid for his specimens. Holmes sold two to the National Museum for $25 each, and two for $20 each. The fifth, an inferior skin, was given to the museum for free. I haven't been able to determine if the National Museum sale was in response to the *Osprey* advertisement, or a separate transaction, but only one of the Hopken birds was not included in the sale to the National Museum. The sixth Hopken bird was sold by Rollo Beck to William Brewster (see below).

Frank Holmes was an avid hunter, particularly of waterfowl [57], and also participated in shooting tournaments [58], but he probably never shot a condor [59]. Apparently, he did not keep a condor specimen for his personal collection; at least, none were included with the mounted specimens that were presented after his death to San Jose State College, and subsequently transferred to the nature center at nearby Alum Rock Park [60].

* * *

Rollo Beck's earliest interest in California condors seems to have been in condor eggs, not skins. In 1894, he corresponded with Charles Bendire at the U. S. National Museum regarding the worth of condor eggs [61], and in 1895 discussed with Harry Taylor (in New York City at the time) the possibilities of finding condor eggs [62]. He made an unsuccessful trip into the Monterey County mountains in April 1895 [63], and was still expressing eagerness to acquire an egg in April 1899 [64]. His hopes were apparently realized in 1900, because he was offering to sell two condor eggs to Georg Girtanner (St. Gallen, Switzerland) late that year. Girtanner did not buy them, and I haven't determined what eventually happened to them [65].

Whereas Frank Holmes' trafficking in condor specimens was relatively passive, Rollo Beck actively sought out condor hunters and condor purchasers. In April 1898, Beck offered two of the Hopken birds to William Brewster. Brewster accepted the offer, but something delayed the shipment [66]. During the delay, Beck hired a second condor hunter who eventually supplied him with six or more condors (probably as many as ten). That man, Simon Castro (1851-ca 1923), spent his life in the Jolon area of Monterey County, and was a neighbor and distant relative by marriage of Frank Blas McCormack: Simon's wife, Sarah Govers, was aunt to McCormack's wife, Maria Govers [67]. Simon's occupation at various times was blacksmith, vaquero, farmer, and rancher. I don't know how Beck first contacted Castro, possibly on Beck's April 1895 egg hunting trip to Monterey County. By early June 1898, Castro was on the job, as he wrote to Beck [68]: *"I write a few lines to let you know that I start today to get them birds for you and I will send them as soon as I can. I don't know how many I am going to send. I am going to send as many as I can, and when I send them please let me know right away how many more you want."*

Castro was able to immediately shoot one condor for Beck, and Beck sent this adult male to Brewster in lieu of the earlier proffered birds, promising to send more as they were obtained [69]. Within a week, Castro had collected two more condors. These specimens were in poor condition, apparently because Beck had not given adequate instruction on how to preserve them. Castro wrote [70]: *"I am sorry to know that the birds were in bad condition. When I killed them I boxed them as quick as possible. I think that the insides should be taken out. I could take them out if you just tell me how, and send me something to put inside so the birds will not spoil... the insides should be taken out for the reason that the Station* [Jolon, where Castro lived] *is about 60 miles from the place where I kill them, and it takes a few hours to get them there."* However, the skins were salvageable and they were sent to Brewster, along with one of the Hopken birds that had been offered in April [71]. Brewster accepted them, but commented that *"the skins are not up to the one you sent before"* [72].

Several California condors were killed in Monterey County in the fall of 1898. These specimens still exist in various museums. It seems likely that most of them were Castro-Beck birds, because no one else is known to have been working in the area during that period. However, the next condor that can with certainty be attributed to them was not taken until January 1899. On 3 January, Simon Castro wrote [73]: *"I start today to get some birds for you. I have been occupied in other work, that is the reason I could not send before. I can go now and kill some. They are coming now almost every day. I have seen a few. Please let me know how many birds you want right away and how long you can wait for them."* In the next year, Castro killed at least four condors for Beck. They were offered to William Brewster, but he was no longer interested, and Beck distributed them to other buyers.

As is the case with other condor hunters, I haven't found any records that show how much Beck paid Simon Castro for the birds he shot. Beck received $25 each for most of the birds he sold, with a high payment of $30 for one adult and $18 for a young bird in "poor plumage."

After 1900, only a few condors are known to have been killed in Monterey County, and sightings of condors there also decreased dramatically [74]. Rollo Beck's activities took him away from condor habitat, and no agent worked that area after him. Emphasis on condors shifted south, where condors were easier to find.

* * *

The first of the "condor people" of the 20th century was Arthur Wilcox. The son of Horace H. Wilcox and Olivia Richardson, he was born in Denton County, Texas, in October 1860, in what turned out to be a brief detour for his family between Henderson County, Illinois, and Butler County, Kansas [75]. If the stories are true, his father - an outspoken Unionist in the opening days of the Civil War - quickly wore out his welcome in Texas, and barely escaped into Kansas ahead of the mobs [76]. In Kansas, Horace Wilcox ran a reported 1,000 head of cattle on the ranges of Butler and Chase counties, an operation in which Arthur Wilcox undoubtedly participated as he grew older.

On 1 November 1881, Arthur married Lillian Heckenlively, daughter of Jacob and Eliza Heckenlively of Chase County, Kansas. Arthur's and Lillian's names do not appear in the 1885 and 1890 Kansas state censuses, so presumably they moved out of state within a few years of their marriage. They were in San Luis Obispo County, California, by January 1888, when a son,

Vincey Arthur Wilcox, was born. Apparently, they moved several times within the county, but dates and places are uncertain. By June 1900 they were living at Arroyo Grande, and Arthur was raising livestock as his father had before him [77].

Most individuals involved with California condors in the 19th and early 20th centuries had a particular interest or specialty. Frank McCormack and Simon Castro hunted condors for the money, but apparently had no other ties to the species. Rollo Beck, although an ornithologist, seemed to have no particular interest in condors beyond buying and selling them. Frank Holmes was principally a middleman between specimen procurers and collectors, but keeping "Ben Butler" and other birds in captivity seems to imply an interest beyond the mere monetary. E. B. Towne (Chapter 14) amassed condor specimens for himself, but apparently made no attempt to share information about them with anyone else. Arthur Wilcox was a little different breed, acting at various times as condor hunter, field agent for a biological supply house, middleman between hunter and collector, and sharer of condor information in print.

I've found nothing in the record that sheds light on how Arthur's interest in California condors developed. He had seen the live condor captured by Austin Hampton and Charles Taylor in early May 1896 [78], that was still alive in Arroyo Grande in June 1897 [79]. He probably read in the local newspaper that David Starr Jordan had written to Hampton about the bird, telling Hampton how rare and valuable it was. He may have been inspired by the editor's comment that *"it would take a big sack of coin to buy the bird from Hampton now"* [80]. In any event, in August 1900 Wilcox killed four California condors, two of which went immediately to the Field Museum of Natural History (Chicago, Illinois) and two to the Milwaukee (Wisconsin) Public Museum.

In 1903, Wilcox wrote [81]: *"Some years ago the Field Columbia Museum asked for a couple of specimens, and as the price was fairly remunerative I outfitted with spring wagon and pack mules, hired a companion and started to secure the specimens."* As Wilcox was unknown to condor collectors before 1900, and as there seems to have been no one in the region that might have given his name to a museum, one wonders how the Field Museum *"asked for"* the condors. Actually, from the paperwork still in existence, it appears that Wilcox killed the condors on speculation, then offered them to the Field Museum [82]. Correspondence in the archives of the Milwaukee Public Museum supports the idea that Wilcox approached both museums after he had the specimens in hand [83]. One wonders how a cattleman from a small community in central California made his decision who to contact to offer his specimens. Even more intriguing than the sales to Chicago and Milwaukee are the 1902 transactions with museums in Sofia, Bulgaria, and Copenhagen,

Denmark, not the most obvious European museums for him to have contacted [84].

Between 1900 and 1905, Arthur Wilcox was involved in acquiring at least seven (and probably nine) condors by shooting, three live condors, and two condor eggs. He personally shot the six condors noted above, and purchased one from the boys who had shot it [85]. Of the living birds, he wrote that he was present when one was taken from its nest [86], but apparently he had no role in its ultimate delivery to the U. S. National Zoo. As described in Chapter 12, he acted as Charles K. Worthen's field agent in procuring the Bronx Zoo's first condor, but he was not involved in its capture. He sent a young condor to John E. Thayer (Lancaster, Massachusetts) in 1903, but his role in acquiring it is nowhere stated. Accompanying a photograph of a well-grown immature condor, he wrote [87]: *"The bird shown here was captured when very young and is very gentle; he eats heartily and seems well satisfied with his surroundings. He has been sold to a gentleman at Lancaster, Mass., and will be in his new home by the time these lines are in print."*

Although museum records show Arthur Wilcox as the collector of the two condor eggs that were in his possession, one was actually collected near Santa Barbara by William Gallaher, Arthur Ogilvy and William Edwards. Wilcox bought the egg from them for $45 [88]. Wilcox wrote about the second egg as if he had been present when it was taken, and photos of the egg and nest site were taken by Wilmot D. Wood, another Arroyo Grande resident, so Wilcox may have been present [89].

About 1905, the Wilcoxes moved from Arroyo Grande a short distance south to Santa Maria, where they opened a meat market. Although they were still living in condor habitat - actually, closer to where Arthur had shot most of his condors - his involvement with condors ended. Perhaps this was because his occupation now kept him mostly indoors. In any event, his ten years in Santa Maria and another 15 years in the San Joaquin Valley at Modesto went by without any known contact with condors. He died 23 May 1932, following the amputation of a leg, made necessary when he developed blood poisoning [90].

Among the condor collectors of the late 19th century and early 20th century, Frank Holmes and Arthur Wilcox were the only ones to publish articles on their condor activities. Holmes had shown an ongoing interest in birds for many years and, although not a very active publisher of his observations, was well known among California ornithologists. Wilcox, on the other hand, seems to have had no particular interest in birds other than the condor, and I've never seen his name associated with the collecting of any other species. Yet, he joined the Cooper Ornithological Society in 1908 and maintained his membership through 1912. Perhaps there is more to be learned about his wildlife interests.

CHAPTER NOTES

1. Judging the reasons condors were killed was not always easy, due to inadequate data or because assigning "motive" is often subjective. In general, if the record merely noted that someone shot a condor and measured its wingspan, I interpreted that as a random shooting for sport or curiosity. If a condor went more or less directly from the shooter to a private collector or institution, I considered that a planned ("on spec") mortality. No doubt some random shootings became opportunistic sales; some I considered as planned may more correctly be in this category.

2. Letter of 16 April 1883 from H. W. Henshaw (Washington, D. C.) to John Bidwell (Chico, California). Special Collections, Meriam Library, California State University, Chico, California.

3. Henshaw, H. W. 1920. Autobiographical notes (continued). *Condor* 22(1):7-10.

4. The birth date for Frank McCormack given in the compiled California death records is 3 February 1863, and 1863 is inscribed on his gravestone at Pleyto, California. His obituary notice (in the Salinas *"Californian,"* 21 May 1953) noted that *"he did not know his exact age as his birth record was destroyed in a fire at the old Santa Clara mission."* I haven't been able to find his family in the 1860 Federal census, but his age as given in the 1870 and 1880 censuses indicates he was born ca 1860. The 1900 census, the only one to give month and year of birth, showed him born in March 1862. Perhaps the most authoritative date is that used by McCormack himself, 19 March 1861, which he used when filling out his 1931 California Indian Census application. [Information supplied to me by his great-granddaughter Suzanne Taylor 17 March 2011.]

5. Page 147 *in*: Taylor, S. P. 2006. The ancestors speak, the remarkable story of an early California Indian family...from ancient times to the present. San Luis Obispo, California: privately printed.

6. Taylor *op. cit.*, pages 148 and 163.

7. U. S. Federal census, 20 June 1880: San Antonio township, Monterey County, California.

8. Catherine (Forbes) McCormack, wife of Lewis McCormack, was an orphaned Miwok Indian from the Sacramento area, adopted in 1838 by James Alexander and Anna Galindo Forbes (Taylor *op. cit.,* pages 115-116).

9. Page 66 *in:* Mason, J. A. 1912. The ethnology of the Salinan Indians. *University of California Publications in American Archeology and Ethnology* 10(4):97-240.

10. Page 402 *in* the Annual Report of the Board of Regents of the Smithsonian Institution for the year ending 30 June 1884. Also, U. S. National Museum accession 15484, 20 December 1884 (Smithsonian Archives, Record Unit 305).

11. U. S. National Museum accession 15757, 27 February 1885 (Smithsonian Archives, Record Unit 305).

12. U. S. National Museum accessions 15766 (2 March 1885) and 15810 (13 March 1885), Smithsonian Archives Record Unit 305.

13. On 18 June 1889, Simon Castro (Jolon, California) wrote to Rollo Beck, asking Beck to send money for the condor skin recently sent to him. *"I got a man to kill it for you, and he wants his money very bad."* (Letter in the Rollo and Ida Beck Collection, California Academy of Sciences, San Francisco.) Castro and McCormack lived near one another, and Castro's wife was aunt to McCormack's wife, so McCormack could logically have been that man.

14. Stephens, F. 1918. Frank Stephens--an autobiography. *Condor* 20(5):164-166.

15. Brewster, W. 1882. On a collection of birds lately made by Mr. F. Stephens in Arizona. *Bulletin of the Nuttall Ornithological Club* 7(2):65-86.

16. Brewster, W. 1883. On a collection of birds lately made by Mr. F. Stephens in Arizona (continued). *Bulletin of the Nuttall Ornithological Club* 8(1):21-36.

17. Frank Stephens field notes, 1886. Box 42, California Academy of Sciences archives (San Francisco, California): one condor near Banning, Riverside County, 22 April 1886; 7-15 June 1886, Bear Valley, San Bernardino County, four sightings, largest group included four condors.

18. Frank Stephens autobiography, *op. cit.*

19. Letter of 21 October 1902 from R. P. Sharples to W. Lee Chambers (Chambers Collection, Bancroft Library, Berkeley, California); C. D. Scott, unpublished manuscript "Looking for California condors" (Huntington Library, San Marino, California).

20. I haven't been able to locate any William Decker in San Diego County between 1880 and 1900. Frank Boring, carpenter living in Julian in 1897, is almost certainly the correct Boring (Directory of San Diego city and county 1897, The Olmsted Co. Printers). He may be the Frank G. Boring in San Diego at the time of the 1900 census: born May 1863 in Massachusetts, single, a machinist.

21. Jefferson D. Swycaffer (1861-1952) lived most of his life in San Diego County, at various times being employed as rancher, stagecoach driver, saloon keeper, hotel owner, and butcher shop operator.

22. Stephens, F. 1899. Lassoing a California vulture. *Bulletin of the Cooper Ornithological Club* 1(5):88.

23. Gilman, M. F. 1907. Measuring a condor. *Condor* 9(4):106-108. Also: Sharp, C. S. 1918. Concerning a condor. *Oologist* 35(1):8-11.

24. Interview notes 6 November 1940: Carl B. Koford interviewing Frank Stephens' widow, Kate Stephens, in San Diego. California condor species accounts, Museum of Vertebrate Zoology (Berkeley, California).

25. Frank Stephens field notes, *op. cit.* California Academy of Sciences archives (San Francisco).

26. Huey, L. M. 1938. Frank Stephens, pioneer. *Condor* 43(3):101-110.

27. Frank Stephens autobiography, *op. cit.*

28. Pages 108-109 *in*: Anonymous. 1889. Historical sketch of the State Normal School at San Jose, California, with a catalogue of the graduates and a record of their work for twenty-seven years (1862-1889). Sacramento, California: State Printing Office.
   The State Normal School operated in San Francisco from 1862 to 1871, when it was moved to San Jose. It was the forerunner of today's San Jose State University.

29. Ahira Holmes' occupation given as stock broker in the Federal censuses for 1870 (San Francisco, California) and 1880 (Oakland, California).

30. Anonymous. 1902. Pioneer educator dies at his San Jose home. Ahira Holmes, principal of the first State Normal School passes away. San Francisco (California) *Call*, 31 December 1902.

31. Barrows, W. B. 1889. The food of crows. Pages 498-535 *in*: Report of the Commissioner of Agriculture, 1888. Washington, D. C.: Government Printing Office. F. H. Holmes of Rio Vista, California, is quoted on pages 506 and 512 regarding crow food habits and damage to crops. The quotes appear to be from 1886.
   Beal, F. E. L. 1907. Birds of California in relation to the fruit industry. Washington, D. C.: Government Printing Office. On pages 15-16, a September 1886 letter from F. H. Holmes (Rio Vista, California) discussed damage to crops done by house finches.
   Sawyer, E. T. 1922. History of Santa Clara County, California: with biographical sketches of the leading men and women of the county who have been identified with its growth and development from the early days to the present. Los Angeles, California: Historic Record Company. On pages 1107-1108, in a biographical sketch of Frank H. Holmes: *"Going to Rio Vista to farm when a boy... In 1886, he moved to San Jose to farm his uncle's ranch which consisted of 160 acres which he developed to prunes and apricots."*

32. Sawyer, History of Santa Clara County, *op cit.*

33. Anonymous. 1900. Took trip with auto. Santa Clara County enthusiast makes record. *Evening News* (San Jose, California), 28 July 1900.

34. Anonymous. 1900. A notable demonstration of serviceability. *The Horseless Age* 6(26):22 (26 September 1900).
Also, page 208 *in*: Farquhar, F. H. 1965. History of the Sierra Nevada. Berkeley, California: University of California Press.

35. Anonymous. 1907. Auto engine made in San Jose works is a marvel of precision. *Mercury News* (San Jose, California), 9 March 1907.
Anonymous. 1909. Sunset car possesses desirable features. *Mercury News* (San Jose, California), 14 February 1909.

36. Anonymous. 1913. Federal truck agency established in City. Frank Holmes has been named as distributor for this section. *Mercury News* (San Jose, California), 23 March 1913.

37. Palmer, T. S. 1921. Notes on some birds of the Berkeley campus. *Condor* 23(4):163-164.

38. With the strong education background of the Holmes family in the Bay Area, one would suspect that Frank Holmes received some kind of higher education, but I haven't found any record of it. Nothing in his family background would seem to have promoted an interest in natural history. His father and uncle were early members of the California Academy of Sciences, but apparently only because of their educational and societal interests in the community.

39. Belding, L. 1890. Land birds of the Pacific District. *Occasional Papers of the California Academy of Sciences*, 2:1-274.

40. Bryant, W. E. 1891. A provisional list of the land mammals of California. *Zoe* 1(12):353-360.
Keeler, C. A. 1891. The geographical distribution of land birds in California. *Zoe* 1(12):369-373.

41. This is based on the dates of specimens he collected that are currently locatable in various museums.

42. Ryon, B. 2006. Betty and the birds. *Livermore Roots Tracer* (Livermore-Amador Genealogical Society), Volume 26, Number 3.

43. Anonymous. 1898. California condor as a lady's pet. Big specimen in the possession of Mrs. Frank Holmes of Berryessa. *Chronicle* (San Francisco, California), 20 May 1898.
Cohen, D. A. 1899. Pet California condor. *Osprey* 3(5):78.

44. The display cases of Austen's birds are shown and described in *Recreation Magazine* in 1896: 4(2):59; 4(3):112; 4(5):220; 5(3):128; and 5(4):224.

45. Anonymous. 1894. Cooper Ornithological Club. *Nidiologist* 2(4):56-57.

46. Barlow, C. 1902. Official minutes, Northern Division. *Condor* 4(4):100.

47. Holmes, F. H. 1897. A pet condor. *Nidiologist* 4(6):58-59.

48. Holmes, F. H. 1899. The old-squaw and fulvous tree ducks at Alviso, Cal. *Bulletin of the Cooper Ornithological Club* 1(3):51.

49. Some biographical notes on Rollo Beck report his family moved from Los Gatos to Berryessa about 1882, but it is clear from the 1870 and 1880 Federal censuses, and from notes accompanying the Rollo Beck archives at the California Academy of Sciences, that the move was made well before 1880.

50. Palmer, T. S. 1951. Obituary: Rollo Howard Beck. *Auk* 68(2):260. Also: Albee, W. E. 1917. R. H. Beck returns from bird expedition. *Mercury News* (San Jose, California), 2 December 1917.

51. Palmer 1951, *op. cit.* Also: Barlow, C. 1899. Prominent Californian ornithologists. II. Rollo H. Beck. *Bulletin of the Cooper Ornithological Club* 1(5):77-79.

52. Abbott, C. G. 1933. Closing history of the Guadalupe caracara. *Condor* 35(1):10-14.

53. Letter of 1 July 1898, Rollo Beck (Berryessa, California) to William Brewster (Cambridge, Massachusetts). William Brewster Collection, Museum of Comparative Zoology archives, Ernst Mayr Library, Harvard University.

54. Anonymous. 1898. A catcher of eagles is killed by an officer. San Jose (California) *Evening News,* 29 June 1898. Additional stories in the *Evening News* of 29 June 1898 ("A Hardy Boy"), 30 June 1898 ("Staid with his victim. Matthews remains while aid is called," and 1 July 1898 ("Crazed by grief, Henry Hopken's father is insane").

55. "California Condor--A fine pair of fresh skins of this species for sale, or would take part payment in desirable rare skins." Advertisement section, *Osprey* 2(10), June 1898.

56. Letter from F. H. Holmes (Berryessa, California) to C. W. Richmond (Smithsonian, Washington, D. C.), 9 November 1898. Smithsonian Institution Archives, Reference Services: Record Unit 305, Accession Folder 34469.

57. Typical of stories occurring regularly in the San Jose *Evening News:* Frank Holmes and party killed 180 geese in two days at Rio Vista, California ("Sportsmen in luck," 14 April 1905); Holmes among locals going to Firebaugh, California, for opening of waterfowl season ("Hunters ready for coming duck season," 30 September 1910); and Holmes killed limit of ducks at Alviso, California, on opening day ("Hunters get limit bag quickly," 14 October 1916).

58. Anonymous. 1895. Ready for the shoot. *Evening News* (San Jose, California), 23 April 1895.

59. Frank Holmes had two California condors in his possession that were reportedly killed in May 1905. These were in the Leonard Cutler Sanford collection, and are now in the American Museum of Natural History. It is unlikely that Holmes shot the birds, but I have found no record of how he acquired them.

60. Ryon 2006 *op. cit.*

61. Letters of 18 August 1894 and 2 September 1894, Charles Bendire (U. S. National Museum, Washington, D. C.) to Rollo H. Beck (Berryessa, California). Rollo Howard and Ida Menzies Beck Papers - Box 1, Folder 7. California Academy of Sciences archives, San Francisco.

62. Letter of 11 March 1895, H. R. Taylor (New York, New York) to Rollo H. Beck (Berryessa, California). Rollo Howard and Ida Menzies Beck Papers - Box 1, Folder 9. California Academy of Sciences archives, San Francisco.

63. Letter of 3 May 1895, Charles Bendire (U. S. National Museum, Washington, D. C.) to Rollo H. Beck (Berryessa, California). Rollo Howard and Ida Menzies Beck Papers - Box 1, Folder 9. California Academy of Sciences archives, San Francisco.

64. Letter of 23 April 1899, Simon Castro (Jolon, California) to Rollo H. Beck (Berryessa, California). Rollo Howard and Ida Menzies Beck Papers - Box 3, Folder 4. California Academy of Sciences archives, San Francisco.

65. Letters of 11 December 1900, 14 January 1901, July 1901, 9 August 1901 and 29 January 1902 from Georg Girtanner (St. Gallen, Switzerland) to Rollo H. Beck (Berryessa, California). Rollo Howard and Ida Menzies Beck Papers - Box 3, Folder 5; Box 4, Folders 2 and 3. California Academy of Sciences archives, San Francisco.

66. Letters of 16 April 1898 and 5 May 1898, Rollo Beck (Berryessa, California) to William Brewster (Cambridge, Massachusetts). William Brewster Collection, Museum of Comparative Zoology archives, Ernst Mayr Library, Harvard University.

67. Taylor 2006 *op. cit.*, pages 149-150.

68. Letter of 7 June 1898, Simon Castro (Jolon, California) to Rollo H. Beck (Berryessa, California). Rollo Howard and Ida Menzies Beck Papers - Box 2, Folder 5. California Academy of Sciences archives, San Francisco.

69. Letter of 10 June 1898, Rollo Beck (Berryessa, California) to William Brewster (Cambridge, Massachusetts). William Brewster Collection, Museum of Comparative Zoology archives, Ernst Mayr Library, Harvard University.

70. Letter of 27 June 1898, Simon Castro (Jolon, California) to Rollo H. Beck (Berryessa, California). Rollo Howard and Ida Menzies Beck Papers - Box 2, Folder 5. California Academy of Sciences archives, San Francisco.

71. Letter of 1 July 1898, Rollo Beck (Berryessa, California) to William Brewster (Cambridge, Massachusetts). William Brewster Collection, Museum of Comparative Zoology archives, Ernst Mayr Library, Harvard University.

72. 69. Letter of 20 August 1898, Walter Deane (Cambridge, Massachusetts) to Rollo H. Beck (Berryessa, California). Rollo Howard and Ida Menzies Beck Papers - Box 3, Folder 1. California Academy of Sciences archives, San Francisco.

73. Letter of 3 January 1899, Simon Castro (Jolon, California) to Rollo H. Beck (Berryessa, California). Rollo Howard and Ida Menzies Beck Papers - Box 3, Folder 3. California Academy of Sciences archives, San Francisco.

74. Pages 13 and 141 *in*: Koford, C. B. 1953. The California condor. National Audubon Society, Research Report Number 4. New York, New York.

75. According to the 1850 Federal census, the Wilcox family had been at Terre Haute, Henderson County, Illinois, since at least 1848. The 1860 Federal census of Denton County, Texas (1 July 1860), showed daughter Mary O. Wilcox, age 2, as born in Illinois. Family records show her birth date as 18 March 1858. Therefore, the family had been in Texas probably no more than two years when Arthur was born.

76. Mooney, V. P. 1916. History of Butler County, Kansas. Lawrence, Kansas: Standard Publishing Company. Several dates are given for the Wilcox arrival in Butler County: summer 1861 (pp. 367-370), 1866 (p. 369), and autumn 1867 (pp. 331-332). If the story is true that their move to Kansas was precipitated by Civil War animosity in Texas, then the 1861 date is most likely.

77. U. S. Federal census, 8 June 1900: Arroyo Grande, San Luis Obispo County, California.

78. Page 44 *in:* Tognazzini, W. N. 1995. 100 years ago, 1896: Excerpts from the San Luis Obispo *Morning Tribune* and *Breeze*. San Luis Obispo, California: self-published.

79. Page 55 *in:* Tognazzini, W. N. 1996. 100 years ago, 1897: Excerpts from the San Luis Obispo *Morning Tribune*. San Luis Obispo, California: self-published.

80. Tognazzini 1995 *op. cit.,* page 49.

81. Wilcox, A. 1903. The California vulture. *Western Field* 2(4):217-219.

82. Armand Esai (Archivist, Chicago Field Museum) found a memo dated 11 October 1900 from C. B. Cory (Department of Ornithology) to Museum Director F. J. V. Skiff: *"I return also, a letter from Arthur Wilcox offering to sell vulture skins. I have written that we would purchase two specimens, if satisfactory after examination, and to forward the same to the Field Columbian Museum, price to be $25 each."* Wilcox's letter could not be found.

83. Susan Otto, Librarian at the Milwaukee (Wisconsin) Public Museum, found five letters from 1900 and 1901, with some details of the purchase of California condors from Arthur Wilcox. Wilcox clearly made the first contact, offering to sell up to four condors to the Museum for $25 each (20 August 1900). Before the Milwaukee museum responded, Wilcox notified them that two of the specimens had been sold to the Chicago Field Museum (19 September 1900). The Milwaukee Public Museum purchased the remaining two on 24 September 1900.

84. It's possible that Arthur Wilcox did not deal directly with the European museums, but sold through a middleman. For one condor sale in 1904 he acted as an "agent" for Charles K. Worthen's biological supply house. No other references to cooperation between Wilcox and Worthen have been found, so far.

85. Page 121 *in:* Tognazzini, W. N. 2000. 100 years ago: January 1, 1901 to December 31, 1901, from the San Luis Obispo *Morning Tribune* and the Arroyo Grande *Herald.* San Luis Obispo, California: privately published.

86. Wilcox 1903 *op. cit.*

87. Wilcox 1903, *op. cit.*

88. Notice in Santa Barbara, California, *Morning Press,* 30 March 1902; also reported by C. B. Koford in interview notes with Arthur Ogilvy, 25 October 1940 (Carl B. Koford condor species accounts, Museum of Vertebrate Zoology, Berkeley, California).

89. Wilcox 1903 *op. cit.;* also: Wilcox, A. 1901. California vulture. *American Ornithology* 1(9):164-168.

90. Anonymous. 1932. Blood poisoning results in death of Arthur Wilcox. *News-Herald* (Modesto, California), 24 May 1932.

Figure 11. Edward B. Towne and son with part of his collection of California condors, circa 1901, Newton, Massachusetts. Photo from Mark Decius.

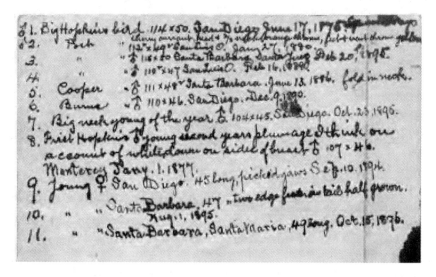

Figure 12. Backside of California condor photo above, with collection details. Photo courtesy of Mark Decius.

CHAPTER 14
KING OF THE CONDOR COLLECTORS

Even if you're read almost every book, magazine article, or newspaper item ever written about the California condor, you may not remember seeing the name of E. B. Towne. If you've looked for condor information in museums, the story will be different. In museum records of condors, his name seems to be everywhere. With at least 21 condor skins and one condor egg to his credit - most of them in his possession simultaneously - he ranks at the top among possessors of condor specimens. Even today, after many private collections have been consolidated in the larger museums, only three institutions can claim a larger total collection of California condor skins, mounts, skeletons and eggs than E. B. Towne had: Harvard's Museum of Comparative Zoology, the Natural History Museum of Los Angeles County, and the U. S. National Museum.

Edward Bancroft Towne, son of Ebenezer Bancroft Towne and Chloe Adaline (Braman) Gilmore, was born in Raynham, Bristol County, Massachusetts, 20 July 1857 [1]. He often identified himself as E. B. Towne Jr., even though he was not technically a "junior." According to one source, this was a family convenience to separate him from a local cousin who was also E. B. Towne [2].

Towne spent his youth in Raynham, and presumably attended schools there. I found no indication that he had any higher education. By 1877 he was living in Nashua, Hillsborough County, New Hampshire, employed as a clerk at the Nashua Bedding Company, operated by his uncle Cleon D. Towne [3]. He married in Nashua 4 October 1882 Emma Grace Stark, daughter of George Stark and Mary Grace Bowers [4], and they moved soon after to West Newton, Middlesex County, Massachusetts. While living at West Newton, Towne worked as a furrier in the Boston establishment of Lamson and Hubbard [5].

I have found nothing in the literature or in family records that describes how E. B. Towne became interested in birds. My speculation is that he was introduced to bird study by ornithologist William Brewster, who between 1870 and 1874 was studying terns on Muskeget Island (Nantucket County, Massachusetts) [6]. Towne's first bird collecting appears to have been in June and July 1874, when at the age of 16 he visited Muskeget and brought back six specimens [7]. It is possible (likely?) that Brewster recruited the local teen to help him with his work. Supporting this speculation is that also on the island with Brewster was Jesse Warren, from West Newton (Middlesex County), Massachusetts and just eight months older than Edward Towne. Towne and Warren became good friends, and from September 1874 into June 1875 all Towne's known bird collecting was in western Middlesex County, a region he is not known to have frequented previously [8]. In May 1875, he found at

Weston what may have been the last known passenger pigeon nest in the county [9]. That same month, at Newton, he collected the nest and eggs of a golden-winged warbler, one of three found that year at Newton, the first ones found in Massachusetts since 1869. Jesse Warren documented this find, including quoting from Towne's field notes [10].

In July and August 1875, Towne was once again on Muskeget with Brewster, Warren, and another birding friend from West Newton, Winchester W. Eager. They collected specimens of what was thought to be a new species of tern, "*Sterna Portlandica,*" later shown to be Arctic terns in immature plumage [11]. Towne collected a few birds around Bristol County in summer and fall 1875, and in February 1876 he, Warren, and Eager were all elected to membership in the Nuttall Ornithological Club of Cambridge, Massachusetts. William Brewster was then President of the Club [12].

Between October 1875 and July 1892, I find no records of Towne collecting any birds, although in 1877 he won a number of prizes for his fancy domestic pigeons and American Plymouth Rock chickens [13]. During those 15 years he had gone to work in New Hampshire, got married, moved back to Massachusetts, started a career in Boston, and conceived four children. Even if he had the inclination to hunt birds, his time was undoubtedly limited. His lack of ornithological activity may also have been tied to the departure from the area of his two birding friends, Jesse Warren to New York State in 1877 and Winchester Eager to Minnesota in 1880 [14].

Something rekindled Towne's interest in birds, and in 1892 and 1893 he collected in a desultory way around Middlesex County. All the specimens I know of from that period were hawks and owls. This may be the period in which he became excited about California condors, and it may be that condors were the reason that, at some time in 1894, he moved with his family to San Diego, California. In March 1897, he wrote to William Brewster from Santa Cruz, California [15]:

"As it is probable we shall go East in the Fall, I dislike to leave the state without killing a Cal. Vulture, and although I have been hunting for this bird for more than two years all the way from the northern part of Mexico, having spent a year in San Diego Co., and been on several extended camping trips where we have killed deer and other animals to bait them, having been assured before outfitting that we would surely get Vultures, I have yet to see a living bird."

The Townes were in California from 1894 until late 1897 or early 1898. As noted in the above letter to Brewster, they were in the San Diego area for a year, then moved north to Santa Cruz. Towne made at least one (and probably a second) trip to Massachusetts in 1895, to pursue a lawsuit against the city of Newton, Massachusetts, for building a highway across his West Newton property [16]. Towne apparently did not have paid employment during the time they lived in California. The three boys attended school, but otherwise it appears Edward and his sons spent most of their California time collecting birds. The oldest son, E. B. Towne Jr., wrote to William Brewster that in three years *"my Father, two brothers and myself collected several thousand birds in California."* In the same letter, he wrote: *"My Father went from Santa Barbara over the Coast range by way of San Marcos toll road into the Santa Ynez valley hunting a Calif. Condor that had been seen by a prospector a few days previous"* [17]. (This probably occurred in summer 1895.) Towne Sr. had written to Brewster earlier [18]: *"My boys and I have rowed hundreds of miles I should think during the last few months to get within gun shot of these birds* [shearwaters]." While living in San Diego, he had made a trip to the Coronados Islands off northern Baja California, Mexico [19]. Once the family moved to Santa Cruz, it appears that most of his collecting was done in the Monterey Bay area. He provided William Brewster with about 20 specimens (mostly seabirds), for which he received in trade about 35 bird skins from Arizona, Texas and northern Mexico [20]. Otherwise, I can find no record of him selling or trading any of the Towne family acquisitions.

Figure 13. Edward B. Towne and sons with what was probably the only California condor Towne killed personally, 1897. Photo from Mark Decius.

The family returned to Massachusetts, but not before Edward finally saw and killed a California condor, in San Luis Obispo County 6 June 1897. How and when he acquired his other 20 birds is a curious mystery. In his letter to

Brewster in March 1897 [15], describing his failure to collect a condor, Towne noted that he had met *"a prospector who has had many years experience and acquaintance in the sheep and cattle raising counties of [the] state who tells me he knows where there are still a few birds over toward Death Valley in San Bernardino Co. and assures me he will get a pair or more skins for me if I will grub stake him for sixty days and furnish pack animals."* Towne planned to make this last attempt, but *"as they are so big and bulky I wish to keep but one skin."* This could mean that he didn't want to carry more than one condor back to Massachusetts with him, but he went on: *"As you have the only specimens I have seen in a private collection I write to ask you your opinion of their value, which I know nothing of except that while collecting with A. W. Anthony two years ago he told me of the British Museum having purchased a skin at a large price."* It is difficult for me to read this passage without concluding that, as of March 1897, E. B. Towne did not have any California condors in his own collection. Yet, a photograph taken at Towne's home in West Newton, Massachusetts, before October 1900 shows Towne and two of his sons posing with 14 condor skins [21]. At least 18 of the 21 condor specimens owned by Towne have collection dates earlier than March 1897; had any of them come into his possession prior to that date, he certainly would have known something about the purchase price and value of a condor skin!

By 1902, Towne had 20 condors. Could he have acquired all of those in just a five year period? It's possible; I know of about 15 condors that were undoubtedly collected during the time period of Towne's specimens (1875-1900), which don't have specific information on where and when they were killed. There were undoubtedly others. But how did Towne locate them? The logical way would have been to inquire at the various biological supply houses, and in fact three were advertising California condors for sale between 1897 and 1901: Charles K. Worthen (Warsaw, Illinois) [22], Walter F. Webb (Albion, New York) [23], and James P. Babbitt (Taunton, Massachusetts) [24]. In 1903, Towne did purchase from Worthen what was probably his final condor skin [25]. I haven't found any advertisements placed by Towne or any correspondence between Towne and biological supply dealers that would positively link them in any other transactions [26]. However, an 1892 letter sent from Charles Worthen to specimen collector Manly Hardy seems like a clue: *"I am told that 'a party' is buying or offering to buy every one* (condor) *that is taken, at a heavy cash price, & will hold all at $100.00 each!! I do not doubt that he will get it if he can afford the loss of use of money for a few years"* [27]. If this refers to Towne - and there is no one else that fits those facts - he must have been seeking specimens for five years before he finally acquired one

Despite the mystery of the origins of Towne's condors, their history beginning in 1900 is well documented, and all but one are identifiable in collections today. On 1 January 1900, Towne wrote to William Brewster:

190

"Expect to take my family back to California to remain permanently, and my collection of skins is so bulky that I am going to dispose of a lot of stuff principally Cal. bird skins" [28]. In a letter to the Smithsonian Institution in September 1900, he elaborated on his personal situation and his plans for part of his bird collection: *"As it is necessary for me to take my family back to California on account of ill health, I wish to loan a series of Calif. Condor skins to some institution where they will be safe. These are good skins, and some of the specimens exceptionally large, as I have devoted much time to this species for many years"* [29]. The Smithsonian agreed to accept the loan, and on 13 October 1900, Towne wrote: *"I ship you today by freight, a case containing eleven Condor skins, an egg and two sternums of exceptionally large birds"* [30].

Robert Ridgway, Curator of Birds at the Smithsonian, acknowledged receipt of the condors 15 November 1900, and asked permission to publish measurements of the birds to compare with measurements he had of Andean condor specimens. He also asked if Towne was interested in selling any or all of the skins, and wondered if Towne had a skin that could be mounted for display at the Pan-American Exposition in Buffalo, New York, in May 1901 [31]. Towne gave Ridgway permission to publish measurements of his specimens, but declined to sell any of the eleven [32]. He did offer to send Ridgway another skin that could be mounted for the Exposition, an offer that Ridgway accepted [33]. When the skin arrived, it was found not to be as good as one the Smithsonian already had on hand, and it was put in storage with Towne's other specimens [34].

Edward Towne and his family moved to California in 1901, and settled in Palo Alto, Santa Clara County. I find no record of him disposing of any specimens before he left Massachusetts (as he had told Brewster was his intention), so he probably took over 1,000 bird skins with him. Additionally, he wrote to Outram Bangs in 1904, *"I have a large collection of sea bird skins stored in my stable at West Newton"* [35]. I haven't located those specimens in any existing collections; they may never have been salvaged.

Among the specimens moved from Massachusetts to California were at least three California condor skins. Five more either moved with him, or were acquired in California after he arrived there. In mid-September 1902, Towne asked the Smithsonian to send six of the condors they were holding for him to the museum at Stanford University (Stanford, California). The skins, plus some condor bones and two drawings Towne had made of condors, were shipped to Stanford in November 1902 [36]. Four months later, Towne asked the Smithsonian to dispose of the rest of his condors, as follows [37]:

"(I) ask you to ship the remaining six skins and egg as per directions below, and wish to say that I am quite willing to pay you for the trouble of shipping. I have ordered sent to you from C. K. Worthen, one Condor skin by express, prepaid. I also send by express, prepaid, a bundle containing four flat Condor

191

skins. When they arrive you will have six made up skins, five flat skins and an egg, which I would like to have you ship as follows - six made up skins to Walter Rothschild, Tring, England, by freight. Five flat skins to Mr. Cullingford, The Museum, Durham, England, by freight, and the egg to Dr. Ernst Hartert, Zoological Museum, Tring Herts, England, by express."

These actions were carried out by the Smithsonian. Probably about the same time as the above transaction, Towne traded one condor to Joseph and John W. Mailliard (San Francisco, California) [38]. That left him with the six condor skins, bones, and drawings on loan to Stanford University, and two skins and a mounted bird retained in his personal collection.

Edward Towne had kept his membership in the Nuttall Ornithological Club until near the time he moved from Massachusetts [39], and in September 1901 he and his son George Towne were elected to membership in the Cooper Ornithological Society [40]. However, and probably due to his worsening medical condition, Edward resigned from the Society just six months later, in March 1902 [41]. He died in Palo Alto 5 February 1905, of a long-term cancer of the skull [42].

In 1907 or early 1908, Towne's widow Emma donated his *"collection of 1260 bird skins"* to the Stanford University Museum [43]. This gift did not include the condor specimens, although there may have been some confusion about that. When Emma Towne offered four of the Stanford condors to the Museum of Vertebrate Zoology in 1912, Joseph Grinnell wrote to John Mailliard [44] that *"there may be a little explaining to do; for I happen to know that the Stanford people believed they owned the Towne series years ago!"* At some point, the three condors left in the Towne personal collection were loaned to John Mailliard. In 1911, Joseph Grinnell learned of these specimens and offered to buy one of them for $25.00 for the "State Museum" (Museum of Vertebrate Zoology). Instead, in May 1912, Mailliard arranged to transfer all three specimens to Berkeley on a loan basis [45].

As noted above, in November 1912, Emma Towne offered four of the Stanford condors to the Museum of Vertebrate Zoology. She wrote to Joseph Grinnell [46]: *"There are six such skins at the Department of Zoology Stanford University. This may be taken as authorization to secure four of these. The remaining two are to remain at Stanford and I would like to have you and Dr. C. H. Gilbert decide the disposition of the individual specimens."* At the same time, she gave the Museum one of the condor skins loaned earlier that year, and instructed Grinnell to give the other two loaned specimens to John Mailliard. Despite Grinnell's concerns that there might be some problems with Stanford, that transfer was made without controversy. At Mailliard's request, the Museum of Vertebrate Zoology retained custody of his two condors until August 1916, when he asked that they be sent to the California Academy of Sciences in San Francisco. That transfer was completed 16 August 1916 [47]. The final two condors from Stanford University arrived at the California

192

Academy of Sciences, along with some of Towne's other bird specimens, when Stanford closed down their natural history museum in May 1964.

Meanwhile, in England, all eleven of the condor skins sent to Joseph Cullingford and Walter Rothschild in 1903 became part of the Rothschild collection [48]. One was sold to W. F. H. Rosenberg, a London dealer in natural history specimens, and was subsequently purchased in 1908 by the Swedish Museum of Natural History (Stockholm) [49]. Three were acquired by the Natural History Museum-Tring (then, British Museum of Natural History), one in 1915 and two in 1939 [50]. Six came to the American Museum of Natural History (New York, New York) when the Rothschild Collection was sold to them in 1932 [51]. The eleventh specimen is not currently identifiable in any collection.

* * *

Despite the good information Edward B. Towne preserved concerning the California condor specimens he acquired, his actual involvement with condors remains mysterious. In a 13 September 1900 letter to the Smithsonian Institution [28], Towne wrote: *"I have devoted much time to this species for many years."* But what does that mean? His 1897 letter to William Brewster suggests to me that the family move to California in 1894 may have come about at least in part because he wanted to collect a condor. If not the actual reason, then perhaps being in "condor country" provided the impetus for his apparent later fascination with condors. I have found nothing he wrote prior to 1897 that mentioned condors, and at that time it appears he had neither seen nor collected one. In 1900, he gave permission to Robert Ridgway to publish measurements of his condor specimens, but never published anything, himself. We know from his youthful collecting in Massachusetts that he sometimes kept field notes, but apparently none have survived, and we don't know if any mentioned condors. Except for the condor specimens themselves and the collection data accompanying them, all we have to show Edward B. Towne's involvement with California condors are a few letters, a few photographs, and two colored drawings

CHAPTER NOTES

1. Massachusetts Vital Records, Volume 105 (1857), page 180.

2. Pages 721-722 *in*: Hurd, D. H. 1883. History of Bristol County, Massachusetts, with biographical sketches of many of its pioneers and prominent men. Philadelphia, Pennsylvania: J. W. Lewis and Co.

3. Page 122 *in*: Greenough's directory of... the city of Nashua for 1879-80. Boston, Massachusetts: Greenough & Co.

4. Anonymous. 1882. Wedding announcement, Towne-Stark. *Daily Telegraph* (Nashua, New Hampshire), 5 October 1882.

5. Edward B. Towne's father, Ebenezer Towne, was a Boston merchant whose business (for many years, under several partnerships) was selling hats, caps, buffalo robes, furs, and straw goods. Ill health forced Ebenezer to retire by 1870, but Edward's familiarity with his father's business undoubtedly influenced his choice of career as furrier when Lamson and Hubbard was incorporated in Boston in 1882.

6. Brewster, W. 1879. The terns of the New England coast. *Bulletin of the Nuttall Ornithological Club* 4(1): 13-22.

7. These specimens - four laughing gulls, one Bonaparte's gull, and one short-eared owl - are now in the collection of the California Academy of Sciences (San Francisco). The Academy has three other specimens from this early period that were acquired with the Towne Collection and that list Towne as the collector: goshawk (Montreal, Quebec, November 1873), razor-billed auk (Grand Manan, New Brunswick, June 1874), and sharp-tailed sparrow (probably Maine, July 1874). Towne, like some other early acquirers of bird specimens, sometimes listed himself as the original procurer, when actually he received the bird from someone else. He may have collected these, but times and places make them questionable, I think.

8. In the Towne Collection now at the California Academy of Sciences there are ten bird specimens, all from the Newton, Massachusetts area.

9. Page 178 *in*: Brewster, W. 1906. The birds of the Cambridge region of Massachusetts. Memoirs of the Nuttall Ornithological Club, Number 4. Cambridge, Massachusetts.

10. Warren, J. 1876. Nesting of the golden-winged warbler (*Helminthophaga chrysoptera*) in Massachusetts. *Quarterly Bulletin of the Nuttall Ornithological Club* 1(1):6-8.

11. Brewster, W. 1876. Some additional light on the so-called "*Sterna Portlandica*," Ridgway. *Annals of the Lyceum of Natural History of New York* 11:201-207.

12. Anonymous. 1899. A list of the officers and members present and past of the Nuttall Ornithological Club of Cambridge. Cambridge, Massachusetts: Nuttall Ornithological Club.

13. Anonymous (1877). "Fifth annual exhibition of the Massachusetts Poultry Association. *The Pet-stock, Pigeon and Poultry Bulletin* 7(11):218-221.
    Anonymous. 1877. The poultry exhibition--some of the premiums awarded. *Daily Citizen* (Lowell, Massachusetts), 19 December 1877.

14. Anonymous 1899, *op. cit.*

15. Letter from E. B. Towne (East Santa Cruz, California) to William Brewster

194

(Cambridge, Massachusetts), 11 March 1897. William Brewster Collection, Museum of Comparative Zoology archives, Ernst Mayr Library, Harvard University.

16. Anonymous. 1894. Newton Boulevard. A long hearing given yesterday. *Daily Advertiser* (Boston, Massachusetts), 20 March 1894.
Anonymous. 1896. Newton Boulevard. Court called to decide on a land assessment and betterment by Edward Towne, who says he did not sign any agreement. *The Journal* (Boston, Massachusetts), 18 January 1896.

17. Letter from E. Bancroft Towne (West Newton, Massachusetts) to William Brewster (Cambridge, Massachusetts), 30 March 1900. William Brewster Collection, Museum of Comparative Zoology archives, Ernst Mayr Library, Harvard University.

18. Letter from E. B. Towne (North Raynham, Massachusetts) to William Brewster (Cambridge, Massachusetts), 24 December 1895. William Brewster Collection, Museum of Comparative Zoology archives, Ernst Mayr Library, Harvard University.

19. Birds collected on the Coronados Islands in May 1895 are now at the California Academy of Sciences (San Francisco).

20. Letter from William Brewster (Cambridge, Massachusetts) to E. B. Towne (Santa Cruz, California, 21 January 1896, listing names and prices of bird skins traded. William Brewster Collection, Museum of Comparative Zoology archives, Ernst Mayr Library, Harvard University.

21. The photograph was sent to the Smithsonian Institution enclosed with a letter of either 13 September 1900 or 2 October 1900. Smithsonian Institution Archives (Washington, D. C.), Accession 37278.

22. Anonymous. 1897a. Note and comment. *Osprey* 1(9):123; Anonymous. 1897b. Note and comment. *Osprey* 1(11-12):149.

23. Webb, W. F. 1898. Advertisement. *The Museum* 4(12):178.

24. Babbitt, J. P. 1901. Advertisement: California condor skin for sale. *American Ornithology* 1(9):157.

25. Letter of 9 March 1903 from E. B. Towne (Palo Alto, California) to C. W. Richmond (Smithsonian Institution, Washington, D. C.). Natural History Museum Archives (London, United Kingdom), Reference TM1/70. Thanks to Robert Prys-Jones and Alison Harding (Natural History Museum, Tring, U. K.) for finding this correspondence.

26. Richard Peek, Director of the Department of Rare Books and Special Collections, Rush Rhees Library (University of Rochester, Rochester, New York) kindly searched the voluminous files of the Henry A. Ward and Wards Natural Science Establishment archives for me, but could find no references to E. B. Towne.

27. Letter of 16 February 1892, Charles K. Worthen (Warsaw, Illinois) to Manly Hardy (Brewer, Maine). Original is in the Ralph S. Palmer Collection, Raymond H. Folger Library, University of Maine (Orono, Maine).

28. Letter from E. B. Towne (West Newton, Massachusetts) to William Brewster (Cambridge, Massachusetts), 1 January 1900. William Brewster Collection, Museum of Comparative Zoology archives, Ernst Mayr Library, Harvard University.

29. Letter from E. B. Towne (West Newton, Massachusetts) to the Smithsonian Institution (Washington, D. C.), 13 September 1900. Smithsonian Institution Archives, U. S. National Museum accession file 37278.

30. Letter from E. B. Towne (West Newton, Massachusetts) to R. Rathbun, Smithsonian Institution (Washington, D. C.), 13 October 1900. Smithsonian Institution Archives, U. S. National Museum accession file 37278.

31. Letter from R. Ridgway (Curator of Birds, Smithsonian Institution, Washington, D. C.), 15 November 1900, to E. B. Towne (West Newton, Massachusetts). Smithsonian Institution archives, RU 105, Box 6, Folder 4 (Volume XXI, pp. 317-318).

32. I haven't found Towne's letter to Ridgway, but Ridgway acknowledged its contents in a return letter of 3 December 1900. Smithsonian Institution archives, RU 105, Box 6, Folder 4 (Volume XXI, pp. 334-335).Towne apparently said that he didn't wish to sell any of his eleven condors but, if he did, he would want $25 apiece. Ridgway replied that, had Towne wanted to sell, the Smithsonian would not have purchased at that price, as they had recently acquired five good skins at $10 apiece.

33. By letter of 26 December 1900 Ridgway acknowledged and accepted Towne's offer of an additional condor skin to be mounted for the Buffalo Exposition: Smithsonian Institution archives, RU 105, Box 6, Folder 4 (Volume XXI, p. 343). I have not found Towne's actual offer but, from later correspondence, he apparently proposed to send the Smithsonian an adult condor for mounting, if the mount was returned to him after the Exposition.

34. Letter from R. Ridgway (Curator of Birds, Smithsonian Institution, Washington, D. C.), 21 January 1901, to E. B. Towne (West Newton, Massachusetts). Smithsonian Institution archives, RU 105, Box 6, Folder 4 (Volume XXI, pp. 363-364).

35. Letter from E. B. Towne (Palo Alto, California) to Outram Bangs (Cambridge, Massachusetts), 7 June 1904. Correspondence archives, Museum of Comparative Zoology archives, Ernst Mayr Library, Harvard University.

36. I haven't found Towne's September 1902 letter, but it was acknowledged as written "yesterday" (19 September) from New York City in the 18 September 1902 response from Charles W. Richmond [Smithsonian Institution archives, RU 105, Box 7, Folder 3 (Volume XXXIII, p. 151)]. The specimens were sent to Stanford University 18 November 1902, as noted in the Smithsonian files for Accession 37278.

37. Letter of 9 March 1903 from E. B. Towne (Palo Alto, California) to C. W. Richmond (Smithsonian Institution, Washington, D. C.). Natural History Museum Archives (London, United Kingdom), Reference TM1/70. It would be fascinating to know how Towne made the arrangements to send (and presumably, sell) his condors to England, but so far no paperwork has been located.

38. I haven't discovered any correspondence concerning this trade, but the condor appears on an undated Mailliard specimen exchange list. Joseph and John W. Mailliard Collections, Box 24, ledger. California Academy of Sciences Archives (San Francisco, California).

39. Anonymous. 1899. A list of the officers and members present and past of the Nuttall Ornithological Club of Cambridge. Cambridge, Massachusetts: Nuttall Ornithological Club

40. Barlow, C. 1901. Official minutes of Northern Division. *Condor* 3(5):136.

41. Anonymous. 1902. Official minutes, Northern Division. *Condor* 4(2):52.

42. Cause of E. B. Towne's death was provided to me by a descendant, Mark Decius, who had a copy of the official death certificate. A brief death notice appeared in the Palo Alto (California) *Times,* 9 February 1905.

43. Anonymous. 1908. Fifth annual report of the President of the University for the year ending 31 July 1908. Stanford, California: Stanford University.

44. Letter of 18 November 1912 from Joseph Grinnell (Museum of Vertebrate Zoology) to John W. Mailliard (San Francisco, California). Letter Archives, Museum of Vertebrate Zoology, University of California, Berkeley.

45. I haven't found all the correspondence relating to this transfer, but the main features can be gleaned from a series of letters in the Archives at the Museum of Vertebrate Zoology: Joseph Grinnell to John W. Mailliard 29 November 1911; Grinnell to Mailliard 29 January 1912; Mailliard to Grinnell 10 April 1912; Mailliard to Grinnell 18 April 1912; and Grinnell to Mailliard 11 May 1912.

46. Letters (2) of 14 November 1912 from Emma G. Towne (Palo Alto, California) to Joseph Grinnell (Museum of Vertebrate Zoology). Letter Archives, Museum of Vertebrate Zoology, University of California, Berkeley.

47. The transfer of the Stanford condors and those loaned by Mrs. Towne in May 1912 are covered in letters in the archives of the Museum of Vertebrate Zoology: Joseph Grinnell to John Mailliard 18 November 1912; Grinnell to Emma Towne 7 December 1912; Grinnell to Mailliard 7 December 1912; Mailliard to Grinnell 18 December 1912; Mailliard to Grinnell 3 August 1916; Grinnell to Mailliard 4 August 1916; and receipt from John Carlson (California Academy of Sciences) to Grinnell 16 August 1916.

48. Probably it had always been intended that all eleven condors were to go to Rothschild, the prepared skins direct to Rothschild and the "flat skins" to Cullingford for final preparation. Joseph Cullingford, a highly respected taxidermist, retired from the Durham University Library in 1905.

49. Information on the condor purchased by the Swedish Museum of Natural History was furnished to me by Goran Frisk of the Museum.

50. Pages 51-53 *in*: Knox, A. G., and M. P. Walters. 1994. Extinct and endangered birds in the collections of the Natural History Museum. London, United Kingdom: The British Ornithologists' Club.

51. A good summary of the Rothschild transfer is: Anonymous. 1935. The Rothschild Collection of birds at the American Museum of Natural History. *Science*, New Series, 81(2097):247-248.

CHAPTER 15
STOCKING THE MUSEUMS

I received some criticism for my 1978 analysis of condor mortality factors, in which I stated that *"I found evidence of 177 condors killed... for additions to collections"* [1]. This was read by some to mean that I was saying all these specimens were collected for "scientific" or other public museum purposes. To the extent that I didn't further explain my terminology, the criticism was deserved.

Two questions were raised by my initial analysis: (1) were all 177 condors taken specifically to sell or give to collections, or were some opportunistic (*i.e.*, were all the condors killed specifically to go to collectors, or were some condors that were initially shot for sport, found sick or injured, etc., later offered for sale?); and (2) how many specimens went to museums with educational or scientific objectives, and how many went into the collections of individuals? Philosophically, this makes a difference because - in contrast to collections made for what might be labeled "public benefit" - many private collectors were gathering up bird skins in the same way one might accumulate coins or stamps, or a modern-day birder might build the largest possible "life list" of species seen.

If the purpose is to fix blame for condor deaths, then clearly public museums were not responsible for the killing of many of the condors now found in their collections. For example, a condor shot in San Diego County in 1888 was sold to an agent for a biological specimen dealer. The dealer sold the condor to a private collector in Maine. Twenty-five years later, that person's collection was purchased by the Rhode Island Audubon Society for the Providence (Rhode Island) Museum of Natural History. Another instance: the 21 condor skins that were in the private collection of Edward B. Towne (Chapter 14), originally collected by various persons between 1875 and 1900, are now in various museums in the United States and Europe. However, none of them reached their current locations before 1903. There are many similar cases in which museums eventually benefitted from the earlier killing of condors, but were not directly culpable.

Also important in deciding the purpose of a condor killing are the definitions of "museum" and "scientific purposes." William Brewster, a private collector but also a noted ornithologist, had at least eight condor specimens, all but one purchased by him shortly after they were killed. His collection eventually went to the Harvard Museum of Comparative Zoology but, during the 20 or more years he had the condors in his possession, he did not "study" them, nor were they available for general public viewing. Does this count as a "scientific" collection? What about the seven condors that Alexander Taylor acquired for John Gurney in England (Chapter 8)? The condors were clearly part of Gurney's personal collection, but from the start they were housed in the

Norwich Museum where they could be viewed and studied. The lines are seldom clear.

In my updated analysis, I've redefined my terms to more clearly differentiate between "hobby collecting" and acquiring specimens for "public purposes" [2]. With a larger total this time around (458 records, versus 300 in 1978), I identified 164 records that probably were of condors specifically acquired to be added to collections. Of those, about 55 (or, roughly one-third) went more or less directly to public or scientific museums. But if this lower figure seems to lessen the impacts that those in the museum community had on condor populations, some of their other actions did just the opposite.

* * *

By the 1880s, general opinion was that the California condor was much reduced in numbers and distribution, and might be approaching extinction. Robert Ridgway wrote in 1880 that the condors *"have become excessively rare in California, having been nearly, if not quite, exterminated in many parts of the State..."* [3]. In 1883, Henry Henshaw opined *"that it is doomed at no very distant day to complete extinction...* [4]. By 1887, Charles Townsend was writing that *"it has probably almost disappeared from Northern California, where it was once certainly common"* [5]. Clark Streator, evaluating the situation in 1888, noted that *"only a few years past it was found common, but now nearly extinct."* He continued: *"I have only found them in two of the counties of Southern California and from making enquiries from practical observers I cannot* [sic] *believe at the present time that the bird can be found only inside a territory of about two hundred miles square and that this limit is gradually diminishing"* [6]. Streator was too pessimistic in his view of the condors' geographical limits, but J. G. Cooper in 1890 certainly agreed with his general assessment of the species' viability. In an article entitled "A doomed bird," he wrote that *"there is no doubt that the species is in the process of extinction... it is evident that the bird is rapidly growing scarce. I can testify myself that from my first observations of it in California, in 1855, I have seen fewer every year when I have been in localities the most suitable for them. There can be little doubt that unless protected our great vulture is doomed to rapid extinction"* [7].

None of these people were qualified to speak authoritatively on the condors' status. Neither Ridgway nor Henshaw had seen a live condor at the time of their pronouncements; in fact, Ridgway had visited California only briefly in 1867, on his way to Nevada to join Clarence King's survey party [8]. Streator and Cooper had traveled extensively in California, and both had seen condors, but clearly neither was an "expert." As I've shown in previous chapters, much of what people believed about condors in the 1880s turned out to be erroneous. What is important here is what they *believed,* and how they reacted to those beliefs. Today, words like those quoted above from noted ornithologists would have been a battle cry for immediate action to save the species. Just the opposite reaction was forthcoming in the 1880s. In the same letter in which Henshaw predicted extinction *"at no very distant day,"* he confessed that this conclusion *"has added much to my desire to procure specimens before it is too late"* [9]. After making a similar pronouncement about the probable fate of the species, Ridgway *"called attention to the fact that several species of North American birds are fast becoming extinct, and has emphasized the desirability of obtaining additional specimens of these species before it is too late."* (Along with the condor, Ridgway's list of desirable collectables included six species now extinct: great auk, Labrador duck, heath hen, passenger pigeon, Carolina paroquet, and ivory-billed woodpecker!) [10]. A year after Ridgway's plea for accelerated collecting, Frederic A. Lucas (destined in three more years to become Curator at the Smithsonian Institution) seemed to offer confirmation that Ridgway's call had been heard: *"The California Vulture is now extremely rare, and in spite of many efforts to obtain specimens of this interesting bird few have been taken of late years, those few coming from southern California"* [11].

Lucas may have been right that Ridgway's urging didn't result in an immediate upswing in condor mortality - although at least 33 condors were taken by collectors between 1880 and 1891 (five specifically for the National Museum!). However, in the last eight years of the 1890s, at least 50 condors were killed for collections, by far the most taken in any decade, before or after. The next ten years accounted for another 33 specimens, most of those going directly to public institutions. After 1905, fewer were collected, partly due to the increasing difficulty of finding birds to shoot, but also because the California Fish and Game Commission was beginning to try to regulate the take [12].

To many of us today, looking back 100 years, this attempt to (using Henshaw's words) *"procure specimens before it is too late"* seems amazingly irresponsible, if not criminal. We often excuse the actions of earlier generations, assuming that - without our historical perspective - they couldn't truly understand the significance of what they were doing. In this case, they very clearly knew what they were doing. Apparently, they saw no way the condors could be saved as a species, and so felt no compunction about speeding along the extinction process.

Lack of interest in preserving condors in the wild - or at least a well-developed fatalism - is blatantly shown by the actions of several major museums between 1917 and 1924, actions that came about in the name of "education." After 1875, but more especially in the early days of the 20th century, museums were changing from mere repositories of specimens, with a few stuffed animals for public viewing, to institutions with an educational function, as well [13]. The principal new feature, apparently first adopted on a large scale by the American Museum of Natural History beginning in 1887 [14], was the "habitat group." Before then, the usual method of display was as

201

individual mounts with no information on how and where the animals lived (and sometimes, depending on the skill of the taxidermist, with little idea of what the species actually looked like!). The new groupings portrayed mounted specimens as they might appear in nature, with painted scenic backgrounds, constructed topographic features, simulated vegetation, and sometimes other species that might be found in similar habitat. The first such California condor exhibit, designed by Frederic S. Webster for the Carnegie Museum (Pittsburgh, Pennsylvania) in 1898, included two condors and several turkey vultures gathered around the carcass of an elk [15]. Later condor dioramas focused on rocky cliffs and nest caves.

This new method of presenting nature to the public fit well with the needs and plans of San Francisco's California Academy of Sciences. The 1906 earthquake and fire had destroyed the Academy's building and all but 2,000 of its specimens, including all of its California condors. A new museum was finally opened in 1916, with a key feature of the North American Hall being a series of large dioramas depicting various California animals and habitats. A condor exhibit had been constructed and the background painted before the grand opening, but it wasn't until May 1917 that the Academy acquired the specimens to go in it. That year, they sent one of their taxidermists, Joseph P. Herring, to Ventura County to acquire the needed three birds. This he accomplished with the guidance and assistance of a local rancher, Frank Arundell [16].

Figure 14. The original California condor diorama at the California Academy of Sciences (now dismantled), with condors collected in 1917.

Between 1920 and 1924, Herring and Arundell collected additional condors from the same area where they acquired the California Academy birds, one of only two areas in the entire condor range where the species could still be considered relatively common. Three condors were killed in 1920 for the Los Angeles County Museum of Natural History, another one in 1923 for the Los Angeles museum, and either four or five more in 1924 for the Denver (Colorado) Museum of Natural History. Also in 1923, Herring and Arundell took one live condor from its nest for the Selig Zoo in Los Angeles [17].

Obviously, this was not the "last straw" for the condors; Carl Koford studied them in the same area in the 1930s and 1940s, and found a small but apparently viable local population. But the museums and collectors didn't know that would be the case; in fact, the expectation was probably just the opposite. What would have happened if a similar level of killing had continued for another decade?

*   *   *

Moralizing about what happened 100 years ago is seldom a profitable use of one's time. Still, it's hard not to wonder why, with the condors' future so uncertain, museum directors would choose to kill more condors rather than trying to make use of some of the specimens already available. There were about 150 condor mounts and study skins in museums at that time. Lack of display space had led to a number of the mounts being relegated to storerooms, where they were of no value for education. Inadequate space, plus concerns that light, air and insects were causing damage, also led to many mounts being relaxed and reformatted as study skins to be used for research only. Many of those specimens had limited research value because the museums had little or no information on where and when they had been acquired. Why couldn't some of the skins of minor scientific or educational value be given a new life in the new habitat dioramas? I'm sure fresh skins were nicer to work with, but by 1915 American taxidermists had been exposed for 30 years to the restoration skills of artists like Frederic S. Webster. Before Webster, as another noted taxidermist, William T. Hornaday, described it, *"there were a score of men who could mount fresh birds exceedingly well, but with old and mummified 'dry skins' their limitations were many."* But to Webster, *"ancient bird mummies had no terrors whatever."* He could construct excellent mounts from small specimens in any condition. *"With larger skins that seemed to defy human skills, he was equally successful... Webster taught his processes to a long line of younger men, who practiced and passed them along for the remainder of their lives"* [18]. The choice to use existing condor specimens wasn't made, but it would have been possible.

*   *   *

Whatever one thinks about the killing of condors for museums at a time when it was clear that the species was in trouble, it seems legitimate to ask what value has been realized over time from having over 150 condors in

203

museums. Presumably (at least before the days of the World Wide Web, with its thousands of photos and stories of California condors), having mounted condors on display increased public understanding of the species and helped build some environmental awareness. Unfortunately, few of the mounted condors were displayed in a way that would attract attention and leave a definite memory. Still fewer had any interpretive story connected to the exhibit to explain the condors' plight. The research value of the specimens has also been minimal. From the original description of Archibald Menzies' condor in 1797 [19] through the 1970s, I found fewer than 25 published papers (out of a total of nearly 2,000 references) that present information gained by examining condor specimens in museums. Almost all the studies were morphological: investigations of such features as the size and shape of bones, placement of feathers, structure of the wing, and the relative size of males and females. Usually the information derived was compared to that of other species, with attempts made to define taxonomic links. Almost nothing gained from museum studies would have been helpful in heading off the decline of the California condor population.

As I wrote in Chapter 7, I think the number of condors killed for sport or out of curiosity was far greater than the written record indicates. In contrast, the numbers I've identified as killed for collections may be close to actual. Most of those specimens are still in existence, and (despite adding almost 150 new mortality records, overall) my estimate of condors killed for collections changed only slightly between 1978 and the present. Did the collecting of perhaps 200 condors over 200 years have a significant impact? Considering the times and places of collecting, and the nature of the species, I think it did.

CHAPTER NOTES

1. Page 20 *in:* Wilbur, S. R. 1978. The California condor, 1966-1976: a look at its past and future. North American Fauna Number 72. Washington, D. C.: U. S. Fish and Wildlife Service.

2. The rationale I used for identifying each type of condor mortality is discussed in Chapter 25.

3. Ridgway, R. 1880. Notes on the American vultures (Sarcorhamphidae), with special reference to their generic nomenclature. *Bulletin of the Nuttall Ornithological Club* 5(2):77-84.

4. Henshaw, H. 1883. Letter of 16 April 1883 to John Bidwell (Chico, California) regarding collecting California condors. John Bidwell Papers, Merriam Library Special Collections, California State University-Chico.

5. Page 201 *in:* Townsend, C. H. 1887. Field-notes on the mammals, birds and reptiles of northern California. *Proceedings of the U. S. National Museum* 10:159-241.

6. Streator, C. P. 1888. Notes on the California condor. *Ornithologist and Oologist* 13(2):30.

7. Cooper, J. G. 1890. A doomed bird. *Zoe* 1(8):248-249.

8. Harris, H. 1928. Robert Ridgway. *Condor* 30(1):4-118.

9. Henshaw 1883 *op. cit.*

10. Page 32 *in:* Goode, G. B. 1890. Report upon the condition and progress of the U. S. National Museum during the year ending June 30, 1888. Washington, D. C: Government Printing Office.

11. Lucas, F. A. 1891. Animals recently extinct or threatened with extermination, as represented in the collections of the United States National Museum. Pages 606-649 *in:* Annual report of the U. S. National Museum, 1889. Washington, D. C.: Government Printing Office. [California condor on pages 629-631]

12. Beginning about 1910, the California Fish and Game Commission began issuing permits for collecting birds and mammals in the State. In the annual permits issued to institutions, the taking of California condors and a few other species was prohibited. (Examples of these early permits [1911-1916] are in the archives of the Museum of Vertebrate Zoology.) However, it was still possible to obtain permits from the Commission for collecting condors or their eggs in specific instances.

13. Evermann, B. W. 1918. Modern natural history museums and their relation to public education. *The Scientific Monthly* 6(1):5-36. Using G. B. Goode's description of the evolution of the U. S. National Museum as an example, Evermann identified three periods of museum history: before 1857, when the museum was viewed as a collection of materials for research; from 1857 to 1876, in which research was still an important reason to amass specimens, but some efforts were made to display specimens for the public to see; and beginning in 1876, when a definite role of the museum as an educational institution began to be realized. The timing varied from museum to museum, and country to country, but the timeline holds, generally.

14. Allen, J. A. 1909. The habitat groups of North American birds in the American Museum of Natural History. *Auk* 26(2):165-174.

15. The Carnegie Museum diorama exists today in essentially its original form. It and some other early habitat groups are described and pictured in: Hornaday, W. T. 1925. Masterpieces of American bird taxidermy. *Scribner's Magazine* 78(3):261-273. The American Museum of Natural History completed its condor exhibit in 1909; next to be opened was at the Field Museum of Natural History (Chicago, Illinois) in 1911.

16. Evermann, B. W. 1917. Report of the Director of the Museum for the year 1917. *Proceedings of the California Academy of Sciences,* Fourth Series, 7:331-346. Joseph Herring's field notes of collecting the condors were copied with Herring's permission by Carl Koford on 7 November 1940. They are preserved as part of Koford's California condor species accounts at the Museum of Vertebrate Zoology (Berkeley, California).

17. The collecting activities of Joseph Herring and Frank Arundell were pieced together from museum specimen records, Carl Koford notes, and news articles. The taking of the Selig Park Zoo was documented in: Wyman, L. E. 1924. A California condor in captivity. *Condor* 26(4):153.

18. Hornaday *op. cit.,* pages 262-263.

19. Shaw, G., and F. P. Nodder. 1797. Vivarium naturae, or Naturalist's Miscellany. Ninth volume. London, England: Nodder and Company.

"FOR SALE.--Fine specimen of the Cal. Condor's egg with data, taken this year. Best cash offer accepted. Egg guaranteed genuine. WILLIS GRIFFITH, Santa Barbara, Calif." [1].

"CALIFORNIA CONDOR EGG for sale. A perfect egg of the California Condor, taken on the 7th of March this year, which we offer for sale at a reasonable figure, cash or installments, to suit purchaser. The price will be furnished to those who think of purchasing. WALTER F. WEBB, Mgr., Albion, N. Y." [2].

"[Wanted:] *eggs in first class sets with data for cash or will exchange extra fine sets with bonus. $150.00 in sets from my Oological collection for a Condor's egg. Dr. M. T. Cleckley, 457 Greene St., Augusta, Georgia"* [3].

In the late 19th and early 20th centuries, advertisements like the above appeared regularly in magazines with names like *The Oölogist, Ornithologist and Oölogist, The Oologists' Record, The Nidologist,* and *The Museum.* Oölogy, the study of birds' eggs, had become a major hobby. Like stamp collecting, acquiring autographs, or (in more recent years) keeping a "life list" of birds observed, the acquisition of eggs became an end in itself. The hobbyists were often wealthy, a desirable attribute when seeking particularly rare eggs or trying to finish up a series (eggs of all the birds breeding in a state, or in the United States, for example). Some private collections grew to tremendous sizes. By far the largest was apparently that accumulated over many years by Joseph Parker Norris, continued after his death by his son. When J. P. Norris Jr. died in 1931, it included over 100,000 eggs [4]. Another hobbyist, Richard Magoon Barnes, eventually donated 39,317 eggs to the Field Museum in Chicago [5], with lesser numbers going to other museums. John Lewis Childs, who in 1901 had a modest 400 sets of eggs, added 30,000 eggs bought from Jean Bell, which she had accumulated on her own and through purchase from others [6]. Childs did not amass eggs, but only wanted one or two sets from each United States species. He took what he wanted from the Bell collection, and sold the rest to Chauncey W. Crandall, bringing the Crandall holdings to *"not less than 50,000 eggs"* [7].

Although hardly a "science" in its early form, oölogy soon attracted serious students. Combining the characteristics of the eggs themselves (size, shape, coloration) with nest construction, nest location, and overall habitat at the nest site, the study of bird nesting became one more source of information for classifying birds and learning their life histories. An early scholar was Thomas Mayo Brewer (1814-1880), medical doctor by training who by 1856 was curator of oölogy for the Boston Society of Natural History. The Smithsonian Institution published Part I of Brewer's "North American Oölogy," subtitled "an account of the habits and geographical distribution of the birds of North America during their breeding season; with figures and descriptions of their eggs" [8]. Unfortunately, the other parts were never published, reportedly because the color plates were too expensive to produce [9].

Charles Emil Bendire (1836-1897), after 30 years in the field combining military duties and wildlife study, in 1883 was appointed "honorary" curator of oölogy for the U. S. National Museum. "Honorary" in his case meant that the position was unfunded, but he held it until his death, and made major strides building up the National Museum egg collection. After Bendire, egg curators became more common, often "honorary" and often curating their own collections which they had loaned or donated to the museums where they worked.

* * *

As might be expected, a California condor egg was much sought after by collectors. Early on, however, they didn't know what they were seeking. In the 1850s, David Douglas' 1827 description of eggs and nesting habitat - information he obtained *"from Etienne Lucien, one of the hunters who has had ample opportunity of observing them"* - was still in vogue:

"They build their nests in the thickest part of the forest, invariably choosing the most secret and impenetrable situations and build on a pine-tree a nest of dead sticks and grass; have only two young at a time; egg very large (fully larger than a goose-egg), nearly a perfect circle and of a uniform jet black. The period of incubation is not exactly known; most likely the same as the eagle. They have young in pairs" [10].

Brewer found Douglas' description unlikely on many counts [11]: *"David Douglas, in the Zoological Journal, speaks of the eggs of this Vulture as nearly spherical, jet-black, and about the size of those of a Goose. Following this authority, all writers who have referred to the eggs of the Californian Vulture have described them in a similar manner. That they should be spherical would be an exceptional case to the whole genus, and is therefore hardly probable, though by no means impossible. Markings of a jet-black color, even to the extent of blotches, spots, or lines, are of very rare occurrence, if not positively unknown. Nor am I aware that any of this family of Vultures ever construct nests. For these reasons, and until the statements of Mr. Douglas can be confirmed by other testimony, I am inclined to discredit his accounts of its nest, eggs, and habits, in every respect. In this unbelief I am in part confirmed by the testimony of Mr. Townsend. He was informed, as he tells us, by the Indians of the Columbia River, that the Californian Vulture, like all others of its genus, breeds on the ground, fixing the place for a nest in swamps, under the pine forests, chiefly in the alpine country, in this conforming with the habits of the family."*

Relying on Townsend's hearsay information didn't help clarify the condors' nesting habits, nor did his replacement of Douglas' egg description with another erroneous one:

"But one instance of the possession of a well-authenticated egg of this species by a naturalist has come to my knowledge. This was one laid in confinement by a female belonging to the Garden of Plants in Paris. An accurate drawing of this was taken by Dr. James Trudeau, and is now in my possession... This egg measured 3 14/16 inches in length by 2 13/16 in its greatest breadth. Its ground color is that of all the known eggs of this genus, a rich cream-color, or a yellowish-white. A ring of reddish-brown confluent blotches surrounds the larger end, leaving the residue nearly free from markings. A few blotches of a smaller size and lighter color are distributed over the whole surface."

It has never been determined what species was responsible for that *"well authenticated egg,"* but it was shown that a California condor egg had no blotches and was considerably larger. No live California condors reached Europe before 1866 (Chapter 10).

* * *

The first certain California condor egg was collected in 1859 [12], when Alexander Taylor obtained one from a Monterey County rancher. Taylor sent this egg to his friend John Gurney in England, so few Americans had a chance to see it. Taylor published a detailed description of the egg [13]:

"The entire egg weighed ten and a-half ounces, and the contents eight and three-quarter ounces. The color of the egg-shell is what painters can 'dead, dull white;' the surface of the shell is not glossy, but slightly roughened, as in the sea-pelican's eggs, but not so much. The figure is nearly a perfect ellipse, being a model of form and shape in itself. It measured four and a half inches in length by two and three-eight inches in breadth (diameter), and was eight and three-quarter inches in circumference around the middle. The egg-shell, after the contents were emptied, (which were as clear, fine, bright and inodorous as those of a hen's egg, with a bright, yellow yolk) held as much as nine fluid ounces of water."

"The egg is a little smaller at one end than the other--in fine, an egg of elegant shape and form. The egg shell is about three times the thickness of a turkey's egg."

Egg collectors now knew what their quarry looked like, but Taylor's description of the nest site left considerable doubt as to where to look for such an egg:

"There was, properly speaking, no nest; but the egg was laid in the hollow of a tall old robles-oak, in a steep barranca [ravine], near the summit of one of the highest peaks..."

A condor nest in a oak tree was not questioned at the time, because there was no other information available. After additional eggs were found, the location was generally discounted. Because Alexander Taylor received the information second-hand, and because Taylor often got his "facts" wrong, or embellished what he was told, some doubt is justified. We now know that condors have nested in hollows formed in the trunks of large coniferous trees [14], and some large oaks could have provided the base for laying an egg. Therefore, the nest site information should not be completely rejected. However, the description was not very helpful to those who might have been seeking condor eggs for their own collections.

Between 1860 and 1889, at least six California condor eggs were taken, five of them by individuals who did not make the existence of their prizes known until around 1900. The sixth was provided to the U. S. National Museum in 1865 or 1866 by Dr. Colbert Canfield, and had been found in the same general area of Monterey County as the Taylor-Gurney egg [15]. If there was ever a written description of that nest site, it was not preserved, so no new insights on the condors' nesting habits were gained by the egg's acquisition. Everyone had to wait until 1895 for a detailed account of a condor egg and nest, published that year by Henry R. "Harry" Taylor, a San Francisco Bay Area ornithologist and specimen dealer. Early that year, Taylor purchased the egg *"at a good round figure from the collector, who took it in 1889, and had since been keeping it as a curiosity (!)..."* [16]. I haven't been able to determine how Taylor learned about the five year old egg, but he followed up the announcement of his oölogical coup with a detailed description of the taking of the condor egg *"in the collector's own words"* [17]:

"In the first part of the month of May, 1889, while out hunting in the Santa Lucia Mountains, San Luis Obispo County, I noticed a large Condor fly from a cave on the south side of a mountain, in a perpendicular cliff about 120 feet high. The altitude was about 3,000 feet. Being of an inquisitive nature, I undertook to enter the cave from below, for I was sure that I had found the nest of the great birds... I could without much trouble get within about 50 feet of the mouth of the cave, but there I was obliged to give up the attempt, as the face of the cliff was too steep for any living man to climb, and I could plainly see that to climb down from above was impossible... Now being sure that I was not mistaken as to the nesting place, I examined the place carefully, and was satisfied that with the aid of a long rope, made fast to a strong manzanita bush above, I could descend the bluff.

"So next morning I returned with ropes enough to reach from top to bottom... I fired a shot at the bird to frighten her away. I pulled off my boots and started down the rope, which at places touched the rock, and reached the cave safely. The cave was about 20 feet wide, 30 feet high, and 16 feet deep. The rock, being of granite, was very rough and jagged. It was free from earth, but was littered with birds' excrement, decomposed stone, and decomposed shells, which are found in nearly all caves in this range of mountains.

"In the back part and to the north side of the cave, in a queer looking nest, was the single egg of the California Condor. The nest was on the bare stone.

In front was a slight ridge of decomposed stone, which had been raked up by the bird to keep the egg from rolling out, while on the other sides was the bare rock. The nest was about two feet across, and contained all the loose feathers obtainable, such as feathers of Owls (which sat blinking in the back end of the cave), and feathers from the bird herself, but not enough to be of much protection for the egg.

"Having secured the big egg I was at a loss to know how to save it, as it took both of my hands to go on down the rope. But I drew up the end of the rope from below, and taking off my overshirt rolled the egg up in it the best I could, and lowered it to the bottom of the cliff. Then I went down myself... Again, going to the top and securing my ropes I went home, and removed the contents of the egg--incubation commenced. "

Specimen dealers seldom revealed the names of their collectors or the locations of nests, not wanting other collectors and dealers working in "their" territory. Harry Taylor didn't identify his collector/correspondent, but from later records it is clear that it was Wallace Mathers. Mathers (1859-1939) was born at Cambria on the San Luis Obispo County coast, and lived in that general area of California all his life. He remained a bachelor and lived an outdoor life, being variously employed as a farm laborer, rancher, miner, and carpenter. Charles Bendire learned his identity (presumably from Harry Taylor), and subsequently employed him to collect several condor eggs for the National Museum, and for Bendire's oölogist friend William L. Ralph (who became egg curator at the National Museum after Bendire's death). Bendire also arranged for Mathers to capture two nestling condors for the Philadelphia Zoo in 1896. These were the first live California condors in an American public institution, although "Grizzly" Adams had live condors in his traveling menagerie 40 years earlier (Chapter 12) [18].

Condor egg collectors were few in number. Four people accounted for a third of the eggs taken; those four, plus 11 others, collected over half of the total. (Actually, some of those 15 always worked together; nine *teams* took more than half the eggs.) In addition to Wallace Mathers, Harry Taylor hired the Harris brothers, sons of Ethelbert Harris and Jane Martin, to search in northwestern San Luis Obispo County and Monterey County. John W. Harris (1852-1927) was born in Texas before the family moved to California in the 1850s; George W. Harris (1859-1926) may have been born in Santa Cruz before the Harrises relocated to San Luis Obispo County. Like Mathers, their neighbor at Cambria and later near San Antonio in Monterey County, the Harris brothers were outdoorsmen, variously employed as farmers, vaqueros, hunters, and miners [19].

The fourth major collector of condor eggs was Willis Edwin Griffith (1871-1945). He was born in Colorado, son of Edwin Griffith and Elizabeth Cave. The family moved a number of times through the Rocky Mountains and Great Plains, mining and farming, before arriving in Santa Barbara County in 1882

Figure 15. The Harris family at Bryson, California, circa 1902. George Harris is at the lower left. Photo courtesy of Ray J. Quigley.

or 1883. Griffith lived the rest of his life in Santa Barbara, working at times as farm laborer, carpenter, and feed merchant [20]. Late in life, he claimed to have taken ten condor eggs [21]; this may not be an exaggeration, as I can account for six of them and suspect that he was the one who took at least two others.

Most of Griffith's condor eggs came from canyons in the Santa Ynez Range, not far from Santa Barbara. At least one egg came from the San Rafael Mountains in the Santa Barbara County backcountry. His earliest known egg was taken in 1888, a year before Wallace Mathers' first egg. Like Mathers, Griffith did not share his discovery with scientists or other egg collectors. He probably took it as a curiosity, as he does not seem to have had other oölogical interests at that time. He kept the 1888 egg until 1943, at which time he sold it to another Santa Barbaran for $25.00 [22]. His next known egg was not collected until 1896, when possibly he was inspired by the news that a condor egg taken in the San Rafael Mountains had been sold the previous year. (At that time, the 1895 egg was regarded as the first one collected in Santa Barbara County [23], oölogists being unaware of Griffith's 1888 accession.) He advertised the egg in *The Museum,* one of several magazines then popular with natural history collectors, for sale for *"best cash offer."* (See the wording of the ad at the head of this chapter.) It was purchased by Walter F. Webb, a specimen dealer in Albion, New York. I haven't found any other advertisements by Griffith, probably because he entered into an agreement to sell all subsequent eggs direct to Webb.

* * *

I haven't determined how much Webb paid Griffith for his condor eggs. Seven records of what other collectors were paid indicate that the going rate in the early 1900s was about $25.00 (range $12 to $50). Dealers at that time usually received $100 to $125 (eight records, range $90 to $200). Four later sales between collectors - after it had become illegal to collect condor eggs - were for $200, $400, and $500 (two sales).

Twenty-five dollars for one rare egg was considerably more impressive in 1900 than it seems now, and was probably "worth it" to the egg hunters. But it was a hard-earned fee. With a few exceptions - an egg found by a little girl on a family picnic, a nest into which one could nearly ride a horse, and an egg found by campers scrambling around nearby rocks [24] - collecting condor eggs was not the kind of "bird nesting" done by grammar school boys. It took a lot of time, good physical condition and stamina, and a certain amount of bravery.

Time alone would have kept many people from hunting condor nests. For example, after capturing two condor chicks in 1896, Wallace Mathers wrote to Charles Bendire: *"I will try the Vultures again next season. For knowing the country well and with my past experience I stand a good show to secure several eggs... I will devote two months to secure the eggs next year..."* [25]. In

213

1898, Harry Taylor wrote: *"My collector, during a ten days' trip into northern San Luis Obispo County, had taken an egg of the California Vulture"* [26]. In 1900: *"Mr. Taylor's field men have come in from another two weeks' trip in which they were successful in taking their second condor's egg of the season..."* [27]. Ten days to two months for a possible (but not guaranteed) income of $25 to $50 was only worthwhile if other money-making options were limited.

Before one could search for condor nests, or take eggs from previously discovered nests, miles of mostly trailless, steep, chaparral-covered hills and canyons had to be traversed on foot or horseback. Just to reach places with names like Los Burros Gorge, The Shut-in, Vulture Rock, The Narrows, and Sisquoc Falls took two to several days. Rugged terrain, heat, little water, rattlesnakes and wood ticks combined to generally discourage all but the most athletic young men. Once they found a nest, the work was not over. Harry Taylor wrote of one egg taken by the Harris brothers:

"Egg was deposited in a pot hole on face of conglomerate bluff about 100 feet from top of bluff and 60 feet above the ground... Quite a hard climb with ropes to secure the egg. My collector and his brother each weigh over 170 lbs and one goes over the cliff while the other adjusts the ropes making the most daring descents with rope ladders and ropes I have heard of in America. The collector often descends 100 feet over the cliff" [28].

An egg taken by L. N. Blackledge in Ventura County came from a nest that *"can only be reached by a rough trail on horseback. The parties procured ropes, and after a fatiguing trip arrived at the Narrows and began at once to ascend to the top of the cliffs by climbing up a side canyon. On reaching the top a sling was made and Hosa, an Indian boy, was lowered on a rope to the nest, which was on the side of a cliff from 300 to 400 feet high, and a perpendicular wall... After the egg had been securely placed in a sack, the boy was hoisted again to the top of the cliff"* [29].

In general, it was not a job for the weak, lazy or faint-hearted.

* * *

Developing a history of California condor egg collecting, and assessing the magnitude and significance of the activity has not been easy. Neither the field men nor the agents who sold the eggs to collectors were likely to disclose nest locations, fearful of competition from others. Some went so far as to print false information about where they found eggs. For example, an egg taken in San Diego County was described as having come from a nest in Monterey County, some 400 miles to the north [30]. Robert Sharples explained in a letter to Lee Chambers: *"The Cal. Condor egg was taken by Frank Stephens, and the location was on the San Luis [Rey] river. In the published article the location was made purposely indefinite because I thought that possibly I might get another egg from the same location"* [31].

Egg-selling agents were less than completely honest with their fellow agents about their clientele, fearful of potential buyers being poached. When Lee Chambers asked Donald Cohen who had purchased his condor egg, Cohen replied: *"As to who got mine I will tell you after I sell him another"* [32]. Agents were also secretive or misleading about their supply of condor eggs, and about the prices they were receiving for them. For obvious reasons, sellers of eggs wanted higher values put on them, while buyers wanted lower prices. When Walter F. Webb published his "Ornithologists' and Oologists' Manual" in 1895, he gave the value of a condor egg at $25.00. Harry Taylor objected in print in an "open letter" to Webb: *"As you price in your new Manual the egg of the California Vulture at $25, whereas there are only four eggs in the world known to me, I hereby offer you for three, or a lesser number, of such eggs, $250 each"* [33]. Webb replied that a condor egg was surely not in the same class as a Labrador duck or great auk, and advised his readers in cases of *"eggs of birds not extinct nor in any wise likely to become so in our generation...to beware of paying over $15.00 for any one egg"* [34]. The war of words continued in their respective magazines for several more issues, but Webb did not change his listing.

Taylor's indignation at Webb's pricing may have been more righteous than it was an attempt to keep prices high. Webb quoted some ridiculously low prices for eggs of extinct birds, and of species for which no authenticated egg had yet been found. Taylor's response was clearly more personal after Lee Chambers published a short note on his attempt to document the number of condor eggs that has been collected: *"I will say here in regard to the eggs of the California vulture, that they are not nearly so rare as supposed"* [35]. Taylor responded to Chambers by letter, citing the article and also referring to a request Chambers had made to review Taylor's notes on condors:

"You mention in the current issue of Condor that you know of 24 perfect eggs, and 35 in all, and that the birds (or eggs) are not so rare as imagined. If you are to enlarge on that idea, your ideas and mine conflict materially, and my notes would be of no benefit to you, nor benefit me for you to have them. But, no doubt, you have no intention of undervaluing the species in your work?" He continued: *"I would ask...that you do not take the erroneous stand that the bird is becoming commoner, or is really not so rare. I have had enough arguments, sometimes, in the past with easterners who took the view that eggs should be cheap, or that it was an ordinary incident to take eggs or birds. I have paid a big price to my collectors for all I secured"* [36].

Prices were not always set low. A story widely circulated in newspapers in 1895 claimed that condor eggs were worth $1,500 apiece [37]. A story in 1900 reported condor eggs had sold for as much as $1,500, but that the most recent sale (allegedly in 1887) had only brought $800 [38]. Herbert M. Beesley, an Englishman in America collecting for Walter Rothschild, was not so definite about the price received for the last egg sold - *"something like $800"* - but stated that *"there are several oologists of my personal acquaintance who* *would not hesitate to pay $1,000 or $1,200 for an egg of the Californian or Sierra condor..."* [39]. As late as 1922, R. Magoon Barnes and "a committee of twenty-five prominent American oologists" put a value of $750 on a condor egg [40]. As already noted, I found no indication that any condor egg sold before the 1920s had brought the seller more than $200; even in later sales between collectors, the highest price I could confirm was $500.

High prices quoted in newspaper stories may have had some influence on the market supply of condor eggs, as a number of new names appeared after 1900 on the roster of successful hunters. In the decade 1900-1909, 28 condor eggs were taken from nests, more than in any other 10-year period, and over one-third of all those known to have been collected. Newspaper interest in condors also led to a rash of tall tales and highly exaggerated stories about taking condor eggs. Some were clearly not meant to be taken seriously, like one about a hunter knocked from the nest by an angry adult bird. Just as he was about to fall a thousand feet to his death, the man grabbed the condor's legs and with the bird as his "parachute" sailed gently to the ground [41]. Other stories are more difficult to judge: a 1930 tale of Carlos Lume finding a condor nest in Baja California, Mexico, and being savagely attacked by the parent birds [42] is curiously reminiscent of a much-repeated article about Frank Ruiz taking an egg near Santa Barbara, with similar vengeance from the adult condors [43]. (Both stories are accompanied with wonderful drawings of the savage condors attacking the egg thieves!) In the latter case, the story is actually true (leaving out the dramatic vulture attack, which California condors have never been known to do), including the egg hunter's real name and almost the actual location (San Royal Canyon in the story, San Roque in real-life). The Baja California incident has been written off as a tall tale (and probably is) but remove the poetry of the condors' attack, and the details could be real.

The best (or worst!) hoax about collecting California condor eggs was perpetrated by Harry H. Dunn (1880-1932), a newspaper and magazine writer with hundreds of articles and columns to his credit. He wrote prolifically on every conceivable topic, including articles on birds for such magazines as *Bird-lore, American Ornithology,* and *The Museum.* He reportedly had a considerable collection of birds' eggs around 1900, but I have been unable to find any specific information about it [44].

In May 1904, newspapers carried a story about a supposed trip the previous February to find and photograph California condors at their nest. Sometimes the story carried Harry Dunn's byline, sometimes it appeared anonymously. Details were the same: two condor eggs were found (handled, but apparently not collected), and the adult birds were photographed (*"believed to be the first ever taken of the great California vulture"),* but the location of the nests and the bad lighting allegedly made it impossible to get photos of the eggs. They photos accompanying the articles were clearly of posed stuffed birds (and not very good ones!) and drawings [45].

216

Donald Cohen (Alameda, California, ornithologist) was skeptical. He wrote to Lee Chambers: *"Did you see account of Dunn finding two eggs: in Sunday Chronical* [sic] *3 or 4 weeks ago. It looks queer to me"* [46].

In November 1904, Dunn was once again in the news, announcing a planned expedition in January 1905 to secure the egg of a California condor. According to the story, Dunn had twice before visited condor nest sites. Accompanying the article was one of the same faked photos used with the previous stories [47]. In May 1905, the triumphant return was announced: a condor egg had been taken, and had already been sold *"for a fat figure to an eastern egg enthusiast and its fortunate finders have already shipped him his purchase."* Not only had they secured an egg, but also *"what are believed to be the first photos ever known of this bird in the wild state were made"* [48]. No pictures accompanied this article, so it isn't known if these were the same *"first photos"* as the previous *"first photos"!*

Harry Taylor, in a letter to Lee Chambers discussing Chambers' proposed condor monograph, commented: *"Hope you are not to depend at all upon records of a certain southern Calif. former egg collector who writes magazine stuff, as to condors which attacked him, etc.!"* [49]. Chambers had written to Dunn earlier, and Dunn sent what must have been a surprisingly honest reply: *"I have no notes concerning the bird (Cal. Vulture) or its nidification. The story portraying taking of the egg of the big bird by myself and others was purely 'hot-air' - a reporter's story, written to keep the pot boiling"* [50]. Despite the confession, the articles continued. In *American Ornithology,* Dunn referred to the nests and eggs he had seen [51]. He also sent to *The Oölogist* [and the editor published] a photo of a truly horribly mounted condor, with the caption, *"Photo from life by H. H. Dunn"* [52]. Two years later, he recycled the condor nest discovery story (with one of the original fake condor photos) for *American Boy Magazine."* This last time around he "discovered" a condor chick, not an egg [53]. He was clearly an unrepentant story teller.

* * *

Despite the fakery, misdirections, and secretiveness, I think the record of California condor eggs collected is fairly complete and accurate. The number of condors killed will always be open to question, because condors could be killed almost anywhere within their range, and because of uneven documentation of the various types of death over time. Egg collecting, on the other hand, was limited to a relatively few locations, and was done for the most part by a very small group of hunters with the time, stamina, and fearlessness needed for success. Another reflection of the completeness of the list may be that, between 1978 and the present, I added 150 new records of condor mortality to my original list of 300 [54]. In contrast, despite an equal amount of searching for egg records, the estimated number of eggs taken has stayed essentially the same - a minimum of 71 in 1978, and a maximum of 80 today.

Taken by itself, collecting condor eggs was a low impact activity. Eighty eggs over 80 years is not many. Some nesting areas were visited repeatedly, but others seldom. A pair with its egg taken one year would very likely nest the next year, and in some cases might even lay a second egg the same season [55]. Although the opportunistic finding of a nest might result in both the egg or chick taken and adult birds killed, the regular collectors knew that their income ceased if there were no condors to lay eggs. Wallace Mathers explained it well in a letter to Charles Bendire: *"The largest Vulture which I have measured was 8 and 1/2 feet from tip to tip of the wings, but one of the old birds which I saw this spring was larger than that. I was tempted to kill him but could not afford to do so as it was one of the pairs which I have located. He was a monster and lit within 60 feet of me"* [56]. Taking eggs deferred productivity, but did not destroy the capability.

In context, the impact of collecting condor eggs can't be ignored. Although not all nesting areas were visited by collectors, eggs were taken from some localities year after year. Certain pairs may have had their productivity deferred for several years in a row. Although the egg collectors weren't killing adult birds, other people were. Deferred production became lost recruitment if the adult birds were killed before they had their chance to replace themselves in the population.

Chapter Notes

1. Advertisement June 1896. *The Museum* 2(8):193.

2. Webb, W. F. 1899. A California condor egg for sale. *The Museum* 5(6):81.

3. Advertisement March 1906. *Oölogist* 23(3):33.

4. Anonymous. 1931. Obituary - Joseph Parker Norris, Jr. *Auk* 48(2):329-330.

5. Page 57 *in:* Gregg, C. G. 1945. Report of the Director to the Board of Trustees for the year 1945. Chicago, Illinois: Chicago Natural History Museum.

6. Burns, F. L. 1901. Editorial. *Wilson Bulletin* 13(3):73-75.

7. Anonymous. 1902. General news and notes. *Condor* 4(3):72-73.

8. Brewer, T. M. 1857. North American oölogy. Part I, Raptores and Fissirosstres. Smithsonian Contributions to Knowledge. Washington, D. C.: Smithsonian Institution.

9. Drobnicki, J. A. 1997. Thomas Mayo Brewer. Pages 107-108 *in:* Sterling, K. B., R. P. Harmond, G. A. Cevasco and L. F. Hammond. Biographical dictionary of American and Canadian naturalists and environmentalists. Westport, Connecticut: Greenwood Press.

10. Page 62 *in:* Douglas, D. 1914. Journal kept by David Douglas during his travels in North America 1823-1827. London, England: William Wesley & Son.

11. Brewer *op. cit.,* pages 6-7.

12. There is a published record of a California condor egg taken from Napa County in 1845: page 177 *in* Berner, M., B. Grummer, R. Leong, and M. Rippey. 2003. Breeding birds of Napa County, California. Vallejo, California: Napa-Solano Audubon Society. This egg allegedly was sent to Russia. Unfortunately, the compilers of the Napa County book retained no record of where they obtained their information.

13. Taylor, A. S. 1859. The egg and young of the California condor. *Hutching's California Magazine* 3(12):537-540.

14. Pages 81-83 *in:* Koford, C. B. 1953. The California condor. Research Report 4. New York, New York: National Audubon Society.
   Snyder, N. F. R., R. R. Ramey, and F. C. Sibley. 1986. Nest-site biology of the California condor. *Condor* 88(2):228-241.

15. Page 161 *in:* Bendire, C. 1892. Life histories of North American birds. Volume 1. Washington, D. C.: Government Printing Office.

16. Taylor, H. R. 1895. Habits of the California condor. *Nidiologist* 2(6):73-79.

17. Taylor, H. R. 1895. Collecting a condor's egg. *Nidiologist* 2(7):88-89.

18. Several letters from Wallace Mathers to Charles Bendire, including details of the capture and rearing of the Philadelphia Zoo condors, have been preserved in the Charles Bendire Papers, Collection MSS12377, Library of Congress, Washington, D. C.

19. Family information on Wallace Mathers and the Harris brothers was gleaned from various censuses, genealogies. and correspondence. The families are frequently mentioned in early central California Coast histories, but there seem to be no detailed records of either the Mathers or Harrises.
   George and James Harris apparently always worked as a team collecting condor eggs. James B. Harris (1857-1920) is cited on only one egg data record, but may have been involved with other acquisitions, as well.

20. Willis Griffith family information taken from various censuses, genealogies, local histories, and correspondence.

21. Koford, C. B. 1946. Interviews with Egmont Z. Rett and Lawrence Stevens, Santa Barbara, California, 15-16 February 1946. Carl B. Koford California Condor species accounts. Museum of Vertebrate Zoology (Berkeley, California).

22. Koford 1946 *op. cit.*

23. Shields, A. M. 1895. Nesting of the California vulture. *Nidiologist* 2(11):148-150. Some references identify this egg as having been collected in San Luis Obispo County, but Ozora W. Howard's collecting notes (copies at the Western Foundation of Vertebrate Zoology, Camarillo, California) are clear as to the date and location. This is also made plain in a biographical sketch of Howard:

"In 1895, when at the age of eighteen, he made a month's trip by team into the head of Sisquoc Canyon, in northern Santa Barbara County, and secured an egg of the almost extinct and much sought for California Condor..." [Pages 755-757 in J. S. McGroaty. 1921. Los Angeles from the mountains to the sea. Chicago, Illinois: The American Historical Society].

24. *"California Condor* [egg]--*collected April 11, 1900, Los Angeles Topanga Mountains, by a little girl who walked up a sloping cliff, easily gotten at..."* W. L. Chambers egg data slip, now at Western Foundation of Vertebrate Zoology (Camarillo, California).

"[The nest site] *was not hard to reach. In fact, we rode our horses to within a few feet of it."* Frank Stephens to C. D. Scott, in unpublished manuscript "Looking for California condors." San Marino, California: The Huntington Library.

"The nest cave was a huge ledge of rocks facing toward the south, the egg was found accidentally by a party of campers climbing among the rocks..." Gallaher, W. 1906. A novel find. *Condor* 8(2):57.

25. Letter from Wallace Mathers to Charles Bendire 25 September 1896. Charles Bendire Papers, Collection MSS12377, Library of Congress, Washington, D. C.

26. Taylor, H. R. 1898. Early nidification of California Vulture. *Osprey* 3(2):29.

27. Anonymous. 1900. Two more eggs of California condor. *Condor* 2(3):60.

28. Information on an egg data slip now at the Museum of Vertebrate Zoology, University of California, Berkeley.

29. Information accompanying a condor egg now at the Chicago (Illinois) Field Museum of Natural History.

30. Sharples, R. P. 1897. The taking of a California Condor's egg. *Osprey* 2(2):21.

31. Letter, R. P. Sharples to W. L. Chambers (Santa Monica, California), 21 October 1902. Willie Chambers Papers, Collection Number BANC MSS 67/131, Bancroft Library (Berkeley, California).

32. Letter, Donald A. Cohen (Alameda, California) to W. L. Chambers (Santa Monica, California), 9 June 1904. Willie Chambers Papers, Collection Number BANC MSS 67/131, Bancroft Library (Berkeley, California).

33. Taylor, H. R. 1895. Open letter to W. F. Webb. *Nidiologist* 2(7):100.

220

34. Webb, W. F. 1895. Notes. *The Museum* 1(6):177-178.

35. Chambers, W. L. 1905. Notes on California Vulture wanted. *Condor* 7(2):56.

36. Letter 2 April 1905, Henry R. Taylor (Alameda, California) to W. Lee Chambers (Santa Monica, California). Willie Chambers Papers, Collection Number BANC MSS 67/131, Bancroft Library (Berkeley, California).

37. Anonymous. 1895. Eggs worth a big sum, genuine condor products that are valued at $1500 each. Cleveland (Ohio) *Plain Dealer,* 14 May 1939.

38. Anonymous. 1900. The busy world. *The School Journal* 61(1):18.

39. Anonymous. 1900. A hunt for a condor's egg, a variety worth $1,000 or more. Charlotte (North Carolina) *Observer,* 19 June 1900.

40. Barnes, R. M. 1922. The American Oologists' exchange price list of North American birds' eggs. Lacon, Illinois: R. Magoon Barnes.

41. Anonymous. 1908. He used condor as a parachute. Baltimore (Maryland) *America,* 18 October 1908.

42. Anonymous. 1930. Battled for his life with giant condors. San Antonio (Texas) *Light,* 23 February 1930.

43. Anonymous. 1899. Desperate fight with condors. Narrow escape of a Santa Barbara man who tried to rob their nest. San Francisco (California) *Call,* 30 April 1899.

44. Robert C. McFadden (Fullerton, California) wrote to me 18 September 1974: *"It is true that I was an infrequent companion of Harry Dunn in his egg hunting trips. Harry was somewhat older than I, but I found that I could gain much from his experience and knowledge. He had at that time what I considered to be a fabulous collection of bird eggs... I have often wondered what became of his egg collection."*

45. Dunn, H. H. 1904. Taking photograps [sic] of the California condor. San Francisco (California) *Chronicle,* 8 May 1904. Also: Anonymous. 1904. Condor hunting with a camera. These pictures believed to be the first ever taken of the great California vulture. *The Sun* (New York, New York), 8 May 1904.

46. Letter, Donald A. Cohen (Alameda, California) to W. Lee Chambers (Santa Monica, California), 9 June 1904. Willie Chambers Papers, Collection Number BANC MSS 67/131, Bancroft Library (Berkeley, California).

47. Anonymous. 1904. Local expedition will seek cave of condors. Los Angeles (California) *Times,* 13 November 1904.

48. Anonymous. 1905. Getting eggs of vultures. How the ornithologists find the condor nest - largest of American birds. Kalamazoo (Michigan) *Gazette,* 27 May 1905.

49. Letter 2 April 1905, Henry R. Taylor (Alameda, California) to W. Lee Chambers (Santa Monica, California). Willie Chambers Papers, Collection Number BANC MSS 67/131, Bancroft Library (Berkeley, California).

50. Letter Harry H. Dunn (Fullerton, California) to W. Lee Chambers (Santa Monica, California). Willie Chambers Papers, Collection Number BANC MSS 67/131, Bancroft Library (Berkeley, California). The date on this letter is clearly 21 August 1902, but I wonder if Dunn inadvertently dated it incorrectly. I have found no indication that Dunn was telling his tall tales as early as 1902. Unfortunately, I haven't found Chambers' original inquiry, so don't know what date it was sent.

51. Dunn, H. H. 1905. The California vulture. *American Ornithology* 5(12):289-292.

52. Dunn, H. H. 1905. The California vulture. *Oölogist* 22(8):118.

53. Dunn, H. H. 1907. How I found the nest of the condor. *American Boy* 8(4):127.

54. Pages 71-88 *in:* Wilbur, S. R. 1978. The California condor, 1966-76: a look at its past and future. North American Fauna Number 72. Washington, D. C.: U. S. Fish and Wildlife Service.

55. Snyder, N. F. R., and J. A. Hamber. 1985. Replacement-clutching and annual nesting of California condors. Condor 87(3):374-378.

56. Letter from Wallace Mathers to Charles Bendire 25 September 1896. Charles Bendire Papers, Collection MSS12377, Library of Congress, Washington, D. C.

CHAPTER 17
CALL TO ACTION

In the summer of 1901, newspapers around the United States reported that the California condors were *"fast approaching extinction"* [1]. Between November 1901 and February 1902, some of the same papers announced that the condor was *"believed to have become extinct"* [2]. Both stories were presented anonymously, and I haven't been able to find the original source of either news feed. In any event, the condors did not disappear to 1901, as amply shown by no less than 20 published reports between 1901 and 1905, with sightings distributed from San Diego County to southern Oregon, and with as many as 11 birds seen simultaneously [3]. Most of those observations were of condors killed or collected for zoos, so there might have been some reason to talk about the threat of extinction!

As it had been in the 1880s (Chapter 15) and at the turn of the century, pronouncements about the condors' status from 1910 to 1920 varied widely. In 1910, they were reported to be *"a rather common bird...in all the spurs of the main mountains of Ventura County"* [4]. While *"not nearly so abundant as formerly,"* they were judged in 1912 to be *"tolerably common"* [5]. That same year, Joseph Grinnell (one of California's best known ornithologists) described the condor as *"...still fairly common, for a large bird, probably equal in numbers to the golden eagle in those regions that are suited to it."* Further, it was his impression *"that the present fatalities from all sources are fully balanced by the natural rate of increase... (and) the mountainous areas where the condor is making its last stand seem...likely to remain adapted to the bird's existence for many years"* [6].

In contrast, Lee Chambers thought a single condor near Los Angeles in 1915 *"was so seldom seen now that I thought it worth reporting"* [7]. A pronouncement in 1918 was that *"with each recurring year the chances that one will see one* (condor) *are diminishing"* [8]. Even as he published Grinnell's assessment, William Hornaday had his doubts [9]: *"I feel that the existence of this species hangs on a very slender thread... Regarding the present status and future of this bird, I have been greatly disturbed in mind. When a unique and zoologically important species becomes reduced in its geographical range to a small section of a single state, it seems to me quite time for alarm."*

Who was correct? To some extent, everyone was. As later study would show, condors were gone, or nearly so, from most parts of their original range. However, they were still *"tolerably common"* in the mountains of Ventura and Santa Barbara counties.

* * *

On 22 August 1927, Robert E. Easton sent a letter to the Smithsonian Institution in Washington, D. C., which read [10]: *"This letter is being addressed to you in anticipation of your interest in the continued existence of the California Condor in this section of California. For many years the writer has been connected with the Sisquoc Ranch, having scattered Government land holdings in the Sisquoc River Canyon as well as on the Montgomery Potreros, having an elevation of 4711 feet, shown on U. S. Geological Survey Topographical Sheet, Santa Ynez Quadrangle.*

"It is the recollection of the writer that about fifteen years ago, by special permit, a specimen of this bird was secured by a taxidermist and forwarded for exhibit in your Institution. For some years these birds have not been reported as being seen. However, it is with much interest that the writer and party, on Saturday, August 20th, enjoyed the opportunity of seeing the beautiful specimens of this bird while on the Montgomery Potreros. These birds were hovering about the stripped carcass of a deer, giving us a closeup view. We estimated that the larger of the two birds measured not less than fourteen feet from tip to tip. Both were wonderful specimens.

"We will be greatly interested in any printed matter available on this bird and its habits and will be glad to investigate and supply you with any information that may be of scientific interest to yourselves.

"One of our party, a resident of the neighborhood, pointed out to the writer a spot in one of the precipitous cliffs, in which he believes the birds have their nest."

At first glance, the Easton letter doesn't seem significant. Two condors don't seem especially noteworthy, and the Santa Barbara mountains seem a logical place to have seen them. The rest of the story is that, during the early 1920s, the condors had almost disappeared from public notice. In the newspapers, there were regular one- or two-sentence space fillers about the size or wing span of a condor, how often condors nested, how much eggs were worth, or what color were their heads. Condors were occasionally mentioned in stories about other species, like the bald eagle or the prehistoric teratorn. The new Lassie movie was showing in theaters in 1926, and the reviews mentioned the villain in the movie, the evil, sheep-killing California condor (by the way, played by a real condor: see Chapter 12). The only time between 1920 and 1927 that California condors had a news story of their own was when domestic chickens were used to try to hatch the eggs of captive condors at the National Zoo (Chapter 12). I have not found any news story between 1920 and 1927 that mentioned a live, free-ranging condor [11].

People were seeing condors during the 1920s, as shown by various unpublished field notes that have subsequently come to light [12]. Only two reports made it into print during that period, the first of sightings in two mountain ranges in Baja California Norte [13], and the second a record of one condor in the Sierra Nevada [14]. Ornithologists, but not the general public, might have read about the Mexico observations. The Sierra report was in an obscure journal that probably was missed at the time by scientist and layman, alike.

Easton received a friendly reply from Alexander Wetmore, Assistant Secretary of the Smithsonian, enclosing a "pamphlet" on condors written by William L. Finley [15]. (This was probably a copy of one of Finley's articles, as I haven't found any evidence that any specially-prepared condor information was available at that time.) Wetmore encouraged Easton to send other observations, and to take some pictures. Reflecting the chief emphasis of ornithology in those days, Wetmore also added a request for a condor skeleton for the museum collections, should Easton ever be fortunate enough to find one. Easton sent a thank-you note, in which he stated his intent to try to bait some condors to a carcass in the spring of 1928 [16].

Six years passed with no known correspondence between Easton and Wetmore or any other ornithologist or conservationist. If Easton went ahead with his plans to bait condors in 1928, I've found no record of it. Easton had recently moved from Santa Maria to Santa Barbara, and it may be that his combined responsibilities as manager of the Sisquoc Ranch, executive of the local telephone company, president of a Santa Maria gas company, and member of various county committees kept him too busy to actively pursue condors [17]. Overall, there was little evidence that the condor had been "rediscovered." There was a minor surge in the amount of coverage the species received in journals and magazines, compared to the previous fifteen years - about 25 articles, most of them brief notes in bird journals, and two longer magazine accounts - but no really new information was forthcoming. Condors were being reported from the Montgomery Potrero–Sisquoc Canyon area, although not in sources available to the general public [18].

The Easton "discovery" started to become significant in July 1934, when stories in the *Los Angeles Times* [19] and other California newspapers reported that Robert Easton was still watching condors in the Sisquoc River backcountry, and that he had seen and photographed 16 of them. The stories, which gave the condors wingspans of 14 to 16 feet and included a drawing of a condor carrying a fawn in its "talons," was reprinted later in the *New York Sun,* where it attracted the attention of The Hawk and Owl Society, an affiliate of the National Association of Audubon Societies. Emerson Stoner, Director of the Society, wrote to the Sisquoc Ranch for confirmation of the story [20]. Easton responded, giving his opinion that there were *"not less than thirty"* condors in the Sisquoc area, but admitting as the highest certain count 11 condors (seen by his son, Robert O. Easton), not 16 as stated in the news stories [21]. The actual facts about the observations were included in an article written by Ernest Dyer, published in the January 1935 issue of *The Condor* [22]. Addressing the newspaper coverage, Dyer wrote: *"Depending, presumably, upon the fancy of the various writers responsible for these literary exercises, the birds were, in some articles, said to be South American Condors and in others: Californian. Accounts differed as to numbers and sizes, but the most favored figure seems to have been 17, both for the number of birds seen and their wing-spread in feet."* As he was, he wrote, *"a member of the party that unwittingly provided the slender basis of fact underlying all this sensationalism,"* he wanted to tell what really happened. The truth he presented was that Robert Easton had invited a small group of friends on a pack trip to Montgomery Potrero, where he had a small blind built and had provided a dead horse nearby, hopefully to attract condors close enough for photographs and motion pictures. The carcass did attract condors, but Dyer saw no more than seven simultaneously, although he was fairly certain there were three others flying in the vicinity. In the article, he expressed concern about the amount of hunting that occurred in the area, believing that *"the presence of hunters, among whom are inevitably many of the irresponsible type, is a distinct menace."* However, he expressed some hope because *"fortunately, most of the areas known as condor country are within the boundaries of National Forests, and it would seem possible to have certain areas set aside within such forests and close them to hunters, keeping them under federal control as sanctuaries."*

Dyer's article prompted two lines of correspondence. Aldo Leopold, newly-appointed professor of game management at the University of Wisconsin and (earlier in 1935) one of the co-founders of The Wilderness Society, wrote to C. E. Rachford, assistant director of the U. S. Forest Service, and to Jay N. Darling, director of the Bureau of Biological Survey. He challenged them both to assure him that the people in the field in both agencies knew about the condors, and were doing the correct things to preserve them. At the same time, John Baker, executive director of the National Association of Audubon Societies, contacted the same two agencies, seeking similar assurances. From the archives I've been able to examine, it isn't clear if these two approaches were generated coincidentally, or if Leopold and Baker had been in contact on the subject previously. In any event, both shared their communications with Joseph Grinnell at the Museum of Vertebrate Zoology. Following a positive response from the Forest Service, the condor became the topic of regular correspondence between Leopold, Baker, Grinnell, Robert Easton, and S. A. Nash-Boulden and Cyril Robinson of the Santa Barbara (now, Los Padres) National Forest [23].

From the start, communications about condors on the national forest were congenial and cooperative. Despite different philosophies, different agendas, and lack of clear knowledge about what condors really needed, this accidental team accomplished good things, and set up the framework for condor preservation that was to be followed for many years.

* * *

LEGAL PROTECTION - One of the first issues identified by the group was a perceived need for stronger laws to protect the condors. The villains in this discussion were those who might steal eggs or chicks from nests, and those who might wantonly shoot condors. Although the Audubon representative took an early position that all the Sisquoc River area might need to be closed to hunting (because hunters might shoot condors) [24], most felt that hunters just needed to be educated about the law, and they would no longer be a threat. As the local Forest Service representatives saw it, *"there are always stupid individuals who will shoot these birds for the so-called sport; however, due to the large amount of local interest and the educational campaign that is being carried on primarily by the Santa Barbara Museum of Natural History cooperating with us we do not believe there is much danger from deer hunters"* [25].

Joseph Grinnell was particularly concerned about the threats from egg collectors. In April 1935, he wrote to the Regional Forester in San Francisco [26]: *"There are doubtless people in the land who would have no hesitancy in raiding nesting sites for eggs or young birds to sell. We often see in the newspapers items, however authentic, to the effect that there is a constant market for condor's eggs at $700 to $1,000 each, and that zoos offer rewards for the young. Of course, a very little activity in disturbing the nesting birds might mean the turning point toward total extinction. There is already a state law protecting the birds and their eggs. But the type of person likely seeking such 'prizes' would probably know nothing of such a law and would not heed it anyway."*

The State law that Grinnell alluded to was Section 637 of the California Penal Code, first added to the Code in 1905. (Its designation became Section 1172 in 1933, when the Fish and Game Code was separated from the Penal Code.) This was the statute used to fine a Los Angeles area man $50 for shooting a condor in 1908, the only time in the history of the wild population that someone was convicted of killing a condor [27]. The 1905 law made it a misdemeanor to kill or capture, or take the nests or eggs of, non-game birds without a State permit. The law included the condor categorically, but did not mention it by name; in fact, the condor was not specifically named in any law until 1953 [28]. (J. G. Cooper reported the passage of a condor protection law prior to 1890 [29], but this was apparently in error. Perhaps there was discussion in the legislature of the need for protection, or perhaps a congressman entered a supportive comment in the record. If so, the pertinent documents are well buried in the State files. Nothing made it into the statutes.)

The new condor team members made an initial overture to the State Division of Fish and Game in April 1935, believing the condor should be specifically named in the state statute, and that the killing of a condor or taking of a condor egg should be made a felony rather than a misdemeanor. The Division's Executive Director Herbert C. Davis responded, assuring them that current law was completely adequate to handle the condor situation [30]. At that point, the need for further legal protection seems to have been dropped from the discussions. This is curious because the team had been so convinced new laws

227

were needed, but perhaps it was a question of timing. There had recently been *"a complete change in the* (California) *Fish and Game Commission"* [31], and the chances of getting any new legislation or state regulation may have been perceived as minimal. For the same reason, the Forest Service was reluctant to invoke their newly-formulated Regulation G-20A, under which they claimed the right to set hunting regulations on national forests that might be different than those set by state agencies [32]. Condor protection did not seem a particularly good "test case" of the controversial new policy [33].

* * *

PUBLICITY – With regulatory changes off the table, discussion turned to publicity and education. The condor team had strongly mixed feelings about the role of publicity in condor protection. Joseph Grinnell was adamant against any publicity. In his first letter seeking Forest Service action on the Sisquoc condors [34], Aldo Leopold had written: *"If you will give me a short summary of what the Forest Service intends to do in this case, I'll get it published where the bird-lovers will see it, and maybe we can spread the idea. Keplinger ought to air this idea in his periodical."*

Grinnell took immediate exception to Leopold's proposal [35]: *"There is just one factor that disturbs me – the danger of giving publicity to the presence of condors in any given territory. Los Angeles is full of movie people, journalists, and alleged sportsmen, and some of these would likely be of the thoughtless or selfish type who would exploit the condors upon one motive or another, to the disturbance, if not immediate destruction, of the birds. There are lots of people who are looking for a thrill from adventure, and they will seek the remotest parts of our still remaining little patches of wilderness to get it."*

Leopold acquiesced [36]: *"Your point about giving no publicity to the hoped-for administrative plan to take care of condors is a very good one. To publicize this remnant might very easily be fatal."* Others were not so sure. John Baker summarized the different opinions and his own ambivalent feelings in a June 1936 letter to the Forest Service [37]:

"There are two distinct schools of thought as regards publicity with relation to threatened species. Some feel that publicity is dangerous, as it calls the attention of profit-seekers and collectors to the rarity of the bird and the exact location at which it or its nest can be found. The majority of our (Audubon) Board of Directors feel this way about it. I have the feeling that if publicity be adroitly directed, it can be made effective in protection of the birds through an aroused public interest in their preservation. However, I am not confident that I am right about this."

The group never agreed on a specific publicity policy, although all (including the conflicted John Baker) leaned strongly toward keeping the condors safe by keeping them secret. They were especially united in trying to limit newspaper coverage (because they felt it was never correct and was usually sensationalized). Baker and Grinnell didn't like magazine or book publicity, either. In a December 1936 letter to the Forest Service [38], Baker reported that he personally had chided freelance writer C. D. Scott, for an article Scott published in *"Nature Magazine"* [39], and that he and Grinnell were putting pressure on Scott not to publish a proposed children's book on condors. Baker wrote: *"I have been in touch with Dr. Grinnell in Berkeley about this, and we are most anxious to delay any publicity by Mr. Scott, until such time, at least, as the Sisquoc area has been definitely set aside as a refuge.*

"The number of people that are involved, in one way or another, in exploiting our wildlife resources, is always a source of distress to me. Mr. Scott undoubtedly means well, but he wants to make a little money out of the Condor by publishing a book about its scarcity, for the children, and so it goes. The National Geographic magazine loves to publish articles about rare species of birds and animals, no matter how much adverse effect such publicity may have on the species in question. We do our best to discreetly as we can restrain all such agencies from giving publicity at a time when it is not helpful to the bird or animal involved."

The Forest Service took (in my opinion) a more realistic approach to the publicity question. While they tried to discourage newspaper coverage, they worked with Egmont Rett (Santa Barbara Natural History Museum) and J. R. Pemberton (who, with Cyril Robinson, had been trying to photograph condors) to educate specific interest groups. Rett prepared an article meant to convince ranchers that condors did not kill livestock [40], and Pemberton planned to show his condor movies to ranchers, hunting clubs, and groups of oil field workers - the people who were most likely to be in areas where they could come into contact with condors [41]. The Forest Service provided basic condor information to their field employees on all the southern California forests, and encouraged them to report all their sightings to the staff of the Santa Barbara National Forest [42].

* * *

USE OF POISONS - Early in the discussions, Aldo Leopold raised the question of condors possibly being killed by eating poisoned ground squirrels [43]. The Forest Service representatives had never heard of squirrel control being a problem for condors, and were reluctant to drop or reduce a program that they felt was so vital to controlling bubonic plague [44]. (Actually, I think the bubonic plague threat was always a peripheral reason for the squirrel killing campaigns. The chief agenda was to keep squirrels from burrowing in farm land, and to save forage for cows.) Because very little squirrel control occurred on the National Forest (none at all in some years), and because most of the agencies who actually were killing squirrels operated on private land and were not yet players in the condor preservation effort, the team didn't put any additional effort into this issue. However, it has remained a background issue in the condor story up to the present day (Chapters 11 and 23).

* * *

ROAD BUILDING - The first big challenge to cooperation involved a road that the Forest Service was constructing deep into the Santa Barbara backcountry. To be used mainly for access to control fires, the road would have crossed through the Hurricane Deck country, then up the Sisquoc River Canyon not far from Sisquoc Falls, a regularly used roosting and bathing spot for condors. At that time, it was thought to be a nesting area, as well.

The issue of the Hurricane Deck road and other roads was first brought up in a June 1935 letter from Warren Eaton (of National Audubon) to the Santa Barbara National Forest [45]. His information was very detailed, likely given to him by Robert Easton. Forest Supervisor Nash-Boulden responded that, while he might agree philosophically with the concept of keeping the condor areas as wild as possible, these roads were vital for fire prevention and control. He assured Eaton that the roads would never be opened to the public, and would be used only for Forest Service administration. Besides, he wrote [46]:

"We do not feel that any roads now being built or contemplated will interfere with the habitation of the Condor. I am of the opinion that the limiting factor in this as in any other bird which is dependent entirely on scavenger material for food is the amount of food supply... The supply has decreased and, therefore, the numbers of Condors which this country once supported can reasonably be expected to be less."

Not convinced by Nash-Boulden's letter, Eaton wrote again to ask that the road building be stopped. The Forest Supervisor remained adamant about the importance of the road, but added some additional justifications [47]:

"The question of disturbing the birds by reason of road building is quite an interesting one. The only road project that is within a few miles of an assumed nesting site (the Hurricane Deck road) *is operated by a comparatively small crew. These men are interested in observing the California Condor, and their reports when questioned indicate that there has not been any decrease in the usual numbers seen daily. Were we to build a road right through, or immediate to an established nesting place, then I believe some apprehension would be reasonable. As stated in a previous letter, we do not feel that any conflict at present has occurred through the introduction of these truck trails or minor roads into hitherto undisturbed areas. You might be interested to know that California Condors have been seen on the U. S. Highway 99, known as the Ridge Route between Los Angeles and Bakersfield. These birds were feeding on the carcasses of jack-rabbits killed by passing automobiles."*

"In conclusion I can state again that in our opinion there is no danger of disturbing the birds by the introduction of roads. If you could see this type of country, and the enormous area between these roadways, I believe you would get a better picture. The assistance your organization could give us in maintaining the rigid closure of roads built solely for purposes of protection

might be a very valuable aid and we will not hesitate to advise you if the matter of public pressure comes up."

Lacking what Audubon considered a positive response from the Forest Supervisor, John Baker wrote to the Chief of the Forest Service [48]. Rather than asking for complete prohibition of the Hurricane Deck road, Baker proposed a realignment that he felt would be better for the condor, taking the road farther away from Sisquoc Falls. He again expressed concern that, once the road was built, it would be difficult to keep closed to the public. He pointed out that *"Mr. Nash Boulden asks for support in maintaining the closure rule on these fire roads. This in itself is an admission that there is danger of them being thrown open."* However, Chief Silcox supported with his field staff, citing the importance of the road for fire control and reiterating that the Forest Service had full authority to keep the public off their roads [49].

Rebuffed by the Washington Office, Audubon took the realignment proposal back to the Santa Barbara Forest staff. Nash-Boulden continued to insist that the road had to be built where they had planned it [50]. Once more, in October 1935, Audubon contacted Chief Silcox [51], this time armed with correspondence from an unidentified person who *"is an engineer* (and has) *reported what appears to us to be the pertinent facts and arguments for either not building the road or re-locating the road."* The "engineer" said nothing about engineering, except to concede that the Forest Service plan was probably a good one, based solely on engineering feasibility. However, he expressed doubts that the Forest Service would be able to stop public use once the road was established:

"When any kind of a road, Service or otherwise, is opened it is but a short time before the public discovers the fact and begins to use it. Eventually pressure is brought to bear which the Forest Service - with the best will in the world - cannot resist, and the road is made definitely public. The next step is for the State Highway Commission - even now glutted with funds from the gasoline tax for which they are seeking an outlet - to step in and make it a boulevard."

The response from the Forest Service [52] quickly disposed of the "engineer's" highly overstated argument that any road built would soon be a public highway. They pointed out that the Forest Service maintained several hundred miles of protection roads in southern California, and had never had any trouble keeping any of them closed. The writer also took a minor swipe at Robert Easton and others who were giving Audubon their information, and who might have a vested interest other than strictly condor preservation: *"Interwoven with the problem of protection of the condor and adequate control of fire is undoubtedly the interest of the stockmen. These users are interested in the maintenance of primitive conditions and have pointed out that this proposed road location would have a harmful effect upon the condor."*

The Forest Service response also suggested out that better fire control might be good for - maybe even vital to - the condors: *"It is felt that fire may have an important relationship to the condor. Large numbers of deer, quail, and doves were killed by the Matilija fire of 1932. It is certain that nests of the condor were disturbed in the vicinity of both Reyes Peak and the Topatopa Mountains, and possibly actual losses sustained due to the homing instinct of the wild species. In practically all cases, death of wild species results from asphyxiation at the time they are seeking refuge. While burning of the carcasses usually follows, it is not the immediate cause of death. It is quite possible that some condors have met death in this way.*

"From the best information available, the egg is laid in March, and the fledglings remain in the nest for about four months, or into the beginning of the most hazardous part of the fire season."

Despite the apparent lack of any flexibility on the part of the Forest Service, it was agreed that construction of the Hurricane Deck road would stop until an on-the-ground discussion could be held between Audubon and the Santa Barbara Forest staff in the spring of 1936. This meeting occurred 13-15 April 1936, during which time Cyril Robinson and Forest Supervisor Nash-Boulden took John Baker on an extended tour of condor country on the National Forest. The record is not clear as to who convinced who of what, but the upshot was that the Forest Service agreed not to complete the Hurricane Deck road until better information was available on its potential impacts on the condors. National Audubon agreed to help fund the necessary studies [53].

* * *

RESEARCH – In a December 1935 letter from the Forest Service to National Audubon concerning the Hurricane Deck road controversy, the problem of making management decisions based on inadequate information on condors was stressed [54]: *"Existing information with regard to the life history of the condor is wholly inadequate. Much additional study is needed to reveal the steps necessary to insure the preservation of the species, if this is now possible. This work must be done by a competent ornithologist, and should be extended to the entire known range of the species."* This wasn't the first time that the need for more information had been discussed. In March 1935, the Audubon Society had suggested that *"one of our own local men spend a couple of months without any noise or taking of pictures or publicity, in the areas involved to find out just exactly how many bird there are, where they are and what proper means can be taken to protect them"* [55]. Aldo Leopold thought the lack of information suggested *"the extreme attractiveness of an actual life history research project...on the remnant of this species"* [56]. In truth, there never had been a study of the California condor. Harry Taylor's egg collectors had supplied some important information about nesting and nest sites 1889-1902 (Chapter 16), and William Finley and Herman Bohlman had made observations and photographed at one nest site on a number of occasions in 1906 [57]. Everything else written about condors to that point was divided

232

between miscellaneous individual observations, and compilations of facts (and a large amount of fiction).

The investigation that grew out of the April 1936 Forest Service - Audubon meeting was the first attempt ever made to study these birds in any detail. Using funds raised by Audubon and by the Cooper Ornithological Club (a grand total of $270!), the Forest Service hired two observers to keep watch daily on the two known condor areas on the national forest, Sisquoc Falls and Whiteacre Peak (in Ventura County). The observers, Walter Maples at Sisquoc and John Jakes at Whiteacre, were regular summer employees of the Forest Service. The Audubon-Cooper money allowed for them to be hired in May, a month earlier than usual. Under the supervision of Cyril Robinson, they both spent that month solely on condor watching. They continued to watch into June 1936, until the money ran out [58]. Robinson continued observations on his own and in company with J. R. Pemberton, who was putting together a film on condors. Robinson arranged through the Regional Forester for all forests in southern California to report condor observations to him, and he continued to compile whatever condor information came his way for several more years. In April 1940, he summarized all the Forest Service observations [59].

As research, the Forest Service study had major flaws. Walter Maples and John Jakes had never done a bird study and, even though they had instructions on what to look for, their information was gathered somewhat haphazardly. Robinson was also at a disadvantage interpreting what was being seen, and drew some faulty conclusions. For example, he thought that males and females could be separated by plumage characteristics. Those he considered females were actually immature birds. His records don't address how he separated what he thought were females from other birds in non-adult plumage. Therefore, his estimated sex and age ratios are meaningless.

One of the highlights of Robinson's work was that he was able to confirm close to 50 condors on the national forest, mainly in the Sisquoc and Whiteacre Peak-Sespe Canyon areas. His count could have been safely increased by quite a number, I think, had he added in the miscellaneous sightings from Monterey County south to Orange and Los Angeles counties, and east into the southern Sierra Nevada. However, he still considered that these were birds that were out wandering, and that eventually came back to one of the two areas on the Los Padres National Forest.

Despite study limitations, Robinson and the Forest Service added considerably to the meager condor knowledge base, and the Robinson reports provided a springboard for the more "professional" study that was to follow (Chapter 18).

* * *

SANCTUARY AT SISQUOC FALLS - The 1936 field observations of Walter Maples, Cyril Robinson, and John Pemberton confirmed that Sisquoc Falls

233

was a significant condor area, being used by as many as 29 condors for roosting and bathing. Nesting in the cliffs near the falls was suspected, but could not be confirmed. The idea of closing the roosting and bathing area at Sisquoc Falls to all public entry arose early in 1936 - perhaps as a result of the meeting between Baker, Robinson, and Nash-Boulden. All the parties appeared supportive of the concept, and sought agreement from the Regional Forester for such a closure. In September 1936, the Regional Forester recommended to the Chief of the Forest Service that administrative regulation T-9 be expanded to permit such action [60]. On 13 January 1937, Section 261.11 of Title 36 of the Code of Federal Regulations, was amended to prohibit *"being on any area which has been closed by the Chief, Forest Service, for the perpetuation and protection of* (among other purposes) *rare or vanishing species of plants or animals..."* Further: *"The boundaries of each area shall be defined by the regional forester and indicated in so far as practicable by posting notices along such boundaries and on roads and trails leading into such areas."* Robinson prepared a brief "report on vanishing species areas," laying out rough boundaries of an area of approximately 1,200 acres around Sisquoc Falls, and on 5 May 1937, Forest Supervisor Nash-Boulden's signature established the Sisquoc Condor Sanctuary.

Symbolically, designation of the Sisquoc Sanctuary was very important, being the first active management ever done specifically for the condors. Practically, it had no effect on condor preservation. The area set aside was too small to have shielded the condors, had there been increases in the amount of human use in the vicinity. (The shield was never needed, because tens of thousands of acres on all sides of the Sanctuary remained lightly-used "wilderness.") Sisquoc Falls was never proven to be a condor nesting site (although several eggs were taken from somewhere in the Sisquoc Canyon around 1900, and condors were nesting within a few miles of the falls into the 1980s). Flocks of over 20 condors used the Sisquoc area at least until 1950, but no more than two or three were reported together at the Falls after 1960. Through much of the time from its establishment until the last wild condors were removed to zoos in the late 1980s, the Sanctuary sat vacant of any endangered birds. Still, the act of designating the sanctuary set a precedent, and probably helped give the Forest Service "courage" to use their authority in the 1950s to set aside the very important Sespe Condor Sanctuary in Ventura County (Chapter 19).

CHAPTER NOTES

1. A story similar to the following was published in newspapers across the United States, usually with titles like "feathered freaks," or "birds that can't fly or sing:" Anonymous. 1901. Some feathered freaks. *Evening News* (San Jose, California), 9 July 1901.

2. In many newspapers, similar to: Anonymous. 1901. Passing of a noble bird. *The Bee* (Washington, D. C.), 9 November 1901.

3. The condor reports were published in various journals and newspapers, and are recorded in my database. The 11 condors were seen in Ventura County: Anonymous. 1904. News and Notes. *Condor* 6(3):83.

4. Pemberton, J. R. 1910. Some bird notes from Ventura County, California. *Condor* 12(1):18-19.

5. Willett, G. 1912. Birds of the Pacific slope of southern California. *Pacific Coast Avifauna* 7:1-122.

6. Pages 22-24 *in:* Hornaday, W. T. 1913. Our vanishing wildlife, its extermination and preservation. New York, New York: Charles Scribner's Sons.

7. Chambers, W. L. 1915. California condor in Los Angeles County. *Condor* 17(2):102.

8. Sharp, C. S. 1918. Concerning a condor. Oologist 35(1):8-11.

9. Hornaday 1913 *op. cit.,* pages 21-25.

10. Letter, 22 August 1927, Robert E. Easton to the Director, Smithsonian Institution. Copy in the library, Santa Barbara (California) Museum of Natural History.

11. I searched through several large on-line archives of United States newspapers, and found 57 references to the California condor 1920-1927. Twelve were stories about condors in the National Zoo laying eggs, five mentioned condors in stories about extinct vultures, and five were reviews of the movie "Night Cry," that featured a live California condor as the villain. The other 35 were short pieces – often only a sentence long – giving "interesting facts" about condors or condors' eggs.

12. Among the unpublished field notes from the 1920s were:
Borrell, A. E. 1925. Field notes on a trip to Baja California, Mexico, 25 March to 23 June 1925. Museum of Vertebrate Zoology, University of California. Berkeley, California. (Several observations, 1-2 condors, Sierra San Pedro Martír.)
Canterbury, R. A. 1926. Notebook of Robert A. Canterbury, Olive Street, Santa Barbara. Library, Museum of Natural History, Santa Barbara, California (several observations of up to 2 condors over Santa Barbara).
Van Rossem, A. J. 1922. Birds seen on Mount Pinos, Kern County, California, 27-31 May 1922. One page typewritten. I have a copy in my files, original source unknown to me. (Condors, at least 4, seen daily.)

13. Huey, L. M. 1926. Notes from northwestern Lower California, with the description of an apparently new race of screech owl. *Auk* 43(3):347-362.

14. Redington, P. G. 1920. A California condor seen near head of Deer Creek.

235

California Fish and Game 6(3):133.

15. Letter, 3 September 1927, Alexander Wetmore, Smithsonian Institution, to Robert E. Easton. Copy in the library, Santa Barbara (California) Museum of Natural History.

16. Letter, 26 September 1927, Robert E. Easton to Alexander Wetmore, Smithsonian Institution. Copy in the library, Santa Barbara (California) Museum of Natural History.

17. Taylor, M. 1986. Mr. Santa Barbara. *Noticias* (Quarterly Bulletin of the Santa Barbara Historical Society) 32(4):60-74.

18. Hoffmann, R. 1930. California condor. *The Gull* (Golden Gate Audubon Society) 12(10):6. (Ten condors seen).
   Page 142 *in:* Koford, C. B. 1953. The California condor. Research Report Number 4, National Audubon Society. New York, New York. (Five condors seen.)

19. Reynolds, H. R. 1934. Gigantic condors with wingspread of fourteen feet found feasting in wild and rugged Cuyama Valley. *Los Angeles* (California) *Times,* 6 July 1934.

20. Letter, 29 December 1934, Emerson A. Stoner to George Begg (Superintendent, Sisquoc Ranch). Copy in the library, Santa Barbara (California) Museum of Natural History.

21. Letter, 4 January 1935, Robert E. Easton to Emerson Stoner. Copy in the library, Santa Barbara (California) Museum of Natural History.

22. Dyer, E. I. 1935. Meeting the condor on its own ground. *Condor* 37(1):5-11.

23. I have found about 150 letters generated following the Dyer article. Specifically referenced correspondence is cited below. All the letters are divided between the following three archives:
   Aldo Leopold Digital Archives, http://digital.library.wisc.edu/1711.dl/AldoLeopold
   Joseph Grinnell correspondence, Museum of Vertebrate Zoology, Berkeley, California
   Robert E. Easton archives, Santa Barbara Museum of Natural History, Santa Barbara, California.

24. Letter, 20 March 1935, Warren F. Eaton (Audubon Society) to Robert Easton. Copy in Robert E. Easton archives, Santa Barbara Museum of Natural History.

25. Memo, 9 March 1935, S. A. Nash-Boulden to Regional Forester, San Francisco. Copy in Robert E. Easton archives, Santa Barbara Museum of Natural History.

26. Letter, 29 April 1935, Joseph Grinnell to J. W. Nelson (Regional Forester, San Francisco). Copy in Joseph Grinnell correspondence, Museum of Vertebrate Zoology.

27. The 1908 killing of a condor in Los Angeles County received considerable

publicity because the bird was killed in the same canyon well-known because of condor photos taken there by William Finley and Herman Bohlman in 1906. It was also of great local interest because a constable had done the shooting. There were many news stories in 1908 and 1909, and a journal summary: Grinnell, J. 1909. Editorial notes and news. *Condor* 11(3):104.

This was the only conviction for shooting a condor prior to the current captive breeding and release program, but there have been several incidents since of people killing or shooting at condors. For example, see: Humphrey, J. 1999. Man pleads guilty to shooting California condor in Grand Canyon. U. S. Fish and Wildlife Service news release, 30 April 1999.

Woodson, J. L. 2003. Killer of condor gets probation, a $20,000 fine. *Los Angeles* (California) *Times,* 16 August 2003.

28. Beginning about 1910, the California Fish and Game Commission began issuing permits for collecting birds and mammals in the State. In the annual permits issued to institutions, the taking of California condors and a few other species was specifically prohibited. (Examples of these early permits [1911-1916] are in the archives of the Museum of Vertebrate Zoology.) However, this was an administrative restriction, and it was still possible to obtain permits from the Commission for collecting condors or their eggs in specific instances.

29. Cooper, J. G. 1890. A doomed bird. *Zoe* 1(8):248-249.

30. Letter, 4 January 1935, Robert E. Easton to California Fish and Game Commission; letter, 30 April 1935, Herbert G. Davis (Division of Fish and Game) to Robert Easton; letter, 7 May 1935, Robert E. Easton to Herbert C. Davis. Copies in Robert E. Easton collection, Santa Barbara Museum of Natural History.

31. Letter, 20 March 1935, C. E. Rachford (Forest Service) to Aldo Leopold. Page 422, Leopold Digital Archives (see note 23, above).

32. Rachford, C. E. 1935. National Forest Regulation G-20A. *Journal of Forestry* 33(1):28-31.

33. Memo, 8 April 1935, Regional Forester (San Francisco) to Chief Forester (Washington, D. C.). Copy in Robert E. Easton collection, Santa Barbara Museum of Natural History.

34. Letter 8 February 1935, Aldo Leopold to Christopher Rachford. Page 425, Leopold Digital Archives (note 23).

35. Letter, 5 March 1935, Joseph Grinnell to Aldo Leopold. Page 424, Leopold Digital Archives.

36. Letter, 12 March 1935, Aldo Leopold to Joseph Grinnell. Page 423, Leopold Digital Archives.

37. Letter, 18 June 1936, John Baker to Cyril Robinson. Copy in Robert E. Easton

237

collection, Santa Barbara Museum of Natural History.

38. Scott, C. D. 1936. Who killed the condors? *Nature Magazine* 28(6):368-370.

39. Letter, 28 December 1936, John Baker to Cyril Robinson. Copy in Robert E. Easton collection, Santa Barbara Museum of Natural History.

40. Robinson, C. S., W. H. Maples, and J. Johns. 1936. A report on study of life habits of the California condor – May, 1936. Unpublished progress report, 10 June 1936, Santa Barbara National Forest. Copy in Robert E. Easton collection, Santa Barbara Museum of Natural History.

41. Letter, 19 October 1936, J. R. Pemberton to Robert E. Easton. Copy in Robert E. Easton collection, Santa Barbara Museum of Natural History.

42. Memo, 9 July 1936, F. P. Cronemiller (Assistant Regional Forester) to Forest Supervisors in central and southern California. Memo, 11 July 1936, S. A. Nash-Boulden to central and southern California forest supervisors.

43. Letter 8 February 1935, Aldo Leopold to Christopher Rachford. Page 425, Leopold Digital Archives (note 23).

44. Memo, 8 April 1935, S. B. Show (Regional Forester) to Chief Forester (Washington, D. C.). Copy in Robert E. Easton collection, Santa Barbara Museum of Natural History.

45. Letter, 26 June 1935, Warren Eaton to G. B. (sic) Robinson. Copy in Robert E. Easton collection, Santa Barbara Museum of Natural History.

46. Letter, 5 July 1935, S. A. Nash-Boulden to Warren Eaton. Copy in Robert E. Easton collection, Santa Barbara Museum of Natural History.

47. Letter, 27 July 1935, S. A. Nash-Boulden to Warren Eaton. Copy in Robert E. Easton collection, Santa Barbara Museum of Natural History.

48. Letter, 16 August 1935, John Baker to F. A. Silcox (Chief, Forest Service). Copy in Robert E. Easton collection, Santa Barbara Museum of Natural History.

49. Letter, 19 August 1935, F. A. Wilcox to John Baker. Copy in Robert E. Easton collection, Santa Barbara Museum of Natural History.

50. Letter, 12 September 1935, Warren Eaton to S. A. Nash-Boulden. Letter, 18 September 1935, S. A. Nash-Boulden to Warren Eaton. Copies in Robert E. Easton collection, Santa Barbara Museum of Natural History.

51. Letter, 30 October 1935, Warren Eaton to F. A Silcox. Copy in Robert E. Easton collection, Santa Barbara Museum of Natural History.

52 Letter, 8 November 1935, F. A. Wilcox to Warren Eaton. Copy in Robert E. Easton collection, Santa Barbara Museum of Natural History.

53. Memo, 17 April 1936, S. A. Nash-Boulden to Santa Barbara National Forest files. Copy in Robert E. Easton collection, Santa Barbara Museum of Natural History.
  Letter, 6 May 1936, John Baker to Aldo Leopold. Pages 357-358, Leopold Digital Archives.

54. Letter, 8 November 1935, F. A. Wilcox to Warren Eaton. Copy in Robert E. Easton collection, Santa Barbara Museum of Natural History.

55. Letter, 20 March 1935, Warren F. Eaton (Audubon Society) to Robert Easton. Copy in Robert E. Easton archives, Santa Barbara Museum of Natural History.

56. Letter, 7 May 1935, Aldo Leopold to Joseph Grinnell. Page 420, Leopold Digital Archives (note 23).

57. Finley, W. L. 1906-1910. Life history of the California condor, Parts I to IV. *Condor* 8(6):135, 142; 10(1):5-10; 10(2):59-65; 12(1):5-11. Although excellent photos and some new information came from the Finley-Bohlman work, it cannot be considered serious "research." The nesting birds were subjected to extreme human disturbance, so their actions in and around the nest site were not entirely natural.

58. Letter, 26 May 1936, S. A. Nash-Boulden to John Baker. Also: Robinson, C. S., W. H. Maples, and J. Johns. 1936. A report on study of life habits of the California condor – May, 1936. Unpublished progress report, 10 June 1936, Santa Barbara National Forest. Copies in Robert E. Easton collection, Santa Barbara Museum of Natural History.

59. Robinson, C. S. 1940. Notes on the California condor, collected on Los Padres National Forest, California. Unpublished report, U. S. Forest Service, Santa Barbara, California.

Figure 16. California condors near Hole-in-the-Wall, Sespe Condor Sanctuary, in the area where Carl Koford made most of his condor observations in the 1930s and 1940s. Photo by Fred C. Sibley.

CHAPTER 18
THE LONG-AWAITED STUDY

While supporting the Cyril Robinson investigations, John Baker and Joseph Grinnell had a greater goal in mind: joining the forces of Audubon and University of California for an in-depth study of California condor biology. As noted in Chapter 17, the idea of a comprehensive study *("in accordance with the Stoddard definition of the term")* was brought up in a letter from Aldo Leopold to Grinnell early in 1835 [1]: *"The ecology of a condor might reveal some startling things from the standpoint of ecological science, and from the standpoint of conservation it should enable us to weigh the comparative value of this or that measure with much more precision than is possible at present."* Grinnell's response [2]: *"Yes, I agree that a full life history study of the condor, along modern lines of attack, would be a highly desirable undertaking. However, just as you say, the project would have to be very specially adapted to this particular kind of animal, and above all, with the danger constantly heeded that disturbance might result in wiping out some of its few remaining individuals—or prevent the birds from reproducing. But who is there in sight, sufficiently well qualified, to undertake this delicate kind of investigation?"*

John Baker and the Audubon Society were also interested in comprehensive studies of certain rare species. In talking about ongoing and proposed projects, Baker wrote to Leopold in November 1936 [3]: *"We are pretty well committed to one* (study) *on the Ivory-billed Woodpecker under* (Arthur A.) *Allen at Cornell. I am also anxious to start one under Dr. Joseph Grinnell with relation to the California Condor, and have written him to that effect."* Grinnell was quite receptive, but was concerned about alienating some of those already engaged in condor projects, namely Cyril Robinson on the national forest, John Pemberton with his condor photography, and Harry Harris. Grinnell seemed particularly concerned about Harris, who had been compiling all the written information on condors for a comprehensive bibliography. Although Baker had reportedly *"sought and obtained"* the Harris approval of a field study of the condor, Grinnell wanted to be sure [4]: *"Now I want to make absolutely sure of your deep-down feeling in the matter. I know full well that you long ago undertook the condor-bird as your special problem for study... Do you feel that if I should agree to Baker's proposition, both of the projects could be brought to completion entirely complementary to one another?"*

All the "condor people" proved supportive, and Baker was able to report in May 1937 [5]: *"The research project in relation to the California Condor has been on the cards for six to nine months and a way has all been cleared through Dr. Grinnell, the Forest Service administration in the Los Padres National Forest, Harry Harris, C. R (sic). Pemberton, Robert T. Moore; in other words, all those whose toes might seem to them to be tread on if they were not brought into the picture as cooperators at the initiation of the project. Three years will presumably complete that job."*

A year passed with no outward signs that the proposed condor study was going forward, but in May 1938 John Baker contacted J. R. Pemberton about showing his condor movies at Audubon's national convention [6]. *"As I think I wrote you before, I have been most anxious to succeed in launching a research project with relation to the California Condor to lay the basis for the most intelligent management in furtherance of their preservation and restoration. I am sure that your showing of your pictures here would be a tremendous help in that connection."*

In September 1938, Baker announced that Grinnell had agreed to supervise the condor research project, and that National Audubon had received a donation of $1,500 to help fund the study. He was seeking ways to raise the remaining $3,000 he felt was needed for the three-year project [7]. Ten days later, he reported that Robert T. Moore had donated $100, and offered *"to serve on a committee of Californians to assist in raising the balance of the necessary funds"* [8]. The remaining money was slow to materialize, much of it eventually coming as donations pledged at showings of John Pemberton's condor movies in 1939 and 1940 [9]. Grinnell did not wait to be fully funded, however, and in February 1939 he announced that he had chosen Carl B. Koford, a graduate student at the University of California, to be the condor researcher [10].

* * *

Carl Koford had an undergraduate degree in Forestry, a year of field work studying ground squirrels, and no knowledge of condors and apparently very little of bird biology. This isn't meant to detract from Koford's work; actually, his inexperience makes what he accomplished even more remarkable than if he had been a seasoned ornithologist. He took the job knowing nothing about his subject; his advisors were 300 miles away, and not very knowledgeable about condors, either; there was very little background information available to get him started; the country he had to work in was extremely rough and extremely isolated; and (for the first year of his study) his only transportation was his own shoe leather and acquaintances with cars. Only a few months into his study, Joseph Grinnell died, and his place as Koford's advisor was taken by Alden H. Miller at the Museum of Vertebrate Zoology. Despite these limitations and problems, his study rates even today with some of the best ever done on a single species of animal.

Grinnell had made it clear that this was to be a life history and behavior study. As he wrote to F. P. Cronemiller of the Forest Service [11]: *"The field work in view will be conducted in such a way as to disturb the condors in the least possible degree. Even photography will not be attempted. The facts that we are after are chiefly those to be obtained through patient long-distance*

242

watching of the birds, in order to obtain knowledge of daily, weekly and seasonal programs of activities, cruising radius, food sources, etc. In other words, it is the ecology of the living birds which we want more accurately to know about; and as a result, we are hopeful that all persons interested in the preservation of this depleted species will better know how to act toward preservation."

Because of Grinnell's emphasis, with which Alden Miller agreed, Koford spent most of the 480 days during which he watched condors in one general area, the Sespe Canyon-Hopper Ridge section of the Los Padres National Forest in Ventura County. There he took copious notes on what individual nesting, roosting, and flying condors did. He made incidental trips into the Sisquoc area, and occasionally visited other parts of the national forest. He had only limited opportunity to observe outside forest boundaries, so his information on condors feeding and flocking was mostly second-hand. To round out his doctoral thesis, he spent perhaps a month's time in libraries and museums, developing preliminary information on former numbers and distribution of condors [12].

Koford worked from March 1939 until June 1941, when he was called to active service in the Navy during World War II. He completed his condor work in 1946, following his discharge. Although he prepared an interim report in 1941, which was made available to the Forest Service and Audubon, he did not complete writing his thesis until 1950 and National Audubon did not publish it until 1953 [13]. By the time the scientific community and the public saw it, over ten years had passed since most of Koford's work had been done, and he had moved on to research in South America, Central America, and Puerto Rico. Late as it was in appearing, nothing significant concerning the condors had been published in the interim years, so his "old news" was still new and important.

According to Koford, John Baker had been disappointed in his report. Apparently, Baker had anticipated something more understandable to the general public, with more conservation and management implications that could be used to garner support for condor preservation. Koford himself admitted that his report was not *"readable and breezy"* [14], but it was exactly what Grinnell had in mind from the start. Three-quarters of it was unlikely to ever be of interest to anyone but an avid bird behaviorist. On the other hand, the other quarter presented the first reliable information on the past and present status of the species, and served as a solid springboard for research that followed. Not all his beliefs and conclusions have stood the test of time, due to his limited focus, but they were a reasoned start:

CONDOR NUMBERS - About 60; probably not much change for 30 years or more - no decrease, but no increase.

DISTRIBUTION - Still found in the counties of San Benito, Fresno, Monterey, San Luis Obispo, Santa Barbara, Ventura, Los Angeles, Kern and Tulare.

243

Almost all the birds seen outside of Ventura and Santa Barbara counties were just wanderers. Apparent local increases were not believed to be increases in the total population, but were responses to food supply.

REPRODUCTION AND SURVIVAL - One-quarter to one-third of the population (15 to 20 condors) were immature (under five years old); about five pairs were nesting each year. An annual survival rate of 90 to 95 per cent was estimated, somewhat higher for adults than for immatures.

PROBABLE CAUSES OF DECREASES - Wanton shooting and museum collection probably most important (although the case against shooting was based more on opportunity and attitude than overwhelming evidence); poisoning not as significant as some had indicated, but its true role still not clear; all other losses important cumulatively, but not individually.

CURRENT THREATS - Wanton shooting; nesting disturbance by photographers and others; increasing habitat disruption from roads, trails and oil wells; and possibly poison.

RECOMMENDATIONS -   Increase the legal protection of condors through Federal laws and strengthened State laws; close to entry the important condor nesting and roosting areas around Hopper Canyon and Whiteacre Peak; and educate about the law and the condors' needs those people most likely to come in contact with condors (ranchers, hunters, government workers).

* * *

Considering the National Audubon Society's objectives of conservation education and advocacy, John Baker's reported response to Koford's work might have been anticipated. The reaction of the Forest Service was not expected. When provided with a copy of Koford's interim report in late 1941 (which had information and recommendations quite similar to what was in the final report), they adopted almost an adversarial position. Whereas Cyril Robinson and S. A. Nash-Boulden had been actively advocating condor protection for a half-dozen years, now they seemed to want to distance themselves and the Forest Service from the bird. Perhaps it was the stresses of the war years, or new direction coming down to them from farther along the chain of command. Whatever it was, it had the sound of a new Forest Service. In a January 1942 letter to Baker, Robinson wrote the following [15]:

"While the Forest Service will assist in every way possible in the preservation of the environmental factors, it must be recognized that our first job, especially now, is the protection and best use of the forest area and the policy of the 'greatest good to the greatest number' cannot be ignored. One must, unfortunately, weigh the practical and economic benefits against the others in cases of this kind. This should not mean any serious disturbance to the condors now, or in the future, but it does mean that certain measures of (watershed) protection planned for and considered necessary must be carried out. I might point out in this regard that considerable development of roads and trails essential for protection and use of the forest area has been done

during the past ten years and apparently no real menace to the Condor has resulted."

Robinson went on to say that a closed area around Hopper Canyon (recommended by Koford) might be possible since most of the area was already closed to the public, but clearly it was not a high priority for the Forest Service. In May 1942, Assistant Regional Forester F. P. Cronemiller wrote to the Los Padres Forest [16]: *"In reviewing the report compiled from Mr. Koford's notes, I found little to indicate a need for sanctuaries or that the important condor problems were found within the boundaries of the National Forest."* He even suggested that the proposed Sespe closed area might be a publicity or fund-raising ploy by Audubon: *"Society officers must keep live issues before their members in order to maintain interest in the organization."* But, in the final analysis: *"Nevertheless, rather heroic measures are essential in saving this species from extinction, and we should probably take every feasible step toward improving survival of the birds within the National Forest area."*

Still, Forest Supervisor Nash-Boulden resisted what he felt would be further condor complications to his forest management. With an odd swipe at the work of both Cyril Robinson and Koford, in September 1945 he wrote to the Regional Forester:

"As to the condors, it seems to me that before we jump out into the middle or attempt to set any further restrictions or a policy other than those now in effect, we must gather many more facts..." He goes on to list how little is known about age of maturity, how often condors nest, how much food they need, and how long they live.

"If we are to secure these facts which are necessary before we can set up further plans or extend the boundaries of the present sanctuary, etc., we should have a qualified man assigned to live on the area or wherever condors may be during the year and secure this information... Mr. Koford made quite a study and has a lot of ideas both factual and theoretical as we all have, but this is not enough if we are to give the type of administration indicated."

CHAPTER NOTES

1. Letter, 7 May 1935, Aldo Leopold to Joseph Grinnell. Page 420, Leopold Digital Archives, http://digital.library.wisc.edu/1711.dl/AldoLeopold.

Leopold's reference to *"the Stoddard definition"* paid homage to Herbert Stoddard Sr. (1889-1970) and his 1931 book, "The bobwhite quail: its habits, preservation and increase." (New York: Charles Scribner's Sons), Stoddard's long-term study of bobwhites, covering their life history and ecology with recommendations for management, is still considered a model for single species research.

2. Letter, 22 June 1935, Joseph Grinnell to Aldo Leopold. Page 413, Leopold Digital Archives.

3. Letter, 7 November 1936, John Baker to Aldo Leopold. Pages 348-349, Leopold Digital Archives.

4. Letter, 4 January 1937, Joseph Grinnell to Harry Harris. Joseph Grinnell correspondence, Museum of Vertebrate Zoology, Berkeley, California.

5. Letter, 26 May 1937, John Baker to Aldo Leopold. Pages 328-330, Leopold Digital Archives.

6. Letter, 18 May 1938, John Baker to J. R. Pemberton. Copy in Robert E. Easton papers, Santa Barbara Museum of Natural History.

7. Letter, 20 September 1938, John Baker to J. R. Pemberton. Copy in Robert E. Easton papers, Santa Barbara Museum of Natural History.

8. Letter, 30 September 1938, John Baker to J. R. Pemberton. Copy in Robert E. Easton papers, Santa Barbara Museum of Natural History.

9. John Pemberton showed his film many times for various gatherings, and National Audubon showed it on occasion without Pemberton. On advice from Lee Chambers, Audubon printed up leaflets to be handed out as donation pleas.

10. Letter, 21 February 1939, Joseph Grinnell to Fred P. Cronemiller (Forest Service, San Francisco). Copy in Robert E. Easton papers, Santa Barbara Museum of Natural History.

11. Letter, 21 February 1939, *op. cit.*

12. Carl Koford's copious notes and journals are on file in the archives of the Museum of Vertebrate Zoology, Berkeley, California.

13. Koford, C. B. 1953. The California condor. Research Report Number 4. New York, New York: National Audubon Society.

14. Koford, C. B. 1981. Interview, Fall 1979. Pages 67-97 *in:* Phillips, D., and H. Nash. Captive or forever free? The condor question. San Francisco, California: Friends of the Earth.

15. Letter, 1 January 1942, Cyril Robinson to John Baker. Copy in Robert E. Easton papers, Santa Barbara Museum of Natural History.

16. Memo, 8 May 1942, F. P. Cronemiller to Forest Supervisor, Los Padres Forest. Copy in Robert E. Easton papers, Santa Barbara Museum of Natural History.

17. Memo, 19 September 1945, S. A. Nash-Boulden to the Regional Forester. Copy in Robert E. Easton papers, Santa Barbara Museum of Natural History.

CHAPTER 19
SANCTUARY IN THE SESPE

Condor use of the Whiteacre Peak-Hopper Canyon area of Ventura County had been known about for some years, but Carl Koford's studies began to show its true significance. While the vast San Rafael Mountains had a handful of condor nest sites and roosts scattered over a wide area (including the Sisquoc Condor Sanctuary), the watersheds of Sespe, Hopper, and Piru creeks formed a major land block of isolated canyons with hundreds of sandstone cliffs and groves of big-cone Douglas-fir. Regularly used condor nests, roosts, and bathing pools were scattered throughout. Whereas the establishment of the Sisquoc Condor Sanctuary turned out to be largely symbolic, preserving the Sespe looked like it could be one of the real keys to condor survival.

As noted in the last chapter, the Forest Service was worried about adopting any proposals by Koford or anyone else that might complicate Forest management. But they never seriously fought against public use closures in the Hopper Canyon - Whiteacre Peak area. Clearly, it was a very important condor area. Much of it was already in the 125,000 acre Sespe Game Refuge (established by the State Fish and Game Commission in 1917 to protect the deer herds of the area) [1], and the area was also seasonally closed for fire protection. The Los Padres forest position was stated by Cyril Robinson in a 1942 letter to John Baker of Audubon [2]: *"The use of Hopper Basin, however, is now well established as a primary nesting and gathering ground, and by reason of its location, public use in this area is light and would not be difficult to control. An extension of the existing State Game Refuge 3-D to cover the Hopper Basin would appear to be justifiable."* The national office of the Forest Service backed up this position later that year in response to an inquiry from the American Ornithologists' Union [3]: *"Considerable protection will be afforded the condor this year so far as the forest areas are concerned. Due to the serious fire hazard on the Los Padres Forest and the danger from sabotage at this time* (because of World War II) *the forest is to be closed to public entry during the fire period. Since the fire period extends beyond the hunting season, this action will automatically close the forest to hunting. The Hopper Mountain area is just within the Sespe State Game Refuge and it is expected that the forthcoming session of the California State Legislature will extend the refuge boundary sufficiently to provide better control in the Hopper Mountain vicinity."*

Probably because of the disruptions of war, and the fact that the Sespe area was closed to the public, anyway, no action was taken on extending the boundaries of the state game area. Deer hunting was closed entirely in San Luis Obispo, Santa Barbara, and Ventura counties in 1942 and 1943 [4]; only 19 deer were reported killed in Ventura County from 1934 to 1945 [5]. However, there were other disruptions. Sometime between the time Koford left the area in 1941 and his return in 1946, a road had been bulldozed into the headwaters of Hopper Creek, and was being regularly driven. Photographers and suspected egg collectors were making regular trips into the area, as were geologists seeking oil. After 1946, the Sespe Game Refuge was again opened to hunting. Some control was needed. All it took to establish a 35,000 acre Sespe Wildlife Area under Regulation T-9-I (the same authorization used for the Sisquoc Sanctuary) was the stroke of a Forest Service pen, which was accomplished 18 November 1947 [6].

With the establishment of the Sespe sanctuary, the Forest Service set up an advisory committee to help decide how to manage the area. The committee included local Forest Service employees, a representative from the National Audubon Society (John Baker, still the active voice in Audubon), one from the Museum of Vertebrate Zoology at U. C. - Berkeley (officially Alden Miller, successor to the deceased Joseph Grinnell, but practically Carl Koford, his student), and the Assistant Regional Forester in charge of wildlife management (F. P. Cronemiller). The committee all wanted to keep publicity about the new condor sanctuary to a minimum (a carryover from the Grinnell - Baker philosophy; *i.e.,* if nobody knows about condors, they won't bother them), but all agreed that a few actions needed to be taken. They agreed that no one was to enter the sanctuary without a written permit (limited to local game wardens, several ranchers who grazed cattle on the Forest, and persons who held oil leases on the land); the road on Hopper Ridge was to be gated and locked at the Forest boundary; all access trails were to be closed; and a patrolman was to be hired to enforce the closure. Audubon provided funds for the patrolman's salary in the spring, then the Forest Service picked him up on their fire control payroll [7].

* * *

The first two years after establishment of the Sespe Wildlife Area were reasonably peaceful. But the Sespe had a complication that the Sisquoc didn't have: oil. In August 1949, Los Padres Forest Supervisor L. A. Rickel wrote to John Baker [8]: *"Within the last few months oil and gas lease applications have been made on nearly every available area not now covered by lease in the condor sanctuary."*

The first oil wells had been drilled in the Sespe area in 1887, in what was known as the Tar Creek oil field (located midway between Hopper Creek and Sespe Creek). By 1900, 33 wells had been drilled in the Tar Creek area, with others in nearby locations in the Sespe district. Not ranked as a major producer of oil, still the Sespe district was estimated to have produced over three million barrels of oil by 1940. There were only 17 producing wells in the district in 1940. At that time, it was believed that *"the peak of production is without question past* (but) *there is no reason to believe that the district will not continue to produce commercially for some years"* [9].

Further development was slow. Oil was present in the Sespe area, but it was in a geologic formation that was not economically developable using the techniques available in the 1940s. (It wasn't until 1963 that hydraulic fracturing, or "fraking," made extraction from the Sespe area economical. In fraking, batteries of aircraft-type engines are used to pump fluid into the ground, fracturing the tight rock seams. Sand is then pumped into the fractures under intense pressure, holding the seams open and allowing the trapped oil to flow out [10].) In the late 1940s, on the heels of a major oil strike in the nearby Cuyama Valley (but in quite a different geologic formation) [11] and with war in Korea looming, speculators began filing on every available acre of government land. This was when Los Padres forest supervisor Rickel advised John Baker of the major increase in oil and gas lease applications on the national forest [12]. Granting new oil leases, and extending the life of existing ones, was in the hands of the U. S. Bureau of Land Management (even on National Forests), and was essentially automatic when an application was filed. The Forest Service had few grounds for recommending denial or cancellation of oil leases, but the Forest Service was taking a proactive stance [13]: *"The Forest Service has followed a policy of recommending rejection of all new applications within the Sanctuary and cancellation of all expiring leases if no active exploratory work or oil production is evident at the time the leases come up for renewal... There has been a considerable amount of correspondence between our Washington office and the Bureau of Land Management concerning renewal of leases in the area. I believe the matter is still not definitely settled."*

It was becoming very clear that invoking Regulation T-9-I was only the beginning of a complicated and controversial process necessary to make the Sespe Wildlife Area a real sanctuary. John Baker took it upon himself to see if it was possible to stop the issuance of oil leases in the condor area. Due in large part to the contacts that Baker made with Department of Interior people, the Forest Service and Bureau of Land Management by early 1950 agreed in principle to pursue withdrawal of the Sespe Wildlife Area from mining and mineral leasing [14]. But opposition from oil operators and speculators was growing. Because of the controversy, the Bureau of Land Management agreed to hold a public hearing on the proposal. It was scheduled for Los Angeles on 21 August 1950.

In June 1950, Spencer Halvorsen, an independent oil operator, announced that he would improve the Hopper Ridge road that had been built in 1946, and begin drilling that summer on his oil lease at "Hole in the Wall," the very center of the condor nesting and roosting habitat in upper Hopper Canyon [15]. There seemed to be no way to stop him, as he could show that he had spent considerable money on his lease in good faith (something most of the speculators could not show). This highlighted the need for some quick resolution of the conflict between condors and oil, and Baker again worked with oil company representatives to see if they could find a compromise that would allow oil development without jeopardizing the key condor habitat. Baker and Rodney Gale, who represented several of the oil interests, drafted a proposal that would have allowed oil development in much of the area under various restrictions [16], but Gale could not sell it to his constituents. The smaller oil interests did not want to act without the consent of the big oil companies, and the big oil companies thought that they could get a better deal by letting the public hearing go ahead [17]. President Truman had just committed our armed forces to allying with South Korea against North Korea, and the oil companies were banking on the Federal Government loosening the restrictions on domestic oil production, not tightening them.

Halvorsen did not drill in Hopper Canyon that summer. The record isn't clear as to why he didn't; perhaps he had merely meant to intimidate. The public hearing went on in August as scheduled, with Audubon, Sierra Club, and the Forest Service speaking in favor of the withdrawal, and almost everyone else speaking against it [18]. Most of those opposed represented the oil interests, but a number of local residents spoke against "locking up" government land so they couldn't use it. Ventura County water interests were concerned that the closure might stop later construction of dams on Piru and Sespe creeks.

Nothing was said at the hearing that added anything pertinent to the record. Much to the surprise of the oil interests, some of who had been counting on war rhetoric to halt the process, the Department of Interior hearing officer suggested the oil people get together with the Forest Service and Audubon to see if they could work out a compromise. Back at the negotiating table, all eventually agreed on stipulations very similar to those worked out several months earlier by Rodney Gale and John Baker, and previously rejected by the oil interests [19].

On 23 January 1951, Secretary of the Interior Oscar L. Chapman signed Public Land Order 695, withdrawing some 35,200 acres of the Sespe Wildlife Area as a condor sanctuary. Approximately one-third of the area, which included the Hopper Canyon - Whiteacre Peak condor congregation area, was completely withdrawn from entry for mining or mineral leasing (although oil extraction was permitted there if oil could be reached by slant-drilling from outside the closed area). The rest of the area remained open to oil leasing, but with the stipulation that no drilling could occur within one-half mile of any condor nest that had been used in the previous three years. (The half-mile limitation might have been adequate protection from the small-scale, low tech drilling operations of the 1950s. It would have been no protection at all from more recent oil "frakking" procedures. Happily, into the 1970s, no attempt had been made to drill on National Forest land that close to a condor nest.)

One final adjustment to the boundary of the Sespe Wildlife Area was made in November 1951, when the Chief of the Forest Service approved changing the boundaries of the sanctuary to include approximately 53,000 acres. This made a more logical boundary for national forest administration, but meant that a portion of the sanctuary was outside the area covered by the public land order [20]

In January 1952, the Forest Service approved a management plan for the Sespe Wildlife Area [21]. It was not detailed, because the emphasis remained on nearly complete closure of the area to human activities. Management continued in much the same vein for the next 20 years, with only one significant problem arising. As part of the compromise on mining and mineral leasing, the Forest Service had left the door open for access through the sanctuary for potential water development and flood control projects. Water development was to become one of the key condor issues of the 1960s.

CHAPTER NOTES

1. Hunter, J. S. 1917. New game legislation. *California Fish and Game* 3(3):100-102.

2. Letter, 1 January 1942, Cyril Robinson to John Baker. U. S. Forest Service files, Los Padres National Forest, Goleta, California.

3. Letter, 5 June 1942, Lloyd W. Swift (U. S. Forest Service, Washington, D. C.) to James Chapin (American Ornithologists' Union). U. S. Forest Service files, Los Padres National Forest, Goleta, California.

4. Pages 21-22 *in:* California Division of Fish and Game. 1944. Thirty-eighth biennial report of the Division of Fish and Game for the years 1942-1944. Sacramento, California: California Department of Natural Resources.

5. California Division of Fish and Game. 1946. Thirty-ninth biennial report of the Division of Fish and Game for the years 1944-1946. Sacramento, California: California Department of Natural Resources.

6. Case, P. C. 1952. Management plan for the Sespe Wildlife Area. Los Padres National Forest. U. S. Forest Service.

7. Letter, 12 April 1949, John H. Baker (National Audubon) to Fred P. Cronemiller (U. S. Forest Service). Copy in Los Padres National Forest files, Goleta, California.

8. Letter, 24 August 1949, L. A. Rickel to John Baker. Copy in Los Padres National Forest files, Goleta, California.

9. Clement, T. 1943. Sespe oil field. Pages 395-399 *in:* Jenkins, O. P. Geologic formations and economic development of the oil and gas fields of California. California Division of Mines Bulletin No. 118.

10. Anonymous. 1969. Fracturing, new drilling aid old Sespe. *Oil and Gas Journal* 67 (12 May 1969):119-120.

11. Hoots, H. W., and T. L. Bear. 1954. History of oil exploration and discovery in California. Pages 5-9 *in:* Jahns, R. H. (editor), Geology of southern California. Chapter IX, Oil and gas. California Division of Mines Bulletin 170.

12. Letter, 24 August 1949, L. A. Rickel to John Baker. Copy in Los Padres National Forest files, Goleta, California.

13. Letter, Rickel to Baker, *op. cit.*

14. Letter, 7 October 1949, John Baker to L. A. Rickel. Letter, 18 February 1850, Baker to Rickel. Copies in Los Padres National Forest files, Goleta, California.

15. Letter, 9 June 1950, L. A. Rickel to John Baker. Copy in Los Padres National Forest files, Goleta, California.

16. Letter, 27 July 1950, Alden H. Miller (Museum of Vertebrate Zoology) to J. R. Pemberton. Also, undated draft (late July or early August 1950), "Suggested form of agreement for the purpose of safeguarding and reconciling interests in the Condor Reserve." Copies in Los Padres National Forest files, Goleta, California.

17. Letter, 5 August 1950, Rodney Gale (Eagle Rock, California) to John Baker. Copy in Los Padres National Forest files, Goleta, California.

18. U. S. Bureau of Land Management. 1950. Public hearing held commencing August 21, 1950...Los Angeles, California, to consider withdrawal from all forms of disposition under the public land laws including the mining and mineral leasing laws, approximately 32,000 acres of land for use as a Condor Sanctuary in the Los Padres National Forest. Three volumes, typed. Copies with U. S. Bureau of Land Management and U. S. Forest Service.

19. Memo, 25 August 1950, Regional Forester to Chief of the Forest Service. Copy is Los Padres National Forest files, Goleta, California.

20. Rickel, L. A. 1951. Proposed revision of boundary, Sespe Wildlife Area (Condor Sanctuary): original report on Vanishing Species Area approved by Chief 11/18/47. Submitted 13 September 1951, approved by Chief, Forest Service 7 November 1951. Copy in Los Padres National Forest files, Goleta, California.

21. Case, P. C. 1952. Management plan for the Sespe Wildlife Area. Los Padres National Forest. U. S. Forest Service.

CHAPTER 20
AN IDEA WHOSE TIME HADN'T COME

In 1949, Belle J. Benchley, Executive Director of the San Diego Zoo, applied to the California Fish and Game Commission for a permit to capture condors to breed in captivity. No condors were captured, and what followed is generally treated as an interesting sidelight in condor preservation history. Actually, the aftermath of that permit application defined condor research and management for the next 30 years [1].

Mrs. Benchley asked for the permit on the basis of the success she and curator of birds Kenton C. Lint had increasing the production of captive Andean condors. Both Andean and California condors in the wild usually raise one young every two years, the result of a one-egg clutch, a long incubation period, and the slowness with which young condors gain independence. The zoo's pair of Andean condors had produced an egg and reared a chick one year, then (as expected) had skipped a year before laying their next egg. That egg was allowed to be incubated by the parent birds, but the nestling was taken after several weeks and raised by hand. Instead of skipping a year, the condors laid an egg the next year. This egg was hatched by the parents, and again the nestling was removed and reared by hand. Once again, the adult laid eggs in consecutive years. This time, the egg was taken and hatched in an incubator; the adults produced a second egg a month and a half later. That nestling was taken from them after four months, stimulating the parents to lay for the fourth year in a row. Through manipulation of egg and young the next year, the pair were again induced to produce two young. In six years, one pair of Andean condors gave rise to seven young, four of them in only two nesting seasons. The potential to produce four young in the time a wild pair of condors would produce only one seemed to the zoo personnel a possible answer to some of the California condors' problems [2].

There is some confusion over what Mrs. Benchley initially requested, and what action was taken by the Fish and Game Commission. It was reported in Audubon Society and Forest Service files that the Zoo had asked for permission to collect either two condor chicks or two eggs, but Zoo and Commission records agree that the application was for trapping two mature condors. The Commission approved the trapping permit at their 6 January 1950 meeting [3], but opposition developed immediately, led by Carl Koford and Alden Miller of the Museum of Vertebrate Zoology [4]. On 27 January 1950, the Commission withdrew their permission, pending a public hearing on the subject. Then followed a 21 February 1950 letter from the Forest Service to the Commission, stating that - under Department of Agriculture Regulation T-9 (see Chapter 17) - they would deny entry onto national forest land for any condor collecting [5]. The public hearing was held in San Diego 28 July 1950; with the Forest Service refusing to allow trapping on the national forest, and with more public opposition than support, the Commission refused to reinstate the permit [6].

Stymied by the Forest Service refusal to allow condor trapping on the national forest, the Zoo put its condor breeding plans on hold for two years. Then, on 28 October 1952, Mrs. Benchley reapplied for a permit. She noted that they had not asked earlier because *"efforts to locate pairs of Condors living outside the Preserve* [national forest], *in areas suitable to their capture without injury were unsuccessful."* However, she continued, *"Leslie F. Edgerton, a game warden who is very familiar with the zoo and its program of breeding Andean condors has located several condors living outside any preserve. He has been watching these birds with care and believes that a pair can be collected safely"* [7]. The Commission considered the request at their meeting on 24 November 1952; despite continuing protests from representatives of the Museum of Vertebrate Zoology, Sierra Club, and Cooper Ornithological Society, the vote was unanimous in favor of the permit [8].

Director Benchley hired Lewis Wayne Walker, a nature writer and photographer, to capture two condors. For three months during the winter 1952-1953, Walker attempted to bait condors to his trap site on a private ranch just south of the national forest. Although as many as 12 condors approached the trap site, none were captured [9]. In the meantime, the opposition had managed to enlist the support of a state senator, and in early April 1953 the California Assembly passed a resolution barring all future attempts to trap condors [10]. The ban did not take effect until 15 January 1954, but the Fish and Game Commission immediately requested that the Zoo delay any trapping efforts until after 15 June 1953, to avoid any possible disruption of nesting activity [11]. The Zoo attempted to shift their efforts away from the controversial refuge area by checking reports of condors around Mojave, California, some 100 miles northeast, but no good trapping location was found [12]. In late 1953, Walker was again attempting to capture condors on the ranch above Fillmore. Cold, snowy weather hampered his efforts and, although he reported seeing condors regularly, none had been captured before the trapping permit expired in January 1954 [13]. With the new law in place, and with Mrs. Benchley retiring from the Zoo, all plans for captive breeding of California condors were set aside.

* * *

Opponents of the Zoo plans - including Miller, Koford, John Baker of National Audubon, Robert Easton of Sisquoc fame (Chapter 17) - received most of the publicity, and eventually "won." Their arguments were that captive breeding wasn't necessary (because, although there weren't many condors, Koford thought the population was stable); that capturing either adult condors or nestlings would likely cut down on the breeding potential of those left in the wild; that, because the sexes were not readily identifiable, probably more than

254

two condors would have to be handled before the Zoo secured a pair; that captive raised birds would never be suitable for release to the wild; and that a zoo was no place for a California condor [14]. However, the Zoo was supported by a number of biologists, aviculturists, and bird lovers who saw the Zoo's success breeding Andean condors as directly applicable to improving the California condors' status. Notable was Jean Delacour, director of the Los Angeles County Museum of Natural History, and one of the best-known and respected ornithologists in the world. William J. Sheffler, a director of the Los Angeles Museum and a past president of the Cooper Ornithological Society, also favored the captive breeding plans. Along with Mrs. Benchley and curator Ken Lint, they argued that the time to start the experiment was while the condor population was "stable" (if indeed it was), rather than waiting until there was little hope of saving the species from extinction [15].

Basically, the "sides" in the argument were those who favored proactive management versus those who expected the condors to make it on their own with minimal help. In his soon-to-be released report, Koford made only three recommendations [16]: enact federal protective laws to supplement state laws; maintain nesting sanctuaries; and educate those people most likely to influence condor survival (government workers, ranchers, hunters, oil men). This was a continuation of the Joseph Grinnell philosophy that the condors would do best if few people knew about them, and they were allowed to peacefully fend for themselves (Chapter 17). To this, Koford added an esthetic slant [17]: *"To put a condor in a zoo greatly diminishes the quality of the recreational value of seeing a California condor in its native habitat. Compared to the Andean condor, the California condor in a cage is ugly, pitiful and uninspiring -- just a big black vulture with a naked head and neck. The beauty of the California condor lies entirely in the magnificence of its matchless soaring flight. No cage is large enough to allow a condor to soar. If some day -- I hope not in our lifetime -- there is only one condor left, would it not be vastly preferable to see it soaring over the Sierra Madre than imprisoned in a city park?"* The contrast between the free-flying condor - the very spirit of the wilderness - and the ugly caged vulture would surface again and again in future years whenever preservation of the condor was discussed.

* * *

Some objections to the San Diego Zoo proposal were justified. For example, there was no way to identify the sex of a California condor in the field at that time, so how would Walker know when he had a pair? Also, if condors were caught, how would one man working alone safely handle them in such a remote location? The objective was obscure, as well: was the purpose to produce condors for other zoos, or was the intent to eventually try to release zoo-produced condors to the wild? If the latter, did Benchley and Lint have the same vision expressed by Walker, of eventually releasing condors on some remote island off Mexico? [18]. The answer to that question might have made

255

a difference to some people interested in the proposal, but the Fish and Game Commission reduced the options by stipulating in the November 1952 permit that condors produced in captivity could not be released to the wild, but could only be given to other California zoos. This had the odd effect of changing the effort from a potential rehabilitation project to merely a zoo program, thereby providing fuel to the opposition viewpoint that California condors did not belong in zoos!

Probably most damning to the zoo proposal was the timing of it. Koford's long-term study was just being made public, and it indicated an apparently stable condor population. Memories of the long fight to improve the security of the Sespe condor sanctuary - a fight based largely on the perceived need to keep the condors safe from disturbance - were still fresh enough to raise questions about how this proposed "disturbance" would differ from other perturbations of the population. Breeding in captivity of any animal had to be considered experimental at that time, and zoos were still perceived as menageries, not scientific entities. Even with much better planning, it's doubtful the project could have happened at that time.

* * *

For the next 15 years, the San Diego Zoo venture was itself a mostly forgotten incident in the annals of the California condor. Not to be forgotten, however, was the California state law that grew out of the controversy. The Assembly resolution, as incorporated into the Fish and Game Code as Section 1179.5, read: *"It is unlawful to take any condor at any time or in any manner. No provision of this code or any other law shall be construed to authorize the issuance of a permit to take any condor and no permit heretofore issued shall have any force or effect for any purpose after January 15, 1954."* The law was so rigid that, even though the condor population was clearly in decline, all innovative thought about condor recovery was repressed through the 1960s and into the 1970s. Isolation and "protection" - although clearly failing as preservation strategies - continued to be the only games in town.

CHAPTER NOTES

1. The San Diego Zoo story played out largely in the newspapers. I've pieced together the sequence of events from a variety of sources, mainly second-hand. The records of the California Fish and Game Commission on this subject are incomplete, but a few items were located in the California State Archives (File F3498:1-13a, Fish and Game Commission records).

2. Lint, K. C. 1951. Condor egg hatched in incubator. *Condor* 53(2):102.
   Walker, L. W. 1953. A naturalist's efforts to save last condors. Los Angeles (California) *Times,* 4 May 1953.

3. Analysis of agenda items, California Fish and Game Commission meeting, 28 July

1950, San Diego. California State Archives (Sacramento, California), File F3498:1-13a, Fish and Game Commission records.

4. Childs, H. E. 1950. Cooper Club meetings, Northern Division. *Condor* 52(2):96.

5. Analysis of agenda items, California Fish and Game Commission meeting, 28 July 1950, San Diego. California State Archives (Sacramento, California), File F3498:1-13a, Fish and Game Commission records.

6. I have been unable to locate minutes of the 28 July 1950 Commission meeting, so the results are inferred from later communications. In a 28 October 1952 letter from Belle Benchley to California Governor Earl Warren, Mrs. Benchley stated that a permit had been issued in July 1950, but that the Zoo had been unable to locate any condors outside of the national forest. However, in a 3 November 1952 response from the Commission it was stated that *"according to our records, no permit was authorized by the Commission when this matter was discussed in 1950."* The letters are in the California State Archives (Sacramento, California), File F3498:1-13a, Fish and Game Commission records.

7. Letter in California State Archives (Sacramento, California), File F3498:1-13a, Fish and Game Commission records.

8. California Fish and Game Commission meeting minutes, 24 November 1952. California State Archives (Sacramento, California), File F3498:1-13a, Fish and Game Commission records.
   Also: Miller, A. H. 1953. More trouble for the California condor. *Condor* 55(1):47-48.

9. Walker, L. W. 1953. A naturalist's efforts to save last condors. Los Angeles (California) *Times,* 4 May 1953.

10. Anonymous. 1953. Bill protecting condors, burros passes Assembly. *Press Courier* (Oxnard, California), 3 April 1953.

11. Anonymous. 1953. Zoo at San Diego asked to delay condor hunt. Los Angeles (California) *Times,* 11 April 1953.

12. Anonymous. 1953. Survey seeks new sites for condor traps. Los Angeles (California) *Times,* 13 August 1953.
    Anonymous. 1953. Mojave area given up in condor hunt. Los Angeles *Times,* 20 August 1953.

13. Anonymous. 1954. Condor hunt in Sespe country fails again. Los Angeles *Times,* 19 January 1954.

14. Miller, A. H. 1953. The case against trapping California condors. *Audubon Magazine* 55(6):261-262.

15. Ainsworth, E. 1953. Hunt starts for pair of California condors. Los Angeles *Times*, 10 February 1953.

16. Pages 135-138 *in:* Koford, C. B. 1953. The California condor. Research Report No. 4, National Audubon Society (New York, New York).

17. During the trapping controversy in 1953, Carl Koford sent copies of his "open letter" to many individuals, organizations, and newspapers, and portions of it appeared in a variety of publications. Copies are preserved in the files of the Museum of Vertebrate Zoology (Berkeley, California).

18. Walker, L. W. 1953. A naturalist's efforts to save last condors. Los Angeles (California) *Times*, 4 May 1953.

CHAPTER 21
DAMS ON THE SESPE?

The flurry of publicity related to the publication of Carl Koford's study, the Sespe oil withdrawal, and the San Diego Zoo controversy was followed by eight years during which the condors almost disappeared from public awareness. From 1954 to 1962, I could find only four magazine articles about condors, two book chapters, 15 "scientific" entries (10 of them archaeological or paleontological), and six brief observational notes (e.g., someone saw a condor in Kern County). Even the agency files are sparse for this eight year period. There was correspondence between the Los Padres National Forest and National Audubon Society about William M. Harper, the first full-time Sespe Wildlife Area patrolman. (Audubon was paying part of his salary.) Also, John Baker (still president of National Audubon) was expressing some concern about water projects proposed near the condor areas - a foretaste of what was destined to become one of the big condor issues of the mid-60s.

About 1961, National Audubon began thinking about a new condor study, a follow-up to Carl Koford's 1939-1946 work. This time, the emphasis was to be on determining what changes, if any, had occurred in condor numbers, reproduction, and mortality since Koford's time. The new researchers were expected to repeat Koford's methods as closely as possible, then evaluate the differences. Alden Miller, Koford's advisor after the death of Joseph Grinnell, was to supervise the study. The field work was to be done by two rancher brothers, Ian and Eben McMillan, apparently on the specific recommendation of Koford [1].

The study began in February 1963 and continued into the summer of 1964. The results were disappointing, but perhaps due most to differences in expectations. According to Miller [2], the primary objective was *"to compare conditions in the condor population with those so fully described by Carl B. Koford...* (to see) *what trends prevailed since 1946...* (and to) *judge the efficacy of the condor refuge and other conservation measures which had been advocated by Koford."* Koford, however, remembered it differently [3]: *"I recommended that Audubon get the McMillan brothers to work on it* (the study), *because I thought the thing that needed to be done then was to appraise the public attitude toward the bird."* The McMillans, with no biological training and with only anecdotal knowledge of birds, clearly were not equipped to gather trend information that could be compared to Koford's findings. In fact, they made no attempt to repeat Koford's methods, making only cursory trips to condor nesting areas, whereas Koford spent almost all his time there (Chapter 18). Instead, they concentrated their efforts on the condors' rangeland feeding habitat. Koford seldom visited those areas, so some of the McMillan observations were useful additions to the overall condor record, but none of them were useful in determining what had happened to the condor population between 1946 and 1963. The final report (prepared by Miller, although he seldom joined the McMillans in the field) had estimates of numbers of condors (40, to Koford's 60) and productivity (one-third of the condors under six years of age, similar to Koford's calculation) [4]. Neither figure was derived from reliable data collecting.

The conclusion of the Miller-McMillan report was that shooting and poisoning had resulted in the loss of one-third of the condor population since Koford's time. The McMillans did find evidence of four condors shot between 1959 and 1964, but most of their discussion of shooting is anecdotal (e.g., one rancher opined that *"80 per cent of the hunters would shoot at a condor if it flew by them within range;"* another said that *"the average hunter, who hunts along the roads, would shoot at any large bird that comes within range")* [5]. Their "evidence" against poisons was mere suspicion [6]. (See Chapter 23). Most of their recommendations for helping the condors were repeats or refinements of the ones given in the previous 30 years [7]: improve law enforcement and legal protection (including establishing Federal laws), limit human use of the Sespe Wildlife Area, don't build any more roads into condor habitat, and curtail the use of poisons in condor areas. New and important was a recognition that large tracts of private land were vital to condors (both as sources of food, and as locations where they might be killed), and that any successful condor preservation program had to include interactions with the owners and managers of these lands. Also new was a recommended change in policy toward publicity. Regarding the 30-year old strategy first voiced by Joseph Grinnell and John Baker (i.e., keep the condors secret, and people will leave them alone), the Miller-McMillan report concluded: *"It is clear now that with heightened interest in the condor, and with much larger numbers of people in southern California, that education and appropriate public notice must be positive and overt."*

Rather than limiting "education" to those groups that might shoot a condor or might invade nesting habitat (hunters, ranchers, oil workers), the Miller-McMillan report recognized a need to involve the general public in the condors' future. They advocated lectures, conferences, and even officially identified and designated observation points where people would have a chance to see the birds without disturbing them. This change in emphasis, which was adopted by National Audubon Society, Forest Service and other agencies, came too late to "save" the condors. But without the publicity and support generated in the years after 1965, I doubt there would have been many opportunities to do anything innovative for the species.

* * *

The Miller-McMillan report was released just as an old condor-related issue was resurfacing, a plan to build a dam on Sespe Creek near the Sespe Wildlife Area. With a greatly expanding human population and the rapid spread of agriculture, arid southern California's demand for water was always on the increase. Sespe Creek, the largest undammed stream in the region, was an obvious target for development. Proposals to dam portions of it and nearby Piru creek date back before 1920, when Sespe Light and Power Company (which had acquired Sespe water rights before 1912) was granted permission to transfer property to Sespe Power Corporation so that hydroelectric facilities could be built [8]. Shattuck Construction Company entered into an agreement to raise funds for dam construction [9], but no dams were built. A dam on Sespe Creek at either the Topatopa or Cold Springs site was proposed again in 1933 [10]. In 1947, the Santa Clara Water Conservation District had filed for year-round water use of both Sespe and Piru creeks [11]. To that point, the welfare of the California condor had not been raised as an issue in water development. However, in 1950, the Ventura County Board of Supervisors became concerned that proposed oil drilling restrictions in the Sespe Wildlife Area (Chapter 19) might interfere with future water developments nearby. At a 21 August 1950 public hearing in Los Angeles, F. P. Cronemiller of the Forest Service assured the Board of Supervisors [12] that: *"It is not intended for the* (oil entry withdrawal) *order to prevent any planned water development or flood control program."* The 1952 management plan for the Sespe Wildlife Area reaffirmed Cronemiller's statement, with a mild caveat [13]: *"Full cooperation will be given to water development and flood control projects. In working with these water and flood organizations we will require that their operations interfere as little as possible with the Condors. Their work, of course, will be mainly confined to major stream channels that are now open corridors."*

In May 1951, surveys were begun on Sespe Creek to identify the best site for a water storage dam [14], and in September 1952 the United Water Conservation District announced that they had selected dam sites on both Sespe Creek and Piru Creek [15]. However, in December 1952, Ventura County voters rejected the bond issue that would have funded the two projects [16]. United Water shelved their Sespe Creek plans, and concentrated on the lower stretches of Piru Creek, where Santa Felicia Dam was eventually built and Lake Piru created. This dam was only a few air miles from the southeastern edge of the Sespe Wildlife Area. However, it was located almost on the Santa Clara River valley floor, close to 3,000 feet lower than the Hopper Canyon nesting and roosting areas, and well shielded from them by the bulk of Arundell Peak. It was never considered a "condor issue."

Only ten months after voters defeated the Sespe dam bond issue, the California Division of Water Resources issued a report citing the seriousness of the water supply in Ventura County, and proposing a number of dam sites, including two on Sespe Creek [17]. United Water was busy on the approval of Piru Dam at the time, and took no overt action on Sespe. However, the Sespe dam issue came back to life in September 1956, when the U. S. Bureau of Reclamation proposed damming Sespe Creek and piping some of the water to

261

the arid Simi Valley 20 miles south [18]. A dispute developed between United Water and the Calleguas Municipal Water District (which served Simi Valley) over which entity would control Sespe water [19]. The State Water Rights Board reviewed the claims in April 1957 [20], and after a five-month study ultimately decided in favor of the Calleguas District [21]. United Water immediately appealed the decision [22].

Before United Water lost the Sespe water fight, they had approached the Forest Service about building an access road to the Topatopa dam site, following the Squaw Flat Road corridor through the middle of the Sespe Wildlife Area. This was of concern to the Forest Service because of the proximity of the route to condor nesting and roosting areas. Apparently those advances were rebuffed with very little publicity, because in March 1957 United Water announced they intended to reach the dam site from the west along Sespe Creek, well away from the sanctuary [23]. Other than the expression of concern voiced by Ventura County during the oil hearings in 1950, this was apparently the first time that Sespe water and condors had been covered together in the news.

Review of the United Water-Calleguas District dispute took almost three years to resolve, during which time there was no action on developing Sespe Creek water. When the Superior Court made their judgment in March 1961, they reversed the earlier ruling that favored the Calleguas Water District and granted Sespe water rights to United Water [24]. Later that year, United Water once again unveiled a proposal for a three-dam complex on Sespe Creek, but apparently some agreement was still required from the State Water Board before action could be taken [25]. The Water Board's final decision was not forthcoming until 29 April 1963; when it came, the ruling stipulated that - for United Water to retain Sespe water rights - dam construction had to begin by 1 December 1967 and be completed by 1 December 1972 [26]. United Water immediately began promoting the Sespe water project, again. In February 1964, the U. S. Bureau of Reclamation recommended that the proposed dams on Sespe Creek serve not only for water storage but become the hub of a major new recreation area for southern California. With this in mind, they entered into a one-year agreement with United Water to develop specific plans for the complex [27]. If controversy had been their aim, they couldn't have timed the announcement any better. National Audubon Society held their annual convention in Tucson, Arizona in November 1964, with one of the highlights being the initial presentation of the Miller-McMillan findings. Word arrived simultaneously of an apparent one-third decrease in the number of condors since Koford's studies - with an indictment of shooters as the main agents of the decline - and a plan to attract great numbers of recreationists - including shooters - into the heart of the condor nesting area. National Audubon immediately took a stand against the dam proposal, and the 900 delegates at the convention quickly spread the word from coast to coast [28]. National

Audubon was soon joined by Defenders of Wildlife in opposing the project [29]; the Committee on Bird Protection of the American Ornithologists' Union expressed their concern [30]; and Santa Barbara condor enthusiasts Dick Smith and Bob Easton published anti-dam articles in a number of periodicals [31].

It was not to be a solid environmentalist front against the water project, however. Reminiscent of the San Diego Zoo captive breeding controversy (Chapter 20), a group of bird "experts" lined up on the side of United Water, proclaiming that the dam and access road could be constructed without negative impact to the condors. Whereas the 1950 proponents of captive breeding had spoken only as individuals, the Topatopa Dam advocates were well organized. In fact, by late February 1965 they were being interviewed as a group [32], and United Water was using them to draft a "management and protection plan" for the condors, to be integrated into the water project plans [33].

United Water's "experts" had a certain credibility, too; in fact, they could claim considerably more experience with condors than could the Topatopa dam opponents. With Carl Koford out of the area on other projects, and John Baker no longer the head of National Audubon, those challenging the Sespe project had only Koford's report and the questionable expertise of Alden Miller and the McMillan brothers to rely on. United Water had Jean Delacour and William Sheffler, internationally known ornithologists (although without condor expertise). C. V. Duff, who had been one of the Cooper Club members opposed to the San Diego Zoo proposal, was solidly with United Water. They also had Ed N. Harrison and Sidney Peyton, both of whom could claim more first-hand experience with condors than almost anyone except Koford. Neither was a trained ornithologist, but both had held leadership roles in the Cooper Ornithological Society, and were well known in southern California. Harrison, working with J. R. Pemberton, had produced the best films ever made on California condors, and Harrison had accompanied Koford in the field on many occasions. Peyton was an active egg collector whose pursuit of condor eggs had taught him much about the nesting habits of the species, and his observations were quoted extensively in both the Koford and the Miller-McMillan reports. No one but Koford could really claim the breadth and depth of study to qualify as an "expert," but the combined credentials of United Water's panel were impressive.

The condor plan prepared for United Water started with a direct attack on National Audubon Society and the recommendations included in the Miller-McMillan report: *"The most that can be said about this so-called program is that it is more of the same unimaginative approach which has been successful in reducing the condor population by one-third in the past 15 years... It fails to assign proper importance to the known reasons for the condor decline and it fails to provide imaginative and aggressive steps based on these reasons."*

263

Truthfully, the criticism wasn't far off the mark. In December 1964, as a follow-up to the Miller-McMillan study, National Audubon had announced a new "five-point program" to protect the condors [34]. The points were: (1) support more diligent enforcement of laws protecting the condor; (2) appoint a full-time "condor warden" (but without law enforcement authority) to work with the Forest Service and State of California on condor issues; (3) increase education efforts to generate more public interest in the condor; (4) work with the Forest Service to increase protection of condor habitat within the sanctuary areas; and (5) encourage pest-control agencies to reduce chemical hazards to condors. There were few specifics to their plan, no standards for measuring success or failure of the efforts, and no contingency plans should those efforts prove inadequate.

In contrast, United Water offered specific proposals that certainly sounded more thoughtful than Audubon's "five point program." Using (selected) wording straight out of the Koford and Miller-McMillan reports, they concluded that: (1) illegal shooting was the main problem for the condors; (2) change in food supply had been an important determiner of condor numbers and distribution in the past century; (3) condors were reproducing successfully within four miles of the town of Fillmore and other human disturbances; and (4) a reduction in mortality of only two birds per year could swing the condor population trend from decrease to increase. With these "facts" as their base, they argued that a year-long supplemental feeding program carried on inside the Sespe Condor Sanctuary would help alleviate any food-related problems, and would also keep condors away from areas where they were more likely to be shot or poisoned. Since condors were reproducing successfully within four miles of Fillmore, then the proposed access road through the sanctuary could not possibly disturb them. To further cut down the incidence of shooting and disturbance, they offered to fence the corridor road so people would have less opportunity to trespass into the nesting areas than they did off the existing Squaw Flat road. Finally, United Water offered to help with the educational effort and to support new research into the condors' needs.

It didn't seem likely that the current "condor people" would be able to reach any agreement on the needs of the condors.

* * *

Before 1965, there is little mention in the condor annals of the U. S. Fish and Wildlife Service (known as the Bureau of Sport Fisheries and Wildlife for a few years of its existence). When it was mentioned, it was likely to be a negative reference to the Service's predator and rodent control program, which was suspected of killing the condors that everybody else was trying to save. Considering the prominence of the Fish and Wildlife Service in endangered species matters in the last 40 years, one might wonder where they were before that time.

The Service and its predecessor, the U. S. Bureau of Biological Survey, had been involved in "endangered species" matters, long before "endangered" became a legal classification. The first national wildlife refuges were established for colonial birds threatened by plume hunters and egg collectors. These sanctuaries had been followed by bison and elk refuges. During the drought and "Dust Bowl" years of the 1930s, emphasis had switched to ducks and geese. With active management and a return to wetter times, waterfowl had recovered to a considerable extent. Still, the Service chose to stay strongly waterfowl-oriented, working closely with the various state fish and game agencies to guarantee a shootable supply of ducks and geese. There were no prohibitions against working with other types of birds; there was just very little interest in them within the Service.

Two circumstances of the 1950s and early 1960s helped bring Fish and Wildlife Service into the condor discussions. The federal Fish and Wildlife Coordination Act, originally passed in 1934, had been amended in 1946 to require consultation with the Service and state agencies whenever any Federal agency proposed actions on waterways that could impact fish and wildlife. The act was further strengthened in 1958 to require that fish and wildlife issues be given equal consideration with other water resource programs (for example, recreation). The U. S. Bureau of Reclamation was involved with funding and development of the Sespe Creek project; therefore, consultation with Fish and Wildlife Service was required.

Also in the early 1960s, the Secretary of Interior had authorized the Service to begin reviewing the status of North American species that might be in jeopardy, a category that certainly included the condor. This assignment produced a "red book" of threatened birds, which provided impetus for passage of the first Federal Endangered Species Act in 1966.

Increasing publicity about the Sespe Creek dam proposal, plus a recent invitation from the U. S. Forest Service for Fish and Wildlife Service to attend their condor advisory committee meetings, prompted Service biologist David B. Marshall to visit condor country in late February 1965. He went with the Forest Service on an orientation trip to the Sespe Wildlife Area, and visited briefly with Ian McMillan. He then attended a condor advisory committee meeting; as expected, the Sespe water project was one of the main topics of discussion. In Marshall's opinion [35], everyone at the meeting seemed generally opposed to the dam construction, but the Forest Service representatives felt that their promise (made during the 1950 oil withdrawal hearings) to not interfere with water development made it difficult for them to fight it. They did think that Koford's conclusions about the need to protect condors from disturbance gave them adequate justification to deny permission for an access road through the middle of the Wildlife Area.

A week after the Advisory Committee meeting, Marshall was once again in southern California, hearing United Water's side of the Topatopa Dam story.

At that time, he met with United Water's "experts" for the first time. He went back to Portland with much food for thought, as is evident in his trip report [36]: *"I was admittedly impressed with the knowledge of the condor shown by the individuals who helped prepare this report* (the United Water Conservation District condor management plan)... *This is the first time I have come into contact (during this controversy) with individuals who have actually had close association with the condor with the exception of Mr.* (Ian) *McMillan, and his experience is limited. In other words we are getting information (which could be slanted) for the first time from the 'horses mouth.' These individuals, however, have never written anything on the condor of any major importance... consequently, they are not considered as authorities on the matter by Dr. Alden H. Miller and others who have worked with the National Audubon Society. I am under the impression that Dr. Miller has not worked with the condor personally at all. All agreed Dr. Koford made an excellent report and it appears the chief conflict is in interpretation of his data."*

"It is obvious that we are faced with having to decipher and interpret conflicting data and opinions presented by two opposing factions of ornithologists who have battled each other for a number of years. No doubt the truth lies somewhere in between."

"It is apparent from this latest meeting that the controversy is even more heated than we had previously supposed. Because of the divergence of opinions between the so-called condor experts, it is going to be most difficult for this Bureau to reach a conclusion as to whether the proposed Topatopa Reservoir would or would not adversely affect the California condor. It is our feeling however that the condor might benefit by some real management practices which are being given study at this time."

* * *

Within a few days of the Director receiving Marshall's review, Ray C. Erickson (a research biologist in the Washington Office) was directed to make a detailed review of the Miller-McMillan report, the United Water Conservation District "condor plan," and other available information, and to recommend Fish and Wildlife Service action. Erickson's 10-page report was sent to the Directorate on 13 April 1965 [37]. In it, he accepted the Koford-Miller-McMillan premise that mortality was a much bigger problem than productivity, and shooting was probably the main mortality problem. He expressed doubt that law enforcement and education would be enough to stop the *"impulse gunners"* and *"out-and-out violators,"* and therefore favored more direct management action, such as supplemental feeding to keep the condors "at home" in the sanctuary. However, he disagreed with the United Water consultants that the road through the sanctuary to the Topatopa dam site would be no problem:

"Development of the reservoir, so long as it did not entail increased public

use, probably would be compatible with the condor preservation program. It is not realistic, however, to believe that the public will allow itself to be denied the use of such facilities, if available, nor does the (United Water Conservation) *District suggest restricting public access. Construction of a public road and increased human travel through the Sespe area without question will increase, to an undetermined extent, the potential for bird loss. Whether increased public information and more intensive and extensive patrol will compensate, no one knows. Based solely on the safety of the condor, therefore, one would have to oppose the proposed development, notwithstanding fence construction, patrol, or other assistance offered by the District, because the condor mortality potential would be increased."*

Erickson's greatest concern about the existing and proposed condor strategies was that no one was looking very far into the future. He wrote: *"Proposed management techniques discussed thus far deal with measures which depend upon reduced mortality in the wild to solve the problem of the decline in condor numbers. Missing are recommendations on action to be taken if the downward trend continues, possibly because of conditions over which there is no control. I believe, therefore, that it would be well at this time to seek agreement among interested agencies and organizations that, if the decline continues until another fourth of the total population is lost, despite continued and intensified efforts to reverse the current trend downward, more direct methods will have to be employed to save this species."* Chief among his *"more direct methods"* was captive propagation. At the time, he was apparently unaware of Belle Benchley's 1949 proposal to breed California condors at the San Diego Zoo, yet his rationale for considering taking condors into captivity was remarkably similar to hers.

* * *

As a result of their preliminary reports, Dave Marshall and Ray Erickson were given the assignment *"to make a major review of the available information on the condor and an analysis of additional research needed to formulate a management plan."* They immediately went to southern California, where between 19 May and 28 May 1965, they visited the Sespe Wildlife Area, then met with the United Water Conservation District staff; John Borneman (new Audubon "condor warden"); Forest Service staff on the Los Padres National Forest and in the San Francisco Regional Office; Ed Harrison; Sid Peyton; Ian McMillan; Ben Glading (California Department of Fish and Game); Waldo Abbott (Santa Barbara Museum of Natural History); San Diego Zoo staff; Alden Miller and Starker Leopold (Museum of Vertebrate Zoology); and the Fish and Wildlife Service biologists in Sacramento responsible for Coordination Act studies. In fact, they talked to almost everyone who had anything to do with condors, except Carl Koford (who was out of the country) and the New York headquarters staff of National Audubon Society.

They reported after their tour that the majority of people they had met with seemed sincerely interested in having Fish and Wildlife Service actively involved in condor preservation [38]. They also reported that, despite the general air of controversy, almost everybody agreed that the condor population was seriously endangered. There even seemed to be general agreement on the kinds of things that should be done. The problems seemed to involve degree of importance, and priority of action. Erickson and Marshall felt that *"This* (condor) *controversy is an important element in a power struggle which has been going on in the Cooper Ornithological Society hierarchy for some time."* They also observed that both factions had decidedly polarized views on what to do about the problem. Further, in referring to both sides: *"Unfortunately, their convictions appear much stronger than the supporting data."*

"Convictions" on both sides had already gelled into canned statements, repeated over and over. Sidney Peyton and Ed Harrison both had first-hand evidence (from their own visits to active condor nests) that condors could sometimes stand considerable disturbance, but they quickly passed over other evidence (even some of their own) that human activity could also be harmful. An often repeated line was that commercial airliners passing over the Sespe Wildlife Area caused more disturbance to condors than would an access road to Topatopa Dam. Alden Miller and his co-worker Starker Leopold did not want to even consider supplemental feeding because they felt it would divert the public from the "real" condor issues and needs (preventing mortality, education, and improving census methods). Miller discounted any value in captive breeding: just because it had been successful with Andean condors didn't mean it would work with their California relatives. Marshall and Erickson reported: *"(Miller said that) efforts to rear California condors in captivity at various times had been unsuccessful. We pointed out that, to our knowledge, no zoo had ever possessed California condors of both sexes at any one time. This remark seemed to surprise him, but he still opposed propagation in principle."*

Their visit to Ian McMillan was a surprise to both of them, after Marshall's friendly meeting with him just a short while previously: *"Despite special efforts at tactful inquiry, we gained the impression that he was extremely emotional and disinclined to speak objectively or with any great measure of logical continuity about condors or proposed methods of preserving them. Any of our questions along any possible line of management other than his own recommendations seemed to irritate him."*

McMillan reportedly told them that he thought condors were on the increase since 1961. When they asked him why the Miller-McMillan report didn't reflect that improvement, he is alleged to have said that, *"in deference to"* National Audubon, the Forest Service, and California Department of Fish and Game, they couldn't *"freely report their findings."* When Marshall and Erickson mentioned this to Alden Miller later, he appeared *"nonplused."* It was just one more confusion to add to the many they were finding among the condor "experts."

The Erickson-Marshall review resulted in a report, *"California Condor Research and Management Program,"* which was sent to the Secretary of Interior for his approval on 14 July 1965 [39]. The report stressed five subjects that needed additional study:

(1) Developing periodic surveys of condor numbers and distribution - There seemed to be no question that a condor decline had occurred recently, but there was still no way to quantify or monitor the decline. *"Authors of the recent population estimate* (Miller-McMillan) *readily admit the possibility of error."* Surveys with repeatable and comparable results needed to be developed. (California Department of Fish and Game and National Audubon Society had already begun work on this need.)

(2) Determining the danger to condors from secondary poisoning - The debate on predator and rodent control continued, but no one had seriously studied it.

(3) Continuing life history and behavioral studies - *"There is sufficient disagreement among authorities on behavioral characteristics of the California condor that further studies are imperative if these differences are to be resolved."* Among the more controversial subjects to be studied: sensitivity of condors to disturbance; the location and success of recently active nests; and the location of condor flight lanes and feeding areas.

(4) More precisely defining condor feeding habits and requirements - Is food supply a problem, either for survival or for production? Would supplemental feeding help cut down on condor killing?

(5) Getting ready for captive propagation - While recognizing the sensitivity of this subject, it was included as a research item because of the lack of any contingency plans, should all else fail to save the condors.

There was one important non-research recommendation in the report: that the Department of Interior decision on whether or not to authorize Topatopa Dam be deferred for two years, pending a serious study of its potential effects on the condors. The memo sending the proposal from the Fish and Wildlife Service to the Secretary of Interior was clear: *"Despite the economic and recreational advantages claimed for the project, the almost certain increase in disturbance to an already gravely threatened species which could be expected to occur with the dam and road construction, augmented by increased public traffic and recreational use, demand that we oppose the project on the basis of existing information and our wildlife preservation responsibilities."*

* * *

Although Department of Reclamation officials assured Ventura County citizens that the California condor would not stop the Sespe Project - *"objections by bird lovers are common to such projects, and seldom defeat them"* [40] - things did seem to be favoring the birds. A month earlier, United

269

Water stopped test blasting at the proposed reservoir site, when a condor was seen to fly from a nest cave after a loud dynamite blast [41]. Then, an engineering company hired to evaluate Ventura County water needs recommended that the Sespe Project be delayed until 1985, due to the controversy, and also because the county needs might be met obtaining water from Castaic Reservoir, which was scheduled to be available by 1972 [42]. When the Bureau of Reclamation's Sespe feasibility study was completed in December 1965, they recommended that the project go forward [43], but in a March 1966 election, Ventura County voted against the proposal [44]. The water project was on hold, the Secretary of Interior granted a two-year study delay, and the Fish and Wildlife Service appointed a biologist to try for more answers to the important condor questions.

CHAPTER NOTES

1. Koford, C. B. 1981. Interview, fall 1979. Pages 67-97 *in:* Phillips, D., and H. Nash. The condor question, captive or forever free? San Francisco, California: Friends of the Earth.

2. Miller, A. H., I. I. McMillan, and E. McMillan. 1965. The current status and welfare of the California condor. Research Report No. 6, National Audubon Society (New York, New York).

3. Koford 1981, *op. cit.*

4. Miller, McMillan and McMillan *op. cit.,* pages 3-10.

5. Miller, McMillan and McMillan *op. cit.,* pages 29-36.

6. Miller, McMillan and McMillan *op. cit.,* pages 36-43.

7. Miller, McMillan and McMillan *op. cit.,* pages 49-54.

8. Pages 936-944, Decision No. 8136, application to transfer property between Sespe Light and Power Company and Sespe Power Corporation. *In:* Anonymous. 1921. Decisions of the Railroad Commission of the State of California, Volume XVIII, 1 April 1920 to 31 October 1920. Sacramento, California

9. Anonymous. 1922. Notice of agreement, Sespe Light & Power Company and Shattuck Construction Company. *Electrical World* 79(8):414.

10. Anonymous. 1933. Calls for two large dams in back country. Oxnard (California) *Daily Courier,* 21 June 1933.

11. California State Water Rights Board. 1963. In the matter of Application 12092 of United Water Conservation District and Applications 13417, 13417A and 13418 of

Calleguas Water District to appropriate from Sespe Creek in Ventura County. Sacramento, California.

12. U. S. Bureau of Land Management. 1950. Public hearing held commencing August 21, 1950...Los Angeles, California, to consider withdrawal from all forms of disposition under the public land laws including the mining and mineral leasing laws, approximately 32,000 acres of land for use as a Condor Sanctuary in the Los Padres National Forest. Three volumes, typed. Copies with U. S. Bureau of Land Management and U. S. Forest Service.

13. Case, P. C. 1952. Management plan for the Sespe Wildlife Area. Los Padres National Forest. U. S. Forest Service.

14. Anonymous. 1951. Four sites surveyed for Sespe Creek dam. Los Angeles (California) *Times,* 15 May 1951.

15. Anonymous. 1952. Santa Clara Valley dams plan speeded. Los Angeles *Times,* 16 September 1952.

16. Anonymous. 1952. New Ventura water supply source sought. Los Angeles *Times,* 18 December 1952.

17. Anonymous. 1953. Water lack felt in Ventura County. Los Angeles *Times,* 8 October 1953.

18. Anonymous. 1956. Sharing of Sespe water proposed. Los Angeles *Times,* 14 September 1956.

19. Anonymous. 1957. Water projects costing $64,000,000 urged. Los Angeles *Times,* 7 February 1957.

20. Anonymous. 1957. Hearing opens on waters of Sespe Creek. Los Angeles *Times,* 17 April 1957.

21. California State Water Rights Board. 1958. Decision No. 884, In the matter of Application 12092 and 15145 of United Water Conservation District and Applications 13417, 13417A and 13418 by Calleguas Municipal Water District. Oakland, California.
    Anonymous. 1958. Simi Valley wins water controversy. Los Angeles *Times,* 16 January 1958.

22. Anonymous. 1958. District will fight Sespe water deal. Los Angeles *Times,* 17 January 1958. Also: Anonymous. 1958. Sespe water suit filed. Los Angeles *Times,* 15 February 1958.

23. Anonymous. 1957. Will condors object? Topa Topa damsite road poses problem. Los Angeles *Times,* 21 March 1957.

24. Anonymous. 1961. State Board's ruling in Calleguas case reversed. Los Angeles

271

Times, 16 March 1961.

25. Anonymous. 1961. Water District proposes three dams on Sespe Creek. Los Angeles *Times,* 15 September 1961.

26. California State Water Rights Board 1963, *op. cit.*

27. Anonymous. 1964. Sespe Creek recreation area sought. Los Angeles *Times,* 6 February 1964.

28. Anonymous. 1964. Audubon Society balks at plans for Sespe Dam. Los Angeles *Times,* 16 November 1964.
   Anonymous. 1965. A Topatopa Dam could destroy the condor. *Audubon Leader's Conservation Guide* 6(1):1-2.
   Buchheister, C. W. 1965. Our campaign to save the condor. *Audubon Magazine* 67(3):180.

29. McMillan, I. 1965. Shall we save the condor or build another dam? *Defenders of Wildlife News* 40(4):39-40.

30. American Ornithologists' Union. 1965. Report of the Committee on Bird Protection, 1964. *Auk* 82(3):490.

31. Smith, D., and R. Easton. 1965. The condor controversy. *Animal Life* 40:22-23.
   Smith, D., and R. Easton. 1965. The condor controversy. *Westways* 57(7):20-21.
   Smith, D., and R. Easton. 1965. The condor controversy: an on-the-spot report. *Defenders of Wildlife News* 40(4):40-42.

32. Ainsworth, E. 1965. Why the fuss over condors? Los Angeles *Times,* 26 February 1965.

33. United Water Conservation District. 1965. The California condor *(Gymnogyps californianus)* management and protection program. Santa Paula, California.

34. Buchheister, C. W. 1965. Meeting the challenges of the "third wave." *Audubon Magazine* 67(1):18-19.

35. D. B. Marshall trip report sent by the Regional Director, Fish and Wildlife Service, to the Director, 17 March 1965. Copy in Fish and Wildlife Service files.

36. D. B. Marshall trip report, *op. cit.*

37. Erickson, R. C. 1965. An analysis of various recommendations for the preservation of the California condor. Report submitted to the Assistant Director-Wildlife, U. S. Fish and Wildlife Service, 13 April 1965.

38. Erickson, R. C., and D. B. Marshall. 1965. Memo to Director, Fish and Wildlife Service, 16 June 1965, subject: Joint report on field trip, California condor problem,

272

May 19-28, 1965. U. S. Fish and Wildlife Service files.

39. Erickson, R. C., and D. B. Marshall. 1965. Management and research plan for the California condor. Report accompanying memo from the Director, U. S. Fish and Wildlife Service, to the Assistant Secretary of Interior, 14 July 1965. Washington, D. C.

40. Anonymous. 1965. Condors won't halt dam, official states. Los Angeles *Times,* 30 July 1965.

41. Anonymous. 1965. Blasts in condor region stopped. Los Angeles *Times,* 24 June 1965.

42. Anonymous. 1965. Engineers urge Sespe Dam delay. Los Angeles *Times,* 13 August 1965.

43. Anonymous. 1965. Bureau gives go-ahead to Sespe Dam project. Los Angeles *Times,* 31 December 1965.

44. Anonymous. 1966. Sespe Dam proposal rejected. Los Angeles *Times,* 16 March 1966.

Figure 17. Hopper Canyon area, Sespe Condor Sanctuary, a major nesting and roosting area for California condors through the 1970s. This area would not have been directly changed by Sespe Creek water developments, but was near enough that condor activity would have been adversely affected by project noise and activity. Photo by author.

* * *

CHAPTER 22
FISH AND WILDLIFE SERVICE RESEARCH

During 1965, Fish and Wildlife Service biologist Ray C. Erickson was able to get approval for the beginnings of an endangered wildlife research program, with the home base to be the Patuxent Wildlife Research Center in Laurel, Maryland. By early 1966, he had his first four research biologists on the job: Winston E. Banko (studying the many threatened bird species in the Hawaiian Islands); Donald K. Fortenberry (working with the black-footed ferret in the Great Plains); Norman E. Holgerson (for everglade kites and other Florida birds); and Fred C. Sibley, the first Fish and Wildlife Service condor biologist. Erickson described their assignment to them this way [1]:

"You are working on subjects of prime concern to everyone. I have never seen anything capture the intense interest and enthusiasm of such a large number of our organization as has research on endangered species. This interest shows no sign of abating, and it seems to have special appeal to the layman. The very reality of endangerment requires no technical knowledge to understand. It is self evident that remedial measures demand higher priority when applied to a preservation of a species than when they concern management efforts solely to change or maintain the numbers of a species whose future already is secure.

"This same public interest, however, will be directed at the results of your ecological investigations so you should continually address your overall program as well as your daily efforts with the question, 'Is this the best way to obtain the information needed to save these species and their habitats?' If the answer is negative, we should have your recommendations for needed changes. These modifications are a natural part of the evaluation of a new field assignment as your familiarity and experience unveil more productive leads."

Fred Sibley's assignment was the outgrowth of Erickson's and Dave Marshall's 1965 orientation to condor issues [2], their preliminary proposals for condor research [3], and the need to better evaluate the effect on condors of the Sespe water project during the two-year moratorium (Chapter 21). Sibley came to the condor project from the remote islands of the Pacific Ocean, where he had been studying albatrosses and other seabirds. He was the first condor investigator to come on the job with a sound ornithological background, and he had already proven himself as someone who could carry out research under difficult field conditions. Like Carl Koford, he would need to be hardy and innovative, because the new program was clearly operating on the proverbial shoestring. When Ray Erickson made his first visit to Sibley's station in Ojai, California, in late May 1966, he reported [4]:

"Mr. Sibley's activities have been only slightly handicapped by restricted funds..., (but) it has been necessary to postpone purchase of an official

automobile and certain other equipment. He does, however, have a Jeep Wagoneer (on loan) *from GSA in Los Angeles, and has purchased a Bausch and Lomb 'scope. He indicated that a war surplus binocular that he obtained in this office* (Patuxent headquarters) *is sufficient for his general viewing needs. A camera and other equipment and supplies will be purchased early in FY* (Fiscal Year) *1967. His office stationery and other supplies are being provided from Patuxent."*

Despite the frugal start Sibley quickly got to work on his principal assignment, assessing the probable effects of the Sespe water project on condors. To begin that task, he had to know the locations of condor nests, roosts, and flight routes in the vicinity of the water project. He also wanted to plot the location of condor use areas in relation to other developments and disturbances, so he could predict condor response to the noise and activity of dam construction, road development, and road and reservoir use after they were completed.

Sibley got help finding condor nests and roosts by studying Koford's field notes [5]; by talking to Forest Service patrolmen, former egg collectors, and others who had been in condor habitat; and by checking the collection records of eggs preserved in various museums. Whereas Koford had concentrated on only one nesting region, Sibley spent much of his time outside the Hopper Canyon area, relocating formerly-known nest sites and watching for condor activity that might indicate nests or roosts in previously unknown locations.

Sibley entered some known and potential nest caves to look for evidence of past or recent use, and to see if he could tell whether (and why) nests had been successful or had failed. This became controversial when Ian McMillan, one of the ranchers employed by National Audubon Society to help with a condor status update, insisted that the nest checking was causing breeding failure. Fish and Wildlife Service responded to the allegations [6]: *"In 1966, no nests were entered by Mr. Sibley until well after their histories were terminated... In 1967, six active nests were found, three of which fledged young and three eggs failed to hatch. Of these, all three nests which successfully fledged young had been visited by Mr. Sibley. Only one of the three nests containing eggs which did not hatch was visited by him. In 1968, only one active nest was found and visited by Mr. Sibley, the young condor fledging successfully.*

"To summarize, of the six nests visited by Mr. Sibley in 1967 and 1968 before fledging took place, five (more than 80%) were successful, while of the two nests not visited by him, neither fledged a young condor. We would also like to note that in an examination of the field notes which Dr. Carl B. Koford, an authority frequently quoted by Mr. McMillan, recorded during his monographic study of the condor in the 1940's, Mr. Sibley found a nest success of approximately 50 percent. This figure is comparable with the 1967-68 success rate of 57 percent during the two years in which Mr. Sibley visited some of the active nests."

276

Not only were Sibley's nest visits limited and occurring mostly when the nests were unoccupied by eggs or chicks, his field notes show that he was in the Sespe Condor Sanctuary on only 48 occasions between January 1966 and May 1969. In contrast, Carl Koford spent over 400 days in the Sespe Sanctuary during his three year study. He not only entered nests that contained eggs and chicks, his field notes show that he sometimes spent long periods of time photographing, handling and leg banding the birds. Despite this activity, he estimated a nest success rate of 50 percent, similar to Sibley's findings. After reviewing Koford's notes, Sibley wrote the following summary [7]:

"The first bird Koford banded, Oscar, was banded August 20, 1939 and rebanded October 7, 1939. On the first occasion it was tied up and pulled to the top of the cliff where it was banded. When rebanded, it was grabbed by the neck and wings and pulled out of a low tree. In both instances the banding, note taking and photographing took 20-30 minutes.

"The second bird, Herkimer, was banded October 17, 1939 during a three hour session of photographing and catching. Herkimer is the bird which Ian McMillan claims had its wing dislocated during the handling. Koford states: 'After we released the chick, the right wing lay on the back on its upper surface, loosely. We had handled the chick gently but thought that the wing might have been dislocated by the birds struggles. I put my feet out and caused the bird to lunge again, and the wing fell into place.' The bird when reexamined on November 4th appeared normal.

"In both cases the birds were disturbed for unnecessarily long periods and were handled far more than needed. Inexperience in handling large birds was part of the reason for the long period taken by Koford, the rest being the seeming lack of worry about handling the birds. Oscar for instance was pulled out of the nest and examined on at least five occasions by different people, including Alden Miller."

In fairness to Koford, it should be noted that most of his research consisted (as did Sibley's and my own) of quiet, long distance watching. It is also worth remembering that both "Oscar" and "Herkimer" fledged successfully.

* * *

Sibley's report on the probable effects of the Sespe Creek Project on the condor was released in August 1969 [8]. In it, he documented that there were nine condor nest sites within 2.5 miles of the Squaw Flat Road, Sespe Creek Road, or proposed Topatopa damsite, most of them along the Squaw Flat Road. He found regularly used roost sites scattered along both access routes, and around the reservoir site. Several condor flight paths crossed over the project area.

Measuring and interpreting a bird's response to disturbance always involves some degree of subjectivity. Sibley considered the effects of disturbance in three situations (flying, roosting, and nesting) [9], and also looked at immediate reactions (i.e., what an individual bird did when disturbed) versus long-term reactions (what the population did). Regarding the several activities and effects:

FLYING - *"Condors in flight show little fear of man and will approach him very closely. Condors will glide to a person walking along an exposed ridge and circle over him: the first approach is the closest and subsequent circles or passes are made at increasing distances. Apparently, the more conspicuous a person is and the more commotion he makes, the more likely the condor is to approach. Whistling and arm waving prolongs the time a bird remains overhead..."*

"Routine ground activity below a flying condor has little apparent effect on the bird. Flight paths from the Sespe Condor Sanctuary pass over Interstate Highway 5 in the vicinity of Gorman and Lebec, and birds fly through Tejon Pass following the highway. Birds have been seen over Bakersfield, Fresno, and even the Los Angeles suburbs."

In other words, condors might very well continue to fly over the reservoir and the improved access road. The problem was not from noise or movement, but from the increased potential for killing the unwary and curious birds.

ROOSTING - Condors are more tolerant of roads and noise at roosts than at nests. For example, there were two well-used roosts in the southern Sierra Nevada that were within one-quarter mile of roads and summer cabins. (These roosts were hard to reach because of rough terrain, and were well-shielded from the limited human noise and activity in the vicinity.) Still: *"The number of permanent roosts is limited, and at each location certain trees or ledges are used while other superficially similar ones are not. The occupied roosts reported in Koford's notes of 1940 are still used today. Roosts may be as important as nesting sites in condor management."*

"Flushing of roosting birds may be important in causing roost abandonment. Very few people are willing to leave a roosting bird unmolested. In over 90 percent of past reports of roosting condors, the observer mentions flushing the bird, even if this required several attempts and considerable effort. After a bird has roosted for the evening, wind conditions usually become progressively less favorable for soaring and any bird flushed may have to soar downhill and take less desirable alternate sites. In any roost close to human activity, condors would be flushed repeatedly and they soon would avoid this site on the basis of experience."

NESTING - Sibley found (as Koford had found before him, and I observed afterward) that condor reaction to noise and movement varied considerably from incident to incident. Sometimes they reacted dramatically; sometimes they seemed not to notice. In general, concluded Sibley: *"The present study provides many new examples to confirm Koford's statements that: 'sound more than motions, disturbs condors,' that condors are '...keenly aware of any man in sight within 500 yards of the nest,' and that 'one man, by disturbing the birds at critical places late in the day, can prevent roosting over an area of several square miles'."* Like Koford, Sibley didn't think that short-term disturbance would lead to abandonment of a nest (i.e., to the bird flying away and never coming back), but that it could keep condors away from the nest long enough that eggs could fail or young could die from neglect. He also expressed concerns about the immediate effects of some big "scares: *"Several observations would indicate that blasting close to a nest might indirectly cause egg breakage. One observer, Fred Truesdale, unexpectedly flushed a condor from its nest and the bird pushed the egg out in leaving. Another individual, J. R. Pemberton, startled an incubating adult and caused it to jump up, with the result that the egg, which had been resting on the bird's tarsi, was thrown several inches forward. On one occasion, I observed a sleeping condor when a sonic boom occurred... The condor 'exploded' to the mouth of the cave and was visibly agitated for the next hour."*

One predictor Sibley used to estimate the probable effects of the water project was the actual location of nest sites in relation to existing disturbances: *"Active nest sites are the best indicators of ultimate tolerance of disturbance. Nests close to roads, trails and oil operations show the amount of noise and movement that a bird will tolerate and yet return to nest again."* Referring to 26 nest sites that had been used by condors after roads, trails, or oil wells had been established in their vicinity: *"Nest sites are selected closer to roads that carry less traffic or that are shielded* (visually) *from the nest. Nests are built a minimum of 0.8 miles from unshielded dirt roads with limited use, and a minimum of 1.2 miles from generally used dirt roads. Only one active nest is known within 3 miles of a paved road, although there are many potential nesting areas near paved roads... Nests are seldom located closer to a road than the distance where traffic noise is at the level of normal background noise."*

"Of the 26 nests in the sample, 15 are within 3 miles of a modern oil well and are known to have been active during the drilling operations. The noise levels produced by drilling operations in the 1940's were lower than those of today, so the earlier data were excluded. No nests were nearer to a well than 1.2 miles and no nests in sight of a well were closer than 2.3 miles. The (recently occupied) *nests are either visually shielded from drilling operations or are sufficiently distant that noise levels would rarely exceed normal background noise."*

"Proximity of a trail does not seem to adversely affect the selection or continued occupancy of a nest site, 14 nests being within one-half mile of a trail and unshielded from it. While the presence of the trails does not seem to interfere with nest selection, their use may seriously interfere with nest success."

* * *

There was no way that Sibley (or anyone else) could positively state the effects on the condors should Topatopa Dam be authorized. Nevertheless, he could present a strong inferential argument that the effects would be bad. He predicted that, with the construction of Topatopa Dam and the access road through the condor sanctuary: *"Seven nest sites and as many important roost sites would be abandoned. A large portion of the prime nesting range would be rendered unsuitable because of traffic noise on the access roads. The present Sespe-Piru area* (the Condor Sanctuary plus adjacent forest lands that together supported 75 per cent of recently used condor nest sites) *would be split into smaller blocks of wilderness habitat that would be less valuable or even useless. Hunting and other recreational use of the area would increase the annual loss of condors, and would disturb additional nesting and roosting sites to an intolerable degree. Loss of this area would result in a great restriction of usable roosts and nest sites and thus reduce the population, which would have no place to go."*

In early February 1970, as a result of Sibley's study and other concerns expressed by the U. S. Fish and Wildlife Service [10], the Secretary of Interior declared the Sespe project suspended [11].

* * *

In addition to studying the effects of disturbance on condors, Sibley added much to overall knowledge of the species. He began to build a network of observers who reported condors throughout California, continued work on developing better survey techniques, and amassed considerable information on the history of condors. He left the condor project in 1969, and I succeeded him as the Fish and Wildlife Service condor researcher for the following ten years.

Unlike Sibley, I did not come to the job with a specific assignment, but was to select and investigate any subjects that might yield information helpful to the condor population. Although condors in the late 1960s were nearly as plentiful as Koford had estimated for the 1940s, this was due to refined estimates rather than to stability in the population. In fact, every indication was that the condor population had decreased by one-third to one-half in the previous 25 years [12], and was not secure. If there was anything else to be done for condors, it needed to be done quickly. Two subjects that appeared to demand attention were assessing the importance of poisons (from animal control and other sources), and determining the role of food supply in the long-term survival of the species.

CHAPTER NOTES

NOTE: References cited as "U. S. Fish and Wildlife Service files" were housed at the California Field Station, Patuxent Wildlife Research Center (Ojai, California), and at Patuxent Research Center (Laurel, Maryland) until 1980. The research function of Patuxent was transferred to the U. S. Geological Survey, the Ojai office was disbanded, and the files were split between several other facilities. I have copies of everything I have cited, and some are in the condor files at the Santa Barbara Museum of Natural

History, but some items may no longer be readily available.

1. Memorandum 5 April 1966, R. C. Erickson to Endangered Wildlife Research Program biologists, subject: Periodic activities reports for September through December, 1965, and project documentation. U. S. Fish and Wildlife Service files, Laurel, Maryland.

2. Erickson, R. C., and D. B. Marshall. 1965. Memo to Director, Fish and Wildlife Service, 16 June 1965, subject: Joint report on field trip, California condor problem, May 19-28, 1965. U. S. Fish and Wildlife Service files.

3. Erickson, R. C., and D. B. Marshall. 1965. Management and research plan for the California condor. Report accompanying memo from the Director, U. S. Fish and Wildlife Service, to the Assistant Secretary of Interior for Fish, Wildlife and Parks, 14 July 1965. Washington, D. C.

4. Memorandum 4 August 1966, R. C. Erickson to Director, subject: Report on inspection of endangered wildlife research program in Hawaii, California and South Dakota. U. S. Fish and Wildlife Service files, Laurel, Maryland.

5. Carl B. Koford field notes and journals are filed at the Museum of Vertebrate Zoology, Berkeley, California.

6. Letter, 25 February 1969, Secretary of Interior to Congressman Burt L. Talcott. U. S. Fish and Wildlife Service files.

7. Memorandum to the files, July 1966, prepared by F. C. Sibley, subject: banding of California condors. U. S. Fish and Wildlife Service files.

8. Sibley, F. C. 1969. Effects of the Sespe Creek Project on the California condor. Administrative report, Endangered Wildlife Research Station, Patuxent Wildlife Research Center, Laurel, Maryland. 19 pages.

9. Condors can be disturbed when they are feeding, and can also be vulnerable to shooting when they are gathered at a carcass. However, very little foraging occurred within the water project boundaries, so no bad effects related to the water project were predicted.

10. U. S. Fish and Wildlife Service. 1969. A detailed report on the Sespe Creek Project. Portland, Oregon. 39 pages.

11. U. S. Department of Interior news release 8 February 1970, carried in papers across the country, for example: Anonymous. 1970. California project posing threat to condor suspended. Baton Rouge (Louisiana) *Advocate,* 8 February 1970.

12. Pages 14-18 *in:* Wilbur, S. R. 1978. The California condor, 1966-1976: a look at its past and future. *North American Fauna,* Number 72. Fish and Wildlife Service, Washington, D. C.

Figure 18. Topatopa, immature California condor at the Los Angeles Zoo, circa 1968. The condor apparently left its nest too early, and was discovered well downstream and in a populated area. A month of efforts to get "Tope" back in touch with the parent birds failed, and the Zoo became a permanent home. "Tope" was still alive in 2012. Photo by Fred C. Sibley.

Of 458 total records of California condor mortality that I have documented, I classified 45 of them as condors found dead, sick, or injured (in ways that did not seem to be caused by gunshot). Half of these were not found until they were mere skeletons, and no cause of death was determined. Of the other half, two were found to have osteomyelitis or arthritis severe enough to have caused, or been a major contributor to, death [1, 2]. Two were apparently killed by hailstones, as they were found dead in an area where *"hailstones as large as walnuts still lay two feet deep in the gullies"* [3]. The rest were either victims of identifiable accidents, or they suffered from undetermined illnesses.

Accidents to adult condors included one flying into a fence and breaking a wing, after being frightened from an animal carcass; another died after it could not escape from a water tank it apparently entered for a drink [4]. Young birds seemed particularly prone to breaking wings when flying into things, probably because it takes them a year or more to fully master the use of their nine foot wingspan. Carl Koford reported one personal observation [5]: *"Early in 1941, I found a dead juvenile on a high grassy ridge near Fillmore. The humerus of the bird was broken but there was no other apparent injury. When found, the bird lay a few yards from a slender vertical pipe which had been used as a surveying marker. I believe that the condor had collided with the pipe in soaring over the ridge."*

Another incident was reported to Koford by a U. S. Forest Service employee [6]: *"Bud Palmer said that for four years he was a guard in the Big Pine Mt. country & often saw Condors there, especially around the lookout & alighting in the pines there. He had seen up to 'about 20' at once. Once he found a young Condor with a broken wing atop the bluffs near the lookout, and he killed it."*

An accident in less usual circumstances occurred in the foothills of the Sierra Nevada in 1965, when an immature condor fell onto a roadway after apparently colliding with a high tension wire. As reported by the California Department of Fish and Game after intensive examination and testing of the carcass [7]: *"From all the evidence we feel the bird collided with a wire, then fell some 40 feet to the pavement... It had severe spinal cord injuries that helped lead to that conclusion."*

* * *

Prior to the 1980s, few sick or recently dead condors had been examined by veterinarians or lab technicians, let alone autopsied, and the descriptions of "sick" are seldom very informative. One condor was *"emaciated and dying when found"* [8]. In another instance, a man observed a condor sitting in a field looking *"sick: ...When he checked later it was dead"* [9]. A condor believed to have died shortly before it was found weighed only 13 pounds (20-

25 pounds would be considered "healthy"), was heavily parasitized, and showed signs of severe arthritis [10]. Another was alive when captured, but *"acted goofy"* and was thought by the rancher who found it to be *"in a poisoned condition or perhaps sick"* [11]. It died soon after capture, and an examination at the Museum of Vertebrate Zoology showed it to be *"desperately thin,"* weighing only 11 pounds 12 ounces [12]. Any of these descriptions might apply to a condor dying of old age or some natural illness, but these could also be the signs of some kind of poisoning. The decline of the condor population, and individual deaths of condors, have often been attributed to the effects of various environmental contaminants. The evidence concerning strychnine was covered in Chapter 11. Here, I look at thallium sulphate, Compound 1080, and lead poisoning.

THALLIUM

The metal thallium was discovered in 1862, but its relative rarity, high cost of extraction, and uncertain properties kept it *"a laboratory curiosity"* for many years. A number of medical uses were experimented with in the late 1890s and early 1900s, but the high toxicity of the metal resulted in early abandonment of such treatments. It was not until about 1925 that thallium sulfate as a poison for mammalian "pests" came into being [13]. Following field trials for ground squirrel control in Santa Clara County in 1926, use spread quickly in California south from Sacramento and the San Francisco Bay area. From July 1927 through June 1928, some 603,000 pounds of thallium-treated grain were spread for squirrel control [14]; the following year the application was 558,000 pounds [15]. Thallium sulphate proved to be a very efficient squirrel killer; unfortunately, it also killed thousands of other small mammals and birds that fed on the treated grain. There was some indication that flesh-eating mammals and birds were also dying after eating the grain-poisoned animals [16]. The California Department of Agriculture by 1931 acknowledged the growing concern about the poison, and promised to attempt better control [17]:

"There is due recognition given to the fact that thallium sulphate is a very dangerous poisonous material and for that reason the agricultural agencies have insisted that its use be permitted only under official supervision. It has not been permitted to gain general distribution such as is the case with the normal rodent poisons. The fact that it is more dangerous to native game species than strychnine has demanded special rules and regulations for its use. The official agricultural agencies have attempted to exercise every reasonable precaution and will continue to exercise such precautions even more vigorously in the future, if it appears necessary, in order to avoid any harm to native or introduced species."

Such assurances that wildlife would be protected in the future were never put to the test, because in 1932 a number of people accidentally ate thallium sulphate-treated grain. Seven of them died, and 30 others developed long-term, debilitating illnesses [18]. Concern about the safety of thallium for humans prompted cutbacks in use, and new restrictions. Thallium became scarce during World War II because almost all the United States supply had come from Europe [19]. By the time it was again available, much of the California ground squirrel poisoning was being done with Compound 1080. Although massive amounts were no longer used, some county agricultural offices continued to apply thallium-treated grain into the 1950s (e.g., Ventura County - 5,862 pounds in 1954-1955, 376 pounds in 1959 [20], and even into the 1960s (e.g., Los Angeles County - 1965, unknown amount [21]).

In his monograph, Carl Koford acknowledged the intensive use of thallium in the condors' range, noting that *"many persons became alarmed about the possible effect of the poison on condors,"* and opined that probably *"some condors have acquired a lethal or near lethal dose of thallium"* [22]. I was unable to find any information on thallium and condors in Koford's journals and field notes (on file at the Museum of Vertebrate Zoology, Berkeley), and suspect that the "alarm" was that caused in 1937 when Junea W. Kelly (Alameda, California) wrote to the National Association of Audubon Societies that six condors had been killed by thallium on the Carrizo Plains in Santa Barbara County. This prompted a series of letters between Kelly, the Audubon Society, U. S. Forest Service, U. S. Bureau of Biological Survey, and others. Mrs. Kelly had received her information second-hand or third-hand, and was never able to provide any details. In July 1937, Stanley P. Young (Chief of the Division of Game Management, Bureau of Biological Survey) wrote to the Supervisor of the Santa Barbara National Forest [23]:

"Recently Mr. A. W. Elder, Deputy Game Management Agent connected with the Biological Survey, received a call from Mrs. G. Earle Kelly of Alameda, California, stating that she had information that a number of condor had been found dead from thallium poisoning on the Carrissa [sic] Plains in Santa Barbara County. In questioning Mrs. Kelly further, she informed Mr. Elder that her information was not complete but that she would submit a report when she had more definite information. Further questioning seemed to indicate that the condor might have been killed by hail or by hunters."

Apparently no additional information was ever forthcoming, and it seems likely that Mrs. Kelly was either misinformed or misunderstood what she had been told. At that time, interest in the California condor was the highest it had ever been, catalyzed by Santa Barbara rancher Robert E. Easton and leading to regular discussions between the Forest Service, National Audubon Society, Joseph Grinnell (University of California) and Aldo Leopold (University of Wisconsin) [24]. Cyril Robinson, of the Santa Barbara (now, Los Padres) National Forest, was in the midst of a five year study (1933-1938) of condors on and near the Forest, and would have been the one in the Forest Service who would have acted on Mrs. Kelly's information. His final report made no

285

mention of thallium, or of any condors poisoned or suspected poisoned. In summarizing the various hazards to condors, he wrote [25]: *"Poisoning is possible if the poisoned baits were also eaten. Strychnine after being in a poisoned carcass for a few days loses its lethal quality. However, very little is known about this and of the actual losses that could be attributed to this cause. Condors can certainly regurgitate as easily as buzzards and thus protect themselves, so we feel that losses from poison can be greatly minimized. Had secondary poisoning resulted from squirrel control work, the condors would have been eliminated many years ago."*

If Robinson was writing his report today, he undoubtedly would not have been so complacent in his assessment of the dangers of poisons to condors. Still, there clearly had been no individual event that had caused him concern at the time. Also, although Carl Koford did not begin his research on condors until 1939, the death of six condors two years previously would have still been prominent news. His failure to even mention Kelly's information, despite his daily contacts with rangers, ranchers, and others who would have known about the report, is significant, I think. Perhaps even more telling is that the brothers Ian and Eben McMillan never mentioned the incident. They were living and ranching not far from the Carrizo Plains at the time, and were already known for their interest in wildlife and agriculture. The report on the status of condors they co-authored for National Audubon Society in 1965 made only passing mention of thallium [26]. Ian McMillan became outspoken about the dangers to condors of ground squirrel poisoning (see below), and missed few opportunities to mention them. Of a 1950 incident in which one condor died and two were sickened, apparently by strychnine (Chapter 11), he wrote [27]: *"Although this incident was of tremendous significance and importance it remained for the next fourteen years a hidden secret."* To become this exercised over the death of one condor from strychnine, then fail to mention six birds killed by thallium, seems highly unlikely to me.

No California condor is known to have died from thallium sulphate, but Koford was probably not wrong in his opinion that condors *could have been* affected. Scavengers have been killed, turkey vultures at least once [28], and lappet-faced vultures (*Torgos tracheliotus*) in Israel [29]. The good news is that major, widespread use of thallium within the range of the condor occurred for only four or five years before being replaced by Compound 1080.

COMPOUND 1080

Compound 1080, a white powdery chemical technically known as sodium fluoroacetate, was developed in the 1940s and was originally used in the United States to poison both rodents and coyotes. The Environmental Protection Agency banned its use for predator control in 1972, at the same time strychnine was banned as a "predacide." Because "1080" was to a large extent replacing the highly toxic thallium sulfate for rodent killing, many people were considering its entry on the scene a good thing. Carl Koford discussed the new chemical in his monograph. While he wisely reserved final judgment, because the chemical was so new, his initial reaction was hopeful [30]: *"Commencing in 1945 a new poison replaced thallium in much of the feeding range of the condor. This poison is Compound 1080 (sodium fluoroacetate). Joseph Keyes and others of the Fish and Wildlife Service watched for the effects of this poison on condors and other birds during trial applications in Kern County. So far, neither condors nor turkey vultures have been found to be killed by eating squirrels poisoned with 1080."*

Koford then cited a study of the effects of feeding "1080" to golden eagles, black vultures and turkey vultures: *"Judged by these results, a turkey vulture would have to eat as much as 40 times its own weight in poisoned squirrels before it would probably be killed. The amount would be less if the contents of the cheek pouches and stomach were eaten or if the squirrel had ingested more than the minimum lethal dose. At least in rats, 'the ingestion of sublethal doses of 1080 has shown no significant cumulative effect...' Perhaps, then, the use of Compound 1080 is less dangerous to condors than the use of thallium."*

Compound 1080 became a condor issue with the publishing of the Miller-McMillan report in 1965. The McMillans furnished information on three condors that had been found dead near Granite Station, Kern County, between 1960 and 1963, inferentially tying the deaths to rodent poisoning that occurred in the vicinity. These are the details they gave on the three birds [31]:

Bird #1, an immature, was found dead in August 1960. It was in an area where "1080" was being used to poison squirrels, but was not found near any poisoned rodents. A rancher discarded the carcass near his house, where it lay in the open until July 1963, when the McMillans were told about it. They sent the remains to the Museum of Vertebrate Zoology (Berkeley, California), where it was determined that the bird had no broken bones (so presumably hadn't been shot). No chemical tests were made; it's doubtful they would have shown anything significant after three years.

Bird #2, an adult, was not seen by the McMillans, although its story was well documented. The bird did not fly and "appeared sick" when found near Granite Station in June 1960. It apparently was not in an area that was being actively poisoned at the time. The condor was taken to a veterinarian, but died a few days later. A gross examination did not reveal any broken bones, but it appeared to have a leg injury. Although the McMillans noted that the condor was "in perfect plumage, such as to indicate that it had been in good health not long before its death," an ornithologist who examined the bird after its death reported it as weighing only 13 pounds (a healthy adult condor should weigh about 20 pounds) and being very emaciated [32].

Bird #3, another adult, was found dead near Granite Station in September 1963. It appeared fairly freshly dead when found, but the rancher who recovered it said there was some indication (an accumulation of excrement in the vicinity) that the bird might have been alive but incapacitated for some time. It was not found in conjunction with any ongoing poisoning project. The McMillans examined the carcass in mid-October, but couldn't say anything about cause of death, except that it did not appear to have any broken bones.

The published Miller-McMillan report was relatively non-committal about these findings: *"In our field study we have obtained no unequivocal proof of recent condor deaths in connection with poisoning for rodents."* But by 1968, perhaps released from the scientific caution of the deceased lead author Alden H. Miller, Ian McMillan had become positive that these were deaths were caused by "1080" [33]. Regarding the first bird: *"In the opinion of local people, including the owner of the ranch, the poison put out for the rodents had killed the condor. The opinion was concurred in by the local official in charge of the poison applications."* Overall, he reported: *"Though toxicological proof was lacking, the circumstantial evidence linking Compound 1080 to the three condor deaths in northern Kern County seemed almost irrefutable."*

But let's look in more detail at what is included in the Miller-McMillan report regarding these three condor deaths. First, only one of the dead condors was associated with an ongoing rodent poisoning campaign. The other two birds were "guilty" of no more than being found in a part of Kern County where poisoning sometimes occurred. Second, the published report makes it quite clear that, even when poison crews were actively working an area, the McMillans seldom saw dead ground squirrels that would have been available for condors to eat. (They did see dead kangaroo rats on the surface of the ground, but the McMillans noted that these could have been poisoned by strychnine, not "1080.") Third, while there was no obvious sign that any of the birds had been shot, one bird did have a leg injury (not mentioned in Ian McMillan's 1968 book). A leg injured by accident or by shooting could have kept the bird from feeding - possibly even kept it from flying, which could have accounted for its emaciated condition when found. From the evidence available, "1080" poisoning is no more likely to have killed the three birds than accidents (as noted above, condors, particularly young ones, have been known to fly into things); other poisons (strychnine-killed kangaroo rats?); steel traps (causing a leg injury); lead poisoning; disease; or even old age. In these three instances, there is no case to be made against "1080."

The "1080" toxicity studies cited by Koford was performed in 1945-1946 by H. L. "Jack" Spencer, a U. S. Fish and Wildlife Service biologist stationed at Gainesville, Florida. *"Concern about the possible effects of field rodent poisoning on vultures and California condors prompted this work"* [34]. Like so much of the popular information on "1080" and condors, Spencer's work has been misrepresented as just a little casual tinkering. In reality, it was a well-designed study that took a year to complete and involved at least 200 black vultures and turkey vultures. A review of some of the highlights of the research will show why Koford (who apparently only saw a summary of the findings, not the study itself) was not particularly worried about "1080" [35].

Spencer found that his vultures were reluctant to eat "1080"-poisoned food, and when they did, they regurgitated it. To determine what a lethal amount of poison might be, he had to force feed the vultures a "shock dose" in water (15 mg/kg for black vultures, 20 mg/kg for turkey vultures). At that dosage, five of 10 black vultures died, as did two of seven turkey vultures. To test this lethal dosage another way, he force-fed 15 black vultures with 15 mg/kg doses of "1080" in 10-gram hamburger pellets. Only one died, because the others all regurgitated the food within seven hours of being forced to eat it.

To test for secondary poisoning, ten Norway rats were given enough "1080" to equal the 15 mg/kg lethal dose for black vultures. The rats were allowed to decompose for 48 hours before being offered to individually caged black vultures. The vultures wouldn't eat them. The test was run again with black vultures caged in a group. They ate all the rats, but there were no symptoms of poisoning.

Next, eighty black vultures were fed 80 ounces of hamburger containing 10.2 mg "1080" per ounce. All food was eaten voluntarily. Within the next 48 hours, three birds developed slight or mild symptoms of poisoning; the other 77 were unaffected. At the end of nine days after the experiment, all birds were in good health again. A new series of sixty black vultures were fed 60 ounces of hamburger containing 20 mg "1080" per ounce. Two vultures died, three showed mild poisoning symptoms, and the other 55 were unaffected. By the fifth day, the three affected birds seemed okay.

Spencer summarized his work in the following two statements in his 1945 and 1946 progress reports: *"As of December 20, 1945, it has been disclosed that this species (black vulture) possesses a tolerance to the poison greater than that of chickens, pigeons and other birds whose susceptibility to '1080' has been determined. Less than 10 percent mortality in black vultures resulted from voluntary ingestion of '1080'-poisoned baits and rodents in which the average amount of '1080' consumed was 25 mg/kg. A mortality of 7 percent in a series of 43 birds resulted from the ingestion by each bird of an average of 25 mg/kg of the poison in fresh ground meat. A mortality of 4 percent in a series of 50 birds resulted from the ingestion by each bird of an average of 25 mg/kg of the poison through the medium of poisoned rat carcasses. These findings lead to the conclusion that the chances are quite remote that any of the vulturine birds would be seriously endangered by properly conducted rodent control operations."*

"Studies to further determine the susceptibility of black vultures to Compound 1080 were continued by H. J. Spencer. A mortality of 11 percent in a series of 100 birds resulted from the voluntary ingestion by each bird of an average of 50 mg/kg of the poison in fresh ground meat. This is further

evidence that vulturine birds possess a tolerance to Compound 1080 considerably greater than that of other birds whose susceptibility has been determined."

A more recent study with captive turkey vultures did not produce any death from "1080" until single doses reached 40 mg/kg of body weight, and that was at temperatures below 50° F. At temperatures above 70° F (a more normal condition when condors would have been feeding on poisoned ground squirrels), it took nearly double that dose of "1080" to kill turkey vultures [36].

To those not familiar with pesticide testing, it may be troublesome that any vultures died in these tests. Remember that the birds were being fed unnaturally high levels of "1080," far greater than they could ever get in a field situation. A lethal dose of "1080" for a ground squirrel is estimated at 0.5 mg/kg of body weight, compared to a minimum of 15 mg/kg dose for vultures. A condor would have to eat a very large number of squirrels to risk getting even a sickening dose of secondary poison, let alone a deadly amount.

As in the case of thallium sulphate, no California condor is known to have been killed or made sick from Compound 1080. That does not completely exonerate it, but it is unlikely that it played a significant role in the decline of the condor population.

LEAD POISONING

Between 1982 and 1985, three California condors were diagnosed as having died from acute lead poisoning [37]. No California condor is known to have died of lead poisoning prior to that time, but few tests were made that would have identified that problem. As early as 1969, lead poisoning had been found in a captive Andean condor, and the authors of the study had warned that California condors might be susceptible [38]. A California condor that died of a gunshot wound in 1976 had a "somewhat elevated" lead level in one tarsus, but low lead levels in liver and kidney. The investigators ruled out recent high level exposure to lead, and conjectured that the source may have been some past high level exposure or perhaps a chronic low lead level [39]. Between 1995 and 2007, two of the captive-reared condors that had been released in California died of lead poisoning, while several others showed very high lead levels in their systems [40]. The number of deaths attributed to lead was much higher in the zoo-released condors in Arizona [41].

The source of lead in condors (past and present) is almost certainly fragmented bullets ingested from the mammal carcasses fed upon by the birds [42]. This type of ammunition came into general use after about 1890. With almost 100 years of exposure to such a potentially lethal agent, it seems inevitable that condors died of lead poisoning throughout the 20th century. (For example, the three condors discussed above as possible victims of "1080" showed symptoms that could have been attributed to lead poison.) Still, there are some troubling questions that need answers before even an educated guess

290

can be made concerning the magnitude of historical losses to lead poison [43].

* * *

All recent discussions of lead poisoning in condors have identified mule deer - either full carcasses of deer shot but not retrieved, or the "gut piles" left when hunters field dress their kills - as the principal source of contamination [44]. This is a curious conclusion because all researchers prior to 1980 concluded that deer were a secondary food source for condors, far behind cattle and sheep. In the 1930s and 1940s, Koford reported that *"the principal food today is Hereford range cattle,"* with *"approximately half of all instances"* of feeding seen by him, reported by others, or cited in literature involving beef cattle, principally calves. Deer were included in the other half, but so were sheep, ground squirrels, horses, and a variety of small mammals [45]. In the 1960s, the McMillan brothers found that *"condor food continues to consist chiefly of the carcasses of cattle and sheep, especially the former"* [46]. In the 1970s, I observed an even greater shift to cattle as sheep numbers decreased in the condor range [47]. I also cited the findings of deer experts who noted that dying deer tend to drift toward canyon bottoms [48]. There, steep terrain and heavy brush would interfere with the ability of condors to see many of the carcasses (since condors find food by sight, not by smell) and also to reach them (because of their large size and wingspread). Even the originators of the idea that most contamination was coming from deer carcasses could only say (without actual observation) that they were *"reasonably confident that a substantial proportion of the species' diet in the fall was hunter-shot deer"* [49].

The idea that condors feed heavily on gut piles came from the same writers, referring (without details) to *"many records of birds feeding on deer gut piles or on crippling-loss deer* [50], and asserting (again, without details) that gut piles *"are well known as favored food for condors"* [51]. Yet Michael Fry, in a detailed evaluation of the threat of lead to condors, concluded [52]: *"There are no documented feeding records of condors using gut piles, with the exception of gut piles of domestic pigs deliberately placed in the field by the MacMillan* [sic] *brothers... in the 1950s."* Apparently there are a few unpublished observations from southern California [53], and condors in Arizona have been seen at gut piles on a number of occasions [54], but the overall record is definitely slim.

Gut piles seem to me an unlikely source of regular condor food. As condors find food by sight, not by smell - and gut piles don't look like "food" - condors likely find most gut piles by seeing other animals at them. *"Gut piles do not remain in the field for long, as both mammalian and other avian scavengers quickly consume them"* [55]. By the time condors - late risers because of their high wing loading - see other scavengers feeding, most of the gut piles would be gone.

While it has been generally found that lead levels in condor blood samples in

California are highest during deer hunting season, they have also been found to be elevated in the same areas six months before and after deer hunting season [56]. (Of the three native condors diagnosed as dying from lead poison, one died in March and one in April, months after the end of deer hunting season.) Lead levels in blood drop quickly to baseline levels if the bird is not re-exposed (half-time 13 days, very high levels reduced to baseline in 30 days or less) [57], so condors must be acquiring lead in substantial amounts clearly not the result of deer hunting.

* * *

The historical record of deer hunting also raises questions. While condor numbers were decreasing during the mid-20th century, nothing suggests an especially precipitous decline during that period. Yet, deer kill within the condor range, which had held relatively steady through the 1930s and 1940s, doubled in the 1950s and 1960s. By the mid-1970s, the kill had returned to pre-1950 levels, and continued to decrease until by the early 1990s the annual kills were only two-thirds those of previous 15 years. There has been no increase in the years since. These are not small fluctuations. Between 1950 and 1969, the annual deer kill in condor range probably exceeded 15,000; before and after, it was perhaps 8,000 annually, and by 1980 less than 5,000. In the 1980s, half of the kill each year was in San Luis Obispo, Monterey, and San Benito counties, areas seldom visited by the surviving condors [58].

Most of the deer that are shot would not have become food for condors, only the "gut piles" left by hunters and those deer that were shot but went unrecovered. This "crippling loss" varies from area to area, but averages perhaps 20 percent of the total kill [59]. Doing some very rough math to determine the potential availability of lead from deer hunting:

- During each hunting season in the 1980s - in Santa Barbara, Ventura, Los Angeles, Kern, and Tulare counties combined - perhaps 500 deer carcasses and 2,500 gut piles would have been left on the range.

- Each hunting season in the 1950s and 1960s, there would have been 3,000 deer carcasses and 15,000 "gut piles" available, and many more condors to find them.

If most lead received by condors was being ingested from deer carcasses and "gut piles," the chances of a condor receiving recurring dosages of lead would have been much greater in the 1950s and 1960s than in the 1980s. Yet - as noted above - there is no evidence of a precipitous drop in the condor population during the early period. It seems that there must be more to the story.

One probability is that deer hunting has not been the main source of lead available to poison condors. For example, the chemical composition of the lead found in condor blood samples is the same as that found in deer hunting ammunition [60], but this is the same type ammunition used by ranchers to kill sick or injured livestock. Many agencies distribute pamphlets describing

292

methods of euthanasia; a typical paragraph on the technique reads [61]: *"A .22 caliber long rifle, 9mm or .38 caliber gun can be used. The muzzle of the gun should be held at least 4 to 10 inches (10-25 cm) away from the skull when fired. The use of hollow-point or soft-nosed bullets will increase brain tissue destruction and reduce the chance of ricochet."* On larger animals: *"Larger mature animals will require at least a .22 magnum hollow- or soft-point bullet or, preferably, a 9mm or .357 caliber bullet"* [62]. The animals are shot in the head, but in a way that maximizes the splintering of the bullets. Ranchers are encouraged to haul animal carcasses to disposal sites, but on the open range far from such facilities, I suspect many animals are left where they die. Livestock carcasses are more likely than dead deer to occur in open terrain where condors can easily reach them.

Another consideration is that lead exposure may not be as critical to condor survival as is often implied. Meretsky et al. [63] stated that any condors having high levels of lead in their blood *"are best considered mortalities"* if not subjected to chelation therapy (chemical binding of the lead in the bird's system, so it can be more readily eliminated). However, and as noted above [64], this is an unsupportable statement: *"It is not true, however, that all condors with high levels of lead in their tissues will necessarily die because they can eliminate lead from blood and some internal organs rather fast unless continually re-exposed"* [65]. Many of the condors exposed to lead may have survived the encounter through their natural resilience.

None of this is meant to deny the fact of lead poisoning of condors, or its probable role in the decline of the species. Without knowing the source of the poison, the magnitude of its historical impact can only be guessed at.

CHAPTER NOTES

1. Rett, E. Z. 1946. Record of another condor death. *Condor* 48(4):182.

2. Specimen data for LACM 36096: study skin and almost complete skeleton, adult male California condor; obtained 27 June 1960 Kern County, California. Natural History Museum of Los Angeles County (Los Angeles, California).

3. Rett, E. Z. 1938. Hailstorm fatal to California condors. *Condor* 40(5):225.

4. Pages 129 and 131 *in:* Koford, C. B. 1953. The California condor. Research Report Number Four. New York, New York: National Audubon Society.

5. Page 131 *in* Koford 1953, *op. cit.*

6. Koford, C. B. 1940. Interview 17 May 1940 with Bud Palmer, U. S. Forest Service, Ojai, California. California condor species account. Carl Koford notes. Museum of Vertebrate Zoology (Berkeley, California).

7. Anonymous. 1965. Shooting is ruled out in Pinehurst bird's death. *Bee* (Fresno, California), 15 June 1965.

8. Lawrence, R. E. 1893. Pseudogryphus californianus. *Auk* 10(3):300-301.

9. Personal communication: letter January 1986 from Janet A. Hamber (Santa Barbara Museum of Natural History, Santa Barbara, California), to S. R. Wilbur., relaying information from Frazier MacGillivray (Paso Robles, California).

10. Specimen LACM 36096 (Chapter note 2, above).

11. Letter 22 January 1937 from J. R. Pemberton (Los Angeles, California) to Joseph Grinnell (Museum of Vertebrate Zoology, Berkeley, California). Historical correspondence files, Museum of Vertebrate Zoology.

12. Letter 25 January 1937 from Joseph Grinnell (Museum of Vertebrate Zoology, Berkeley, California) to J. R. Pemberton (Los Angeles, California. Historical correspondence files, Museum of Vertebrate Zoology.

13. Waggaman, W. H., G. G. Heffner, and E. A. Gee. 1950. Thallium: properties, sources, recovery, and uses of the element and its compounds. U. S. Bureau of Mines Information Circular 7553. Washington, D. C.

14. Linsdale, J. M. 1931. Facts concerning the use of thallium in California to poison rodents: its destructiveness to game birds, song birds and other valuable wildlife. *Condor* 33(3):92-106.

15. Shaw, P. A. 1932. Studies of thallium poisoning in game birds. *California Fish and Game* 18(1):29-34.

16. Linsdale 1931, *op. cit.*

17. Jacobsen, W. C. 1931. Ground squirrel control in California. *California Fish and Game* 17(3):240-246.

18. Munch, J. C., G. Olden, H. M. Ginsburg, and C. E. Nixon. 1933. The 1932 Thallotoxicosis outbreak in California. *Journal of the American Medical Association* 100(17):1315-1319.

19. Waggaman et. al., *op. cit.*

20. From Agricultural Commissioners' annual crop reports for Ventura County, compiled by the California Department of Food and Agriculture, Sacramento.

21. Memo 16 July 1965 Ronald A. Thompson (Riverside, California) to Malcolm N. Allison (Sacramento, California), subject predator and rodent control activities in

California condor range within Los Angeles County. U. S. Fish and Wildlife Service files.

22. Koford 1953 *op. cit.,* page 130.

23. Copies of the letters about the alleged thallium poisoning are in the California condor files maintained at the Santa Barbara (California) Museum of Natural History.

24. Details of these early discussions are covered on pages 45-56 *in:* Wilbur, S. R. 2004. Condor tales: what I learned in twelve years with the big birds. Gresham, Oregon: Symbios.

25. Robinson, C. S. 1940. Notes on the California condor collected on Los Padres National Forest, California. Santa Barbara, California: Los Padres National Forest. 22-page typed manuscript.

26. Page 36 *in:* Miller, A. H., I. I. McMillan, and E. McMillan. 1965. The current status and welfare of the California condor. Research Report No. 6. New York, New York: National Audubon Society.

27. McMillan I. I. 1966. Poisoned condors. *Defenders of Wildlife News* 41(2):115-116. McMillan alleged that this incident had been purposely "hidden," because Carl Koford had never heard of it. Actually, it was reported to Fish and Wildlife Service officials within a day, and a full report was prepared for the Director of Fish and Wildlife Service within three weeks. At the time of the incident, Carl Koford was in Mexico, and he spent much of the next two years in Central and South America. During that time period, there was no one studying condors, and interest in the species did not revive until Koford's work was published in 1953. By that time, the incident was old news buried in government files until the 1960s, when the next investigation of condors occurred.

28. Linsdale 1931, *op. cit.*

29. Mendelssohn, H., 1972. Ecological effects of chemical control of rodents and jackals in Israel. Pages 527-544 *in:* M. T. Farvar, and J. P. Milton (editors.), The Careless Technology: Ecology and International Development. New York, New York: Natural History Press.

30. Koford 1953, *op. cit.,* pages 130-131.

31. Pages 40-42 *in:* Miller, McMillan and McMillan, *op. cit.*

32. Specimen LACM 36096 (Chapter note 2, above).

33. Pages 118-122 *in:* McMillan, I. 1968. Man and the California condor. New York, New York: Dutton and Company.

34. U. S. Fish and Wildlife Service memorandum 24 March 1965, James W. Caslick

(Gainesville, Florida) to Director, Patuxent Wildlife Research Center (Laurel, Maryland), describing Compound 1080 studies done in 1945-1946.

35. Spencer, H. J. 1946. Progress reports, Second and Third quarters, Fiscal Year 1946, effects of Compound 1080 on vultures. Gainesville (Florida) Field Station, Denver Wildlife Research Center. U. S. Fish and Wildlife Service.

36. Fry, D. M., G. Santalo, and C. R. Grau. 1986. Final report for Interagency Agreement: Effects of Compound 1080 poison on turkey vultures. Department of Avian Sciences, University of California - Davis. 44 pages.

37. Janssen, D. L., and M. P. Anderson. 1986. Lead poisoning in free-ranging California condors. *Journal of the American Veterinary Medical Association* 189(9):1115-1117.
Wiemeyer, S. N., J. M. Scott, M. P. Anderson, P. H. Bloom, and C. J. Stafford. 1988. Environmental contaminants in California condors. *Journal of Wildlife Management* 52(2):238-247.

38. Locke, L. N., G. E. Bagley, D. N. Frickie, and L. T. Young. 1969. Lead poisoning and aspergillosis in an Andean condor. *Journal of the American Veterinary Medicine Association* 155(7):1052-1056.

39. Wiemeyer, S. N., A. J. Krynitsky, and S. R. Wilbur. 1983. Environmental contaminants in tissues, foods, and feces of California condors. Pages 427-439 *in:* Wilbur, S. R., and J. A. Jackson, Vulture biology and management. Berkeley, California: University of California Press.

40. Hall, M., J. Grantham, R. Posey, and A. Mee. 2007. Lead exposure among reintroduced California condors in southern California. Pages 163-184 *in:* Mee, A., and L. S. Hall (editors), California condors in the 21st century. Series in Ornithology No. 2. Nuttall Ornithological Club and American Ornithologists' Union. Cambridge, Massachusetts.

41. Parish, C. N., W. R. Heinrich, and W. G. Hunt. 2007. Lead exposure, diagnosis, and treatment in California condors released in Arizona. Pages 97-108 *in:* Mee, A., and L. S. Hall (editors), California condors in the 21st century. Series in Ornithology No. 2. Nuttall Ornithological Club and American Ornithologists' Union. Cambridge, Massachusetts.

42. Church, M. E., R. Gwiazda, R. W. Risebrough, K. Sorenson, C. P. Chamberlain, S. Farry, W. Heinrich, B. A. Rideout, and D. R. Smith. 2006. Ammunition is the principal source of lead accumulated by California condors re-introduced to the wild. *Environmental Science and Technology* 40(19):6143-6150.
Hunt, W. G., W. Burnham, C. N. Parish, K. K. Burnham, B. Mutch, and J. L. Oaks. 2006. Bullet fragments in deer remains: implications for lead exposure in avian scavengers. *Wildlife Society Bulletin* 34(1)167-170.

43. Nothing in this discussion is intended to cast doubt on the reality of lead poisoning

296

in California condors. My purpose throughout this book is to evaluate through time the contribution that various agents made to the near-extinction of the species. This has been difficult to do in the case of lead poisoning because the discovery very quickly became ammunition (of another sort) in the national campaign to reduce and eventually eliminate lead in the environment. This is undoubtedly a worthy cause, but the demands for immediate action effectively quelled scientific inquiry into the issue as it affected condors, and a number of key questions have gone unanswered.

44. Hundreds of newspaper, magazine and journal articles could be cited, but almost all arose from speculations of Noel and Helen Snyder, for example:
Page 206 *in:* Snyder, N. F. R., and H. A. Snyder. 1989. Biology and conservation of the California condor. Pages 175-267 *in:* Power, D. M. Current ornithology, Volume 6. New York, New York: Plenum Press.
Page 252-253 *in:* Snyder, N., and H. Snyder. 2000. The California condor, a saga of natural history and conservation. San Diego, California: Academic Press.

45. Koford 1953 *op. cit.,* page 55.

46. Miller, McMillan and McMillan 1965, *op. cit.,* page 26.

47. Pages 24-27 *in:* Wilbur, S. R. 1978. The California condor, 1966-76: a look at its past and future. North American Fauna Number 72. Washington, D. C.: U. S. Fish and Wildlife Service.

48. Blong, B. 1954. A South Coast deer range. Los Angeles, California: Department of Fish and Game.
Taber, R. D., and R. F. Dasmann. 1958. The black-tailed deer in the chaparral. Game Bulletin Number 8. Sacramento, California: Department of Fish and Game.

49. Snyder and Snyder 2000 *op. cit.,* page 152.

50. Meretsky, V. J., and N. F. R. Snyder. 1992. Range use and movements of California condors. *Condor* 94(2):313-335.

51. Snyder and Snyder 2000 *op. cit.,* page 253.

52. Page 58 *in:* Fry, D. M., and J. R. Maurer. 2003. Assessment of lead contamination sources exposing California condors. Species Conservation and Recovery Program Report, 2003-02, California Department of Fish and Game. Sacramento, California.

53. Cited on page 10 *in:* Johnson, C. K., T. Vodovoz, W. M. Boyce, and J. A. K. Mazet. 2007. Lead exposure in California condors and sentinel species in California. Report for the California Department of Fish and Game. Wildlife Health Center, University of California, Davis.

54. Personal communication, 28 January 2012, Grainger Hunt (The Peregrine Fund) to S. R. Wilbur: *"Yes, the guys in Arizona have seen condors feeding on ungulate gut piles* (and) *there have been numerous radio fixes of condors at gut piles."*

55. Fry and Maurer 2003, *op. cit.*, page 58.

56. Hall *et al.* 2007, *op. cit.*
   Sorenson, K. J., and L. J. Burnham. 2007. Lead concentrations in the blood of Big Sur California condors. Pages 185-195 *in:* Mee, A., and L. S. Hall (editors), California condors in the 21st century. Series in Ornithology No. 2. Nuttall Ornithological Club and American Ornithologists' Union. Cambridge, Massachusetts.

57. Fry and Maurer 2003, *op. cit.*, page 32.

58. California Department of Fish and Game has compiled records by county of reported deer kill back to 1927: Mohr, R. C., and M. Parker. 2008. 2007 California deer kill report. Deer Management Program, Wildlife Programs Branch. Sacramento, California. Reports for subsequent years are also available. According to Craig Stowers, Deer Program Coordinator, reporting procedures have changed only in minor ways through the years (personal communication, 24 January 2012).

59. The Department of Fish and Game uses various weighted correction factors to convert reported deer kill (from their various surveys) to an estimate of the actual kill. The estimated kill is not shown by county in the Department's compiled reports, so these figures are my estimates.

60. Church et al. 2006, *op. cit.*

61. Anonymous. 1999. The emergency euthanasia of sheep 7 goats. Sacramento, California: California Department of Food and Agriculture.

62. Jensen, W., and J. Oltjen. 2007. Beef care practices. Davis, California: University of California Division of Agriculture and Natural Resources.

63. Meretsky, V. J., N. F. R. Snyder, S. R. Beissinger, D. A. Clendenen, and J. W. Wiley. 2000. Demography of the California condor: implications for reestablishment. *Conservation Biology* 14(4):957-967.

64. Fry and Maurer 2003 *op. cit.*, page 32.

65. Cade, T. 2007. Exposure of California condors to lead from spent ammunition. *Journal of Wildlife Management* 71(7):2125-2133.

CHAPTER 24

FEEDING CONDORS, AND BEYOND

Over the years, whenever the status of condors had been talked about, a likely subject for discussion had been food supply. In the 1930s, the Forest Service suggested that lack of food was a much more important problem for condors than any threat posed by new road building [1]. While Carl Koford didn't think condors were in danger of starving in the 1930s and 1940s, he concluded that food supply was the second most important factor affecting distribution and numbers of condors, direct persecution being the first [2]. In one of the few significant papers on condors from the 1950s, Raymond Cowles put forth his idea that control of wildfires in the Sespe area had seriously reduced condor food supplies [3]. In the 1960s, supplying food for condors was suggested as a way to keep condors safe from shooting, poisoning, and effects of the Sespe Water Project [4]. With so many ideas expressed about the importance of the condor food supply, it didn't seem like a subject to be ignored.

My initial evaluation did show that the condors' feeding area was shrinking [5]. It was true that the acreage was still extensive in the Coast Ranges and in the Tehachapi Mountains. It also appeared adequate in the Sierra Nevada foothills, but rangeland there was being rapidly replaced at the edges by houses and citrus groves. Rangeland had decreased drastically south of the Sespe Condor Sanctuary (the nearest feeding area to the best nesting area), and was still decreasing as the Los Angeles suburbs moved north to join the Ventura County suburbs.

The available food supply was also decreasing. Sheep and cattle grazing were almost non-existent in the once dependable grasslands south of the Sespe Sanctuary. Yearlong livestock operations in the Tehachapis, Sierra Nevada, and Coast Ranges were being replaced with seasonal "stocker" cattle herds. Second-home land schemes in the Tehachapis were another problem. Most of them failed, and few homes were built, but the big land holdings that had been sold were divided into smaller parcels and fenced. The land still looked like grazing land, but there was little grazing done on it. Deer populations were sparser than they had once been, and they were healthy; few disease die-offs occurred to provide carcasses for condors. Deer hunting had experienced a significant decrease since the 1950s and early 1960s, reducing the number of deer that hunters killed but did not retrieve. Ground squirrel and kangaroo rat poisoning was still common, but refined techniques seemed to be leaving fewer dead rodents where condors could find them. All of these changes appeared to make food finding, particularly in summer, more difficult than in former years.

Despite the evidence that condor food resources were shrinking, intuitively it didn't look like a population of perhaps 50 condors could be starving. Even with decreases in habitat, they had some 10.8 million acres of the State of California to forage over in their search for food [6]. Daily food need per bird was estimated at 3 pounds or less [7]. Fifty condors would need only 150 pounds of food per day, which potentially could be obtained from one Hereford steer, two big mule deer, or three or four lambs or calves [8]. Obviously, they would need more carcasses than that if the food was to be available at the right times and right places for all the condors but, overall, quantity of food did not appear to be an issue. If there were problems, they involved the geographical or seasonal location of food.

A condor free to fly throughout the range of the species should have had little trouble finding food, even in summer. Non-breeding birds, although traditionally bound to certain regions at certain times of year, were able to disperse widely [9]. Breeding pairs, on the other hand, had critical time restrictions to deal with. Without easily found food near nest sites, pairs might chose not to nest, or might spend so much of their time foraging that they could not adequately attend to a nest. They might nest less often or less successfully. The southern portion of the Sespe-Piru area, including the historic nesting locations in Hopper Canyon and the Sespe Creek side canyons, had suffered the most loss of nearby feeding habitat. It appeared to me that shortage of food could be - or could soon become - limiting to condors attempting to nest there. With few other options available to slow the condor population decrease, an experimental feeding program was initiated. It appeared that provision of a dependable food supply near known nest sites might be beneficial in one or more ways.

1. It could make it possible for breeding birds to spend less time looking for food and more time attending to their nests, thus increasing the chances of nesting success.

2. When carcasses were scarce, the most dominant condors could keep birds lower in the "peck order" from getting adequate food. Increasing the overall food supply, and feeding in several locations concurrently, might decrease intraspecies strife, and make it possible for more pairs to establish territories in the area.

3. Having food available at several sites near nests might make it possible for young birds to become independent at an earlier age, permitting their parents to nest more frequently. One of the reasons that condors were not breeding every year is that the young ones could not compete against older birds at carcasses. The adults fed their young long after the immature birds were physically capable of taking care of themselves, and so were not free to begin a new nesting attempt. Having additional carcasses available near nesting areas might break down the "peck order," and let the younger birds feed in peace.

4. More theoretically, it seemed like supplementing the local food base could help maintain the tradition of condors using historical nesting areas. For long-

300

term integrity of the population, it might be important to keep condors doing what they had been doing since at least the 1930s, and probably for hundreds of years previous to that. They had been reaching their peak numbers in the Sespe-Piru nesting area in winter, the logical time and place for unpaired condors to meet and mate. The nesting terrain itself was undoubtedly a magnet for the birds, attracting them and keeping them as long as other conditions (e.g., local food) were good. In the spring, the non-breeding condors dispersed into the northern rangelands, leaving the nesting pairs alone to raise their young in peace, without "peck order" strife and with full use of a local supply that (even in past times) was less reliable in summer than in winter. In the 1970s, the nesting terrain still looked pretty good. Supplemental feeding couldn't replace the lost rangelands of Moorpark-Simi Valley, but perhaps it could partially recreate them.

5. The old argument about feeding condors in the Sanctuary to keep them safe from shooting or poisons seemed to have some life in it, still. As food became scarcer, condors would be forced to congregate more often, perhaps increasing their vulnerability. It looked like it might be worthwhile to see if feeding condors in secure locations was even a viable technique.

* * *

The supplemental feeding program began in February 1971, and was carried through the 1970s, using whatever deer and domestic livestock could be obtained. The results from the first two years were moderately encouraging [10]. Of 83 carcasses hauled to the two feeding sites, condors had definitely fed on 47 of them. Indications were that another 27 had probably furnished food for condors. As many as nine condors fed together, but the usual numbers seen were from two to six birds. Immature condors fed regularly, sometimes by themselves. During the feeding period, three condors were known to have been reared in the Sespe Condor Sanctuary, compared to only one certain fledgling in the previous three years. After only two years, there was no way to determine if the extra food had been an influence, but presence of the regular food supply was the only obvious change in circumstances.

The program was relatively expensive, requiring about 6.5 hours of somebody's time each week just to get the food to the condors. Much of the food went to scavengers other than condors - particularly bears, which could be troublesome because they dragged off entire carcasses - but condors seemed to get their share. As for a chief concern of the feeding critics - that regular feeding might cause condors to become tame and dependent - we summarized this way: *"The fear that condors would become overconditioned to the feeding site, and would fail to forage naturally, proved groundless. As stated, nine condors were the most seen at a carcass simultaneously, and usually there were less, even though others were known to be in the near vicinity. Condors occasionally came to the freshly placed carcass with their crops already bulging with food, indicating they had been out on normal foraging flights. And, while condors sometimes showed up at the feeding site with remarkable promptness when a new carcass was set out, there were other occasions when a carcass was untouched for a day or more before finally being eaten by condors. Even after 2 years of regular feeding, the condors continued to behave like wild condors - sometimes wary, sometimes bold and inquisitive, and always unpredictable."*

* * *

The next four years of the supplemental feeding program resulted in regular condor use of the "cafeterias," but without increases to "unnatural" numbers and without attracting non-breeding birds in summer and fall when they were expected to be out of the Sanctuary area. Young condors sometimes fed by themselves at carcasses, without having to defer to older birds. However, only 20 to 30 per cent of the 246 carcasses provided were used by condors, compared to more than 50 per cent use in 1971-1973. Also, the increase in condor production noted in the first years of feeding had not been repeated. In four years, only two young were known to have been produced from nests within reasonable range of the feeding stations. It wasn't a particularly optimistic report [11].

So far, there had been no overt signs that the feeding program was helping the condors. On the other hand, there might be some positive effects that weren't measurable, such as preventing mortality that might have occurred in less secure locations. Reproductive response within the condor population would not manifest itself immediately, so there was still a chance that local food was making the nesting area more attractive. More to the point, we were running out of ideas on how to stop the more and more obvious population decline. We kept the feeding going into the 1980s, but began preparing for a more drastic intervention.

* * *

The California Condor Technical Committee, with membership from various government agencies and National Audubon Society, had developed a "recovery plan" for the species [12]. The prime objective of the plan was *"to maintain a population of at least 50 California condors, well distributed throughout their 1974 range, with an average natality (production) of at least 4 young per year and with the lowest possible annual mortality"* [13]. To reach the objective, six sub-objectives were identified:

(1) To provide adequate nesting conditions for each subpopulation of condors;

(2) To provide adequate roosting sites for each subpopulation of condors;

(3) To provide optimum food and feeding habitat;

(4) To maintain condor mortality at the lowest levels possible;

(5) To monitor the condor population to determine the success of management; and

(6) To conduct a widespread conservation-education program.

302

Unfortunately, most of the tasks included in the plan were completed by the mid-1970s, with no indication that the decline of the condor population was slowing. It appeared that the only actions that might save the species involved taking condors into captivity, getting them to produce young at a capacity beyond that possible in the wild (as proposed by the San Diego Zoo in the 1950s: Chapter 20), and attempting to introduce the captive-reared birds into whatever remained of the wild population.

This was obviously not going to be easy to implement. To begin with, State law in California prohibited the capturing of condors for any purpose. With the passage of the Endangered Species Act, federal law could override the state statute, but none of the agencies involved with the condor wanted to attempt that. As had occurred at the time of the San Diego Zoo proposal and later during the Sespe Dam controversy (Chapter 21), those interested in condors were split into two camps: those that wanted the condors left to fend for themselves, no matter what the outcome, and those who favored some degree of active management. The symbolism of the wild condor - the keeper of the wilderness - figured strongly in the stand taken by many opponents of captive breeding, but there were other concerns. Some felt that the task was impossible, and the small wild population would be further jeopardized by removing condors for a project doomed to failure. Others felt that a long-term captive breeding program would be far too expensive, considering all the other environmental needs that might be funded instead. Despite the controversy, the proposal moved slowly forward. By 1980, the U. S. Fish and Wildlife Service was committed to a captive breeding program [14].

As initially formulated, the captive breeding plan did not envision taking all the remaining condors into captivity. It seemed like leaving a few condors in the wild was good strategy, both biologically and socio-politically. Although the condor population of 1980 was not stable (*i.e.,* the long-term death rate was exceeding the long-term birth rate), the decline was slow and some of the condors were still successfully rearing young. While a slightly larger gene pool in the captive population would not be bad, there was no indication that all the birds were necessary for program success. If even a small number of wild condors survived until captive-reared birds were available to release into the wild, the remaining wild condors might have helped the new birds acclimate to their environment.

From the public standpoint, it seemed desirable to have a few wild condors. Even if they didn't contribute anything to the ultimate recovery effort, wild condors were a reminder of what the captive breeding program was trying to attain. Having a chance to see a condor during the 10 years, 20 years, or potentially longer time period before there were new populations could have been of great psychological value to the interested public, and could have helped keep interest in the project alive. A few wild condors might also provide some assurance to the public that (contrary to what some people were suggesting) this was not trading free-living condors and their habitat for a perpetual zoo program.

Regardless of the apparent advantages of having wild condors and captive condors concurrently, in 1986 the U. S. Fish and Wildlife Service decided to capture all the remaining birds. The wild California condors ceased to exist, hopefully to be replaced at some later date by the captive-reared carriers of their genetic makeup. Whatever happened in the future, "the annals of *Gymnogyps*" had come to a close.

CHAPTER NOTES

1. Letter, 5 July 1935, S. A. Nash-Boulden (Santa Barbara National Forest) to Warren Eaton (National Audubon Society). Copy in Robert E. Easton collection, Santa Barbara Museum of Natural History.

2. Page 72 *in:* Koford, C. B. 1953. The California condor. Research Report Number 4. New York, New York: National Audubon Society.

3. Cowles, R. B. 1958. Starving the condors? *California Fish and Game* 44(2):175-181.

4. United Water Conservation District. 1965. The California condor management and protection program. Santa Paula, California.

5. Pages 27-31 *in:* Wilbur, S. R. 1978. The California condor, 1966-76: a look at its past and future. *North American Fauna* Number 72. Washington, D. C.: U. S. Fish and Wildlife Service.

6. Rieger, S. F. 1973. California range land study. California Department of Fish and Game, Sacramento, California. 13 pages.

7. Wilbur 1978 *op. cit.,* page 26. Also: Hiraldo, F. 1983. Breeding biology of the cinereous vulture. Pages 197-213 *in:* Wilbur, S. R., and J. A. Jackson. Vulture biology and management. Berkeley, California: University of California Press.

8. Information from commercial meat cutters: a 160 pound mule deer would have perhaps 80 pounds of meat and viscera; a lamb or fawn might yield 40 pounds of food; and a 1,000-pound steer would yield about half its weight in condor food.

9. Pages 233-240 *in:* Wilbur, S. R. 2004. Condor tales, what I learned in twelve years with the big birds. Gresham, Oregon: Symbios.

10. Wilbur, S. R., W. D. Carrier, and J. C. Borneman. 1974. Supplemental feeding program for California condors. *Journal of Wildlife Management* 38(2):343-346.

11. Wilbur, S. R. 1978. Supplemental feeding of California condors. Pages 135-140 *in:* Temple, S. A. (editor), Endangered birds: management techniques for preserving

threatened species. Madison, Wisconsin: University of Wisconsin Press.

12. Wilbur, S. R., W. D. Carrier, B. K. Muldowney, R. D. Mallette, J. C. Borneman, and W. H. Radtkey. 1974. California condor recovery plan. Washington, D. C.: U. S. Fish and Wildlife Service.

13. Some had asked why the recovery objective - a mere 50 condors - had been set so low. For a long-lived species like the condor, a population of only 50 is not necessarily the end of the road. There is always the potential for a major catastrophe to affect a large number of individuals. On the other hand, all a pair of condors has to do during their long lifetime is produce two more condors that live approximately as long as they do, and that produce two more condors to replace them. Even genetics - the various dangers of inbreeding - do not seem to affect large, long-lived species in the drastic ways seen in some smaller and more prolific animals. One hundred condors would be better than 50, and 1,000 would be better than 100. Still, if births and deaths are more or less balanced, even the smallest of these three populations could remain stable over a long period of time.

14. Full details of the efforts to develop a captive breeding plan for condors, and to get the plan implemented, are included in Chapters 38 to 49 of "Condor Tales" (Wilbur 2004, *op, cit.*).

Figure 19. Immature California Condor, Sespe Condor Sanctuary. Photo by author.

CHAPTER 25
WHAT HAPPENED TO THE CONDORS?

In the preceding chapters, I surveyed the history of California condors from before human presence until the early 1980s, when management emphasis changed from preserving the remaining wild population to a captive breeding program. The presentation was meant to entertain and inform, and also to correct or further analyze some of the popular condor stories that had developed through the years. Also, I planned the chapters in the book to lay the groundwork for asking - and to the extent possible, answering - the question: why did the California condor population decline to the point at which extinction was almost certain?

Many different opinions about the causes of the condors' decline have been expressed over time. Varying ideas about history are inevitable; those who actually *live* the history seldom leave behind the records that would be most useful to those who later try to *interpret* it. With the condor, we have - at best - a very fragmented record to work with. A further complication arises because most writers of the 20th and 21st centuries haven't known that the popular record of condor history has been badly tainted since the 1850s. Few recognize the name of Alexander Taylor today, but few books and articles written about condors in the last 150 years have not been influenced by Taylor's imagination and exaggeration (Chapter 8). No condor researchers or historians other than myself, Harry Harris, and Carl Koford have spent any significant amount of time looking at primary and secondary references. New books may have new research findings, but the authors almost always refer back to earlier books for their historical information.

For the following analysis, I reviewed some 3,000 sources. Two-thirds of them specifically mention condors; the others provided information on historical conditions within the condor range, or supplementary data to help interpret the condor material. The types of condor records (with the approximate percentage of the total shown for each) were: published books (15%), articles in serial publications (45%), newspapers (15%), library and museum archival records (20%), and various government documents and unpublished matter (5%). Chronologically, the records date from: before 1850, 2%; 1850-1900, 25%; 1901-1930, 25%; 1931-1960, 15%; 1961-1980, 20%; and after 1980, 13%.

From the compiled record, I identified specific agents known or suspected to have impacted the condor population, and have looked at their potential effects both chronologically and geographically. I considered three general circumstances that might have had a significant effect on the condors' ability to maintain a viable population over time: major changes in habitat, making areas unable to support condors; changes in productivity great enough to have caused an unnatural decline in numbers; and excessive mortality.

HABITAT CHANGE:

There is no evidence (and little likelihood) that habitat loss or degradation caused significant changes in the condor population. Certainly, useable acreage - particularly of feeding habitat - has been lost over time, but I don't think there is any region that was occupied in 1800 that could not support condors today. Even in Baja California, Mexico - where in the past I have questioned whether food supply was adequate to support a condor population [1] - recently released condors have been regularly finding natural food (mule deer, bighorn sheep, burro, cattle, horses) to supplement that artificially provided to them [2].

DEPRESSED PRODUCTIVITY:

Changes in productivity - either within the population generally, or for individual birds - does not appear to have been a significant problem for condors. Nevertheless, there are several ways the species could have been affected: by loss of genetic diversity, from the effects of the chemical DDT, or as a result of group limitations brought about by fewer condors living in a region.

GENETICS - Reduction in genetic diversity is a potential problem with any declining species, and some loss has occurred over time with the captive flocks of California condors [3]. Nevertheless, the current population of nearly 400 condors are all derived from six breeding pairs, with little or no evidence of genetic decline. One would think that in the past, with many more breeding pairs and greater geographic distribution, genetic problems would have been less significant than currently.

DDT - Beginning about 1944, massive amounts of the organochlorine DDT were applied to kill insects in the United States and around the world. Peak use in the United States occurred about 1959, but continued at high levels until DDT was banned in the U. S. in 1972. One result of this pesticide use was "thin eggshell syndrome," in which DDE - the principal metabolite of DDT - interfered with calcium production in birds, causing extreme production failure in some species due to their laying fragile thin-shelled eggs [4]. Eggshell thinning was most strongly associated with birds that fed heavily on fish or other birds (brown pelicans, bald eagles, ospreys, peregrine falcons). Therefore, it came as a surprise that comparisons we did between condor eggshells from before DDT use and those collected 1964-1969 showed the DDT-era samples to be 32% thinner than those from before 1944. This was quite high compared to most other species that had been studied; average thinning of more than about 18% has been associated with population declines. The deterioration of the shell layers in the thin condor eggs was spectacularly evident through the electron microscope. Also, we found significant residues of DDE in the more recent eggshells [5].

Historically, condor egg breakage occurred regularly; about 10% of eggs known to have been taken by collectors were reportedly found punctured or otherwise damaged at the nest site [6]. If it was natural for 25-pound birds laying eggs on hard rock floors to sometimes damage the shells, it seems inevitable that DDE-thinned eggshells would be even more vulnerable.

Shell thinning contributing to egg breakage is the most obvious sign of DDE influence on avian productivity, but disruption of normal breeding behavior is also possible. Among changes noted in various species have been decreases in nest attentiveness, lessening of courtship activities, and changes in expected nest defense [7]. There is no evidence that DDE contamination disrupted condor behavior, and only one condor egg was found that was so thin-shelled that it crushed immediately after laying. Nevertheless, considering the potential for egg breakage, and the possibility of aberrant behavior by breeding birds with high DDE levels, it seems to me likely that DDE had some role in the reduced productivity observed in the 1960s and 1970s.

POPULATION CHARACTERISTICS - Observations made by me and by Fred Sibley in the 1960s and 1970s suggested that - considering the size of the condor population - average annual production was only about half of what seemed possible [8]. At the time, I thought that decreased productivity was principally due to less reproductive activity rather than lack of nest success [9]. As noted above, I may have been wrong in not considering DDE contamination at least a part of the problem. With or without chemicals in the equation, as the numbers of condors decreased, chances of successful pair formation could have been reduced by uneven sex ratios, disparate age structure, and varying sexual experience. With a natural tenacity by individuals to certain nesting, roosting and feeding sites, potential to meet prospective mates would have been reduced by each fragmenting of the population. In general, the larger the reservoir of condors, the better the chances would have been for pair formation.

If decreased productivity was a significant factor in the near demise of the California condor, the effects would have been greatest in the last 20-25 years, when the combined impacts of DDE and reduced population size would have been most likely. It is possible that, even in the late 19th century, some localized groups of condors could not sustain themselves as other factors isolated them from former outside recruitment. Whatever productivity issues occurred, I think their impact was minor compared to the measurable toll of human-related mortality.

EXCESSIVE MORTALITY:

I was able to document 458 instances of California condor mortality occurring between 1602 and 1985, 450 of them in the 190 years after 1793. An average of approximately two condors lost per year does not sound particularly significant, but there is more to the story. For example:

1. Because of the condors' low reproductive potential, population stability required long life for individual birds, with almost all mortality the result of old age and "natural" deaths (accidents, diseases). Even minor changes in the balance between birth and death would be reflected in the species to a much greater degree than in most birds.

2. The record of human-related mortality is almost certainly far from complete. After what seemed like a fairly exhaustive search between 1966 and 1978, Fred Sibley and I compiled a list of some 300 deaths [10]. The 150 records added since then were made possible by today's sophisticated internet search engines and by the continuing digitization of historical newspapers, allowing access to information previously unavailable to the average researcher. Even now, many California newspapers published between 1850 and 1950 are not readily searchable. A number of these were published in communities in the heart of "condor country," and it would be surprising if more records are not eventually found in them. Of course, even if all the *documented* losses were discovered, they would still constitute some unknown (but I suspect, small) portion of the *actual* number of human-related mortalities.

3. Of the mortalities documented, 334 (74%) occurred in only 30 years, 1880-1909. Of these, approximately 90 (over 25%) were from just two parts of the total condor range, the Monterey County area and the San Diego County area. Even without knowing how recorded losses compare to actual mortality, it is clear that certain segments of the condor population suffered major upsets to their natural gain:loss balance during that 30-year period.

* * *

CAUSES OF MORTALITY - Of the 458 mortalities documented, 14 were "natural" losses - deaths that would have occurred with or without human presence (disease, collision with cliffs). The reasons for another 88 losses could not be positively ascertained from the information available [11]. The remaining 356 records have been divided between eight categories.

Killing for sport or curiosity - Forty percent of the records were of condors killed merely because they were big and interesting. Most were shot, but six were lassoed and a few were killed by other means. Killing for sport was documented in every decade through the 1970s, with over 50 percent recorded between 1880 and 1909. This is probably a true representation of when sport killing reached its peak, but it is also the period during which - with no stigma attached to killing a condor, and with newspapers actively soliciting unusual local stories - such events were most likely to be reported. By 1900, there was a decided change in public sentiment about killing wildlife, and groups such as local (and eventually, national) Audubon societies were pressing for laws against unregulated killing. Opinions favoring "birds of prey" were slower to develop than for some other avian groups, but the number of reported killings fell sharply after 1910.

I searched on one popular historic newspapers website for the phrase "from tip to tip" (a common measure of a bird's wingspan or a mammal's length). Among the species interesting enough for their "tip to tip" measurement to warrant mention in the news were eagles, hawks, owls, herons, pelicans, swans, mountain lions, and of course, condors. From 1800 to 1850, I found some 300 "tip to tip" citations. The number of records increased every decade until 1901-1910, when the number exceeded 3,000. After 1910 - even though the number of digitized, searchable newspapers increased with each decade - the number of "tip to tip" references (for all wildlife) in the 1930s was down to around 500 nationwide, and only 300 in the 1940s. Some of the change undoubtedly reflects a real decrease in the number of large birds shot for sport or curiosity. Some unknown portion is a result of more wildlife law enforcement and more public concern about killing "birds of prey," both of which made it much less desirable to openly praise one's shooting prowess.

The first prosecution for killing a condor occurred in 1909 [12]. This undoubtedly contributed to a decrease in reporting shooting incidents, if not necessarily to an actual decrease in shooting. Both Carl Koford in the 1930s and 1940s [13], and the McMillan brothers in the mid-1960s [14], thought that shooting was still taking a significant toll. Only a few certain condor deaths were recorded, but both studies documented considerable shooting at large soaring birds within the condor range.

Killing for private collections - Close behind sport killing as a cause of mortality was the acquiring of condor specimens for private collections (31% of the total). In fact, some of this number may actually have begun as killings for sport, after which the hunters found there was a market for selling their trophies. In most cases, the records of these condors indicated they went more or less directly from the hunter to a taxidermist, a known private collection, or to a natural history supply house that sold specimens. As discussed in Chapter 15, many of these specimens eventually were acquired by public institutions, and a number of the collectors later became curators of public museums. Initially, however, these were condors taken by or for hobbyists.

Only a few bird collectors were operating before the 1870s, and only John Gurney in England had more than one or two California condors (Chapter 8). As collection laws tightened in the early 1900s, legal taking of condors ceased, and only a few are known to have been acquired after 1910. Like sport killing, hobby collecting was at its peak between 1880 and 1910 (over 86% of the specimens taken). Unlike sport killing, which continued opportunistically and surreptitiously in ensuing years at unknown levels, hobby collecting ended. Many of the specimens taken by hobbyists are still in existence, and the record of this particular impact is probably nearly complete.

Collecting for museums and scientific investigation - I consider only 55 condor mortalities (16%) attributable to scientific study or specific acquisition for public museums. The record appears to be nearly complete, and no more than 10 specimens were taken for this purpose in any decade. Even though considerably less significant than sport killing or hobby collecting, scientific collecting was one more drain on the condor population. Perhaps most important is that 20 percent of losses in this category came after 1910, when there was no question that the species was in trouble (Chapter 15).

Live capture for zoos and menageries - Beginning with at least two condors in Grizzly Adams' live animal show in the late 1850s, 16 condors (5%) are known to have been taken into captivity for display purposes (Chapter 12). Usually only one or two were captured in any decade, although there were six taken 1900-1909. Most of the captive condors were taken from nests, leaving the adult birds to produce additional eggs. While adding to the general disruption occurring in the late 19th and early 20th centuries, the taking of these nestlings would have had little direct impact on the condor population.

Losses associated with predator and rodent control - Nine accidental deaths (2%) were attributable to animal control activities: five from ingestion of poison (probably strychnine), three from being caught in leg-hold traps, and one possibly from cyanide gas released by an M-44 "coyote getter" [15]. Only one of the incidents occurred before 1880, by which time it was being regularly reported that poisoning was the principal cause of condor deaths. As explained previously (Chapter 11), both chronologically and geographically, it is almost impossible for strychnine to have been a major killer of condors in the 19th century. A much better chance for poison to have taken a significant toll would have occurred after 1915, when the U. S. Bureau of Biological Survey (BBS) began establishing formal predator control programs in the West. *"By 1917, the BBS had established districts throughout the US and initiated cooperative funding with states and counties... In time, the field men worked in both predator and rodent control. After 1917, this type of activity ramped way up"* [16]. Because it was no longer fashionable to publicize the death of big birds - and because animal control already received enough adverse publicity without adding condor deaths - the chances of a fatality being reported were probably less than in earlier times.

Killing allegedly to protect livestock - Eight condor fatalities (2%) occurred because the shooters reportedly believed that condors were attacking their calves, lambs, or hogs. In a few cases, there may have been a real fear of depredations; for example, one herder admitted he mistakenly shot a condor because he thought it was an eagle. In most instances, I'm inclined to think that herd protection was a stated excuse for what were really shootings for sport. Granted that many ranchers were wary of any large soaring bird around their flocks, the stories told about the shootings were sometimes so outrageous they seem like after-the-fact justifications: e.g., the condor was flying off with a calf when killed; it had killed 30 pigs before being shot; etc.

Accidental human-related deaths - In contrast to such natural condor losses as from disease, hailstones, or flying into canyon walls, ten deaths (3%) would not have occurred without a human element. Typical were deaths caused by flying into power lines, or into other man-made objects. Also in this category were three cases of lead poisoning, the result of bullet fragments in food eaten by condors. Obviously, the opportunities for such losses would have increased with each succeeding generation, as human presence in condor habitat grew. Even so, with the exception of lead poisoning, the likelihood of such deaths was relatively low. Deaths from lead ingestion could have occurred regularly without being detected (Chapter 23).

Killing for quills - The often-told story of condors being killed so that miners would have receptacles in which to store their gold is just that: a story (Chapter 9). There are no specimens, or even reliable narratives, that suggest the practice occurred in California. There are four records (1%) from Baja California, Mexico, in which quill collecting was reported to have been the objective for killing the birds. All four accounts are suspect in some way (Chapter 9); lacking proof one way or the other, I've included them here as a possible minor source of condor mortality.

* * *

With the exception of localized killing of condors by Native Americans - apparently of regular occurrence only in the lower Sacramento Valley and adjacent hills, and mostly before 1850 (Chapter 2) - almost all human-related losses of condors can be placed in one of the categories above. Every non-natural loss had a greater effect on the condor population than would have been the case with most other species, so no factor can be considered neutral. As the range of the species contracted and the numbers of condors decreased, the effect of any loss for any reason would have been magnified. Nevertheless, the only factor that spans all generations and locations was killing for sport. Combined with hobby and institutional collecting between 1880 and 1910, the losses were great enough to extirpate condors in some areas and to seriously depress their survival potential throughout their range.

Old stories die hard, particularly if they are romantic (Indians sacrificing condors, miners carrying gold in condor quills) or if they support a particular belief or point of view (poisoning predatory mammals must have poisoned many condors, also). When presented in books that appear authoritative, it is often because the writers have done inadequate historical research, and have just repeated readily available information. Sometimes, writers resort to acknowledging that there is little support for a belief they favor, but suggest that "we simply don't know enough to make a judgment" [17]. Framed as "the absence of evidence is not evidence of absence," or "absence of proof is not proof of absence," credit for the quote is usually given to the poet William Cowper, who allegedly presented the argument to explain his belief in God [18]. Used for everything from supporting the potential existence of extraterrestrial life [19], discussing the archaeological excavation of London [20], to lampooning religious arguments by introducing the Flying Spaghetti

Monster into the debate about teaching creationism and evolution in schools [21], the argument does have some logical validity. For example, lead poisoning appears as a minor source of condor mortality if only actual records through 1986 are considered. However, based on recent findings, it appears possible (likely?) that death from ingesting lead bullet fragments has been a long-term, potentially serious problem for the condor population. The historical "absence of evidence" is the result of such deaths being inconspicuous, and of our not having the ability to monitor that aspect of condor survival until the 1980s when condors could be trapped and blood samples analyzed (Chapter 23).

The lead poisoning example notwithstanding, scientific investigation - like the law - depends on evidence. Without some strong support, invoking the "absence of evidence" mantra *"might be used to deflect criticism away from one's failure to provide such positive justification for a claim one has made. The requirement of fulfilling the burden of proof for a claim one has made is a fundamental principle of argument..."* [22]. A flea and elephant comparison illustrates: *"If someone were to assert that there is an elephant on the quad, then the failure to observe an elephant there would be good reason to think that there is no elephant there. But if someone were to assert that there is a flea on the quad, then one's failure to observe it there would not constitute good evidence that there is no flea on the quad. The salient difference between these two cases is that in the one, but not in the other, we should expect to see some evidence of the entity if in fact it existed. Thus the absence of evidence is evidence of absence only in cases in which, were the postulated entity to exist, we should expect to have some evidence of its existence"* [23].

In Chapter 11, I showed that the original story of major condor losses to strychnine poisoning was erroneous; that later authors embellished the story with no additional information; that geographically and chronologically the use of strychnine does not match with the decrease in condors; and that regular deaths of condors in the 19th century would have been documented. In Chapter 9, I deconstructed the tale of condor quills and gold dust to show that there is no basis for treating feather harvesting as significant in the decline of the condor population. The story of Indians sacrificing condors (Chapter 2) stems from incorrect interpretation of early records of eagles; completely without merit is the recently-stated belief that Indians may have been responsible for *"a potential annual take on the order of 700 condors"* [24]. All three - strychnine, condor quills, and Native Americans - have been treated as "elephants" in the near extinction of the California condor; there is not even enough support to treat them as "fleas." Strychnine use and sport killing after 1910 - when it was no longer wise to talk about condor deaths - may well qualify as "fleas," and lead poisoning might qualify as a significant infestation of that bug. The "absence of evidence" argument may be valid in those three cases. As for "elephants" on the condors' "quad," there were only two: sport killing, and specimen collecting.

CHAPTER NOTES

1. Wilbur, S. R., and L. F. Kiff. 1980. The California condor in Baja California, Mexico. *American Birds* 34(6):856-859.

2. Wallace, M. P., M. Clark, J. Vargas, and M. C. Porras. 2007. Release of puppet-reared California condors in Baja California, Mexico: evaluation of a modified rearing technique. Pages 227-242 *in:* Mee, A., and L. S. Hall (editors). California condors in the 21st century. Series in Ornithology No. 2. Nuttall Ornithological Club & American Ornithologists' Union. Cambridge, Massachusetts, and Washington, D. C.

3. Adams, M. S., and F. X. Villablanca. 2007. Consequences of a genetic bottleneck in California condors: a mitochondrial DNA perspective. Pages 35-55 *in:* Mee, A., and L. S. Hall (editors), California condors in the 21st century. Series in Ornithology No. 2. Cambridge, Massachusetts, and Washington, D. C.: Nuttall Ornithological Club & American Ornithologists' Union.

4. Cooke, A. S. 1973. Shell thinning in avian eggs by environmental pollutants. *Environmental Pollution* 4(1):85-152.
   Stickel, W. H. 1975. Some effects of pollutants in terrestrial ecosystems. Pages 25-74 *in:* McIntyre, A. D., and C. F. Mills (editors), Ecological toxicology research. New York, New York: Plenum Publications.

5. Kiff, L. F., D. B. Peakall, and S. R. Wilbur. 1979. Recent changes in California condor eggshells. *Condor* 81(2): 166-172.
   Kiff, L. F. 1989. DDE and the California condor *Gymnogyps californianus*: the end of a story? Pages 477-480 *in:* Meyburg, B. U., and R. D. Chancellor (editors), Raptors in the modern world. *Proceedings of the 3rd World Conference on Birds of Prey and Owls*.

6. Kiff 1989, *op. cit.*

7. Peakall, D. B. 1996. Disrupted patterns of behavior in natural populations as an index of ecotoxicity. *Environmental Health Perspectives* 104 (Supplement 2):331-335.
   Haegele, M. E., and R. H. Hudson. 1977. Reduction in courtship behavior induced by DDE in male ringed turtle doves. *Wilson Bulletin* 89(4):593-601.

8. With no way to positively identify individual condors or to track pairs over time, my "life tables" were developed from population census estimates, direct observations of nesting activity, determination of the success of known nests, and changes in the percentages of immature-plumaged condors in the population. While admittedly rough, my conclusions were deemed reasonable by several population modelers.

9. Pages 22-24 *in:* Wilbur, S. R. 1978. The California condor, 1966-76: a look at its past and future. *North American Fauna* Number 72. Washington, D. C.: U. S. Fish and Wildlife Service.

10. Wilbur 1978, *op. cit.,* pages 71-88.

11. It appears that most of these losses were the result of either random shooting or purposeful acquisition of specimens for private collectors. There isn't quite enough information on these deaths to confidently assign causes of death.

12. Anonymous. 1909. Condor without mate. Hunter who shot great rare bird is found guilty and will be sentenced tomorrow. Los Angeles (California) *Times,* 24 January 1909.

13. Page 129 *in:* Koford, C. B. 1953. The California condor. Research Report Number 4. New York, New York: National Audubon Society.

14. Pages 29-36 *in:* Miller, A. H., I. I. McMillan, and E. McMillan. 1965. The current status and welfare of the California condor. Research Report Number 6. New York, New York: National Audubon Society.

15. Laboratory tests after initial evaluation raise doubts of cyanide from an "M-44" being the cause of death: Wiemeyer, S. N., E. F. Hill, et al. 1986. Acute oral toxicity of sodium cyanide in birds. *Journal of Wildlife Diseases* 22(4):538-546.

16. Personal communication, 23 March 2012, from Nancy Freeman, Archivist, National Wildlife Research Center (Fort Collins, Colorado).

17. Page 3 *in:* Walton, D. N. 1996. Arguments from ignorance. University Park, Pennsylvania: Pennsylvania State University Press.

18. There must be thousands of sentences written that contain the phrase "as Cowper said;" however, no one seems to know where the "quote" originated!

19. *"All we can safely conclude is that intelligent life has evolved at least once. Even if it existed elsewhere, we might not recognize it. Intelligent extraterrestrials may lead contemplative lives, and have no motive for signaling their presence to us: absence of evidence cannot be evidence of absence."* Page 23 *in:* Rees, M. J. 1997. Before the beginning: our universe and others. Reading, Massachusetts: Addison-Wesley.

20. Regarding *"the ever-intriguing question of post-Roman London; and on this, even while remembering the important fact that absence of evidence is not identical with evidence of absence, it does at least* seem *significant that* (so many additional excavations) *have still produced no positive evidence of life continuing through the late fifth and early sixth centuries."* Burn, A. R. 1969. Book review: The excavation of Roman and Mediaeval London, by W. F. Grimes. *The Classical Review,* New Series, 19(2):229-232.

316

21. Henderson, B. 2006. The gospel of the Flying Spaghetti Monster. New York, New York: Villard Publishing.

22. Walton 1996 *op. cit.,* page 2.

23. Evans, C. S., and M. Westphal. 2003. Religious epistemology. Pages 155-170 *in:* J. P. Moreland and W. L. Craig. Philosophical foundations for a Christian worldview. Downers Grove, Illinois: Inter Varsity Press.

24. Page 44 *in:* Snyder, N. F. R., and H. Snyder. 2000. The California condor, a saga of natural history and conservation. San Diego, California: Academic Press.

* * *

Figure 20. Map of Western Oregon, showing county names and boundaries.

317

Figure 21. Map of California, showing county names and boundaries.

As noted in Chapter 15, there were pronouncements as early as 1880 that condors were becoming rarer. The statements were more intuitive than factual, because no one had knowledge of the entire range of the species. The most authoritative opinions were still based on changes observed in local situations. Still, when in the 1940s Carl Koford made the first species-wide analysis of condor populations, he concluded that condors had become rare in much of their range before 1910. He felt they were *"extinct or very rare"* in all areas north of San Francisco by 1890; in the central Coast Ranges by 1900; and south of Los Angeles before 1910. While he thought there might have been some increase in numbers after 1930 in the uplands around the southern San Joaquin Valley, he suspected this could have been due to changing foraging patterns, rather than changes in population size. The only areas where he felt confident that *"the incidence of condors has remained about the same since the 1880s"* were central Ventura County and northern Santa Barbara County [1].

Koford identified various factors that were known, or suspected, to have killed condors [2], a list essentially the same as given in Chapter 25. In general - except for the area north of San Francisco Bay - he did not try to rank their individual impacts nor did he try to explain why condors had disappeared from the various regions. Below, I look at each region to see if Koford's unasked questions can be answered.

NORTH OF SAN FRANCISCO

Carl Koford speculated that the total loss of condors north of the San Francisco Bay area occurred - at least, in large part - because condors had never been resident in that vast area. He conceded that *"the occurrence and disappearance of condors along the Columbia River* (in Oregon and adjacent Washington) *cannot be satisfactorily explained on the basis of available facts,"* but he thought all condor records north of San Francisco had been of non-breeding birds that periodically or irregularly wandered out of their usual range. He believed that as condors became rarer to the south, there were no longer birds to travel north [3].

Early in my condor research, I proposed that condors in the Northwest were not merely wanderers, but were resident at least as far north as the Columbia River between Washington and Oregon [4]. I discussed my reasoning with Koford, but he remained convinced there had been no resident condors north of San Francisco Bay [5]. His main objections remained that there was not enough supporting evidence of continuous occupancy of the region from prehistoric to recent times, and that no one had discovered nesting north of Monterey County. He continued to support his earlier hypothesis that condors flew north in search of food, either in times of food scarcity in the south or because there was some particularly attractive source in the north.

PREHISTORIC AND PRE-CAUCASIAN RECORDS

The record is complicated somewhat by uncertainty as to whether or not there was any break between the occupancy of prehistoric and modern California condors in the early West (see Introduction and Chapter 1). *Gymnogyps* bones have been recovered from Samwel Cave and Potter Cave in Shasta County, California, associated with materials carbon-dated at around 15,000 to 20,000 years before present [6]. At The Dalles, Wasco County, Oregon, bones from at least 22 different condors have been excavated, most of them from strata dated at 7,500 to 8,500 years old, with a few in older and a few in younger deposits [7]. A condor bone found on Pender Island, British Columbia, Canada, is about 2,900 years old [8]. These few records do not prove continuous occupancy, but they do show a long tenure.

Native American records of condors were reviewed in Chapter 2. They show a strong connection between Indians and condors throughout the Sacramento Valley and northern Coast Ranges; a weak record in western Oregon (but perhaps due to lack of a deep oral history); no ties in Washington away from the Columbia River [9]; and none in British Columbia [10].

RECORDS BY EUROPEANS: OREGON-WASHINGTON-BRITISH COLUMBIA.

Chapter 5 has most of the records of condors in Oregon and adjacent parts of Washington. I can add a few later observations to the Oregon narrative. James Clyman reported condors in the Willamette Valley 1844-1845 [11]. Roselle Putnam, a settler at Yoncalla, Douglas County, saw condors around 1851-1852 (no date or numbers given), and saw one dead condor in that area [12]. A condor was rumored to have been killed on the southern Oregon coast ca 1890 [13]. There are several records of 2-4 condors near Drain, Douglas County, in July 1903 and March 1904 [14]. *"Several well-informed woodsmen described accurately"* condors in southwest Oregon in the early 1900s [15].

In Washington State, in addition to the records cited in Chapter 5, one condor was tentatively identified near Fort Vancouver in January 1854 [16]. A September 1897 sighting of a condor near Coulee City, Washington, was made by someone who had seen condors in California [17]. There are no other later records for Washington. There are several sightings from southwestern British Columbia between 1860 and 1890. None of them are particularly well documented, but all were within about 20 miles of one another, and only about 25 miles from where the condor bone was found on Pender Island [18]. J. K. Lord, who was in British Columbia 1858 to 1862, reported condors at the "mouth of Frasar River," but there is no indication this was his own observation [19]. John Fannin wrote that *"in September 1880, I saw two of these birds at Burrard Inlet;"* he suspected they were "accidental visitants" [20]. Samuel Rhoads visited British Columbia in 1892. He did not see condors, but learned from long-time Lulu Island postmaster William London that they "used to be common" in the area, the last seen on Lulu Island "three or four years ago" [21].

RECORDS BY EUROPEANS: NORTHERN CALIFORNIA

To 1850. In extreme northwestern California near the present town of Klamath, Humboldt County, Jedediah Smith in May 1828 recorded *"large and small buzards* [sic]" [22]. As he also listed *"Crows...Ravens, several kinds of hawks, (and) Eagles,"* it seems likely he saw condors. Between July 1840 and September 1841, Russian naturalist Ilya Voznesenskii collected a number of condors and (from the Indians) condor artifacts in the Coast Ranges and Sacramento Valley. There is only one certain date and place: May 1841, when Voznesenskii was in the Russian River area of Sonoma or Mendocino counties [23].

The Wilkes Expedition traveled south through the Sacramento Valley in October 1841. They recorded several condors in the hills between Mt. Shasta and present-day Redding on 5 October; and saw "numbers" of them in the Valley at about the latitude of Red Bluff on 13 October [24]. Charles Pickering, one of the expedition naturalists, described a condor in immature plumage, when the party was in the vicinity of the Sutter Buttes [25].

"Several" condors were seen near Fort Ross, Sonoma County, ca 1845-1846 [26]. In Napa County, condors were seen "in great abundance" in August 1845, and one was killed there in September 1845 [27]. A condor egg was reportedly collected in Napa County in 1845 [28]; unfortunately, there is no documentation of the actual event. Condors were seen in the Sacramento-San Joaquin delta area in spring 1847 [29]. In Marin County in July 1847, more than a dozen condors came to feed on a deer carcass [30]. In August 1849, one was shot in the Sacramento Valley near the junction of the Sacramento and Feather rivers [31], and in September of that year "several" were seen in the Yuba River canyon above Sacramento [32]. In October 1849, another was shot in the hills northeast of Marysville, and were seen regularly seen in that vicinity in November 1849, February 1850 (as many as 12), and March 1850 [33].

The 1850s. -In July and August 1854, members of the Pacific Railroad Survey saw condors daily on their march up the Sacramento Valley and through the Siskiyou Mountains to the Klamath Basin (but "very few" there), and had *"many opportunities of shooting them"* [34]. Indeed, at least two had been shot in the Sacramento Valley earlier that year, one in March near Sacramento [35] and one in June near Chico [36]. Another was shot "in the coast ranges" sometime before April 1856 [37]. Between 1857 and 1860, condors were frequently seen in the Napa Valley, usually two or three together [38]. One was shot in Napa County in January 1858 [39], and others were reported in the hills "east of Marysville" in August 1858 [40].

The 1860s. A condor was killed in June 1861 "in the coast range," apparently in the Russian River area [41]. Another was shot in Plumas County in November 1865 [42], and a third in Mendocino County sometime before October 1867 [43]. Numbers in Napa County seemed to have declined after 1860 [44], but one was collected in nearby Marin County in August 1868 [45].

The 1870s. Lyman Belding observed "a few" condors in Mendocino County [46], possibly in August 1870, when he spent several days in the Coast Ranges near the head of the Eel River [47]. He also saw condors on two or three occasions in the Sacramento Valley near Marysville, in winter but with no specific records given [48]. A condor was reported killed in Mendocino County in February 1872 [49], and one was shot in Marin County February 1873 [50]. One was reported flying near Mt. Shasta in September 1873 [51].

The 1880s. In March or early April 1880, a condor was killed by an unspecified poison near the South Fork of the Eel River, Humboldt County [52]. One was shot in late April or early May 1880 in Tehama County [53]. Condors were seen "in the foothills southwest of Mount Lassen" between 1880 and 1884, probably by the same person who killed the condor in Tehama County [54]. A condor shot in the Feather River canyon was reported in November 1880, but may not have been killed then [55]. There was a condor held captive at San Rafael, Marin County, in the summer of 1882, that likely was acquired in the vicinity [56]. By the mid-1880s, Charles Townsend believed that the condor *"has probably almost disappeared from Northern California, where it was once certainly common"* [57].

The 1890s and beyond. Early settlers in far northwestern California claimed that condors were plentiful there at one time. The last confirmed records were of individual birds shot in the hills east of Eureka in the fall of 1889 or 1890, and in the fall of 1892 [58]. I found no other confirmed reports of condors in California north of San Francisco until between 1900 and 1905, when one was killed in Marin County [59].

* * *

Because the above listing is not a *sampling* of condor records north of San Francisco, but is every apparently reliable record I could find, one might be left with the impression that condors were unusual in the northern part of their range. I think the dearth of records is more a reflection of the numbers and types of people who were in the area before 1900 than it is the number of condors present. The entire area of Oregon had only 52,000 people in 1860 [60]. The population had grown to 415,000 by 1900, but most of those people were still congregated around a few population centers in the Willamette Valley. The Umpqua River-Rogue River area of southwest Oregon - where condors were observed in 1826, 1841, 1903 and 1904 - in 1860 had less than

4,000 residents. In 1900, there were still less than 25,000 people in an area of over 8,000 square miles of rugged habitat in which condors were unlikely to be conspicuous [61].

In northern California, the 1860 federal census of Del Norte, Humboldt, Mendocino, Trinity and Siskiyou counties recorded less than 25,000 people, most of whom were either miners or people living in the lowlands around Humboldt Bay. By 1900, that population increased to 70,000, but many lived at Crescent City, around Humboldt Bay, and around Ukiah, leaving some 18,000 square miles of mountains essentially uninhabited. In 1860, there were an average of less than two people per square mile; the density had increased only to four per square mile by 1900 - and considerably less over much of the area away from the main population centers [62].

Human numbers were greater in the Sacramento Valley (85,000 people in 1860; 151,000 in 1900) and in the North Bay (33,000, growing to 108,000) than they were on the northwest coast. Population densities were also greater, increasing from four people per square mile to seven in the Sacramento Valley (23,000 square miles), and from seven to 23 in the North Bay counties (4,700 square miles). However, if you subtract that part of the Sacramento Valley population that lived in the city environment of Sacramento, as late as 1900 most of the Valley supported only about four people per square mile.

All these numbers are presented to show that vast areas of northern California and western Oregon were so sparsely inhabited through the 19th century that condors could easily have gone unreported. Add to this a consideration of the type of people inhabiting the northern areas. In all the area west of the Cascades and the northern Sierra Nevada, the scientific surveys had ended by 1855, and for the next 50 years the sparse Caucasian population had little time for the pursuit of natural history. The climate and the cultural environment of central and southern California attracted many people with the time and interest to study wildlife and collect birds' eggs. In contrast, the Northwest was populated mainly by homesteaders, miners, and the city merchants needed to support them. Few of these people left any kind of systematic records, and few mentioned birds. I have found no publications on birds of northwestern California between 1828 and 1887, and only five significant papers on birds of that area between 1887 and 1906 [63]. For western Oregon, I found only six papers on birds written between 1855 and 1895, and most of these were brief notes of birds seen near the Willamette Valley population centers [64]. After 1855, the first bird reference I can find for southwestern Oregon was from 1893 [65]. In other words, for the last fifty years of the 19th century almost no one was looking for any kinds of birds or birds' nests in the Pacific Northwest.

Combining this information with the pre-Caucasian record I think presents a clearer picture of condor occupancy. The prehistoric record is scant, but shows early condors in the same localities as later representatives of the species.

Remains of at least 22 condors at one spot (The Dalles, Oregon) suggests either a significant local population, or regular visitation over a period of time. The detailed presence of the condor in myth, religion, medicine and celebration of a number of regionally separated aboriginal groups (at least in northern California, if not farther north) indicates a greater familiarity with condors than would have been gained from occasional visits of vagrant birds. (This contrasts with the aboriginal record of some other regions, in which unusual birds show up from time to time – often as harbingers of events to come – but do not have a solid place in the group ethos.)

Many of the historic records are of individual condors that were shot or otherwise killed, and most give no indication of how many other condors were in the vicinity at the time. However, each region (Columbia River-Willamette Valley, southern Oregon-northern interior California, north coastal California, Sacramento Valley) has at least two reports that describe condors as common or of regular occurrence. Also, three of the four regions have records from every season (southern Oregon-northern California is missing specific winter reports) and from most months (Columbia River, 8 months; southern Oregon, 5 months; coastal California, 8 months; Sacramento Valley, 9 months). Clearly, in the area north of San Francisco, there were more condors at more times and in more places than would have been the case had all been vagrants or seasonal migrants from the south.

LACK OF NESTING RECORDS

The farthest north confirmed nesting records of California condors are from Santa Cruz County, California [66]. There is one alleged nest record from Napa County [67]; other than that, there are not even any credible rumors. (See Chapter 16.) It isn't surprising to me that no nest sites have been identified; no one looked for them while condors occurred in the northern areas. Explorers affiliated with fur trading companies or government expeditions made many of the condor observations. These explorers spent most of their time in the river valleys, the main travel routes through the region, so most condor observations were made of birds flying or feeding, not associated with potential nests or roosts. The few scientists who made their way deeper into mountainous areas (for example, David Douglas and Titian Peale in the Umpqua River area of southwest Oregon; Chapter 5) merely passed through, with no time for pursuing birds away from the expeditions' established travel routes. The one early exploring party in northwestern California, Jedediah Smith's group in 1828 [68] saw condors. Smith recorded the sighting, but his party was too busy trying to survive to look for birds' nests. If the chances of even seeing a condor were slim, the likelihood of someone finding and reporting a nest was much, much slimmer.

AVAILABILITY OF FOOD FOR CONDORS.

As already noted, Carl Koford speculated that condors went north of what he considered their breeding range either because there was a particularly desirable food source that attracted them, or because they were forced north by food shortages in central and southern California. He opined that the first trip was made because of vital need for food. Finding not only food, but an especially attractive source, they returned even when there was no impetus for long-distance travel. Making regular sorties out of the breeding range eventually developed into a learned behavior within the condor population [69].

Some aspects of condor population behavior go against a migration-for-food hypothesis. First, although condors are capable of traveling great distances, there are no 20th century records of condors (breeding or non-breeding) farther than 150 to 200 miles from a known nesting area [70]. In the 1930s and 1940s, Koford [71] found that most foraging by condors occurred within 35 miles of regularly used roosts, similar to what I observed in the 1970s. In the early 1980s, Meretsky and Snyder [72] equipped several condors with radio transmitters, and found most activity to be within 50 miles of nesting areas. Food for condors was drastically reduced in the 20th century compared to the previous hundred years [73], yet no scarcity forced condors to move beyond their expected range.

Also, in the 20th century, condors were quite predictable in their seasonal movements north and south, away from and back toward nesting areas. Expected changes occurred regardless of local food availability. For example, condors moved south from summer roosts in the Sierra Nevada by September, although there was more potential food (dead livestock) in fall and winter than in summer. Similarly, movements north from nesting areas began by April, at which time local food supplies were still near their peak [74]. Regular provision of carcasses in one feeding area from 1972 through 1977 failed to disrupt these expected movements. When condors were in the area, they used the supplemental food; when it was "time to go," they left [75].

* * *

Considering the tenacity with which 20th century condors maintained their close ties to known nesting and roosting areas, and the seasonal regularity of their movements, it is difficult to picture a food situation either so dire in one area or so attractive in another that condor behavior would have been modified in the way Koford hypothesized. Actually, there is no evidence that any food shortage occurred in central or southern California that might have been severe enough to cause unusual movement of condors. The abundance of both wild and domestic large mammals there has been documented in Chapter 6, as have similar potential food supplies in the Sacramento Valley. If scarcity of food had been the impetus for condor travel north of San Francisco Bay, they would have had no need to go farther north than the Sacramento Valley. Had they gone on to Oregon during that period of "abounding" game in California, they would have found elk, white-tailed deer and black-tailed deer sometimes (as reported by human travelers) "plentiful" or "abundant." More often, however, they would have found what the human travelers found: only scattered herds, often not plentiful enough to provide adequate food for themselves [76].

Koford [77] suggested two special food situations, either of which he felt might have been the original attraction that drew condors north from central California. The first was the potential availability of many mammals killed during the extensive fires set each year by Native Americans. The other was the tremendous biomass of spawned salmon that died along the Columbia River and its tributaries. Widespread burning throughout the Northwest is well-documented, and was done in part to improve habitat for game and in part to help with the hunting of game [78]. However, I could find no evidence of large numbers of mammals being killed in the frequent fires. In any event, burning of the land by Native Americans was also extensive and long-term in California [79], so the practice conferred no particular advantage on Oregon or elsewhere in the northern part of condor range.

In hypothesizing about the importance of the Columbia salmon runs, Koford himself expressed concern that the actual record of condors feeding on salmon was confused because *"hearsay is not always separated from fact"* [80]. A close examination of the written record shows that John Kirk Townsend was the only person who ever claimed to have seen condors feeding on dead salmon. All other reports are apparently hearsay, based either on Townsend's one specific comment on the subject [81] or on a letter from Townsend that was included in Audubon's "Ornithological Biography" [82]. Even Townsend's reports on the subject are confusing. In his 1848 paper, he said *"during the spring (1835), I constantly saw the Vultures at all points where the Salmon were cast upon the shore."* In his letter to Audubon, he repeated the information that condors were most common in spring, but later in the same letter, he wrote: *"It* (the condor) *is seen on the Columbia only in summer, appearing about the first of June, and retiring, probably to the mountains, about the end of August. It is particularly attracted to the vicinity of cascades and falls, being attracted by the dead salmon which strew the shores of such places"*

Vultures are opportunistic scavengers, and condors may have eaten dead salmon along the Columbia River more often than is factually documented. Whether they did or not, spent salmon could not have been the special attractant that lured condors north. During the same period that condors were found along the Columbia River, salmon were abundant in the Sacramento-San Joaquin rivers drainage. Use of the salmon by Native Americans throughout interior California is extensively documented. The spring run of Chinook salmon in the San Joaquin River in the early 1800s has been described as *"one of the largest Chinook salmon runs anywhere on the Pacific*

Coast," possibly numbering 200,000 to 500,000 spawners annually. Similar claims have been made about the Sacramento River, which had *"the sole distinction among the salmon-producing rivers of western North America of supporting four runs of Chinook salmon – spring, fall, late-fall and winter runs"* [83]. Chinook were the most abundant salmonids, but the Central Valley river system also supported four other species [84]. Condors were never reported feeding on fish in California, but there was no need to go to Oregon for them, had the condors wanted them.

* * *

Even if there had been a food incentive for long distance movement, it seems as if there had to have been resident condors beyond San Francisco Bay. The farthest north verified nest sites were in Santa Cruz, San Benito, and Tulare counties. Points approximately 200 miles north of those locations (considerably farther from nesting areas than any condors - breeding or non-breeding - would be expected to forage) are southern Mendocino County in the Coast Ranges, Yuba County in the Sacramento Valley, and Calaveras County in the Sierra Nevada. Practically speaking, there must have been additional nest sites in that 200-mile stretch. Even supposing that all condors reaching those northern locations had been birds from already confirmed nesting areas, that still leaves some 500 air miles to the Columbia River (and over 700 miles to British Columbia). Seventy-five percent of the documented condor sightings north of San Francisco were made in that 700-mile stretch, and those observations were made during all seasons. Breeding condors were either regularly spaced throughout the northern area, or there were denser populations somewhere in every 100 to 200-mile segment.

Condors were nearly gone from all areas north of San Francisco by 1900, but records found since Koford's study show the disappearance wasn't as early as he believed. Condors may have disappeared from the Columbia River area before 1850, as Koford thought, but there were condors in the Sacramento Valley at least into the 1880s (Koford thought 1860 at the latest). Koford tentatively accepted 1904-1905 records from southern Oregon, and into the 1890s for Humboldt County, California, but he could find no reports for the North Bay counties after 1870. I've been able to add records to show that condors were seen (and killed) regularly in Marin, Napa and Mendocino counties until at least 1900. Although there is general agreement that, by the 1880s or 1890s, condors had become scarce in areas where they had once been common, it's possible that there were still remnant populations scattered throughout their former northern range into the early 1900s.

* * *

Why did condors disappear from the northern portion of their range? Of the three broad categories of impacts potentially affecting condors - decreased productivity, habitat change, and excessive mortality (Chapter 25), depressed recruitment seems unlikely. Condors were gone before the advent of chemical

327

pesticides. If genetic bottlenecks were not a significant problem in the second half of the 20th century, greater numbers of condors and broader distribution would seem to have rendered it even less of an issue.

There were habitat changes, but none that seem extreme enough or at the proper time to have greatly affected the northern condor populations. For example, the story of Caucasian America is often told as one of the pioneers clearing primeval forests, creating more open lands in what had been continuous woodland. In fact, in much of the United States – including the Pacific Northwest - the sequence was reversed. Regular, extensive burning by Native Americans slowed growth of trees and shrubs over vast acreage west of the Cascades from British Columbia south through Oregon, and through the Coast Ranges of northern California [85]. With major decreases in the aboriginal population after 1840, and with purposeful intent by Caucasian settlers to stop the burning, prairie lands began to revert to forest. For example, at the time of the 1853 land survey, prairies dominated the Willamette Valley. *"The surveyors found no trees at all in the flat of the Valley, and had to utilize marking systems other than the traditional witness trees... Frequently, the surveyors, when working on the prairie, made the statement that there were no trees in sight"* [86]. There appears to be no record of how quickly vegetation changed after the suppression of fire, but invasion of woody growth was being reported by the early 1850s [87], and by 1946 the Valley supported "large numbers of trees of the 90-year age class" [88].

Of a smaller scale, but perhaps significant to any local population of condors, the "bald hills" of Humboldt County, California may be only half the size they were in the mid-1800s. Using the public land survey transects done 1875-1886: *"Less than half (43.8 percent) of the nineteenth-century prairie points are found in prairie today. The conversion of historic prairie points is closely split between oak woodland or open timber (24.7 percent) and coniferous forest (31.5 percent)... The majority of prairie boundaries have shifted, representing a significant reduction in the areal extent of the Bald Hills prairies. Two-thirds of the prairie units have one or more nineteenth-century boundary points located more than 100 m from the modern prairie boundaries... Fifty percent of these historic prairie boundaries are now found in logged coniferous forest, 10 percent in encroached coniferous forest, 5 percent in uncut coniferous forest, and 27.5 percent in oak woodland"* [89].

I bring up this habitat modification just to discuss all possibilities, but I think it highly unlikely that either the amount or the timing of vegetation change affected the condors. It may have been that any detrimental effects of open land reduction were offset by increases in food supply as more domestic livestock were brought into the Northwest. If condors really were gone from the Willamette Valley and lower Columbia area by the 1850s, habitat changes could not have figured greatly in their disappearance there.

* * *

Condors were killed by humans, but I only found 38 specific instances north of San Francisco. Twenty-five occurred before 1860, with not more than four verified in any later decade. Thirty-six were shooting casualties; two-thirds of the ones before 1850 were taken for more or less scientific purposes, all the rest were shot for sport. One condor died of an unnamed poison (but probably strychnine); the cause of death of the final bird is unknown.

The low number of reported deaths could be interpreted two ways. One is that the much sparser human population, compared to central and southern California, would have resulted in relatively few encounters between people and condors, with fewer chances for condor deaths. The other is that in the more rural north, with people living in more isolated situations and with fewer sources of published local news, a smaller percentage of condor deaths would have been reported than was the case in the south. If the first situation prevailed, then it is difficult to see human-caused mortality as an overriding reason for the disappearance of condors. If a significant number of deaths went unreported, then we need to consider the likely reasons for additional losses.

Scientific collecting of condors ended in the northern areas before 1850, and almost all of it occurred in the Columbia-Willamette area of Oregon and Washington. Several people who killed condors had them mounted for display, but there was no real "hobby collecting" of condors north of the Bay Area. One condor was reported killed because of the belief it had killed livestock; losses from that motive would likely go unreported, but it is difficult to see it as cause for significant mortality. The only factors that are likely to have been more important than the record indicates are accidental poisoning from predator control, and sport shooting.

Strychnine Poisoning. No condor is known to have been killed by strychnine in Oregon or Washington, and there is only one record from northern California. That doesn't entirely rule out the possibility that condors succumbed after eating poisoned meat. However, it appears that condors had become rare in the Columbia-Willamette region long before strychnine came into use. In southwestern Oregon in the last two decades of the 19th century - with more people, more livestock, and apparently more strychnine - poisoning may have been more of a threat to condors than at any time previous. Nevertheless, the odds of a condor being poisoned in that vast area seems small.

The situation in northern California was similar to southwest Oregon. Although people and livestock both increased in the region through the second half of the 19th century, northern California had more than one-third of the State's beef cattle in only one decade (the 1870s). The North Bay and northwest coast counties through 1900 never had more than about 15 percent of the northern California total. The sheep situation was similar: even as total sheep numbers in the State increased 1860-1880, there were never more than about one-third of the population north of the Bay Area. Perhaps more significantly, even when sheep numbers were high, the majority were found congregated in limited area. In 1860, over 50 percent of the sheep were in three counties, comprising less than 15 percent of the total northern California acreage. In 1870, three counties had 50 percent of the sheep on 10 percent of the available acreage. In 1890 and 1900, over 60 percent of the sheep were on 25 percent of the land. Only in 1880 were the sheep more widely distributed; even then, six out of the 22 northern California counties had almost 70 percent of the sheep, on 30 percent of the acreage [90].

While strychnine was widely used for predator poisoning in western Oregon and northern California - and while much more was undoubtedly used than was strictly necessary - the popular belief that virtually every animal carcass on the range was laced with strychnine is clearly erroneous (Chapter 11). Granted that one poisoned carcass might kill a number of condors, in most places and at most times it would have been almost coincidental that any condor should find any strychnine bait. Strychnine was also used for rodent control, but apparently much more extensively in central and southern California than in the northern areas. It seems to me that, even if reporting was less frequent and less likely in the north than in the south, dead condors were so eye-catching that some losses would have been documented.

Shooting. Thirty-six condors known shot in 100 years does not seem alarming. What gives these shooting losses more significance is that, while deaths from poisons are speculative, condor deaths from shooting are documented in every decade and in all parts of the northern range. Whereas the greatest likelihood of condor poisoning would occur in only those areas of highest perceived need for predator or rodent control, shooting could occur anywhere. Condor shooters were not driven by just one motive, either. The desire to see a giant bird up close, or the desire to show off one's shooting skills, were just the most obvious reasons. Although only one record specifically mentions protecting livestock as the reason for shooting a condor, many cattlemen and sheepherders were wary of any large birds around their charges. Vultures spreading disease did not seem to be a widely held belief on the Pacific Coast, but it was prevalent in some parts of the United States, and it might have provided another excuse to shoot big birds. Finally, as detailed in Chapter 5, early trappers and explorers saw condors and eagles as competitors for food. Apparently, it was not uncommon for scavengers to get to shot game before it could be salvaged. Living off the land was seldom easy for these early travelers. Finding their hard-earned and much needed food devoured by condors and eagles would have been frustrating, but could also have been life-threatening if it was a regular occurrence. Reducing condor and eagle populations may have been both retaliatory (for past deeds) and preventative (to forestall future problems).

Even after food for human survival became less of an issue, the spirit of competition between condors and hunters lived on. As Andrew Jackson

330

Grayson wrote in the late 1860s: *"In the early days of California history it [the condor] was more frequently met with than now, being of a cautious and shy disposition the rapid settlement of the country has partially driven it off to more secluded localities. I remember the time when this vulture was much disliked by the hunter because of its ravages upon any large game he may have killed and left exposed for only a short length of time. So powerful is its sight that it will discover a dead deer from an incredible distance while soaring in the air"* [91].

It seems to me that condor losses to shooting are much understated in the available record. Nevertheless, even if the loss from gunfire was much more than the actual record shows, and even if strychnine poisoning was much more prevalent than seems likely, it's still doubtful there would have been enough impact from both combined to have caused the disappearance of condors over such a vast area. The truth about the losses in the northern condor range probably is much more nuanced and complicated.

* * *

AN HYPOTHESIS

During my studies of California condors in the 1970s, it appeared to me that – even within the relatively limited range of the species by that time – the condors were not acting as a single population. To be sure that my surveys were adequately covering all parts of the range, I made special effort to increase condor records from the Coast Ranges between Santa Barbara and the Bay Area, by spending more time there myself and by recruiting new condor reporters. Yet, between 1966 and 1974, out of a total of 2,586 condor records, only 356 (13.7 per cent) were in the Coast Ranges, the rest being in the "Sespe-Piru" area of Ventura and Los Angeles counties, and northeast through the Tehachapi Mountains into the southern Sierra Nevada. Of even more significance, the largest group seen in the Coast Ranges during that period included only five condors, and that high a number was recorded only once in the 9-year period. In contrast, there were groups of over 10 birds seen every year in the eastern part of the condor range, groups of 15 or more in eight years, and groups of over 20 in four years. The Carrizo Plains, one of the most used feeding areas in the Coast Ranges during Koford's research in the 1930s and 1940s, did not produce any records of more than four condors together. The area still supported considerable livestock, and was less than 25 air miles from highly used condor areas at the south end of the San Joaquin Valley.

These findings led me to write the following [92]: *"The regularity with which condors are observed in certain areas at specific times of year, and in relatively predictable numbers, indicates that at least two subpopulations of condors exist. The division in the population occurs near the Santa Barbara-Ventura County line."* Later writers erroneously stated that I believed *"condors existed in two main subpopulations with a line of separation that was, at most, rarely crossed"* [93]. Actually, I did not define a "line," but a

331

strip of land perhaps 25 miles wide, including parts of Santa Barbara, Ventura, and Kern counties, in which I considered the *"subpopulation affinity unknown."*

Support for the subpopulation hypothesis came in the 1980s, when researchers were able to put radio transmitters on 11 condors, and follow their movements for from one to four years. Only four of the condors from my "Sespe-Sierra" subpopulation area had traveled more than a few miles into what I considered "Coast Range" habitat. One of these was a bird whose home territory was within my *"subpopulation affinity unknown"* area, and only one of the four birds made more than two trips outside the range I would have expected them to occupy [94]. It's unfortunate that there were no radioed Coast Range birds farther away from the mixing area. Had there been, the hypothesis could have been better tested.

It should not be surprising that, with birds as traditional in their movements as condors, groups associated with various nesting, roosting and foraging areas would - over time - develop their own seasonal movements. Time constraints would preclude long distance foraging by breeding condors, and a combination of distance and learned behavior seemed to define where and how far non-breeders would go. It would have been likely for condors from the Sisquoc area to mix on occasion with birds from the Sespe (nest area to nest area of about 40 miles). Condors from nests and roosts in central San Luis Obispo County might share habitat with Sisquoc birds (40-50 miles apart), but it would have been much less likely that they would regularly travel into Sespe territory. Similarly, condors resident in central Monterey County probably mixed regularly with San Luis Obispo birds, less regularly with Sisquoc condors, and rarely with the Sespe population. Each leg north (or south from the Sespe and Sisquoc areas) would render each group more isolated from those farthest from them, until distance alone would have precluded certain condors from ever meeting with one another.

Without definite nest and roost site records, one can only speculate on the location and interrelationships of condor subgroups. Based on the historical record, I think that condors were yearlong residents from the Sierra San Pedro Martír in Baja California Norte, Mexico, north in the western mountains of California and Oregon at least to the Columbia River, perhaps farther. There were also condors resident in the foothills east of the San Joaquin and Sacramento valleys in California. Within their total range, subgroups of condors occurred where suitable nesting and foraging habitat existed together. Condors in each of these subgroups "homed" to their specific nesting areas, with their seasonal wandering taking them no more than 150 or 200 miles from "home base." No condor in Oregon ever met a condor from Mexico, but there was undoubtedly regular interchange between the nearest neighbor groups (probably in foraging areas seasonally populated by two or more groups, as occurred in the 20th century). Tenacity to a home nesting habitat gave cohesiveness to the subgroup, and for much of the year isolated its members from other condors. However, the seasonal mixing of subgroups improved the chances of new pair formation, and likely helped maintain diversity in the gene pool of each group [95].

Subgroups such as I hypothesize for condors have been identified in many species of birds. In fact, because habitats are often fragmented naturally or the result of human land use, it has been suggested that it is *"often relevant to consider populations as collections of subpopulations in heterogeneous environments rather than continuous entities,"* the relationships of the subpopulations to the whole depending on such factors as the distance between subpopulations, the relative sizes of the individual habitat areas, and the relative densities of the subpopulations [96]. Oliver Austin was one of the first to identify these subpopulations, noting that common terns live in small colonies, each of which maintains its membership, even though located only a few miles from other colonies [97]. More recent studies of gulls have shown even stronger affinities to the home site. For example, in black-legged kittiwakes *"movement between their colonies was extremely rare once an individual bred,"* and *"though this effect is more precise in the male, most females which change site move only a few meters from their nest site of the previous season"* [98]. Sabine's gulls *"showed strong tenacity to their breeding site from year to year, with most pairs nesting within approximately 100 m of the previous year's site* [99]. Among waterfowl, pink-footed geese *"form closed groups occupying small, well-defined areas"* in which *"the scale of mixing is negligible"* [100], while among common eiders nearly all surviving females homed to the same breeding island year after year [101]. Ducks, crows, ravens, eagles, hawks, falcons, ospreys, owls, great tits, and flycatchers are other groups that have been shown to have strong "homing" instincts to a particular area and particular group of companions [102].

In addition to the obvious limitations of birds separated by great distances getting together, the ties developed to a home habitat could inhibit the chances of pioneering into new or vacant habitat. For example, consider what is known about Canada geese. They're one of the most abundant and most successful species of waterfowl in the world. Yet, if a local population of geese is removed from a marsh (by overshooting, for example), that marsh may not be nested in by Canada geese for many years. Other members of the species from other subpopulations may fly over the area and see that suitable habitat still exists. Yet, their ties to their own home marshes are too strong for them to break, even for a marsh that might be much better than their own [103]. Hesitancy in re-pioneering areas formerly occupied by their species has been shown in various other waterfowl [104], in the common crow [105], and in the great tit. In the latter case, adult tits did not move from what was considered "suboptimal" habitat when better habitat became available nearby, but returned and reused their previously occupied locations [106].

* * *

Considered on a subpopulation basis, the relatively meager record of condors in the northern part of their range takes on more significance. Condors along the Columbia and Willamette rivers were probably living near the margin of habitable range. The environment was not unsuitable in any way, and condors survived there for hundreds of years. As observed by David Douglas and members of the Lewis and Clark expedition (Chapter 5), the condors were not noticeably affected by the cloudy, rainy weather of Northwest winters. Nevertheless, their body characteristics and behavior are clearly better suited to areas with greater amounts of open space and sunlight. Condors have high wing loading (the ratio of weight to supporting surface [107]), which results in a relatively short period each day when the atmosphere has warmed enough to develop the ascending currents needed for soaring flight. This "soarability" [108] is only 5 to 6 hours in winter in the southern part of their historic range, and 7 to 8 in summer [109]. Not only is the amount of time for foraging limited, the condors' late rising insures that they will be left with whatever food the earlier, more efficient scavengers leave them. In practice, this has meant that most of their food supply comes from large mammals, native or domestic, which most often inhabit grasslands and other open habitat. They were more likely to have this kind of habitat and type of food in the valleys of California than farther to the north. Comparing equal acreages of the Northwest and central California, the latter would almost certainly have a higher scavenger carrying capacity, and likely could support more condors per unit of land than the Northwest habitat.

In fact, it appears that - although condors were widespread throughout the north - numbers were relatively low in any given area. Sometimes, words like "common" were used to describe local populations, but seldom were more than two or three reported together. The largest actual numbers recorded were of nine in a group [110], and "more than a dozen" [111]. No one north of San Francisco referred to the (probably exaggerated) "hundreds" regularly recorded in central and southern California.

Under pristine conditions, the number of condors locally would not have been a problem. Although each population segment was relatively small, presumably they could sustain themselves as long as natality and mortality remained "natural." However, if a substantial number of condors were lost from a local group, there might not have been eligible birds nearby to join the remaining condors. Even if there were other condors within 150 miles or so, their ties to their own area could have inhibited them from pioneering into vacant habitat.

I think the losses of condors in the Columbia River area - 10 positive in a 29 year period, and more suspected - could have been enough to destabilize that population enough to lead to its eventual disappearance. Perhaps the losses of condors in Marin, Napa, and Mendocino counties, or in the mountains

334

surrounding the Sacramento Valley, were enough to begin the decline at that end of the northern range. With the Monterey County condor population nearly exterminated (see below), there would be no close source of new recruits for the northern areas.

There is too little information on the condors of northern California and the Pacific Northwest to bring this discussion to a very satisfactory conclusion. The population losses to the south are much easier explained.

SAN FRANCISCO SOUTH

Overexploitation of subgroups of condors may explain the major declines in condor numbers in the central Coast Ranges (Monterey, San Benito, Santa Clara, and Santa Cruz counties), and in the area between Los Angeles and the Mexican border (Orange, Riverside, San Bernardino, San Diego, and southern Los Angeles counties).

In the central coast region, I have records of 68 condors known killed between 1850 and 1910. Forty-three of the deaths occurred between 1880 and 1900; 12 were killed in 1898, alone. Twenty-eight were killed as additions to private collections, while 15 went to zoos and public museums. Ten were victims of random shooting. Other losses are identifiable only as occurring in "southern California;" a number of them undoubtedly occurred in this region, also.

This level of loss to a species that had no significant natural enemies, and which died mainly of old age, disease or accidents, had to have a major impact. If, as I believe, there was little interchange between condor groups to the north and south, the losses would have been disastrous. In fact, this is borne out by the record. The region including Monterey County was once a major condor nesting area, perhaps rivaling the Sespe-Piru area of Ventura County in the number of pairs supported. One-third of all the condor eggs known to have been collected came from Monterey County and adjacent parts of extreme northwest San Luis Obispo County. There are no certain nesting records after 1910, and after that condors were seldom seen except in the far southeastern corner of the county. The former nest sites were within 50 miles or so of condors nesting to the south, but there was apparently little or no pioneering of new pairs into the vacated area.

In the area south from Los Angeles, there were 69 mortalities documented between 1870 and 1910. Half of those were random shootings, and 18 were believed taken for collectors. Only a few went to public museums. As had occurred in the central coastal counties, there were only a handful of condor reports for the vast southern coastal region after 1910. Condors remained relatively common just to the north of the Los Angeles Basin for 60 more years, and both nesting and feeding habitats were still available. No condors emigrated to fill the vacant niches [112].

After 1910, most of the remaining California condors nested in Ventura and Santa Barbara counties, and adjacent areas of Los Angeles and San Luis Obispo counties. The disappearance of condors from much of their former range concentrated condor mortality - both legal and illicit - in that area. No condors are known to have been purposely killed in Santa Barbara or Ventura counties until the 1870s (one record); during the 1880s and 1890s, the kill increased to 15 percent of the total. During the first decade of the 20th century, 30 percent of the loss occurred in those two counties; it was 50 percent between 1910 and 1920, and almost 70 percent in the 1920s. Although condors were still relatively "common" there for another 30 years, one wonders what would have been the case if collecting for zoos and museums had continued through another decade. The "annals of *Gymnogyps*" might have ended, with no chance to write any more chapters.

CHAPTER NOTES

1. Pages 7-19 *in:* Koford, C. B. 1953. The California condor. National Audubon Society Research Report Number 4. New York, New York.

2. Koford 1953 *op. cit.,* pages 129-135.

3. Koford 1953 *op. cit.,* pages 8-11.

4. Wilbur, S. R. 1973. The California condor in the Pacific Northwest. *Auk* 90(1):196-198.

5. Personal communication between Carl Koford and Sanford Wilbur, June 1974.

6. Miller, L. 1911. Avifauna of the Pleistocene cave deposits of California. *University of California Bulletin of the Department of Geology* 6(16):385-400.
   Feranec, R. S., E. A. Hadley, J. L. Blois, A. D. Barnosky, and A. Paytan. 2007. Radiocarbon dates from the Pleistocene fossil deposits of Samwel Cave, Shasta County, California, USA. *Radiocarbon* 49(1):117-121.
   Feranec, R. S. 2009. Implications of radiocarbon dates from Potter Creek Cave, Shasta County, California, USA. *Radiocarbon* 51(3):931-936.

7. Miller, L. H. 1957. Bird remains from an Oregon Indian midden. *Condor* 59(1):59-63.
   Hansel-Kuehn, V. J. 2003. The Dalles Roadcut (Fivemile Rapids) avifauna: evidence for a cultural origin. Master of Arts in Anthropology, Washington State University (Pullman, Washington).

8. Specimen at the Royal British Columbia Museum, Victoria, British Columbia, Canada.

9. Nine Indian middens in the Puget Sound area yielded some 500 bones and bone fragments of various birds, but there were none from either California condors or turkey vultures. [Miller, L. 1960. Some Indian midden birds from the Puget Sound area. *Wilson Bulletin* 72(4):392-397.]

10. David Moen tried to connect the California condor to the mythical "Thunderbird" of various northwestern Washington and British Columbia aboriginal groups (Moen, D.B. 2008. *Condors in the Oregon Country: exploring the past to prepare for the future.* Masters degree project, Portland State University (Portland, Oregon). However, he did not cite (nor could I find) any reference that stated or implied that the condor was a model for the Thunderbird. The various Thunderbird motifs bear strong resemblance to raptorial birds, not vultures. If any "real" bird was the source of the myths, it would seem to me most likely to have been an eagle.

11. Page 65 *in:* Clyman, J., and C. L. Camp. 1926. James Clyman: his diaries and reminiscences (continued). *California Historical Society Quarterly* 5(1):44-84.

12. Pages 255-256 and 262 *in:* Putnam, R. 1928. The letters of Roselle Putnam. *Oregon Historical Quarterly* 29(3):242-264.

13. Finley, W. L. 1908. Life history of the California condor, Part II – historical data and range of the condor. *Condor* 10(1):5-10.

14. Peck, G. D. 1904. The Cal. Vulture in Douglas Co., Oregon. *Oologist* 21(4):55.

15. Page 180 *in:* Gabrielson, I. N., and S. G. Jewett. 1940. Birds of the Pacific Northwest. Corvallis, Oregon: Oregon State University.

16. Page 141 *in:* Cooper, J. G. 1860. Report upon the birds collected on the Survey. Chapter I, Land birds. Report on explorations and surveys to ascertain the most practicable and economical route for a railroad from the Mississippi River to the Pacific Ocean. Volume 12, Book 2. Washington, D. C.: Thomas H. Ford, Printer.

17. Page 166 *in:* Jewett, S. G., W. P. Taylor, W. T. Shaw, and J. W. Aldrich. 1953. Birds of Washington State. Seattle, Washington: University of Washington Press. *"The last record of the species for the state appears to be that of Dr. C. Hart Merriam (letter of January 4, 1921). In the early morning of September 30, 1897, Dr. Merriam saw a condor on the ground in open country a few miles east of Coulee City, Washington."*
Even though Merriam had seen condors previously, I'm uncomfortable with this record. It is so relatively recent, and so far to the northeast of any other records, it seems anomalous. Researcher Maria Brandt reviewed for me the extensive Merriam archives at the Bancroft Library (Berkeley, California), but couldn't find correspondence about the sighting, and no journals or field notes that might have given additional information about the observation.

18. Credit is sometimes given to William Tolmie for a California condor sighting much farther north in British Columbia, at Ft. McLoughlin. On 24 November 1834, he wrote: *"What I supposed a large species of vulture at the northern end* [of the lake], *along*

with some white-headed eagles attracted probably by the dead salmon. "[Page 293 *in:* Tolmie, W. F. 1963. William Fraser Tolmie, physician and fur trader. Vancouver, British Columbia: Mitchell Press Ltd.] The far northern location and the late time of year makes this unlikely; also, Tolmie made no mention of immature bald eagles, the logical large dark bird to be with adult bald eagles.

19. Page 291 *in:* Lord, J. K. 1866. The naturalist in Vancouver Island and British Columbia. Volume II. London, England: Richard Bentley.

20. Page 22 *in:* Fannin, J. 1891. Check list of British Columbia Birds. Victoria, British Columbia: Province of British Columbia.

21. Page 39 *in:* Rhoads, S. N 1893. The birds observed in British Columbia and Washington during spring and summer 1892. *Proceedings of the Academy of Natural Sciences of Philadelphia* 45(1):21-65.

22. Page 92 *in:* Sullivan, M. S. 1924. The travels of Jedediah Smith, a documentary outline including the journal of the great American pathfinder. Lincoln, Nebraska: University of Nebraska Press.

23. Two of Ilya Voznesenskii's California condors are still at the Zoological Institute, St. Petersburgh, Russia (confirmed by Wladimir Loskot, Curator of the Department of Birds, 28 April 2008). Two others have been gone from the Institute for many years, probably traded to other museums within a few years of Voznesenskii's return to Russia.
The general timetable for Voznesenskii's collecting is given in: Alekseev, A. I. 1987. The odyssey of a Russian scientist: I. G. Voznesenskii in Alaska, California and Siberia 1839-1849. Translation by W. C. Follette. Kingston, Ontario: The Limestone Press.

24. Poesch, J. 1961. Titian Ramsay Peale 1799-1885 and his journals of the Wilkes Expedition. Philadelphia, Pennsylvania: The American Philosophical Society.

25. Page 72 *in:* Cassin, J. 1858. Mammalogy and ornithology: United States Exploring Expedition during the years 1838, 1839, 1840, 1841, 1842, under the command of Charles Wilkes, U. S. N. Philadelphia, Pennsylvania: J. B. Lippincott & Co.

26. Page 406 *in:* Finley, E. L. (editor). 1937. History of Sonoma County, California: its people and its resources. Santa Rosa, California: Press Democrat Publishing Company.

27. Pages 137-138 *in:* Clyman, J. 1926. James Clyman, his diaries and reminiscences. *California Historical Society Quarterly* 5(2):109-138.

28. Page 177 *in:* Berner, M., B. Grummer, R. Leong, and M. Rippey. 2003. Breeding birds of Napa County, California. Vallejo, California: Napa-Solano Audubon Society.

29. Page 42 *in:* Wilbur, M. E. 1941. A pioneer at Sutter's Fort, 1846-1850. Los Angeles, California: The Calafia Society.

30. Page 52 *in:* Bryant, W. E. 1891. Andrew Jackson Grayson. *Zoe* 2(1):34-68.

31. Page 27 *in:* Johnson, K. 1967. The Gold Rush letters of J. D. B. Stillman. Palo Alto, California: Lewis Osborne.

32. Page 135 *in:* Clark, T. D. 1967. Gold Rush diary: being the journal of Elisha Douglass Perkins on the Overland Trail in the spring and summer of 1849. Lexington, Kentucky: University of Kentucky Press.

33. Pages 204-311 *in:* Reed, G. W., and R. Gaines. 1949. The journals, drawings and other papers of J. Goldsborough Bruff, April 2, 1849-July 20, 1851. New York, New York: Columbia University Press.

34. Page 73 *in:* Newberry, J. S. 1857. Report upon the zoology of the route (mammals and birds). Volume 6, Part 2, Report of explorations and surveys to ascertain the most practicable and economical route for a railroad from the Mississippi River to the Pacific Ocean. Washington, D. C.: Beverly Tucker.

35. Anonymous. 1854. California vulture. Sacramento (California) *Daily Union,* 11 March 1854.

36. Anonymous. 1854. A California vulture. Sacramento (California) *Daily Union,* 21 June 1854.

37. Anonymous. 1856. Nomen Laken Reservation. Sacramento (California) *Daily Union,* 1 April 1856.

38. Leach, F. A. 1929. A turkey buzzard roost. *Condor* 31(1):21-23.

39. Anonymous. 1858. Vulture. *Daily Alta California* (San Francisco, California), 4 February 1858.

40. Anonymous. 1858. The California vulture. *Daily Alta California* (San Francisco, California), 22 August 1858.

41. Anonymous. 1861. A large bird. Sacramento (California) *Daily Union,* 18 June 1861.

42. Anonymous. 1865. A huge bird. Sacramento (California) *Daily Union,* 25 November 1865.

43. Anonymous. 1867. A huge blow. San Francisco (California) *Chronicle,* 16 October 1867.

44. Leach 1929 *op. cit.*

45. Anonymous. 1868. Proud bird of the mountain. San Francisco (California) *Bulletin,* 19 August 1868.

46. Letter from Lyle Belding to Robert Ridgway 21 March 1878: *"I have never shot a Cal Condor, have seen a few along Feather River in former years & a few in Mendocino Co."* Smithsonian Institution archives (Washington, D. C.), Division of Birds records 1874-1959, Record Unit 105.

47. Belding, L. 1918. Autobiographical sketch. *Proceedings and Collections of the Wyoming Historical and Geological Society* 16:127-184.

48. Belding, L. 1879. A partial list of the birds of central California. *Proceedings of the U. S. National Museum* 1:388-449.

49. Anonymous. 1872. Untitled ["vulture eagle" killed in Mendocino County]. Chicago (Illinois) *Tribune,* 24 February 1872.

50. Anonymous. 1873. California condor. Sacramento (California) *Daily Union,* 19 February 1873.

51. Avery, B. P. 1874. Ascent of Mount Shasta. *Overland Monthly* 12(5):466-476.

52. Anonymous. 1880. State news in brief. San Francisco (California) *Bulletin,* 5 April 1880.

53. Anonymous. 1880. State news in brief. *Daily Evening Bulletin* (San Francisco, California), 7 May 1880.

54. Page 201 *in:* Townsend, C. H. 1887. Field-notes on the mammals, birds and reptiles of northern California. *Proceedings of the U. S. National Museum* 10:159-241.

55. Seabough, S. 1880. Gold Lake, search for a mythical bonanza in the Sierras. San Francisco (California) *Chronicle,* 21 November 1880.

56. Page 89 *in:* Gassaway, F. H. 1882. Summer saunterings, by "Derrick Dodd." San Francisco, California: Francis, Valentine & Company.

57. Townsend 1887 *op. cit.*

58. Smith, F. J. 1916. Occurrence of the condor in Humboldt County. *Condor* 18(5):205.

59. Specimen records, FMNH 39613, Chicago (Illinois) Field Museum of Natural History: collected in mountains north of San Francisco, Marin County, California, between 1900 and 1905.

60. Oregon population figures in this chapter were compiled from the Federal censuses, taken at ten year intervals throughout the United States.

61. The observations of California Condors in Douglas County, Oregon in 1903-1904 are usually considered to represent vagrant birds from far to the south, or misidentifications. However, William Finley conceded that, if condors were resident in the Northwest, *"the last of these northern birds seem to have taken refuge in the rough mountain regions of southern Oregon."* [Finley, W. L. 1908. Life history of the California condor. Part II, historical data and range of the condor. *Condor* 10(1):5-10.

62. Compilations by California counties for each federal census 1860 to 1950, as well as the county size (in square miles), are given in: Gibson, C. 2007. Population totals by township and place for California counties: 1860 to 1950. Alexandria, Virginia.

63. Grinnell, J. 1909. Bibliography of California ornithology, First installment. Pacific Coast Avifauna Number 5. Berkeley, California: Cooper Ornithological Club.
  Grinnell, J. 1924. Bibliography of California ornithology, second installment to end of 1923. Pacific Coast Avifauna Number 16. Berkeley, California: Cooper Ornithological Club.
  Grinnell, J. 1939. Bibliography of California ornithology, third installment to end of 1938. Pacific Coast Avifauna Number 26. Berkeley, California: Cooper Ornithological Club.

64. Jobanek, G. A. 1997. An annotated bibliography of Oregon bird literature published before 1935. Corvallis, Oregon: Oregon State University Press.

65. Andrus, F. H. 1893. A nest (plum) full. *Oologist* 10:300.

66. Specimen records, FMNH 2909, Chicago (Illinois) Field Museum of Natural History: two California condor eggs collected July 1879, Santa Cruz County, California, by or for William A. Cooper.

67. Berner *et al.* 2003 *op. cit.*

68. Sullivan 1924 *op. cit.*

69. Koford 1953 *op. cit.,* pages 9-11.

70. Page 27 *in:* Wilbur, S. R. 1978a. The California condor, 1966-76: a look at its past and future. North American Fauna 72. Washington, D. C.: U. S. Fish and Wildlife Service.
  Page 236 *in:* Wilbur, S. R. 2004. Condor tales: what I learned in twelve years with the big birds. Gresham, Oregon: Symbios.

71. Koford 1953 *op. cit.,* page 52.

72. Meretsky, V. J., and N. F. R. Snyder. 1992. Range use and movements of California condors. *Condor* 94(2):313-335.

73. Wilbur 1978a, *op. cit.,* pages 27-31.

74. Wilbur 1978a, *op. cit.,* pages 7-12.

75. Wilbur, S. R., W. D. Carrier, and J. C. Borneman. 1974. Supplemental feeding program for California condors. *Journal of Wildlife Management* 38(2):343-346.
   Wilbur, S. R. 1978b. Supplemental feeding of California condors. Pages 135-140 *in:* Temple, S. A. (editor), Endangered birds: management techniques for preserving threatened species. Madison, Wisconsin: University of Wisconsin Press.

76. In addition to descriptions in the journals of the Corps of Discovery, Wilkes Expedition, and others, see discussions of the Northwest "game sink," for example:
   Lyman, R. L., and S. Wolverton. 2002. The late Prehistoric-early Historic game sink in the northwestern United States. *Conservation Biology* 16(1):73-85.
   Kay, C. E. 2007. Were native people keystone predators? A continuous-time analysis of wildlife observations made by Lewis and Clark in 1804-1806. *Canadian Field-Naturalist* 121(1):1-16.

77. Koford 1953 *op. cit.,* page 9.

78. Johannessen, C. L., W. A. Davenport, A. Millet, and S. McWilliams. 1971. The vegetation of the Willamette Valley. *Annals of the Association of American Geographers* 61(2):286-302.
   Fritschle, J. A. 2008. Reconstructing historic ecotones using the public land survey: the lost prairies of Redwood National Park. *Annals of the Association of American Geographers* 98(1):24-39.
   Bjorkman, A. D., and M. Vellend. 2010. Defining historical baselines for conservation: ecological changes since European settlement on Vancouver Island, Canada. *Conservation Biology* 24(6):1559-1568.

79. Anderson, M. K., and M. J. Moratto. 1996. Native American land-use practices and ecological impacts. Pages 187-206 *in:* Sierra Nevada Ecosystems Project: Final Report to Congress. Volume II, Assessments and scientific basis for management options. Davis, California: University of California, Centers for Water and Wildland Resources.
   Keeley, J. E. 2002. Native American impacts on fire regimes of the California coastal ranges. *Journal of Biogeography* 29(3):303-320.

80. Koford 1953 *op. cit.,* page 9.

81. Townsend, J. K. 1848. Popular monograph of the accipitrine birds of N. A. – No. II. *Literary Record and Journal of the Linnaean Association of Pennsylvania College* 4(12):265-272.

82. Pages 240-245 *in:* Audubon, J. J. 1839. Ornithological biography. Volume 5. Edinburgh, Scotland: Adam & Charles Black.

83. Yoshiyama, R. M., E. R. Gerstung, F. W. Fisher, and P. B. Moyle. 2001. Historical and present distribution of Chinook salmon in the Central Valley drainage of California. Pages 71-176 *in:* Brown, R. L. (editor), Contributions to the biology of

Central Valley salmonids. Fish Bulletin 179. La Jolla, California: Scripps Institution of Oceanography.

84. Williams, J. G. 2006. Central Valley salmon: a perspective on Chinook and steelhead in the Central Valley of California. *San Francisco Estuary and Watershed Science* 4 (3):1-398.

85. In addition to the references cited in Notes 78 and 79 above, see:
   Habeck, J. R. 1961. The original vegetation of the mid-Willamette Valley, Oregon. *Northwest Science* 35(2):65-77.
   Gregory, S., L. Ashkenas, D. Oetter, P. Minear, K. Wildman, J. Christy, S.Kolar and E. Alberson. 2002. Presettlement vegetation ca. 1851. Pp. 38-39 in: Hulse, D., S. Gregory and J. Baker (editors), Willamette River Basin Planning Atlas: trajectories of environmental and ecological change. Pacific Northwest Ecosystems Research Consortium. Corvallis, OR: Oregon State University Press.
   Dubrasich, M. 2010. Stand reconstruction and 200 years of forest development on selected sites in the Upper South Umpqua watershed. South Umpqua headwaters precontact reference conditions study. Western Institute for Study of the Environment (Lebanon, OR), White Paper No. 2010-5.

86. Johannessen *et al., op. cit.*

87. Gregory *et al., op. cit.*

88. Sprague, F. L., and H. P. Hansen. 1946. Forest succession in the McDonald Forest, Willamette Valley, Oregon. *Northwest Science* 20(4):89-98.

89. Fritschle 2008 *op. cit.*

90. California livestock information is based on figures given in Appendix II, pages 251-256 *in*: Burcham, L. T. 1981. California range land: an historico-ecological study of the range resources of California. Publication Number 7, Center for Archaeological Research at Davis (California).

91. 91. Page 52 *in*: Bryant, W. E. 1891. Andrew Jackson Grayson. *Zoe* 2(1): 34-68.

92. Wilbur 1978a, *op. cit.,* pages 9-11.

93. Meretsky and Snyder 1992, *op. cit.*

94. Meretsky and Snyder 1992, *op. cit.*

95. Wilbur 1973 *op. cit.;* Wilbur 1973a, *op. cit.* pages 7-13; Wilbur 2004 *op. cit.,* pages 229-240.

96. Grosbois, V., and G. Tavecchia. 2003. Modeling dispersal with capture-recapture data; disentangling decisions of leaving and settlement. *Ecology* 84(5):1225-1236.

97. Austin, O. L. 1949. Site tenacity, a behavior trait of the common tern (*Sterna hirundo* Linn.). *Bird-banding* 20(1):1-39.
  Austin, O. L. 1951. Group adherence in the common tern. *Bird-banding* 22(1):1-15.

98. Fairweather, J. A., and J. C. Coulson. 1995. The influence of forced site change on the dispersal and breeding of the black-legged kittiwake *Rissa tridactyla*. *Colonial Waterbirds* 18(1):30-40.

99. Stenhouse, I., and G. J. Robertson. 2005. Philopatry, site tenacity, mate fidelity, and adult survival in Sabine's gulls. *Condor* 107(2):416-423.

100. Boyd, H. 1972. British studies of goose populations: hindsight as an aid to foresight. Pages 251-262 *in:* Population ecology of migratory birds: a symposium. U. S. Bureau of Sport Fisheries and Wildlife, Wildlife Research Report 2. Washington, D. C.

101. Wakeley, J. S., and H. L. Mendall. 1976. Migrational homing and survival of adult female eiders in Maine. *Journal of Wildlife Management* 40(1):15-21.

102. Hickey, J. J. 1942. Eastern populations of the duck hawk. *Auk* 59(2):176-204.
  Sowls, L. K. 1955. Prairie ducks: a study of their behavior, ecology and management. Harrisburg, Pennsylvania: Stackpole Company.
  Brown, L. H. 1972. Natural longevity of wild crowned eagles, *Stephanoaetus coronatus. Ibis* 114(2):263-265.
  Jenkins, J. M., and R.E. Jackman. 1993. Mate and nest site fidelity in a resident population of bald eagles. *Condor* 95(4):1053-1056.
  Switzer, P. V. 1993. Site fidelity in predictable and unpredictable habitats. *Evolutionary Ecology* 7(6):533-555.
  Doncaster, C. P, J. Clobert, B. Doligez, L. Gustafsson, and E. Danchin. 1997. Balanced dispersal between varying local populations: an alternative to the source-sink model. *American Naturalist* 150(4):425-445.

103. Hochbaum, H. A. 1955. Travels and traditions of waterfowl. Newton, Massachusetts: Charles T. Branford Co.

104. Sowls 1955 *op. cit.*

105. Emlen, J. T. 1940. The midwinter distribution of the crow in California. *Condor* 42(6):287-294.

106. Switzer 1993, *op. cit*

107. Page 572 *in:* Fisher, H. I. 1946. Adaptations and comparative anatomy of the locomotor apparatus of New World vultures. *American Midland Naturalist* 35(3):545-727.

108. Page 26 *in:* Hankin, E. H. 1913. Animal flight. London, England: Iliffe and Sons.

109. Koford 1953 *op. cit.*, page 52.

110. Page 216 *in*: Douglas, D. 1914. Journal kept by David Douglas during his travels in North America 1823-1827. London: William Wesley & Son.

111. Bryant 1891 *op. cit.*, page 52.

112. The situation in Mexico is unclear. Probably California condors nested at a number of locations between San Diego County and the Sierra San Pedro Martír in Baja California Norte. Some survived at least into the late 1930s, likely because they were more isolated and less subject to killing than were the condors in California. Periodic killing was reported, however, and all of Baja California Norte was subjected to a long-term drought that likely reduced the food supply. With no possibility of recruitment from the north, the Mexican population was eventually extirpated.

Figure 22. California condor mount, Museum d'Histoire Naturelle (Geneva, Switzerland), collected in Monterey County, 1901 or 1902. Photo courtesy Francois Baud.

346

AFTERTHOUGHTS

As history, I find the story of the California condors fascinating. They saw the end of the Age of Mammals, and were given a place in the myths and traditions of the earliest known people on the West Coast of America. They viewed the Spaniards, the Russians, and the British in turn, as these foreigners sailed the Pacific and occasionally set foot on the lands that would become Washington, Oregon, and California. The condors were there as the Spanish missions were established, perhaps getting a new lease on life from the food provided from the expanding livestock herds - at the same time that the first human inhabitants of California were being destroyed by the actions taken against them by an alien religion. They accompanied the Lewis and Clark expedition from the Cascades of the Columbia to the sea, and soared overhead as westward-bound settlers and gold-seeking '49ers poured over the mountains and across the deserts into "condor country." They became enticing targets for men with guns, unique trophies for hobby collectors, and the relics of a probable lost race to the administrators of public museums. In the end, they disappeared from rocky canyons and grassy hillsides into city zoos, hopefully to raise new generations to begin another history of the California condors.

As a story of conservation, the condors' tale is not a satisfying one. Extolled for their size, and viewed with alarm in their increasing rarity, the condor was relegated to the role of "doomed bird" even before the end of the 19th century. Entering the 1900s, action was not toward study or preservation, but to getting more specimens while the getting was good. Not until the 1930s was there any move toward learning about the species and considering how it might be saved.

Preliminary studies, and the setting aside of a token sanctuary, raised awareness of the condors' plight. The increased interest made it possible to fund, and eventually carry out, the first in-depth investigation of the species. Unfortunately, the results of the study (which had been done in the 1930s and 1940s) were not finalized and made public until 1953. Part of the delay was due to the intervention of a World War, part to inertia on the part of the writer and the sponsoring organization. In any event, time had marched on for the condors without any significant help forthcoming for them. The eventual establishment of a much larger sanctuary undoubtedly bought the species a few more years. Yet, the same public awareness and sentiment that created the refuge also brought about extreme legal protection that made it nearly impossible to do anything proactive for the condors for the next quarter-century. By 1955, the lines were indelibly drawn between active "management" of the birds or letting them "take their chances." By the time of the second major investigation of the condors (1966-1980), there was really little to do but document the past, and fight for one meaningful intervention on behalf of species survival.

History - bad, good, or neutral - is what happened. Personally, I'd like to change parts of it, but it can't be done. History *is* history. How it gets remembered is something else, again. History can be written from ignorance, arrogance, faulty research, sloppiness, to support a cause, to "prove a point," to earn a diploma, to make a living, to discredit other ideas: the list goes on. Even disregarding capability and motive, we can never get it entirely right. By the time history becomes interesting, most of those who actually lived it are long gone. By that time, all we can do is the best we can.

I've devoted over 40 years to the study of the California condor. Obviously, in that time, I've developed a lot of opinions about the bird and the people involved with it. Those opinions have already been published ("Condor Tales:" Symbios, 2004). In the book you've just finished, I've tried to tell history just for the sake of telling history - to "get it right," in so far as it is possible to ferret out the whole truth about anything in the past. Some of what I found revises even what I wrote in "Condor Tales" as recently as 2004, illustrating that "getting it right" can be an ongoing process.

I can remember a day back in the mid-1970s, as I was walking near the Sespe Condor Sanctuary with a young friend who had just hitch-hiked his way 3,500 miles from northern New Hampshire to southern California. He was on a personal vision-quest, and we talked about a lot of weighty things. At one point, he challenged me on my interest in historical research. What good is history, he asked? I don't remember how I responded. I probably used the line about those not knowing history being doomed to repeat it - which, by the way, I believe is one justification, even if as human beings we often seem incapable of not repeating past mistakes. My answer today would include that admonition, but it would be more visceral: history is fun; history is fascinating; and some of us seem to have an insatiable desire to "get it right." I could have finished writing this story two years ago, but I kept finding new sources of information, and kept questioning myself as to whether or not I *really knew* what I just wrote. I've had a lot of fun - and learned quite a bit more about condors than I knew after my ten years of field research. I hope you have, too.

Sandy Wilbur
Gresham, Oregon
August 2012

ACKNOWLEDGMENTS

When one has been working on a project for 40-plus years, it follows that there have been many contacts made, and much information shared. The long list of contributors includes librarians, archivists, museum curators, historians, co-workers, relatives of early-day "condor people," and a lot of general condor enthusiasts who have found and sent along items that "I might be interested in." (I usually was.) There are also the experts in fields that I only dabble in - ethnologists, archaeologists, paleontologists, geneticists, taxonomists - just to identify a few. Whether we communicated once, or 50 times, I thank you all.

The compiling of a history of the California condor didn't begin with me. As acknowledged in the Preface, Harry Harris got the project jump-started in a major way. Carl Koford and Fred Sibley added significantly to the gathering, abstracting, and analyzing of data. I added a lot, but because of those three I had a solid foundation from which to start.

Two people deserve special note for their help going through archives and gathering obscure references for me: Ellen Alers, Research Archivist at the Smithsonian; and Jan Hamber, long-time friend, condor biologist, associate curator, and keeper of the official condor files at the Santa Barbara Museum of Natural History. Thanks to you both for your interest, willingness, and patience to take on the archival challenges I tossed to you.

The cover photo of California condors in the Sespe Condor Sanctuary - clearly showing their "nine feet from tip to tip" - was taken by Fred C. Sibley, my predecessor as leader of Fish and Wildlife Service condor research.

Figure 23. California condor mount at the Swedish Museum of Natural History (Stockholm). Acquired in 1903, Edward B. Towne bird.

INDEX

ABOUT THE AUTHOR

Sanford (Sandy) Wilbur was from 1969 to 1980 in charge of the U. S. Fish and Wildlife Service's California condor research program, and was leader of the condor recovery effort. His research also included studies of the endangered clapper rails, least terns, and Bell's vireos. He served as leader of the Light-footed Clapper Rail Recovery Team, and was a member of the recovery teams for California least terns and peregrine falcons. During the rest of his 34 year career with Fish and Wildlife Service, he worked on National Wildlife Refuges in Nevada, Idaho and California; began the Wilderness Act studies of National Wildlife Refuges in the West; was Regional Refuge Biologist for 12 Southeastern states; was Chief of Endangered Species for the Service's Pacific Region; and was Refuge District Supervisor for Oregon, Washington, and Idaho.

Sandy is the author of many scientific publications, including *"Birds of Baja California"* (University of California Press 1987). *"Condor Tales: What I Learned in Twelve Years with the Big Birds"* (SYMBIOS 2004), companion volume to *"Nine Feet from Tip to Tip,"* is his personal narrative of the "Condor Years." With Jerome A. Jackson, he co-edited and contributed to the volume *"Vulture Biology and Management"* (University of California Press 1983). He has also authored a novel *"If God is God"* (SYMBIOS 1996), and with his wife Sally, an Oregon Trail narrative *"The McCully Train: Iowa to Oregon 1852"* (SYMBIOS 2000).

Sandy was born in Oakland, California, and has spent most of his 70+ years in the Pacific Coast states. He has lived in Oregon since 1981.